James E. Killer

# Urban Transportation
# Modeling and Planning

# Urban Transportation Modeling and Planning

**Peter R. Stopher**
Northwestern University

**Arnim H. Meyburg**
Cornell University

**Lexington Books**
D.C. Heath and Company
Lexington, Massachusetts
Toronto          London

**Library of Congress Cataloging in Publication Data**

Stopher, Peter R
    Urban transportation modeling and planning.

    Includes bibliographical references and index.
    1. Urban transportation—Mathematical models. 2. Traffic
estimation—Mathematical models. I. Meyburg, Arnim H., joint
author. II. Title.
HE305.S84        388.4'01'84        74-21876
ISBN 0-669-96941-9

*Copyright © 1975 by D.C. Heath and Company*

Published simultaneously in Canada

Printed in the United States of America

International Standard Book Number: 0-669-96941-9

Library of Congress Catalog Card Number: 74-21876

**To our wives, Valerie and Lee**

# Contents

# List of Figures

# List of Tables

# Preface

This book has evolved from the notes developed for three courses offered at Cornell University and Northwestern University over the last several years. These courses are offered to senior undergraduates and first- and second-year graduate students in transportation and planning programs. It is at these levels that this book is aimed, although it should also be useful to many practicing professionals who wish to pursue the areas of urban transportation planning and travel-demand modeling.

The treatment of subject matter in this book assumes certain rudiments of knowledge in various disciplines. It is assumed that the reader or student is familiar with basic microeconomics (i.e., consumer behavior in economics), has an understanding of probability and statistics, and can handle relatively simple calculus. Beyond this, we have attempted to provide the necessary background in the text, although some minimal knowledge of systems analysis and linear programming will also be helpful in some sections.

The purpose of this book is to examine in detail the available techniques and current research in travel-forecasting procedures. This is done within the broader construct of the transportation-planning process, in the hopes of maintaining some perspective on the primary uses to which such procedures are to be put. Thus, in the early part of the book, we have outlined the evolution of the transportation-planning process, particularly within the United States, and have discussed some of the fundamental underpinnings of the process and its associated forecasting procedures. These underpinnings are largely derived from systems analysis and economics, which form the basis of chapters 2 and 3. In addition, since the primary focus of the book is on modeling the demand for travel, we have interjected into these chapters a number of fundamental concerns related to model-building in general.

Chapter 4 provides a broad overview of the transportation-planning process. This overview is a generalization of current practice, but is not without substantive controversy. The chapter is intended, however, to provide a coherent picture of the position, relative importance, and interactions of the forecasting or modeling procedures. The next seven chapters take the individual steps, identified in chapter 4, and subject them to a close scrutiny. The emphasis here is placed on the travel-forecasting methods (chapters 7, 8, 9 and 10), with a relatively less detailed examination of the other three steps in the process. Chapter 12 provides a critical review and summary of the travel-forecasting process.

The remainder of the book—chapters 13 through 16—is concerned with four recent approaches to replacing the conventional travel-forecasting process. Again, we have attempted to provide a detailed treatment of these approaches, providing information on the theory and concepts of the approaches and evaluating them from the viewpoint of both academic satisfactoriness and implementability within the constraints of the transportation-planning process. At no point in the book do we attempt to provide detailed discussion of policy issues or the strategies of planning. This neglect is intentional and is based on two premises: First, there are a number of texts available that deal with questions of policy and strategy, but generally ignore the question of available methodology for examining policy issues or accomplishing strategy. Second, there is an almost-complete absence of books that consider the theory, concepts, and derivations of available modeling procedures. We feel that this absence of such a technical treatment leaves the average student or professional helpless to implement the policies and strategies that might be appropriate. Furthermore, an understanding of the technical limitations that are imposed on the planning process by the models is an essential element of the education of any professional transportation planner.

In summary, this book concentrates upon the development of the theories, concepts, and structure of travel-forecasting models and methods, and of current research concerned with developing new methods. Policy issues are dealt with only peripherally, where such issues may place limiting constraints or special demands on the forecasting models. However, we must also emphasize that it is not possible for a book such as this to provide an exhaustive treatment of these topics. It is clear that there are so many modifications, improvements, and revisions of the models we have discussed here that no single book could contain them all. We have attempted to cover a sufficient range of the models to whet the appetite of the reader and encourage him to explore the wealth of literature that exists in this area. We have also endeavored to provide a starting point for such exploration by the reference notes in each chapter.

Finally, we feel that it is appropriate to note here our general conclusions about the material in this book. In examining the conventional travel-forecasting procedures, we are drawn to the inevitable conclusion that these procedures are conceptually and theoretically barren, while yet they represent the only fully operational procedures for travel-forecasting. They are, therefore, important to the professional because they comprise the only available procedure for practical use. It is also important, however, that their shortcomings be understood fully by the planner so that the products of the procedure are interpreted carefully and an open mind is kept towards possible new developments. Among these latter, we do not perceive major potential to be offered by any of the procedures except that of behavioral travel demand. At present, we feel that this area of endeavour holds the greatest promise of providing a new, more accurate, more responsive travel-forecasting procedure. However, it is also possible that a newer approach, perhaps only now being formulated, might replace behavioral travel-demand as the basis for a future operational procedure of travel forecasting.

# Acknowledgments

A number of individuals and agencies have contributed their time, expertise, and cooperation in the preparation of this book. The authors express their sincere appreciation to all of them. We would like to acknowledge the special efforts of Valerie Stopher and Patricia Apgar, who typed and retyped several drafts of this manuscript, and the drafting skills of Wilfred R. Sawbridge of Cornell University who prepared all drawings for this book. We thank Dr. Andrei Rogers, and Messrs. James Clark and Thomas Zlatoper of Northwestern University for their critical comments on parts of this manuscript.

We thank Dr. Peter L. Watson of Northwestern University for his helpful suggestions and comments, particularly on chapter 3, and Dr. Richard B. Westin of the University of Toronto for explaining the theoretical derivations in chapter 16. In addition, we would like to thank the many students who, through their responses to earlier drafts of this book, their questions during classes, and their term-paper efforts, were responsible for generating the impetus to write this book and have inspired many elements within it.

The authors also acknowledge the use of material from various publications of the Transportation Research Board, the Chicago Area Transportation Study, and the Metropolitan Toronto and Region Transportation Study. Finally, we gratefully acknowledge the cooperation of the following publishing companies and authors: the McGraw-Hill Publishing Company for permission to quote and use illustrations from *Systems Analysis for Engineers and Managers* by R. deNeufville and J.H. Stafford, and from *Traffic Systems Analysis for Engineers and Planners* by M. Wohl and B.V. Martin; the Van Nostrand-Reinhold Company for permission to quote from *A Methodology for Systems Engineering* by A.D. Hall; Academic Press for permission to use an illustration from *Mathematical Theories of Traffic Flow* by F.A. Haight.

The authors accept complete responsibility for any errors that might still exist in the text.

# 1 Introduction and Background

**Historical Background**

The formalized process of urban transportation planning, as it is described in this book, is relatively new, having evolved largely during the last 25 years. However, the problems to which it is applied have existed almost since the beginning of civilization. Almost without exception, the automobile age is plagued with the same broad types of problems as was the era of the Roman Empire. Problems of traffic congestion in urban areas were prevalent during the eighteenth and nineteenth centuries, and also during the heyday of the Roman Empire. As early as the time of Julius Caesar, congestion and its attendant impacts on urban life were generating legislation to restrict or control vehicular movements in the center of Rome.

In the same way, problems of noise, pollution, and other undesirable impacts of transportation are not new with the automobile age. Traffic noise was a serious problem in ancient Rome, and probably in many other cities of the era. It was also a problem in European and North American cities during the eighteenth and nineteenth centuries, particularly, and very probably was also a problem in Europe back to the fourteenth century and earlier. In fact, at any state in history where man has congregated in cities and has relied on any form of transportation other than his feet, noise, congestion, and pollution have been perennial problems. It is true that the pollution problem has changed radically with the automobile, particularly with a substantive change from obvious solid, liquid, and odiferous pollution to the more subtle gaseous pollution that can be neither easily seen nor (in many cases) smelled.

Again, a further constant can be identified in the continuing interactions between urban form and transportation. The changes in urban form of our present civilization, particularly during the last 250 years, have run hand in hand with changes and technological advances in transportation. Both the size and pattern of urban developments have been affected extensively by the existing transportation technology. Thus, it is clear that the needs to plan, control, and restrict traffic and the means of transportation have existed for many hundreds of years although the current methodology is very new.

There are several reasons for the recent development of the urban

1

transportation process. Perhaps the most obvious reason is the development of the high-speed computer. Before the advent of electronic computers, it was not possible to collect, store, and analyze the vast quantities of data needed to carry out transportation planning for an entire urban area, within a time period and at a cost less than that of experimenting with the real-world transportation system. Thus, prior to the advent of modern computers, planning could only be carried out for specific transportation facility improvements (e.g., the widening of a mile or two of highway, an intersection improvement, etc.), without the capability of assessing the wide local and regional implications of the improvement. However, it was not the computer alone that provided the impetus for regional planning of the type described here. Rather, the computer was one of the enabling factors. To understand the need for regional planning, it is necessary to consider another aspect of the history of transportation—the responsibility for its provision.

Until the early nineteenth century, all transportation within an urban area was provided largely by the private individual, with some limited for-hire transportation. Public transportation was limited entirely to interurban movements and was provided by the stage coach. Provision of rights of way for either public or private transport was not, in the past, the primary motivation for road construction. Rather, throughout those parts of Europe that were within the influence of the Roman Empire, the motivation to provide roads for interurban travel was a military one—to provide a ready means to transport troops and weapons for conquest or defense. Even now, one of the criteria for providing interstate highways in the United States is that of national defense. Thus, the origins of much of the original intercity network of highways was a military one. Even within many of the older cities of Europe, the origins of the intraurban network were tied into the concept of a fortified, walled city and were, first and foremost, intended to provide ready access to the city walls and major defense points under conditions of attack. Elsewhere, the provision of local highways was a more ad hoc procedure, based upon common usage, with many rights-of-way beginning as little more than footpaths.

By the early eighteenth century, changes were already taking place in this pattern, and more coherent attempts were being made to design rights-of-way as an integral part of the city. This form of planning was most successful in the then European colonies, such as North America and Australia. In these countries, where few permanent settlements had been erected by the indigent populations, the settling Europeans were able to design entire cities. The hallmark of many of these city highway systems is the rectangular grid, which replaced the totally haphazard location of streets and highways that occurred over many centuries in most European towns. However, the responsibility for providing the streets and roads at this time was usually held by the developer of the urban area. In other words, it was largely a private industry responsibility and was concerned primarily with providing the necessary accessibility between residences, workplaces, and urban services.

The advent of steam locomotion did little to change this. Provision of rights-of-way was largely still a private industry concern, dictated in Europe by commercial motivations and in North America by the combination of commercial motivation and exploration of an unknown hinterland. The development, subsequently, of public transport on its own right-of-way—elevated rapid transit, underground railway, etc.—did little to change this, although government at both the local and national level began to become increasingly involved at least in approving or licensing rights-of-way. The proliferation of intraurban public transport in the late nineteenth and early twentieth centuries, however, began the process of the collapse of public transport as a successful private enterprise. Proliferation of competing lines occurred at a rate greater than the growth of the market for travel, and often at the expense of service to the public. The resulting economic collapses of many private operators and the lack of good service gradually forced the intervention of government in the provision of mass transport. Thus, both in Europe and in North America, the advent of the automobile also led to the gradual absorption of public transport into the public sector and to government control. This process is almost complete in Europe and is accelerating rapidly in North America.

At the same time public transportation was becoming a government-owned business, the provision of new roads and highways was also moving into a more tightly controlled era, in which most provision and maintenance was being assumed by government at the local or regional level. In the United States, this process was accelerated by the commencement of taxation on gasoline sales and other aspects of automobile ownership and use with the creation of the Highway Trust Fund in 1956. This legislation dedicated the proceeds of all such revenues to the provision of rights-of-way for the automobile and to certain aspects of the maintenance of existing rights-of-way. A similar process of governmental assumption of responsibility for providing and maintaining highways occurred in most European countries in the early twentieth century, but without the legislative push administered by the United States Highway Trust Fund. In large measure, the change in responsibilities for streets and highways was a result of increasing pressures on existing road space, coupled with technological advances in road surfacing materials and rapid population increases that generated major pressures for new residential, commercial, and industrial development throughout Europe and North America.

Thus, by a quarter of a century ago, the responsibility for the provision of most urban area transportation services had been assumed by various levels of governmental jurisdiction throughout most countries of Western culture. This assumption of responsibility also had the effect of changing the entire procedure for providing transport services and rights-of-way. Before public ownership of public transport services, a quasi-free market situation had existed for providing such services, and roads were provided for access without much consideration of the ability of the arterial street network to handle increased traffic loads. Governmental responsibility for urban area transport changes all the rules of the game. Since such services have to be paid for from general taxation revenue, allocation of funds has to be considered among all public services, such as education, health care, provision of water, sewage and refuse disposal, together with public transport services and roads. Similarly, criteria for the allocation of transport funds have changed since government does not have a profit-making responsibility to shareholders, but has, instead, a broad responsibility to the taxpayer to use resources sensibly. Clearly, those changed criteria lead to a requirement that the provision of all aspects of transport be planned by the local jurisdiction in such a way that allocation of funds to transport can be made effectively and that transport projects can be selected on an informed basis and with some knowledge of the probable consequences of undertaking certain projects while not undertaking others.

**Legislative Background**

As discussed in the previous section, most transport legislation in the past was aimed at limited control of the private enterprises providing transport services. This took the principal form of requirements for licenses or franchises to operate public transport services, together with limited controls on the planning of subdivisions in and around urban areas. However, the increasing involvement of government in the transport sector of the economy has brought with it major changes in the legislative situation. In order to simplify the discussion of the legislative background, this section is concerned with the situation that obtains in the United States, although the student will find many parallels in the legislative patterns of other Western culture nations.

With respect to streets and highways, one of the first requirements in a multilevel jurisdiction is to determine what levels of government will have what degree of responsibility for the provision and maintenance of different streets and highways. This has given rise to a hierarchy of classes of roads. In the United States this classification has defined at least six broad groups of highways with responsibilities divided between the federal government (Federal Highway Administration of the U.S. Department of Transportation); state government (State Department of Highways or Transportation); counties; and cities, towns, or villages. In order of decreasing federal involvement in the capital expenditure, these classes are:[1]

1. Interstate highways, defined by legislation in Congress in 1956, for which capital expenditure is apportioned as 90 percent federal and 10 percent local (including state, county, city, etc.).
2. Major interurban arterials, including all designated United States routes, for which the federal government provides 60 to 75 percent of the capital funds and the local jurisdictions provide the balance.
3. State highways, not classified for national defense, for which the federal government provides 40 to 60 percent of the capital funds.
4. Local feeder routes and intracity arterials receive 10 to 40 percent federal funding and the balance comes from local sources.
5. County roads, which generally form a secondary network in both urban and rural areas, receive generally no federal funding, but are the joint responsibility of the state and county, with some funds shared by local communities, depending upon state legislation.
6. City, town, or village roads, which generally comprise the remainder of the highway system and provide access between land areas and the secondary and primary highway systems, are generally the responsibility of the local city, town, or village, with additional funding from the county or state, depending upon local legislation.

In terms of the maintenance of each class of highway, the federal government appoints the states as its agents for the maintenance of all principal federal-aid routes, these being classes 1 and 2 as defined above. Federal funds are not provided to the states for the maintenance of these highways.[2] In general, the state provides all funds for the maintenance of state highways, and local feeder routes, and intracity arterials. Similarly, maintenance of county roads, and local roads, is primarily the responsibility of the county and the local community, respectively. However, there may be funds available from state sources for certain types of maintenance work, dependent upon fiscal policy approved at that governmental level.

The picture for public transport is much less clearly defined. Broad programs for capital and operating expenditure have not been defined in quite the same form as the programs for highway expenditure, and there is no equivalent of the Highway Trust Fund for public transport. The provision of urban public transport services has been defined as a local responsibility with the availability of federal funds for certain types of expenditure administered through the Urban Mass Transportation Administration of the U.S. Department of Transportation.[3] In general, the acquisition of a public transport company by a local government agency qualifies for substantial federal funding, and may range up to 67 percent of the acquisition costs. Purchase of new equipment can also receive federal funding through the Capital Grants Program, which provides up to 67 percent of the costs from federal sources. New equipment purchases may also qualify for federal assistance under the Demonstration Program of the federal government, under which federal assistance may be provided at a rate of 67 percent of capital expenditure. This source of funding is, however, restricted to capital expenditure on new or novel transport systems, where the expenditure can be used to demonstrate the potentials of such a system. Finally, under recent legislation, two further sources of funds have been created. The first of these is the use of the Highway Trust Fund for capital expenditure on certain types of public transportation investments.[4] Generally, expenditure of these funds is restricted to road-based public transport and to other nonauto transport, such as bicycles. The second source of federal funds is the National Mass Transportation Assistance Act of 1975, which provides $11.8 billion for transportation hardware and operating subsidies.[5] Until 1974 the federal government had considered that it was the role of state and local governments to provide such subsidies. However, with the increasing costs of maintaining existing public transport systems, the increased awareness of detrimental impacts of proliferated private auto use, and the service pressures resulting from recent shortages and price increases of fuel, it has become apparent that local and state resources are insufficient to provide the size of subsidies now required.

Legislation and funding for interurban mass transport has generally taken a different form, particularly since private industry is still much more heavily involved in this market than in the urban arena. Airlines and railroads are still privately owned, although the federal government has assumed responsibility for interurban rail transport through AMTRAK. Similarly, interurban bus companies are still under private ownership. Federal legislation has continued to be concerned with control and licensing of this transport sector, with financial aid provided only through direct negotiation with, and special appropriation by, Congress. However, since the major emphasis of this book is on urban transport, this sector will not be considered any further.

Finally, there has been considerable legislation affecting the transport of freight, both within and between urban areas. The concern of this book is with the intraurban element, where most freight transport is by truck, apart from pipeline and power line distribution systems. The primary legislation here takes the form of the licensing of carriers both in terms of commodity groups and routes. Generally, however, legislation over routing is undertaken at the interurban level. Freight transport is conducted as a profit-making private industry subject to local, state, and federal controls. Freight distribution and collection within urban areas is handled, for the most part, independently of interurban hauls and is less subject to federal control but more subject to local and state control, which varies in nature from city to city. Financial provisions of legislation affecting freight transportation are primarily taxation of vehicles and exclusive rights-of-way, and provision of highways and streets for road-based vehicles.

**Need for Transportation Studies**

As stated earlier, the increasing involvement—particularly financial—of the federal government (in the U.S.) in urban area transportation led to increasing pressures to carry out planning for transportation on a fairly long-term basis and in a way that would allow fairer assessment of federal fiscal allocations between public sectors, as well as between alternative transportation projects. These pressures produced federal legislation in 1952, based on the current federal involvement in highway provision, that required urban areas to conduct metropolitan-area studies of transportation as a prerequisite to receiving federal funds for urban highway construction. In effect, this legislation created the "Urban Transportation Study" for which the technology—principally in the form of high-speed digital computers—was just becoming available. The initial concern of these metropolitan-areawide studies was with highway travel and particularly with provision for the private automobile. This should not be construed as being a necessarily short-sighted or narrow-minded view by the federal government of the United States but rather as a natural consequence of the fact that the federal government was relatively uninvolved with public transport (in financial terms) in the early 1950s while it was heavily involved in the provision of highways. It should also be recognized that the requirement to plan highways at a metropolitan-area level was a major progressive step since most highway planning prior to 1952 was conducted at a much more local level and without any concept of the impacts of individual projects on areawide travel and urban structure.

Thus, although this chapter started by pointing out that the need for transportation planning has existed for hundreds of years and in probably every major civilization on this globe, it has only been the combination of factors—public spending on transport provision, computer technology, and finance-based legislation—that have arisen in this century that have been able to produce the art of transport planning as it is dealt with in this book.

**Urban Transportation Problem**

Many papers and treatises on transportation talk of "the" urban transportation problem. So far, little more has been done than to identify a few of the symptoms of the problem and to attempt to define what the problem is. It is, perhaps, inappropriate or inaccurate to talk of a single problem since it has not been established that there is but one problem. Therefore, the topic of this section is the identification of urban transportation problems.

To understand the actual problems that have arisen, it is necessary, first and foremost, to determine what transportation is. Transportation may be defined as the movement of objects (goods and people) in the three dimensions of space, time, and state.[6] The dimensions of time and space have traditionally been considered in definitions of transportation. The concept of state, however, is of relatively recent vintage in this context. In this usage, state may also be defined as market value (or utility; see chapter 3). Thus, a good may have a specific value in one time and location, and another value in a different time and location. This represents a change in state. A similar rationale applies to changes in time and location of people, although market value may not necessarily be the correct synonym for state in that case. In summary, transportation is not only a change in time and location, but also a change in state. By considering these three dimensions, some estimate can be made of the demand for transportation as each of the three dimensions vary.

With the exception of certain recreational trips, transportation is not required simply for its own sake. It is, rather, a means of accomplishing some other purpose. Thus, people make trips in order to get to their place of work; to shopping centers; to friends, clubs, or social activities; etc. Similarly, transportation of goods serve the purpose of collection of raw materials and distribution of finished items. These purposes represent the change in state of the transported item. Basically, transportation can be considered largely as an undesirable necessity. It is undesirable in that it requires expenditures of money, time, and energy, all of which are scarce resources, and it may be considered in certain ways to be basically unproductive. It is necessary because of the spatial separations that exist in the physical environment.

If transportation of people and goods is necessary, then presumably it is desirable to minimize the total costs (money, time, and other expenditures) of transportation. At the same time, there is a general desire to live in residential locations that are not close to the industrial and commercial centers of cities, while the jobs of the residents frequently are found in these centers. Thus, the locational shifts of jobs and residences tend to place greater distances between home and work and so require more transportation. Furthermore, other land uses, such as shops and stores, and recreational areas, also tend to be grouped, and their use entails further transportation. Population patterns have been shifting and central area populations have diminished or have changed radically in their socioeconomic composition over the past few decades. The richer city dwellers, willing and able to pay for transportation to and from work, and to pay a premium for residences located in suburban areas, have tended to move out of the central cities. Their migration has left the central city populated with a disproportionately larger number of the poorer people and has brought about a subsequent decline in the tax base of the central city. Again, the erosion of the tax base has become even more damaging because the population changes bring rising welfare rolls, prolonged unemployment, and racial barriers in education, housing, and public facilities, all of which demand greater expenditures by the city.

While the tax base of the central city is being eroded, the rapid growth of the suburbs is increasing the demands for certain urban amenities normally furnished by central cities. Because both the political institutions and municipal boundaries were set up before current suburban growth, the municipal and political organization intensifies the problems of the central city. Hence, economically the central city is being called upon to make considerably greater and ever increasing expenditures while at the same time it suffers a continuous erosion of its tax base.

It is clear that there is not simply one urban transportation problem, just as there is not one urban problem. Transportation problems represent a number of the constituent factors of a complex of urban problems. In fact, in many respects, transportation may be considered one of the major causes of present urban problems and also one of their symptoms. Although attempting to solve urban transportation problems may often be only a matter of tackling one of the symptoms of these urban ills, there is still a strong case for solving transportation problems in their own right. Because of the central role that transportation plays in the proper functioning of our highly industrialized and commercialized society, it is deserving of a considerable amount of attention, effort, and investment to improve its performance in this vital role. Even a partial paralysis in one of the components of the national transportation system leads to severe economic and social consequences, nationwide (e.g., strikes by air traffic controllers, longshoremen, bus and truck drivers, etc.).

However, it must also be noted that, with this very rapid growth of transportation methods and availability of transportation, cities have been extremely slow to adapt themselves. Even now, after a period of some 25 years of so-called transportation planning, cities are relatively poorly adapted to the automotive age. In 1973 the United States had a total of more than 110 million motor vehicles.[7] Yet for this total population of motor vehicles, there is only a relatively limited mileage of urban highways that have been built to adequate standards. For the most part, traffic still moves on an antiquated gridiron of streets laid out long before the needs of the automobile were known. In addition to this, little provision has been made for parking motor vehicles and for allowing people to perform loading and unloading activities. Typically, excellent design standards and plenty of capacity are provided by the rural highways, but as soon as these enter the urban area, a considerable reduction of the total level of service of the highways is experienced. One of the major symptoms of this type of level of service and provision of facilities is that of the extremely serious accident rate—the number of people killed and injured on our highways.

The separation between homes and work that was alluded to earlier has also created another feature of the urban transportation picture. This is the considerable movement of people between home and work each day. Because of the pattern of concentration of home locations and work locations, considerable volumes of traffic along relatively narrow corridors are generated by trips to and from work. At the same time, most working hours are similar through the whole spectrum of jobs, and thus people travel between home and work at approximately the same times in the day. This is what gives rise to the typical peaking of traffic volumes (Figure 1-1). It has been shown in a number of studies of cities, varying in size from less than 5,000 to several million, that between 40 and 60 percent of the total travel in the urban area each day comprises trips between home and work. The results of this heavy concentration of trips both in terms of time and space are the typical problems of commuting traffic: congestion, frustration, delays. Neglect of public mass-transportation facilities, lack of coordinated planning between highways and mass transport, and the overriding investments made in highway transportation over the last few decades have combined to present a considerably increased problem in the urban area.

The urban transportation problem can be summarized as comprising a number of facets. While being tied very deeply into the total urban problem, the urban transportation problem itself is concerned principally with the ever rising costs of frustration and congestion, the impetus of expansion within the urban area, the attendant increased requirement for transportation facilities within the total urban area, and a desire, at the same time, to minimize the outlay of time and money involved in transportation.

**Possible Solutions**

There are a number of alternatives that present themselves for tackling this problem. The first of these is simply to do nothing on the assumption that the problem will go away or alternatively that its worsening will itself generate solutions. Improbable as it may at first sound, this may be not only a plausible alternative, but may occasionally be the best alternative. There is a growing body of data that suggests that certain symptoms of the urban transportation problem have no cure. Almost regardless of the provision of additional road capacity where there is serious congestion, levels of con-

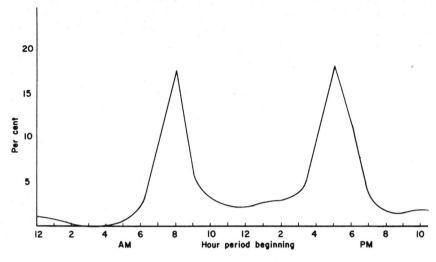

**Figure 1-1.** Typical Traffic Peaking Pattern.

gestion in many parts of our urban areas seem to remain more or less constant. This suggests that people will tolerate certain levels of congestion and beyond these levels will either cease to make the trip or will make it by a less congested means of travel or in a less congested direction. Similarly, there is evidence to suggest that an hour of travel time (in one direction) represents the normal limit for commuting travel. Improved travel speeds thus generally have had the effect of pushing the residential limits of cities further and further out from the city center, generally to about one hour's commuting time. Thus, it may be futile to suppose that there is any policy alternative, except one of constraint, that can shorten commuting time or reduce some levels of congestion. A "do-nothing" alternative may then be a completely sound and reasonable option.

The second alternative is to tackle the urban ills that have produced, in large part, our present transportation problems and to cure these urban ills directly. This sounds like a good approach. However, the expertise and knowledge are both lacking for making a concerted effort at combatting these urban ills and, at the same time, the total cost of so doing would probably be very considerable, and possibly beyond the bounds of present resources. The third alternative, which is the one with which this text is primarily concerned, is that of attempting to understand the phenomenon of transportation and, through that understanding, to be able to devise methods by which the present dimensions of the problem can be attacked effectively and by which future probable transportation can be catered for by present investment.

The fourth alternative, which may well also form a part of the third one, is that of attempting to see how far it may be possible to substitute other forms of communication for transportation. It is clear that transportation, to a large extent, performs basically the function of a form of communication. For instance, it allows people to gather in one place to perform a job of work. It also performs the function of allowing people to interact socially, or in business, in recreation, or in other activities. In all these ways it performs simply the task of being a channel of communication. It is, therefore, logical to look at transportation within the entire spectrum of forms of communication.

This aspect of transportation, as a part of the total communication system, is something that obviously warrants some further study. A number of proposals have been put forward in the past for substitution of various types of transportation by means of modern electronic communication systems. Among these it has been suggested that it may be possible for the housewife to shop for groceries and other household necessities from her home by means of telephone and closed circuit television that would allow her to view the products and choose them, and place her order. The order itself would then be delivered, possibly by means of some form of freight transportation but also conceivably by means of a communication line existing between her house and the store. Such communication lines might comprise some form of tube able to carry mail, groceries, and a number of other commodities and items that regularly have to be delivered to residences. Similarly, many social interactions may well be substituted for by the same combination of telephone and closed circuit television. It is also conceivable that a number of jobs may be performed remotely by means of television and telephone. Any developments of this type must certainly have a major impact upon the necessities and types of provision of transportation in urban areas.

As well as considering the ways in which communications of different forms such as telephone, television, etc. can substitute for transportation directly, it is also worthwhile to look at the way in which other activities may be substituted for the activities that currently generate the need for transportation. For example, television, radio, and other forms of home entertainment have formed somewhat of a substitute for the dance hall, the theater, and the cinema. It is possible that further technological advances may provide yet additional nontransportation activities that may substitute for activities currently requiring transportation. Again, it may be noted that the basic core of this argument is the fact that urban transportation should be regarded not as a single isolated system by itself, but as a subset of a much larger system. It is clear also that all attempts that may be made to try to understand this phenomenon of transportation, to cater for it, to predict it for the future, and so forth, are predicated upon the fact that it is a subsystem, rather than a system alone.

In the past it has been quite common that most transportation planning has been carried out in isolation. It is for this reason that such a high emphasis is being placed here on the necessity of viewing transportation planning as the planning of a subsystem within a very large total system. It is, therefore, necessary to bear in mind that urban transportation planning must be set up in such form that it interacts consistently with total urban planning, with technology developments, with communications developments, etc.

Finally, consideration should be given as to how travel patterns in the United States have been changing. It should be noted that these changes are not confined solely to the United States, although they are very clear and obvious there. First, total travel growth in urban areas has been occurring at a fairly alarming rate. In the period from 1950 to 1960, urban travel grew by 52 percent, from 218 billion vehicle miles to 332 billion vehicle miles. By 1970 this had grown to over 550 billion vehicle miles, or two and one-half times the 1950 figure and 66 percent over the 1960 figure. This rate of increase has only recently been slowed by energy shortages, but 1980 figures are expected to show a further substantial increase over 1970.[8] Second, mass transit travel as a whole is decreasing. Mass transit use is extremely important in carrying central city residents to work or in carrying central city workers to work in outlying suburbs. However, mass transit service has been curtailed time and time again in the past, and it is not suited to carry central city residents to outlying business areas because of the high degree of dispersion of destinations in such areas. It should also be noted, in relation to mass transit, that the major area of growth in travel is non-CBD (central business district) oriented trips. These are largely trips that are not particularly well served by existing systems of mass transit.

Within the context of attempting to understand and provide for total travel in the urban area, there are two basic approaches that can be taken to solving these problems. The first of these includes measures such as using traffic engineering techniques to obtain the most efficient use of existing streets; using price mechanisms to ration the use of streets, freeways, and parking by time and location; and using measures to keep cars out of the downtown area.

The other approach would include the construction of new facilities such as freeways, rapid transit, commuter rail systems, off-street parking, downtown distribution systems, truck, rail, and air terminals, all planned to fit into urban development patterns of the future. It might also require massive urban renewal that would involve redevelopment of the central cities and ghetto areas with new transportation facilities as an integral part of the new city. Technological changes could be part of the development of more efficient urban transportation, and governmental reforms may be needed to facilitate regional planning and financing of transit as well as freeways. The approach would imply the development of goals and the planning of systems that are best suited to urban area goals and objectives. It may also require the utilization of land-use zoning to reserve space for the future to develop traffic facilities, and the provision of federal grants and loans for balanced transportation systems, and federal legislation facilitating the creation of balanced systems in much the same way as it exists now for highways (Highway Trust Fund) and airports (Airports and Airway Trust Fund) individually. In order to achieve either approach to solving this problem, it is necessary that the engineer and the planner work together effectively. It is also necessary that legal, administrative, and financial impediments be overcome. The need for the planning process for transportation and areawide development must be recognized to take full consideration of processes that influence social and economic opportunities. All of these alternatives should be expressed in goals in a cost-effective manner. A range of choices should be provided for residents in terms of places to live, work, find recreation and entertainment, shop, and also a range of choices should be provided in modes of travel and levels of service, and for industrial and commercial locations.

Thus, urban transportation planning should comprise an attempt to provide a procedure that will permit the achievement of planning goals. It should be a process directed towards the generation and evaluation of alternative investment policies, in terms of the consequences that would follow from the adoption of such policies. Urban transportation planning also should include attempts to obtain a clearer understanding of the processes that lead to a demand for travel. It is the various aspects of these constituent parts of the urban transportation planning process that are the concern of the rest of this book.

# 2

## Systems Analysis and Principles of Modeling in Transportation

**Introduction**

The planning, provision, and operation of transportation systems constitutes an essential and sizeable component of a properly functioning society. The monetary resources required for these transportation processes are substantial. Other societal needs compete for the available funds. It seems, therefore, justified to spend some time discussing the appropriate approach to be utilized when analyzing these processes.

Originally, transportation planning, as it then was, comprised the planning and provision of isolated facilities such as a bridge or a street, or the widening of an existing street, or a line of a mass transportation facility. As such, facilities were provided by looking only at the specific facility as being the entire spectrum of the planning and construction process. Little or no attempt was made to investigate the impact of such facilities on the rest of the transportation system and most certainly no attempt was made to investigate the impact on the wider urban system. More recently, developments in transportation planning have concentrated not on individual facilities, but on an examination of the total transportation system. Rather than concentrate on just a bridge, a parking garage, or a single transit line, they have dealt with whole networks. However, for the most part, these transportation planning efforts have still not considered the impact on the rest of the transportation system and have still not looked in detail at the impact on the wider urban system. As a consequence of this, the alternatives that are put forward, as a result of the transportation planning process, have largely been evaluated with only a partial set of consequences available. Such evaluation tends to lead to serious and erroneous conclusions and may result in a serious misinvestment of resources in a specific transportation plan.

The reason for this apparent deficiency in approach and investigation in the past lies not only in the fact that short-sighted hardware orientation frequently dominated the thinking of transportation planners and engineers. It also was a consequence of the absence of appropriate planning tools and theories as well as analytical and computational techniques that permit the quantitative analysis of complex systems. The development of the concept and tools of systems analysis as a way of analyzing complex problems has opened up new possibilities for better transportation planning.

15

Conventionally, what are termed transportation facilities comprise such things as highways, railway lines, bus routes, and terminals. These together constitute an extraordinarily complex system within which each element has effects on the performance of the other elements, and in turn is affected by the performance levels of all of the other elements. At the same time this transportation system is only a subset of a larger total communication system. In general, travel is not demanded for its own sake, but is rather a derivative of a more basic demand for goods and services. The pattern of urban travel demand is largely determined by the pattern of urban activities. Again, the urban transportation system is also a component or subsystem of the much larger urban system. As discussed in the first chapter, the transportation system both influences and is influenced by each of the other subsystems that make up the total urban system. Throughout the entire transportation planning process, it is necessary that the interactions between the transportation subsystem and the other subsystems in the urban system are observed and allowed for. The objectives of the transportation system are closely intermingled with overall planning objectives and should be considered together with them rather than isolated from them. Similarly, the transportation objectives can be attained in a wide variety of ways and not all of these will necessarily require substantial investments in the construction of new facilities. There may also be significant trade-offs between transportation investment and investments in other urban subsystems. Given this highly complex system of interactions, there is one technique available that may be employed usefully as a basis for setting up the process of urban transportation planning. This technique is known as systems analysis. The first half of this chapter will be concerned with this technique, particularly as it may be applied to the planning of transportation facilities.

## Systems Approach

First, it should be clarified what systems analysis is and does. In very brief terms, *systems analysis* is a technique or framework for setting about the solution of a problem. It is not, itself, a solution. Rather, it permits the development of a systematic and comprehensive approach to a specific problem and provides a frame of reference that should hopefully ensure a balanced and reasoned solution to a problem. At this point it seems appropriate to point out some of the semantic difficulties the student of systems analysis might run into. A quote from Charles J. Hitch and Ronald N. McKean serves as an illustration of the problem:

Systematic effort to determine preferred courses of action is called "operations research" when applied to problems in military or industrial operation. It is called "systems analysis" when applied to certain broader or longer-range problems, particularly the comparison of weapons systems. It is called "cost-benefit analysis" when such things as water-resource developments are being considered.[1]

And to complicate matters, in computer design the term systems analysis is used to describe detailed computer programming. In the meantime, a more meaningful differentiation between the concepts has evolved and is briefly presented here. As stated previously, systems analysis is a term used to describe an approach to the study of large complex systems, where a system can be characterized as a group of interdependent elements that function together for a purpose. Operations research developed into a set of tools, namely of mathematical optimization techniques, which prove to be useful and are typically applied in the model-building phases of a systems analysis. It has also developed into a separate discipline in the academic curriculum. Cost-benefit analysis is now generally considered as one particular technique in the evaluation phase of a project or in the evaluation of alternative plans in a systems analysis. To gain further insight into systems analysis, it may be useful to look at some statements that have been made about it in connection with its application to transportation in particular:

[An approach] . . . in which we fit an individual action or relationship into the bigger system of which it is a part, and one in which there is a tendency to represent the system in terms of a formal model.[2]

. . . inquiry to assist the decision-maker to select a course of action by systematically investigating his proper objectives, comparing quantitatively, where possible, the costs, effectiveness and risks associated with the alternative policies or strategies for achieving them, and formulating additional alternatives if those examined are found wanting. Systems analysis represents an approach to, or way of looking at, complex problems of choice under uncertainty. In such problems, objectives are usually multiple and possibly conflicting, and analysis designed to assist the decision-maker must necessarily involve a large element of judgement; . . .[3]

. . . the more important objectives of systems engineering:

  (i) Provide management with as much information as possible needed to guide and control the over-all development program.

 (ii) Formulate long-range plans and objectives as a framework for tying together individual projects.

(iii) Balance the over-all development program to assure progress along all needed lines, at the same time making the best use of development manpower and other resources.

(iv) Develop objectives and plans for individual projects and make those consistent with long-range objectives. Know the present needs of the organization. Look ahead to anticipate future needs to be fully prepared when the time comes for action.

 (v) Keep abreast of new ideas, principles, methods, and devices. Ensure the best and most timely use of new technology.

(vi) Carry out each operation in the systems engineering process in the most efficient manner possible, recognizing that the requirements for detail, accuracy, and speed depend upon the phase of the process one is working in.[4]

. . . procedures for planning, designing, and managing large-scale physical systems . . .[5]

The key words in these definitions are that systems analysis provides a framework for a *systematic* approach to solving *complex problems* under conditions of *uncertainty*. The technique provides an approach in which *objectives* are defined and *alternatives* are assessed against these objectives. The entire process is carried out in the framework of identified *systems* and *subsystems*.

A number of the above words, and several additional ones, have some specific connotations in the framework of systems analysis. These terms need to be defined in order to be able to understand fully the systems analysis procedure.

*System*: A set of objectives, fixed or mobile, meaningfully connected and satisfactorily bounded, that interact for a common purpose.

*Subsystem*: A smaller system that is a component of the larger system. All systems are composed of subsystems and are themselves elements of a larger system. The definition of system boundaries is a function of the analytical purpose.

*Environment*: The set of objectives or relationships external to a system, including all external influences and conditions that may interact with the operation of the system.

*Closed System*: One that is not influenced by its environment.

*Open System*: A system whose performance is influenced by its immediate environment.

*Interface*: The points at which interaction occurs between a system and its environment or between two separate systems.

*Values*: Irreducible qualities upon which individual and group preferences are based.

*Goals*: Idealized end states toward which a plan might be expected to move. The desired eventual end states of a planning process.

*Objectives*: Operational statements of goals, measurable and attainable. (Attainability is defined without reference to availability of resources or to budgetary restrictions.)

*Alternatives*: Means of accomplishing a specified objective; a plan, design or program.

*Criteria*: Indices expressing the degree of goal or objective attainment.

*Resources*: The available inputs to the system, monetary, labor, and physical.

*Constraints*: Limitations on resource inputs and undesirable systems outputs.

*Model*: An abstraction of reality, formulated in either conceptual, physical, or mathematical terms and used as a mechanism for reproducing the operation of a real world system for analytical purposes.

*Direct Output*: Performance outputs directly related to the attainment of system objectives, (desirable).

*Indirect Output*: Concomitant outputs that result from the operation of the system but are not directly related to its immediate objectives, (desirable or undesirable).

*System Consequences*: The entire set of consequences that stem from the operation of the system, including the effects of resource consumption, the consequences of system output, and the impact of the system on its immediate environment.

**Strategy of Systems Analysis**

Having defined systems analysis and the various terms associated with it, the operation of systems analysis may now be examined. Definition of the problem constitutes the first task. After that, it is necessary to define and bound the system under consideration. This requires the identification of the elements of the system, the isolation of pertinent subsystems, the definition of the environment and interfaces.

The next process required is one that will lead to the specification of objectives. This is perhaps the single most intransigent element in the systems analysis procedure. There is no foolproof technique for generating an appropriate set of objectives. The process of specifying objectives can probably best be achieved by utilizing the links between values, goals, objectives, and criteria. Each of these represents a restatement, in more operational terms, of the preceding element. For example:

*Value*: Equity.

*Goal*: Equal accessibility to workplaces for all urban residents.

*Objective*: Equal incidence of travel costs for all workers irrespective of income or location.

*Criterion*: Constant ratio of cost of travel to work to daily wage; all workers, all points of residence, and employment.

Each stage has become more definitive and restricted, and more readily adapted to a quantitative assessment. In defining or generating objectives it is useful to proceed through the stages of values and goals. The definition of criteria from the objectives is required to enable a comparison to be made between the original objectives and the consequences of alternatives. This issue is pursued again a little later in this chapter.

The next step in the systems analysis process is the allocation of resources to the problem. In this step, the resources are evaluated in terms of their availability for the problem being considered. This would include, for instance, the determination of the monetary and manpower budgets applicable to the problem.

Following this, it is necessary to develop a system model. This involves the formulation, calibration, and validation of a basic system model. The model is designed to permit the prediction of the consequences of alternative plans without the necessity of direct experimentation on the real-world system. This concept is used later in attempting to develop criteria for model building.

At this point, the basic requirements for predicting the consequences of various alternative plans have been developed. However, before generating alternatives, a set of criteria is required by which to assess goal achievement of the alternative plans. This requires a restatement of objectives in a form that will permit evaluation of alternatives and assessment of system performance and goal attainment. Having selected criteria, the next task is to generate alternative system designs and methods of achieving the specified objectives.

The various alternatives generated need then to be evaluated. For evaluation purposes, it is necessary to predict the consequences of each alternative plan. These are predicted by feeding the pertinent system parameters into the system model. The full spectrum of consequences stemming from each alternative have to be predicted. The next stage in the process is the evaluation and comparison of the alternatives in terms of their effectiveness, efficiency, and costs. With this output, the "best" alternative can be selected and implemented. In the event that none of the alternatives are deemed to be satisfactory, the process may be recycled to generate new alternatives, specify consequences, and evaluate further alternatives until an acceptable best alternative can be selected. The strategy is represented in Figure 2-1.

This process also can be adapted to a goal-seeking mechanism. As discussed earlier, the specification of goals and objectives is about the most intransigent element of the process. In many cases, it is possible to use the process to generate or reduce the goals. In the first case, the process can be initiated with a minimal set of goals and objectives. In the processes of identifying consequences and evaluating alternatives, further goals may be generated. Alternatively, a large set of goals may be identified initially, and

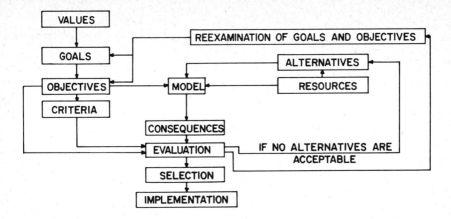

**Figure 2-1.** Systems Analysis Procedure in Flow-Diagram Form.

the same stages in the process used to discard these goals and objectives that are unattainable with the resources available, and to increase the precision of specification of those goals that are feasible and desirable.

Finally, one further feature of systems analysis should be noted, particularly when it is applied to transportation. Typical transportation "goals" might include efficiency, economy, safety, speed, comfort, convenience, etc. These goals are meaningful in the context of transportation and the transportation system, but they cannot be considered independently of the total urban system. It must always be remembered that the urban transportation system is required to facilitate movement in an urban area and that that movement is not an end in itself. Therefore, the goals for the transportation system must be considered only in reference to the goals of the urban system, and should frequently be considered subservient to the urban goals. This also reveals one further important facet of the process. Clearly, no matter how hard the analyst may strive to be completely impartial, the goals will reflect his own individual biases. The systems analytic approach permits the inclusion of a greater number of factors interacting within the transportation system itself and between that system and its environment. It could be said that transportation systems analysis was necessitated by the rise of environmental and social concerns over transportation system changes. On the other hand, such an approach is also the enabling factor that allows for the inclusion of such concerns in the transportation planning process.

The systems approach is appropriate and essential in the area of transportation planning because of the fact that the analyst typically does not have the opportunity and ability to conduct physical experiments in the laboratory in order to evaluate the performance and functioning of alternative transportation hardware or operations. Aside from the prohibitive costs such experiments would also be operationally infeasible.

### Example of the Application of Systems Analysis

Consider now a transportation problem in order to see how this technique of systems analysis may be utilized.

1. Problem:
   a) To examine the feasibility of providing an improved public transport system in a large urban area.
   b) In global terms, this problem is one alternative solution to the problem of providing for efficient movement and communication.
   c) In specific terms, within the mass transportation system, the problem is that of determining the best alternative method of improving mass transportation so that it will be competitive with the private car.

2. Values:
   a) Equity
   b) Accessibility
   c) Safety
   d) Amenity
   e) Economy
   f) Privacy
   g) Flexibility

3. Goals:

   To develop a mass transport system that will be *efficient, economic* to use and operate, *attractive* and *safe* to ride, *convenient* and *reliable*, and that will have a *minimal disruptive* effect on the environment through which it passes.

4. Objectives:
   a) Equal incidence of costs for all users
   b) Uniform level of service in all areas
   c) Acceptable noise levels inside and outside the vehicle
   d) Minimal neighborhood disruption
   e) Minimal pollutant emission
   f) Minimum cost for a given level of objective attainment
   g) Minimal schedule sensitivity to external effects (e.g., highway congestion, vehicle breakdown, etc.)

5. Criteria:
   a) Equal ratio for cost/income for all users
   b) Probability of wait $> t$ minutes $\leq p$ in all areas.
   c) Internal noise $\leq 35\,dB$; external noise $\leq 60\,dB$ at 75 ft.
   d) Amount of right-of-way required, number of buildings taken to be minimized.
   e) CO emission $\leq x$ ppm per minute; hydrocarbons $\leq y$ ppm per minute; nitrogen oxides $\leq z$ ppm per minute at idle speed.
   f) Total annual operating cost, including amortization of capital expenditure $\leq \$Q$ thousand.

6. Alternatives:
   a) Modify and extend existing mass transport services, maintaining existing technology but improving level and quality of service and introducing new fare services and modifications of engine
   b) Ban or tax the use of autos in congested areas and modify engines of existing mass transportation vehicles
   c) Integrated line-haul/distributor system
   d) Demand bus system
   e) Rail pallet
   f) Multimode capsule
   g) Automated highway
   h) Do nothing.

7. Models:
   a) Computer simulation
   b) Mathematical program
   c) Econometric demand model
   d) Preference model

   The evaluation process would then require an analysis of the alternatives and an assessment against each of the specified criteria. Also, the available resources should be specified and any alternatives requiring greater resources than those available would be rejected immediately.

   The specification of goals and objectives is somewhat difficult and tends to reflect the biases of the analyst. Since the professional planner might be expected to perceive the structure of the urban system with more clarity than the layman, his role in the planning process should be an active one. However, it should also not be allowed to dominate since the planner's perceptions and values may not entirely replicate community values, governmental values, etc. Failure to account for an explicit goal set at the outset of the process also causes problems. In effect, such an omission forces the analyst to place his own arbitrary weightings on both the elements included and those excluded, with the additional problem that such weightings will usually be implicit and not explicitly stated. For instance, in the above example, the goal of minimum pollutant emission may have been omitted. In such a case, there is an assumed weighting on the included goals that they are of considerably greater importance than pollutant emission.

Several approaches could be suggested for goal formulation, particularly with reference to the foregoing paragraphs. These include:

*Iterative Concensus*: The political process, the use of expert panels.

*Free Competition*: Advocacy planning and the free pursuit of individual goals, constrained only by preventative legislation.

*Deficiency Identification*: Goal formulation by specifying the deficiencies of the present system and using the elimination of these as goals for a new system.

*Inductive Planning*: Goal specification on the basis of attitudinal and preference analysis.

*Enlightened Design*: Goal specification by knowledgeable specialists, utilizing specific familiarity with system performance and operational constraints.

*Constrained Analysis*: Goal specification limited to transportation system goals, with nontransportation objectives acting as constraints on the transportation system.

*Hierarchical Evaluation*: Specification of hierarchical objective structure and identification of complementary and contradictory goals.

*Goal-seeking Analysis*: Repetitive use of the systems analysis procedure, generating alternative systems to seek out feasible and desirable goals.

In the previous discussion some rather optimistic and normative statements were made about the role of systems analysis. A number of reasons for the optimistic tone about the power and potential of the systems analysis approach can be stated. The rapid development of computer technology has enabled the analyst to evaluate the implications of a number of alternatives characterized by multidimensional descriptors. Partly as a consequence of increased interdisciplinary training and cooperation, the concepts of economic theory are being included in and have made possible the evaluation process. The relatively recent developments of powerful optimization techniques in operations research constitute another reason for the rather optimistic outlook on the use and applicability of the systems approach in the solution of complex problems facing the urban transportation planner.

**Summary of the Systems Analytic Approach**

The systems approach to transportation planning can be summarized in the following terms. The concept of systems analysis applied to transportation planning requires that the problems that are dealt with are identified initially. Given that the problem can be identified, a statement of values has to be made and the pertinent goals developed from these. Given the goals that were developed, they can be restated as a series of objectives for achieving these goals and these objectives may then be further defined by a series of criteria. These criteria enable the planner to generate sets of alternatives. The alternatives so generated must be evaluated in terms of their ability to achieve the objectives. The mechanism by which this is done is to construct some form of models of the system. It is the construction of these models that is the concern of the remainder of this chapter and of much of the remainder of this book. Having generated models and evaluated the alternatives in terms of their ability to achieve or not achieve the objectives, the analyst then has a set of alternative solutions to his problems and he must go through the decision process to determine which of these solutions he will adopt. This basically then covers the entire range of the systems approach to transportation planning and sets the scene for the remainder of the development of transportation planning as it is seen in this book.

**Principles of Modeling Systems**

*Basic Modeling Precepts*

As just discussed, one of the major elements of the systems approach to transportation revolves around an assumption that the system can be modeled. First, it is necessary to consider just exactly what it is that is meant by an ability to model the system. The idea of modeling was raised in the previous discussion in the context of being able to evaluate the ability of possible alternative solutions to achieve a specific set of objectives. This modeling has as its objective an attempt to determine whether or not a specific solution will have a particular effect when implemented in the system. Clearly, the first and most obvious way of evaluating this is to carry out an experiment on the real system. Thus, if one of the objectives is to move people more efficiently and at lower cost within an urban area, and one of the alternatives that is proposed is that of building a large number of new freeways, then clearly one of the ways in which the ability of this alternative to fulfill the objective may be evaluated is to build those freeways. Clearly, though, this type of experimentation with the real system is extremely expensive, has only very limited ability to look at a range of alternatives, and may well produce a considerable spectrum of undesirable consequences. As a result of this, models of the system are required. These models would be such that they allow one to manipulate a number of alternatives without expensive experimentation on the real-world system, and assess the effects of these alternatives on the system. In fact, this may not necessarily be the only reason why models are required. There are at least five basic requirements or uses for models:

1. To enable forecasts to be made
2. To be able to evaluate alternative plans
3. To investigate the makeup of the system and the structure of interactions within it
4. As an aid to explain the principles of operation of the system
5. To improve on decision making based exclusively on intuitive judgement

These purposes of model building are highly interrelated. In general, it is not possible to begin to forecast a future system, or to evaluate alternatives, without first investigating and explaining the structure and operation of the system. By and large, attempts to do the former without the latter lead to false results and erroneous conclusions.

It is important to clarify the terminology used here in reference to functions of models. Three basic functions may generally be carried out by a model: description, prediction, and forecasting. *Description* comprises the use of a model in the location where it was calibrated and for circumstances that are not changed from those that exist at the time of calibration. Causality is not required in such a model, and understanding of the underlying mechanisms is not necessary. *Prediction* is the process of estimating the changes in the performance of the system being modeled that result from changes in characteristics of that system. It is also the process of estimation for a location that is different from the one used for model calibration. Finally, *forecasting* is the use of a model to estimate system performance for a specified time in the future, usually for the location where the model was calibrated. Forecasting is, therefore, a special case of prediction in which the system changes are determined by considering the elapse of a specific time period.

There are basically three forms of models that might be considered as candidates for this process. The first of these would be a purely conceptual model. Such a model would largely have uses in structuring a problem. Second, one may try to build a mathematical model, which would provide a convenient mechanism for simulating the operation of the system and evaluating its performance under a variety of input conditions or environmental constraints. Finally, one might consider a physical model, which would probably be a small-scale version of the real system, on which some form of simulation could again be performed; and this may be required in order to be able to examine the final form and design of the solution that is being generated.

Certain assumptions are implied by asserting that the transportation process can be modeled. First, it is assumed that the traffic phenomenon that is to be modeled is repetitive and predictable; repetitive implies that the process of travel or of traffic, whichever it is that is actually being modeled, has only a relatively small random element, and that basically it represents a phenomenon that repeats itself in a pattern which is susceptible to investigation and quantification. The fact that the phenomenon is stated to be predictable implies an element of rationality in this repetition, such that the repetitions can be reproduced, and predictions can be made because of the regularity of what is being investigated.

Second, it is assumed that the phenomenon exhibits dependence on a number of more easily measured and predicted parameters. Furthermore, this implies that its dependence on these parameters is either independent of time or that its dependence on time is known.

Each of these model types may be seen to have a specific role to play in the total modeling process. In an ideal modeling situation, the conceptual model would represent the first stage in the modeling effort. This would probably take the form of a flow diagram, which shows the interactions of various parts of the total system that is to be modeled. An example is Figure 2-1, which represents a conceptual model of the systems analytic approach.

From here, some form of mathematical model would next be built, which would quantify the various interactions of the systems and subsystems. An example of a mathematical model would be:

$$T_i = 0.12 + 0.76C_i + 0.33I_i + 0.74W_i$$

where  $T_i$ = the number of trips made by household $i$

$C_i$ = the number of cars owned by household $i$

$I_i$ = the annual income in thousands of dollars of household $i$, and

$W_i$ = the number of workers in household $i$

Finally, some form of physical model may be built to represent the way in which the selected alternative—or perhaps two or three alternative solutions—might actually appear in the physical world.


*Dimensions of Models*

Models can be categorized in a number of ways, dependent upon their structure. These categories or dimensions are helpful in determining the appropriate uses to which various models may be put and will be used in later chapters as a partial basis for assessing models in the urban transportation planning process. Eight dimensions may be proposed to describe, in a reasonably formalized manner, the types of models that might be constructed. These are:

1. Descriptive, predictive, or planning models
2. Deterministic or probabilistic models
3. Analytical or statistical, or simulation models
4. Cross-sectional or temporal models
5. Aggregate or disaggregate models
6. Unidirectional or multidirectional models
7. Analogue, homomorphic, or isomorphic models
8. Backward-seeking or forward-seeking models

**Descriptive, Predictive, or Planning Models.** The basic purpose of a *descriptive model* is to attempt to replicate certain relevant features of an existing phenomenon. They have two major achievements: First, good descriptive models reveal the structure of the phenomenon being observed. They reduce the apparent complexity of the observed world to the coherent and rigorous language of mathematical relationships. Second, they may possibly offer a shortcut to field work, by generating reliable values of hard-to-measure variables from considerably easier-to-measure variables. Basically, however, they only describe the existing phenomena, and give no key to future prediction.

*Predictive models*, on the other hand, attempt to provide understanding of the relationship between various features within the system. In descriptive models, it may be sufficient to know that $y$ equals $10x$, or—alternatively—$x$ equals $0.1y$; however, this does not specify the sequence of cause and effect. A predictive model, to have validity, must specify the causal sequence in which events occur. In other words, it must be known whether a unit change in $y$ will *cause* a change of 10 units of $x$, or whether a unit change in $x$ will *cause* $0.1$ units change in $y$. The predictive model is then used in a manner such that, given values of the causes for some future time, the effects may be predicted. In building a model of any particular system or subsystem that is a predictive model, it becomes necessary to classify the variables in the system into one of two types: endogenous or exogenous. *Endogenous* variables are those variables which undergo change within the system. *Exogenous* variables are those variables that are affected only by events outside the system being modeled. In other words, the exogenous variables may be considered as having values provided from outside the system. It then becomes necessary to construct the model in such terms that the endogenous variables are the "effect" variables, and the exogenous ones are the "cause" variables. This follows from the requirement that the models are to predict effect on the basis of cause. It is also necessary to ensure that values of the exogenous variables can be plausibly predicted as far into the future as predictions are required.

Finally, the last category of models in this dimension is that of planning models. The *planning models* go one step further than the basic predictive models. Instead of just attempting to predict what will occur in the future, a planning model incorporates an attempt to evaluate the outputs of the model in terms of the planner's goals. Effectively, a planning model performs four steps:

1. Specification of alternative programs or actions that might be chosen by the planner
2. Prediction of the consequences of choosing each alternative
3. Scoring these consequences according to a metric of goal achievement
4. Choosing the alternative that yields the highest score

The models are usually built on linear or dynamic programming methods.

**Deterministic or Probabilistic Models.** A *deterministic model* is one that specifies the actual outcome of certain events. If it is a predictive model that is deterministic, then it effectively specifies the actual outcome in rigid terms. In other words, a deterministic predictive model of travel demand will specify that, given certain levels or values of the various systems parameters—whether these are descriptions of people or of the transportation system, or of the environment within which people live—then it will predict that a certain total number of people will travel between certain points by certain modes and by certain routes. More specifically, there is only one possible outcome for a deterministic model—an event either occurs or does not occur. On the other hand, a *probabilistic model* would indicate a likelihood of certain events following. Thus, a probabilistic model will indicate a probability of certain outcomes as a result of certain causes.

**Analytical or Statistical, or Simulation Models.** The most satisfying form of solution is an *analytical or statistical solution*. Such a solution could be obtained only where the system to be modeled exhibits a very tight logical structure, and where the internal functional relationships within the system are uncomplicated by discontinuities. Such models may be built by utilizing any of a number of strict mathematical techniques and a set of data as a basis for evaluating the relationships represented within the model. Where such strict relationships do not hold, the next form of solution that may be possible is that of an iterative solution. This is effectively a search technique for a set of output values that satisfy all the constraints of the model. It usually will proceed by assuming certain values for some of the variables and solving analytically for the remainder. These first-round solutions are then used as the basis for computing second approximations to replace the initial estimated values. The process will continue until such time as convergence is achieved, that is, where further iterations fail to make significant changes in the values being solved for. Finally, if the system being modeled does not fall into either of these two categories, the main solution method left open is some form of simulation. In simulation the model specifies an inventory of possible events and indicates the immediate consequences of each event for one or more variables. A change in the magnitude of these variables has specified consequences in the form of inducing new events. Characteristically, however, the major source of new events is exogenous to the system; and in sophisticated simulations such as Monte Carlo, the exogenous events are generated by a random choice from a given frequency distribution of possibilities. The simulation may be made entirely by a computer, or it may be made by a combination of a computer and human intervention.

**Cross-sectional or Temporal Models.** The types of models that have been considered thus far attempt to represent the outcome of a process with temporal dimensions. Beginning at some time in the real-world, say time $t$, the model attempts to indicate what will be the situation at time $t + 1$, $t + 2$, or $t + n$. Two alternatives are possible in building models, given this aspect. In the first place, a model may be built as a *cross-sectional model*. In this case, it is assumed that the temporal dependence of the phenomenon is determined exogenously. In other words, time is not included as an element of the model, and it is assumed that all dependencies upon time can be determined outside the model. Such models are often calibrated on cross-sectional data, which are data collected at a single point in time. Such data do not reflect the dynamic process that may possibly underlie the phenomena. Alternatively, the model may be designed as a *temporal model*. In this case, time is an essential element of the entire model process, and a set of data over a considerable time period is required.

**Aggregate or Disaggregate Models.** If it is *aggregate*, it is possible to consider the process as being that of a mass or group of people, vehicles, or whatever. At this level, the collective behavior and properties of the phenomenon are to be modeled. At a *disaggregate* level, the concern is more with the actual behavior of each separate element of the population that is being modeled. These differences can be illustrated briefly by considering the prediction of travel demand. This may be considered at the level of an entire urban area, in which the requirements are to determine the total number of trips that will be made. This may be modeled at an aggregate level where the area is divided into zones and the total travel demand from each zone is predicted, where these zones may contain as many as 10,000 people. Alternatively, the models may be built by investigating the behavior of each single individual, and then building up the model system for the whole urban area on the basis of each individual. These two demonstrate, respectively, aggregate and disaggregate modeling.

**Unidirectional or Multidirectional Models.** A *unidirectional model* effectively specifies a single process of cause and effect acting in one consistent direction. If the system is modeled in a series of processes, a unidirectional model or model system would require that each step in the process can only affect those steps yet to come. On the other hand, a *multidirectional model* allows interactions to occur in any direction through the system.

**Analogue, Homomorphic, or Isomorphic Models.** In the case of an *analogue model*, a similarity is proposed between some existing phenomenon and the particular system phenomenon to be modeled. For example, an analogue may be proposed between fluid flow in a network of pipes and traffic flow on a road network. Mathematical techniques are then employed to define the precise relationship being sought. A *homomorphic model*, however, is one that behaves *like* the process, but not necessarily for the same reason. In other words, it forms some form of approximation to the process that is being considered. However, it does not necessarily specify the exact cause and effect processes which underlie the phenomenon. Both homomorphic and analogue models are more useful for descriptive modeling than for predictive or planning modeling. An *isomorphic model*, on the other hand, attempts to model the process exactly, by finding the causes and effects and simulating the process of interaction between cause and effect.

**Backward- or Forward-Seeking Models.** A *forward-seeking model* moves ahead one step at a time, and seeks to determine the eventual outcome of a sequence of events. In contrast, a *backward-seeking model* determines a goal that is desired and works backwards to determine the events that must occur between the present time and the goal in order to realize that goal. Alternatively, these different forms may be specified by considering that a forward-seeking model is effectively a goal-seeking model, that is, it moves forward to attempt to find what alternatives may exist as a result of present actions, and allows the planner to seek from these the goals that he would desirably wish to achieve. On the other hand, a backward-seeking model starts with goals and attempts to demonstrate the methods that may be used to achieve those goals.

This by no means represents an exhaustive set of dimensions that may be used to describe models; however, the concepts that have been discussed here are extremely useful in describing the types of models that might be built, and in indicating the ways in which one may go about building them.

*Model Aims*

Before leaving the basic concepts of the modeling process, it is well worthwhile to attempt to describe in fairly brief terms some aims that might be defined to be met by any modeling efforts. It is clearly of no use at all to build models based on precise mathematical theories and techniques when the resulting models are possibly unusable, irrelevant, or too complex and time-consuming to be economically worth using.

A number of basic constraints may be considered that should always be imposed on attempts at model-building:

1. *Simplicity*: It is of prime importance that the model should be as simple as possible, within the terms of the further constraints that will now be discussed.
2. *Utility*: The model should be able to carry out the task for which it was designed.
3. *Validity*: The model should formulate a set of interactions that are valid and noncontradictory. It should also be applicable not just to the specific situation in which the model has been formulated.
4. *Suitability*: The model must be able to accept as input the data that are available for use in the model, now and in the future. It must also generate as output information that is of clear meaning and that can be utilized in other, subsequent models.
5. *Accuracy*: The model should be able to produce answers that fall within a stated error range.
6. *Economy*: The model should be no more expensive to use than is necessary to meet the other constraints imposed. It should be cheaper than direct observation or experimentation.
7. *Sensitivity*: The model should be sensitive to the parameters whose influence is being modeled.
8. *Realism*: The model should be similar to the real-world situation it is attempting to model, and should be behavioral in form.
9. *Decisive*: It should supply the necessary answers for decision making on the basis of the model's output.

These constraints may be accepted as being the basic criteria against which models should be built. It is difficult to give these items an order of importance, since in many ways they are all of equal importance. However, validity, utility, and simplicity might be considered as the most important ones—particularly since several of the other requirements are then likely to be implicitly attained.

**Error Analyses in Transportation Modeling**

*Introduction*

This section is concerned with considerations of error properties of models. Two specific ideas will be developed within this general area. The first of these is the development of the concept of the types of errors that exist, and an examination of the effects of certain of these errors on the calibration or estimation processes used in building models.[6] Second, the way in which certain types of errors are propagated through a model will be examined, together with the implications that this propagation has on the accuracy of the predicted variable.

In general, two basic types of error can be identified. These are two completely distinct forms of error and will generally be present in any model, having very distinct effects upon the model. These two types of error are measurement error and specification error. *Measurement error* is simply the error due to the fact that the processes of estimating the values that are used for the independent variables have some level of error associated with them. In general, in transportation modeling, the data that are available for the independent variables have resulted from the collection of data in a sample survey. As such, either the values from the survey may be used directly for each individual who was surveyed, or alternatively the data set may be expanded to apply to the entire population from which the sample was drawn. In both cases, certain errors are present. The process of collecting information about people is generally subject to errors of reporting. Thus, it can be expected that reported information on such things as income, the number of trips made on a specific day, and various other socioeconomic and transportation variables will be erroneously reported by the people interviewed. In addition to this, a certain amount of information is generally collected in aggregated groupings, where it would only be known that a particular individual or household possessed an attribute that lay within a specific range. This obviously applies most frequently to things such as income, where a series of income ranges may be used that may be as large as \$2,000 to \$5,000.

The other major source of measurement error in this type of data results from the survey process itself. If the sample data are to be applied to a total population, there are errors of expansion of the data-base to the total population. These result from the fact that only a small section of the population has been sampled, and that this small sample is to be expanded to represent the entire population. Thus, there will be present in such data an error that may be termed a sampling error. No matter how accurately and how well-accomplished any sample survey is, it must contain a sample error when expanded to the entire population. This survey-sampling error should not be confused with a bias (which might result from incorrect sampling or from various other sources) that commonly occurs during a survey process.

The other form of error, specification error, may briefly be defined as that error which arises from the simplification process adopted in building a model. In general, a minimum number of explanatory variables is aimed for, together with the simplest mathematical form that will do a reasonably good job of explaining the phenomenon which is to be modeled. In most cases, it is not possible to model the phenomenon exactly by this means. The simplification process is the process that gives rise to specification error. As an illustration of this concept, consider the situation that arises in placing a mathematical form on a physical law, as opposed to the placing of a mathematical form on some associative relationship. Clearly, a physical law such as Ohm's Law or Newton's Law of Gravitation is not subject to a specification error. The mathematical models that represent these laws are clearly completely correct in terms of both the form of the relationship and the inclusion of variables to describe the relationship. On the other hand, an attempt to build a trip generation model (see chapter 7), for instance, requires that certain simplifying assumptions are made, both in terms of a finite number of variables to be used in the model, and upon the actual mathematical form of the relationship. In general, a linear formulation is aimed for, at least initially, but this may be an approximation to what correctly should be a curvilinear relation. Similarly, the number of variables in the model is kept to a minimum; and, in so doing, again the process is being simplified and it therefore tends to introduce specification error.

*Measurement Errors in Estimation*

The simplest way of investigating the effects on estimation of measurement errors in the independent variables is to examine a simple case. The best-documented and probably simplest case is that of an estimation procedure that uses simple multiple regression. The existence of errors in the independent variables may be expected to have two principal effects: First, estimates of the model parameters may be expected to be affected; and second, prediction of the dependent variable will be affected.

A simple two-variable case, where both the dependent and independent variables are subject to measurement error, is presented in equation 2.1 and 2.2.

$$X = x + u \qquad (2.1)$$

$$Y = y + v \qquad (2.2)$$

where $X$ and $Y$ are the observed values, $x$ and $y$ are the true values, and $u$ and $v$ are the errors of measurement in the observations. The parameters of the relation between the true values of the variables is to be estimated, as shown in equation 2.3, rather than the relation between the observed values.

$$y = \alpha + \beta x \qquad (2.3)$$

Substitution of equations 2.1 and 2.2 in 2.3 results in equation 2.4.

$$Y = \alpha + \beta X + w \qquad (2.4)$$

where

$$w = v - \beta u \qquad (2.5)$$

It is assumed that $u$ and $v$ are independent of each other and also of $x$ and $y$, and further that the expectations (or means) of $u$ and $v$ are zero. The covariance of $X$ and $w$ is shown in equations 2.6 and 2.7.[a]

$$E\{w[X - E(X)]\} = E[(v - \beta u)u] \qquad (2.6)$$

$$E\{w[X - E(X)]\} = -\beta \operatorname{var} u \qquad (2.7)$$

Since the covariance of $X$ and $w$ is not zero, unless $u$ is zero (i.e., no measurement error), then clearly there is a dependence between $X$ and the total error term of equation 2.4. This means that the usual application of least-squares analysis to equation 2.4 will yield biased estimates of the parameters $\alpha$ and $\beta$, which will, furthermore, be inconsistent. For instance, the least-squares estimate of $\beta$, based on $n$ observations, is shown in equation 2.8.

$$b_n = \frac{\sum_i (X_i - \bar{X})(Y_i - \bar{Y})}{\sum_i (X_i - \bar{X})^2} \qquad (2.8)$$

The terms in equation 2.8 can be rewritten in terms of the true value, $x$ and $y$, and the error, $u$ and $v$, as shown in equations 2.9 and 2.10.

---

[a] This is so since $\quad w = v - \beta u$
and $\quad E[X - E(X)] = E[x + u - x] - E(u)$
hence $\quad E\{w[X - E(X)]\} = E[(v - \beta u)u]$

$$\sum_i (X_i - \bar{X})^2 = \sum_i (x_i - \bar{x})^2 + 2\sum_i (x_i - \bar{x})(u_i - \bar{u})$$

$$+ \sum_i (u_i - \bar{u})^2 \tag{2.9}$$

$$\sum_i (X_i - \bar{X})(Y_i - \bar{Y}) = \sum_i (x_i - \bar{x})(y_i - \bar{y})$$

$$+ \sum_i (x_i - \bar{x})(v_i - \bar{v})$$

$$+ \sum_i (y_i - \bar{y})(u_i - \bar{u})$$

$$+ \sum_i (u_i - \bar{u})(v_i - \bar{v}) \tag{2.10}$$

As the sample size increases, the second term in equation 2.9 and the last three terms in equation 2.10 will tend to zero. Thus, in the limit,

$$p \lim_{n \to \infty} b_n = \frac{\sum_i (x_i - \bar{x})(y_i - \bar{y})}{\sum_i (x_i - \bar{x})^2 + \sum_i (u_i - \bar{u})^2} \tag{2.11}$$

Denoting

$$\frac{1}{n}\sum_i (x_i - \bar{x})^2 \qquad \text{by} \qquad \sigma_x^2$$

and

$$\frac{1}{n}\sum_i (u_i - \bar{u})^2 \qquad \text{by} \qquad \sigma_u^2$$

then equation 2.11 may be rewritten as shown in equation 2.12.

$$p \lim_{n \to \infty} b_n = \frac{\sum_i (x_i - \bar{x})(y_i - \bar{y})}{\sum_i (x_i - \bar{x})^2} \left[ \frac{1}{1 + \sigma_u^2/\sigma_x^2} \right] \tag{2.12}$$

The true estimate of $\beta$ is shown in equation 2.13.

$$\frac{\sum_i (x_i - \bar{x})(y_i - \bar{y})}{\sum_i (x_i - \bar{x})^2} = \beta \tag{2.13}$$

Hence it follows that the estimate, $b_n$, will approach the value shown in equation 2.14 for very large samples and thus will generally be an underestimate of the true value $\beta$.

$$p \lim_{n \to \infty} b_n = \frac{\beta}{1 + \sigma_u^2/\sigma_x^2} \tag{2.14}$$

Clearly, the problem becomes more complex as the number of variables is increased, but in general the parameter estimates will tend to be underestimates of the true estimates.

The second result of measurement errors that was hypothesized was an effect on the value of the predicted dependent variable. Clearly, there are two problems that arise here. In the first place, it was already established that there will be errors in the parameter estimates of the model. Second, the value of the new observation of the independent variable(s) will be subject to error, in the same manner as those in the original estimation process.

There are methods by which one can obtain consistently biased estimates of $\beta, \hat{\beta}$, and so two alternatives for the estimation of a future $Y$ are available. These alternatives are to use the equation of 2.3 (together with its disturbance term, $\varepsilon$), or to use the estimated equation 2.15.

$$Y_i = a + bX_i \tag{2.15}$$

In general, equation 2.15 will be the known equation, and it would generally be used for the estimates. Bearing in mind the error in estimating $b$ for $\beta$, 2.16 develops.

$$E(Y_j | X_j) = E(a + bX_j) \tag{2.16}$$

In the limit, $b$ converges in probability to

$$p \lim_{n \to \infty} b_n = \frac{\beta}{1 + \sigma_u^2/\sigma_x^2} = \frac{\beta \sigma_x^2}{\sigma_x^2 + \sigma_u^2} \tag{2.17}$$

Then the expected value of $X_j$ is given by equation 2.18.

$$E(Y_j | X_j) = a + \frac{\beta \sigma_x^2 X_j}{\sigma_x^2 + \sigma_u^2} \tag{2.18}$$

Assuming no bias in $a$, equation 2.18 can be rewritten as equation 2.19.

$$E(Y_j | X_j) = \alpha + \frac{\beta \sigma_x^2 X_j}{\sigma_x^2 + \sigma_u^2} \tag{2.19}$$

Now the objective is to determine the error in $E(Y_j | X_j)$ calculated by this means. Suppose $E(Y_j | X_j)$ is estimated, given the true values of $\alpha$ and $\beta$. Then $E(Y_j | X_j)$ may be expressed in terms of $\alpha$, $\beta$, and $x_j$, as shown in equations 2.20, 2.21, and 2.22, where the values of $E(\varepsilon_j)$ and $E(v_j)$ are both assumed to be zero.

$$y_i = \alpha + \beta x_i + \varepsilon_i \tag{2.20}$$

$$E(Y_j | X_j) = E(\alpha + \beta x_j + \varepsilon_j - v_j | X_j) \tag{2.21}$$

$$E(Y_j | X_j) = \alpha + \beta E(x_j | X_j) \tag{2.22}$$

However, $X_j$ may be written in terms of $x_j$ and $u_j$, equation 2.23.

$$X_j = x_j + u_j \tag{2.23}$$

Therefore, it follows that $E(x_j/X_j)$ can be written as equation 2.24.

$$E(x_j|X_j) = \frac{\sigma_u^2 x + \sigma_x^2 X_j}{\sigma_x^2 + \sigma_u^2} \tag{2.24}$$

Thus, equation 2.22 can be rewritten as equation 2.25.

$$E(Y_j|X_j) = \alpha + \frac{\beta\sigma_y^2 \bar{x}}{\sigma_x^2 + \sigma_u^2} + \frac{\beta\sigma_x^2 X_j}{\sigma_x^2 + \sigma_u^2} \tag{2.25}$$

This would be the correct estimation of $Y_j$, given the correct estimation of $\beta$ and $\alpha$ and knowledge of $\sigma_x^2$, $\bar{x}$ and $\sigma_u^2$. The comparison of equation 2.25 with 2.19 shows that equation 2.19 amounts to an underestimate of $E(Y_j|X_j)$ by a quantity given by equation 2.26.

$$E(Y_j|X_j) = \frac{\beta\sigma_u^2 \bar{x}}{\sigma_x^2 + \sigma_u^2} \tag{2.26}$$

At this point, it has been established that the direct use of independent variables with errors will result in biased, inconsistent estimates of both the model parameters and prediction estimates from a simple regression analysis. This can be put into a more general framework, which will not be derived here. In general, given a function of the form $X$ of equation 2.27,

$$Y = f(X_1, X_2, \ldots, X_n) \tag{2.27}$$

then the error in $Y$, $e_y$, caused by errors of measurement in the $X$'s is given by equation 2.28.

$$e_y^2 = \sum_i f_{x_i}^2 e_{x_i}^2 . + \sum_i \sum_j f_{x_i} f_{x_j} e_{x_i} e_{x_j} r_{ij} \tag{2.28}$$

where $f_{x_i}$ is the partial derivative of $f$ with respect to $x_i$; $e_{x_i}$, $e_{x_j}$ are the errors in $x_i$ and $x_j$, and $r_{ij}$ is the correlation between $x_i$ and $x_j$. When $f(X_1, X_2, \ldots, X_n)$ is a linear function, this formula is exact. When it is a nonlinear function, it becomes an approximation, but generally a quite good approximation. Equation 2.28 will be used later in this text in order to investigate specific properties of certain functional forms.

*Two Types of Error*

As was mentioned at the beginning of the section, there are two types of error that may affect a model. The first is measurement error, whose quantitative effects have been illustrated above; and the second is specification error. In general, specification error is the error that is caused by the simplifying processes inherent in modeling. It may arise from two principal sources: simplification of the model structure, and simplification by reduction of the number of variables (Figure 2-2).

Assuming that there is, in any phenomenon to be modeled, a minimum unexplainable variance, then as complexity increases, specification error will decrease and asymptotically approach the minimum error. However, as model complexity increases, the effects on measurement error have to be considered. This may be examined by considering the effects of adding to the complexity of a simple model, using equation 2.28 to show what will happen. A simple model is represented by equation 2.29.

$$y = ax_1 \tag{2.29}$$

Assume first that $x_1$ has an error, $e_1$, associated with it. Then the error in $y$ is shown by equation 2.30.

$$e_y^2 = a^2 e_1^2 \tag{2.30}$$

Now, adding a second variable, $x_2$, equation 2.31, with error $e_2$, and a 0.4 correlation with $x_1$, the error in $y$ is now given by equation 2.32.

$$y = ax_1 + bx_2 \tag{2.31}$$

$$e_y^2 = a^2 e_1^2 + b^2 e_2^2 + ab\, e_1 e_2 0.4 \tag{2.32}$$

Clearly, the error has increased quite considerably by adding $x_2$. Even had $x_1$ and $x_2$ been totally uncorrelated (a very improbable situation), the measurement error of $y$ would still have increased by $b^2 e_2^2$. Now suppose that, instead of adding a new variable, $x_1$ is raised to a power, as shown in equation 2.33.

$$y = ax_1^2 \tag{2.33}$$

In this case, the error is given by equation 2.34.

$$e_y^2 = (2ax_1)^2 e_1^2 = 4a^2 e_1^2 x_1^2 \tag{2.34}$$

Or, perhaps another equation that could have been used is equation 2.35, for which the error is given by equation 2.36.

$$y = e^{ax_1} \tag{2.35}$$

$$e_y^2 = a^2 e^{2ax_1} e_1^2 \tag{2.36}$$

It would be useful to put some values in the error equations that were just derived. Assume that $x_1 = x_2 = 10$; $a = 0.5$; $b = 0.8$; and $e_1 = e_2 = \pm 1$. Then equation 2.30 results in equations 2.37 and 2.38.

$$e_y^2 = 0.25 \cdot 1 = 0.25 \tag{2.37}$$

$$e_y = \pm 0.5 \tag{2.38}$$

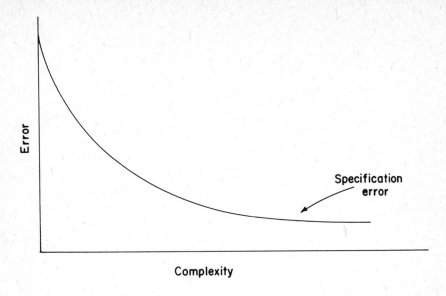

**Figure 2-2.** General Relationship between Specification Error and Model Complexity.

Equation 2.32 develops as equations 2.39 and 2.40.

$$e_y^2 = 0.25 \cdot 1 + 0.64 \cdot 1 + 0.40 \cdot 0.40 \cdot 1 = 1.05 \qquad (2.39)$$

$$e_y = 1.025 \qquad (2.40)$$

This represents an increase in the error of $y$ by a factor of over 2. Equation 2.34 results in equations 2.41 and 2.42.

$$e_y^2 = 4 \cdot 0.25 \cdot 1 \cdot 100 = 100 \qquad (2.41)$$

$$e = \pm 10 \qquad (2.42)$$

This is a clearly startling increase over 2.38, amounting to an increase by a factor of 20. Finally, using equation 2.36, the following results shown in equation 2.43 and 2.44 develop

$$e_y^2 = 0.25 \ e^{10} \cdot 1 = 5507 \qquad (2.43)$$

$$e_y = \pm 74.2 \qquad (2.44)$$

All the errors that were calculated here are *absolute* errors. The values of the relative errors should also be examined; that is, the percent error of $y$ in each case. These relative errors are:

1. For $y = ax_1$, $e_y = \pm 10\%$ (the error in $x_1$ is $\pm 10\%$)

2. For $y = ax_1 + bx_2$, $e_y = \pm 7.9\%$ (the errors in both $x_1$ and $x_2$ are $\pm 10\%$)

3. For $y = ax_1^2$, $e_y = \pm 20\%$

4. For $y = e^{ax_1}$, $e_y = \pm 50\%$

With the exception of adding further variables, all the relative errors of $y$ are larger than those of the $x$'s. As the complexity increases, the absolute error increases, and generally the relative error also increases. This phenomenon is represented in Figure 2-3. Thus, if measurement and specification errors are combined using the fact that $E = \sqrt{(e_m^2 + e_s^2)}$, Figure 2-4 results.

This figure appears to indicate that there may be an optimum level of complexity in terms of the compound of specification and measurement errors.

Figure 2-5 illustrates a situation where a second data set, in which measurement errors are greater, is superimposed on the hypothetical situation represented in Figure 2-4. The same basic model is assumed for both cases.

Obviously, the total error, $E_2$, is consistently higher than the total error, $E_1$. But the important fact here is that the curve reaches its optimum at a lower level of complexity. This clearly demonstrates the necessity of designing simple models when the data are subject to even relatively small measurement errors. The danger of actually increasing total prediction error becomes obvious, if refinements of models are made by adding to their complexity.

Finally, the effects of chains of models can also be seen, such as those used in conventional sequential travel forecasting (see chapters 7 through 10). Each model has a prediction error associated with it, while the prediction from one model is used as the basis for the next model.

### Summary of Error Analysis

Three different types of errors were determined that will generally be liable to affect the models that are built and used. These three are: measurement error, calibration error, and specification error. *Measurement error* arises from the fact that the values of all the variables that may be considered in the modeling process have been obtained by some means of measurement, such as a survey. As a result, their values are subject to some degree of error. *Calibration error* arises from the use of variables with measurement errors to determine the value of parameters in a model. This process introduces biases in the estimates of parameters, and removes the possibility of obtaining estimates of the true relationship. Thus, estimates from the

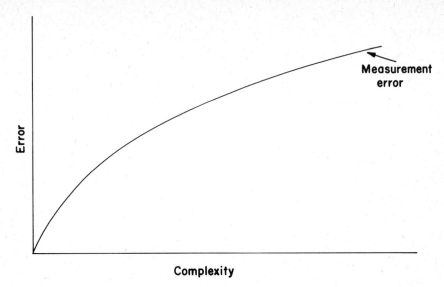

**Figure 2-3.** General Relationship between Measurement Error and Model Complexity.

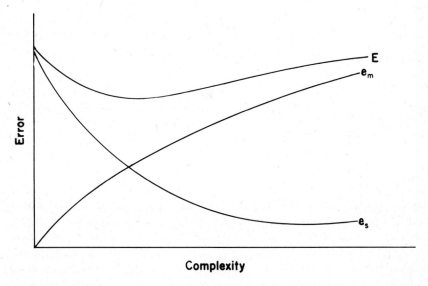

Source: William Alonso, ''The Quality of Data and Choice and Design of Predictive Models,'' *Highway Research Board Special Report* 97, National Academy of Sciences, Washington, D.C., 1968, p. 184.

**Figure 2-4.** General Relationship between Combined Measurement and Specification Errors and Model Complexity.

43

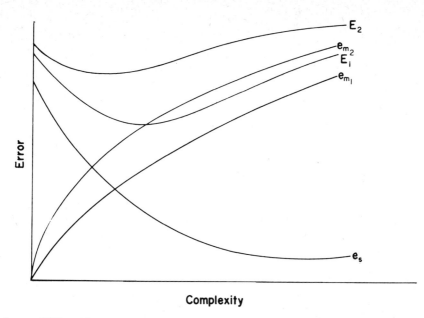

Complexity

Source: William Alonso, "The Quality of Data and Choice and Design of Predictive Models," *Highway Research Board Special Report* 97, National Academy of Sciences, Washington, D.C., 1968, p. 185.

**Figure 2-5.** General Relationship between Combined Measurement and Specification Errors, and Model Complexity, for Two Data Sets.

models will be subjected to both the errors in new values of the independent variables and also errors in the estimates of the parameters due to the measurement errors of the original data set. The final form of error, *specification error*, arises from the simplification process that is adopted in attempting to build mathematical models.

From all these forms of error, it was established that it is possible to determine, to some extent, the effects of measurement errors on the predictive estimates. In certain cases, it also appears to be reasonable to obtain estimates of the errors introduced by biases in the calibrated parameters. However, this generally applies only to the more simple statistical modeling techniques, and becomes considerably more difficult to determine as the calibration procedure becomes either more arbitrary or more complex. Finally, it was noted that in general it is not possible to determine estimates of the specification error, since this requires prior knowledge of the exact relationship that should have been built. In general, however, it would appear that the specification error will drop off rapidly as complexity increases.

From this study of the measurement errors and their propagation through a model, certain desirable rules of model building can be identified that would appear to be useful to bear in mind when considering a new modeling effort. It was noted that if variables with measurement errors are added, the proportional or relative error of the dependent variable is generally less than the individual errors in the independent variables. Also, as the complexity of the model increases, by the inclusion of multiplicative terms or of terms raised to powers or even relationships involving powers of $e$, the relative and absolute errors rise very rapidly. From all of these observations, some basic rules can be developed for modeling attempts. These are:

1. Avoid intercorrelated variables. This can be seen to be desirable because of the second term in the general expression for predicted errors, equation 2.28. Clearly, if $r_{ij}$ in that equation is zero or close to zero, the total error in the dependent variable will be considerably reduced.

2. Add, where possible. On the basis of the fact that addition is the only general mathematical operation that reduces the proportional error of the dependent variable in relation to the value of the proportional errors on each of the independent variables, addition appears to be the most desirable mathematical operation.

3. If addition is not possible, multiply or divide. Clearly, both multiplication and division lead to somewhat lower order increases in the predictive errors propagated through a model than do some of the more complex mathematical manipulations.

4. Avoid, as far as possible, taking differences or raising variables to powers. Again, this follows directly from the observations. It is perhaps noteworthy, however, that in using differences within a model form such as the logit model (see chapter 16), the effect of taking differences has been considerably mitigated by the model in terms of the errors that may be expected in the dependent variable.

5. Avoid, as far as possible, models that proceed by chains. Models that use the outputs of preceding models as their independent variables are subject to considerable propagation errors.

Finally, some basic mathematical formulae were developed from which it appears to be possible to obtain estimates of the errors of prediction for any model that has measurement errors in the independent variables. There appears to be no basic reason why these formulae could not be applied to almost any modeling process that is to be investigated. The major difficulties that arise are those resulting from the calibration of a model, where for any technique other than simple multivariate regression, the estimation of calibration errors becomes an extremely difficult and tedious task.

# 3

## Economic Theory and Travel Demand

### Rationale

The previous chapter concluded with discussions of the basis of modeling. The primary emphasis there concerned the purposes and basic principles of model building. However, the way in which models are actually conceived and constructed was not discussed. Clearly, there must exist some prior basis for building a model of a real-world phenomenon. This prior basis may be one of several alternatives: a series of hypotheses of relationships between the phenomenon and certain measurable characteristics: an hypothesis of a total relationship between the phenomenon and a number of measurable characteristics: or an hypothesis based upon one or more theories applied to the specific modeling situation.

The first of these alternatives tends to yield a badly structured model, since interactions among the measurable characteristics are ignored in the initial hypothesis. Second, the relationships hypothesized are generally constrained to be overly simple, mathematically, due to the complexity of putting forward numerous hypotheses that must be fitted into a single model. The second alternative is a somewhat unusual one, since prior information that would permit an hypothesis generally does not exist, particularly in transportation work. The third alternative provides such prior information by calling upon theoretical knowledge from different areas and using these to build the modeling hypothesis. The result of this alternative is likely to be a well-structured model. The task now becomes that of identifying where bodies of theory exist that might be useful and applicable to transportation.

It has been found that one of the most useful of such bodies of theory to transportation exists in the field of economics. One may consider transportation as a commodity that is bought and sold, and therefore it may be regarded as an economic good. Since transportation has a market, it follows that one may consider the mechanisms by which its price and volume of sale are determined. Economics has a considerable amount of theory that can be applied to any marketable commodity to determine its price and volume, and these theories can clearly be applied to transportation. The remainder of this chapter is concerned with developing the basic economic theories in the context of transportation, and these theories are used later in the text for specific modeling purposes.

45

**Supply and Demand in Transportation**

In order to be able to use consumer behavior theory in transportation, it is necessary to establish whether it is a reasonable premise that travel behaves like an economic good. First, it may be asserted that, in most cases, travel is not demanded for its own sake, as was discussed in chapter 1. There is a joint demand for travel and an activity that can be carried out at the end of the trip. Therefore, in an economic sense, the utility gained by the individual is the total utility of the trip and the activity, and the total cost or price expended is the total cost or price of the trip and the activity. Thus, if the total utility gained from the trip and the activity could be observed, and the total prices of both could be estimated, a demand curve could be constructed, for the joint good of travel and activity. To estimate the separate demand curves would require that the utilities are separable and can be observed separately, and that the prices can likewise be separately estimated. Where the demand for only one of the jointly demanded commodities can be estimated readily and separately, the demand for the second commodity can be derived from the joint demand. This would appear to be the necessary strategy for determining the demand for travel, if it is, indeed, an economic good.

Second, it may be postulated that decreases in the price of travel will, all other things being equal, lead to increases in the amount of travel. This may be observed in the overall traffic increases that occur with the opening of a new expressway. It is also observed in the reverse when patronage of public transport declines in response to an increase in fares. However, it is clear that the changes in trip making identified here are highly dependent upon the actual activity to be indulged in. For example, both in response to increased highway capacity and increased transit fares, the changes in trips to work will generally be slight. On the other hand, changes in trips for recreational purposes, social visits, some types of shopping, etc. may be much more significant.

Both of these considerations have led transportation planners to define "trip purposes," which represent groups of activities that may require travel from home for their execution. These trip purposes are defined first as a proxy for determining the price and utility of activities and second as a means of identifying activities that have fairly common response patterns to transport system changes.[1] The set of trip purposes usually employed by the transportation planner is:

1. Work trip
2. School trip
3. Shopping trip—soft goods
4. Shopping trip—hard goods

5. Employer's business trip
6. Personal business trip
7. Social trip
8. Trip to eat meal
9. Recreational trip

Since trips are defined as one-way movements, a tenth trip purpose of "home" is added to this set. Finally, two intermediate trip purposes may be defined. These are "serve passenger" and "change travel mode." As will be explained in the next chapter, these purposes are dropped at a subsequent stage of the analysis.

*Demand*

It appears that it is perfectly consistent with economic theory to postulate that travel behaves like any economic good and, indeed, revealed behavior seems to bear out this postulate. Thus, we may assume a downward-sloping demand curve[2] when plotting on the normal reverse axes of price and quantity (see Figure 3-1). The exact shape of the curve cannot be determined at this time, and will depend upon the anticipated elasticity[3] of demand for travel with price, as it varies over the range of prices. It should be remembered that the point elasticity is defined by equation 3-1.

$$\varepsilon_p = \frac{dv}{v} \cdot \frac{p}{dp} \tag{3.1}$$

In words, the point elasticity of demand with price is the percentage change in volume that results from a one percent change in price. The point elasticity is generally defined at the mean of the observed price. The assumption of a constant elasticity generates a hyperbolic demand curve, as shown in Figure 3-2a. A straight line demand curve (Figure 3-2b) gives a continuously varying elasticity from infinity at the price intercept to zero at the quantity intercept. A similar range of elasticities results from a convex (quadratic) curve of the form shown in Figure 3-2c. However, in this case relatively little change in elasticity occurs at low quantities, while change in elasticity accelerates rapidly when quantity exceeds a certain value. The concept of elasticity is an important one in the development of demand relationships and assumptions of the form of the elasticity are frequently keys to the structuring of such relationships.

When the price of travel changes, demand for travel changes by a shift along the demand curve, all other things being equal. If the price of travel is measured in monetary terms only, then changes in the income of the traveler will shift the position of the demand curve (and may alter its

48

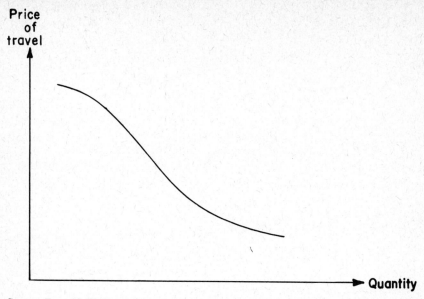

Source: From M. Wohl and B.V. Martin, *Traffic System Analysis for Engineers and Planners*. Copyright © 1967 by McGraw-Hill Book Co., New York. Used with Permission.

**Figure 3-1.** General Form of Demand Curve for Travel.

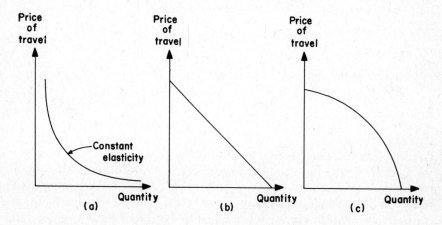

**Figure 3-2.** Important Demand Curve Shapes.

shape). An increase in real income will move the demand curve rightwards and upwards, while decreases will shift it downwards and leftwards. As will be seen later, the price of travel is not strictly monetary, but includes a number of other scarce resources. Changes in these resources will also induce similar shifts in the demand schedule.

*Supply*

In the standard microeconomics approach[4] the supply and demand "stories" are told in a situation of perfect competition, wherein there are a large number of buyers and sellers such that no one buyer or seller can influence disproportionately the price of the good. It is then recognized by most economists that perfect competition rarely occurs and that the prevailing market situation is one of imperfect competition. It is clear that, in the case of transportation facilities, there is a situation of extremely imperfect competition, which is perhaps closer to monopoly than any other economic market condition. Under these circumstances, it is, perhaps, somewhat questionable as to whether an application of consumer economics is appropriate. The concern with this aspect arises principally because of the few suppliers and many buyers. Thus, it is not possible to tell the supply story of the economist in relation to supply of transportation facilities. In the public transport situation of, say, seventy-five years ago, a condition of imperfect competition did exist, wherein the economic concept of supply could be applied approximately. For example, a given set of public transport operators would be willing to provide capacity for travel at a more or less constant fare for a fairly substantial range of capacities. Beyond a certain point however, the fare would have to rise fairly rapidly in order to induce the operators to increase their supply of transportation. This is shown in Figure 3-3. This supply curve would arise because of the law of diminishing returns and concepts of profitability in a competitive market situation.

The concept of the supply curve is that of determining the response of price to supply volume. In other words, the supply curve tells what price will potentially be charged, if a given volume of good is produced. The transportation planner has extended this concept to allow an "engineering supply curve" to be defined as the response of price to volume in a noncompetitive market.[5] To do this, it is first necessary to define "price of travel," in terms of its constituent elements. The price of travel is defined as the outlay of resources required in order to consume travel. These resources include money, time, energy, discomfort, hazard, etc.

The price-volume curve (a more correct terminology for this curve than "supply curve," for the reasons given above) may now be defined by considering the price response on a fixed portion (link) of, say, a highway system. (An identical argument can be developed for public transport either on the highway or on its own right-of-way.) For this link, the capacity is fixed, while the input volume (the number of vehicles entering the link in a given time period) is varied.

If there is a very low input volume (low enough that a traveler entering the facility will not see any other travelers as he carries out the trip) then the price that he will perceive will be the lowest possible. The time taken will be

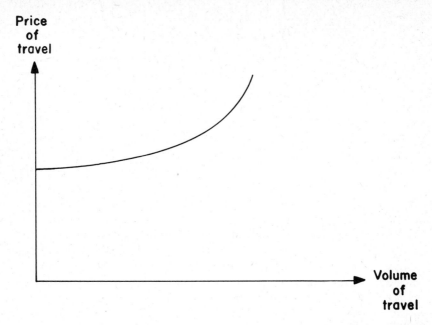

**Figure 3-3.** Hypothetical Supply Curve for Public Transport, circa 1900.

a minimum, there will be no hazards from other vehicles, energy costs will, depending upon posted speed limit, be at or near their minimum, etc. As the volume increases, the price of travel will increase only slowly. Over quite a wide range of input volumes, travel time and direct travel costs will barely change, although hazards, and consumption of human resources will increase somewhat. As the volume increases still further, the price will begin to increase at a more and more rapid rate.

In order to understand clearly what is happening, a consideration of some fundamental ideas of traffic volume, speed, and density is helpful. Consider first the relation between volume and density, where density is the number of vehicles per unit length of roadway. Clearly, at zero density, volume is also zero. As volume increases, density increases, until some maximum volume is reached. When maximum density is reached (i.e., vehicles packed end-to-end), volume is again zero (since no vehicles are moving). Thus, volume must decrease for increasing density after the maximum volume is reached. This is shown in Figure 3-4.

Defining *space mean speed* as volume divided by density, then the space mean speed can be determined by drawing a line from the origin, in Figure 3-4 to a point on the curve, for example, $OA$. It is also clear that there are two possible space mean speeds for volume $V_A$, where the speed given by $OB$ is clearly higher than $OA$. At very low traffic volume and density, the

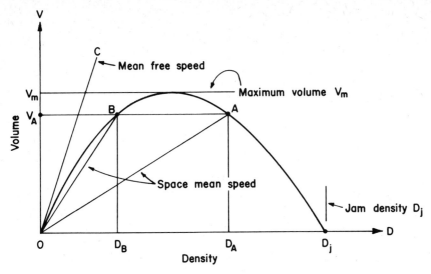

Source: F.A. Haight, *Mathematical Theories of Traffic Flow*, New York, Academic Press, 1963, p. 72. Used with Permission.

**Figure 3-4.** Fundamental Diagram of Road Traffic.

space mean speed approaches the maximum, the mean free speed, shown as *OC* in Figure 3-4.

By considering the variations of space mean speed with volume, a relation between these two variables can be graphically represented as shown in Figure 3-5.[6] Mean free speed occurs at zero volume, and speed falls continuously as volume increases to $V_m$. As volume now falls, while density increases, speed continues to drop to zero at zero volume and jam density. Since speed and price perceived by the traveler are related, it is clear that these relationships provide a basis for inferring the shape of the price-volume curve.

At near zero volume, a traveler will be able to drive at mean free speed, and will thus incur the lowest possible price. As the input volume approaches the output volume capacity, congestion will begin to occur and the price will rise very rapidly. Near capacity, the increase in price, for each vehicle in the system resulting from the addition of one more vehicle, is very large. This curve is shown in Figure 3-6. This is the correct price-volume curve, given the present methods of charging for highway use. A toll facility would simply yield a curve that would be displaced upwards on the price axis by the amount of the toll. Other forms of charging, relating price to the input volume or to the actual costs of providing, maintaining, and administering the facility, would give rise to other forms and shapes of price-volume curve.

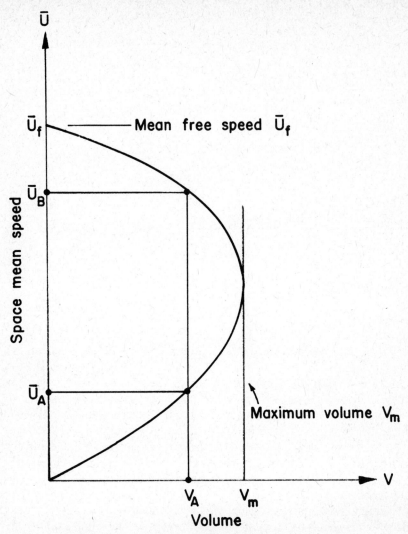

**Figure 3-5.** Idealized Speed-Volume Relationship.

In this discussion two different types of volume have been introduced, the input and the output volume. The *input volume* is the total volume that attempts to enter the facility in a given period, and either succeeds in entering the facility or queues at the entrance (e.g., at an intersection, a freeway ramp, etc.). The *output volume* is the total volume that moves through the facility in a given period. Therefore, clearly input volume may equal or exceed output volume both reckoned over the same time period. However, output volume must be less than or equal to output capacity.

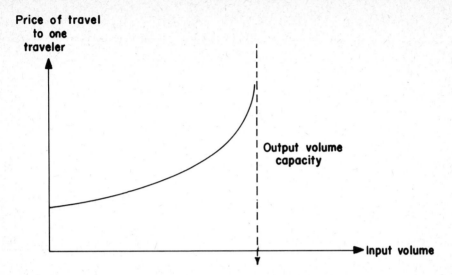

**Figure 3-6.** Price-Volume Curve for a Highway Link.

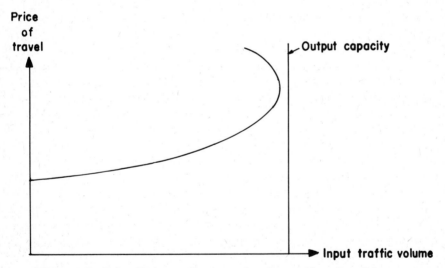

**Figure 3-7.** Price-Volume Curve under Congestion Conditions.

The price-volume curve indicates the price for a trip through the specified link at some given volume. Because of the speed-flow relationship, it is clearly possible for low output volumes of traffic to have associated with them much higher prices of travel, under conditions of congestion. This would give rise to a "backward-bending" price-volume curve, as shown in Figure 3-7. It should be stressed, however, that such a

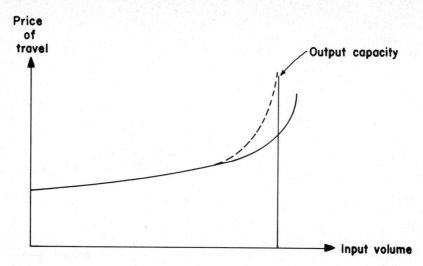

**Figure 3-8.** Price-Volume Curve for Short Duration Excess Input Volume.

curve only arises from consideration of a price-volume relationship, and would not be consistent with concepts of economic supply in a competitive market.

The measures of input volume, output volume, and capacity are clearly time-dependent. Assuming that all are expressed in vehicles per hour, it is also possible for input volume to exceed output capacity for a short period without generating much higher prices. Under these conditions, a price-volume curve of the form shown in Figure 3-8 may occur. Sustained excess input volume will result in the standard price-volume curve shown by the dashed line in Figure 3-8. Since input volume will be expressed as an hourly rate, the extent to which the price-volume curve can shift to the right of the output capacity is very limited.

At this point relationships have been developed that tell how the price of travel will vary with the input and output volumes. Thus, for a given facility, if the level of utilization is known, the average price of travel encountered by the traveler can be determined. It must be emphasized that this curve does *not* indicate the volume of travel for a particular price, which would constitute a demand curve.

*Equilibrium*

In order to determine the actual volume of travel and its price, the demand and price-volume curves can be plotted on the same axes (at the same scales), in the same way that this is done for supply and demand in standard microeconomics. This joint plotting of the curves represents visually, the

55

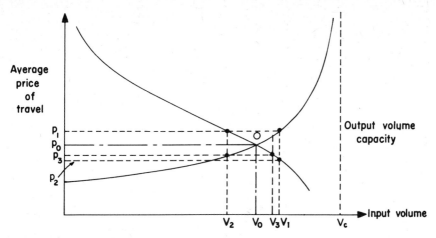

Source: From M. Wohl and B.V. Martin, *Traffic System Analysis for Engineers and Planners*. Copyright © by McGraw-Hill Book Co., New York. Used with Permission.

**Figure 3-9.** Equilibration of Demand and Price-Volume Curves.

simultaneous solving of demand and price-volume equations and is shown in Figure 3-9. The intersection of the two curves at $O$ gives the estimate of the appropriate price and travel volume for the link under consideration. If a higher volume, $V_1$, were to use the facility, the price of travel would be $p_1$ according to the price-volume curve. However, the volume $V_1$ would only occur at price $p_2$ according to the demand curve, so an instability occurs. At price $p_1$, a volume $V_2$ will use the facility, instead of $V_1$. At volume $V_2$, however, the price of travel is $p_3$, and therefore an instability again exists. At a price of $p_3$, the volume on the facility will increase to $V_3$, and the price will again rise. This cycling will continue until the point $O$ is reached, at which time the price-volume and demand curves are in equilibrium. It should be noted, however, that an average price of travel and an average demand curve are discussed here. The price of travel is averaged over a period (depending upon the detail of the study), while the demand curve is averaged over the users of a facility during a particular time period. Both these averages may be calculated from a wide variation in both travel price and demand curves. Clearly, this means that there should be a confidence interval around both the price-volume and demand curves, and a two dimensional confidence range around $O$.

**Changes in Capacity**

The effect of changes in the capacity of a link should be considered next. For a fixed volume, travel price varies with capacity according to a curve

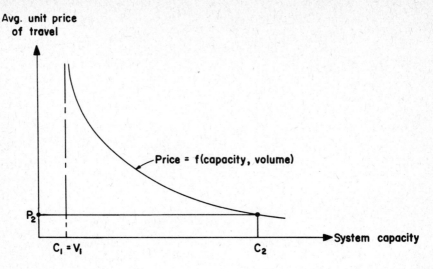

Avg. unit price
of travel

Price = f(capacity, volume)

$P_2$

$C_1 = V_1$

$C_2$

System capacity

Source: From M. Wohl and B.V. Martin, *Traffic System Analysis for Engineers and Planners*. Copyright © by McGraw-Hill Book Co., New York. Used with Permission.

**Figure 3-10.** Variations of Price with Capacity at Fixed Volume.

that will be a mirror image of the price-volume curve. Where $C_1 = V_1$, the price of travel will be indefinitely large. As capacity is increased, the price of travel will drop, rapidly at first, and then more and more gradually. The resulting curve is shown in Figure 3-10. Clearly, for a range of volumes, there will be a family of parallel curves. As system capacity is increased, there comes a point (say $C_2$) where additional capacity barely affects travel price at that volume.

The addition of capacity to the network produces a new price-volume curve. Consider a family of price-capacity-volume curves, as shown in Figure 3-11. From this it can be seen that at some capacity $C_3$, a volume $V_4$ can be accommodated at price $p_3$. At a greater capacity, say $C_1$, the volume $V_4$ can be accommodated at price $p_1$. Demand and price-volume curves for a change in capacity will thus appear as a shift in the price-volume curve alone, as shown in Figure 3-12. The price-volume curve 1 refers to the time before the addition of capacity, and the price-volume curve 2 to after the addition of capacity. The result of the addition of capacity, in this case, is an increase in the demand that can be accommodated and a concomitant drop in travel price. It should be noted that the demand curve in this example has not shifted. In fact, the demand at any given price is still the same as it was before. However, a change in volume of travel has occurred, and it is due entirely to a change in the price of the travel that is being offered. This change is based on an assumption that the utility of a trip, or the value of

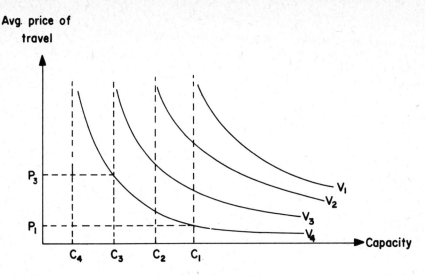

**Figure 3-11.** Price-Capacity-Volume Curves.

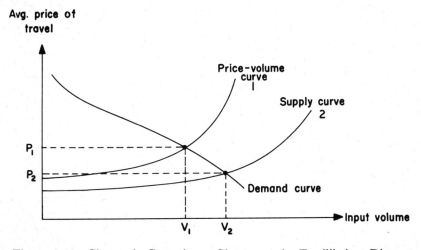

**Figure 3-12.** Change in Capacity as Shown on the Equilibrium Diagram.

making it, is unchanged by the nature of the transportation involved. It is entirely dependent upon the consumer preference pattern and the satisfactions to be gained from the activity to be consumed. Again, however, it should be emphasized that this is based on an improvement in an existing facility, not the addition of a new facility.

In order to handle the addition of a new facility, price-volume curves must first be aggregated over a section of the transportation network. The addition of a new facility will now be seen to alter network capacity and will generate a similar shift to that discussed above. However, it must be noted that this aggregation over the network introduces averaging errors in examining travel responses to transportation system changes.

**Application of the Theory**

The preceding sections of this chapter have outlined a theory of travel demand. This theory provides a basis for the development of models for forecasting and predicting amounts of travel. The basic requirements are clearly to develop both demand and price-volume relationships, in the form of mathematical models, which can then be solved simultaneously or iteratively to yield an equilibrium estimate of travel volume. Projected changes in socioeconomic characteristics of the population can be taken into account through shifts in the demand curve, while alternative transportation system changes will be reflected in price-volume curve shifts.

The theoretical base developed here also provides postulates of the likely variables for inclusion in the models. Both demand and price-volume curves should provide relationships between the price (in a general, non-monetary sense) and volume of travel. As has already been discussed, the constituents of price are likely to include money cost, travel time, comfort, convenience, etc. Second, it can be postulated that socioeconomic characteristics will interact with the relative weights (or coefficients) of the system variables in the demand curve. This interaction will serve to shift the demand curve in the price-volume space. On the other hand, capacity would appear to be the interactive term in the price-volume equation, causing bodily shifts of that curve in the same space.

In addition, the demand and price-volume relationships can only be calibrated if there are observations of a range of prices and volumes, with all other things held equal. In general, such observations can only be obtained by extremely careful data collection design. Furthermore, the locus of shifts in either curve will require variations in the interactive characteristics. Such variations will generally require time-series data.

As will be seen in subsequent chapters,[7] this theoretical basis for travel forecasting has been employed only sketchily in the development of the conventional travel forecasting procedures. Specific criticisms relating to this aspect will be brought out in the appropriate chapters.

# 4

## The Urban Transportation-planning Process

### Transportation Studies

Over the past 23 years, most of the metropolitan areas in North America, as well as a number of those in Europe, have conducted large-scale transportation studies. The primary intent of these transportation studies has been to provide the information necessary for long-term planning of the metropolitan area. These studies have set a pattern in major investments in the planning and design of future transportation systems. Out of these studies there has evolved a more-or-less standardized system, referred to usually as the transportation-planning process. Although the process has become somewhat standardized, it is subject both to continuing, incremental change and development, and also to much controversy among some professionals, relating to whether the process has any merit or influence on planning decisions. This section is concerned with the way in which this transportation-planning process has its backing in the transportation study. The remainder of this chapter comprises a brief examination of the transportation-planning process itself, and its various constituent parts.

The first of these major studies was conducted in Detroit, Michigan in 1953, followed within the next two or three years by studies in Washington, D.C. and Chicago. Since then, almost all of the major metropolitan areas in the whole of North America, as well as the capital cities of most countries in Europe and a number of their other metropolitan areas, have conducted major studies. Initially, these studies had as their intention the development of a comprehensive highway plan. This emphasis has been changed over the years to now include a comprehensive plan for the whole transportation system. In addition to this change in emphasis on the various modes of transportation, greater emphasis has been attempted on the integration of land use and transportation plans, and the comprehensive evaluation of policy alternatives. In all of these studies, there has been a heavy emphasis on data and on building computerized models. These emphases have not necessarily resulted in a collection of particularly good and useful data, nor in the development of foolproof, or good scientific, computerized models.

The major objectives (not necessarily realized in practice) of these studies could be summed up as follows: to provide comprehensive and continuing guidance for the development, evaluation, and implementation

59

of future transportation-planning proposals, emphasizing the broad role of transportation in urban activities; the comprehensive evaluation of alternative planning policies; and the allocation of priorities for future investment and development.

The Urban Transportation Planning process can usually be seen to be accomplished in a three-stage study. The first stage comprises an inventory of existing travel throughout the whole urban area, together with inventories of land uses, socioeconomic characteristics of the population, and the existing facilities for travel. The second stage constitutes a set of forecasts, first of the land uses that should occur in the forecast period, and then of the travel demand that may be anticipated and the way in which this will occur throughout the region. The final stage comprises the detailing of a number of alternative strategies for providing transportation and changes in land uses, together with evaluations and, hopefully, an eventual selection of a particular form or policy for future planning.

The conduct of these transportation studies and their general structure is based on the premise that the demand for travel is repetitive and predictable, and that future transportation systems should be designed to meet a specific, predicted travel demand. This demand is itself based on an analysis and extrapolation of current travel, and an investigation of its relationship to the patterns of population, employment, and socioeconomic activity. The structure is essentially forward-seeking, and relies heavily on an assumed ability to predict with a known degree of error, which is, hopefully, small.

It is a necessary step within the structure outlined above that a series of models of travel demand are included within it. These models allow the use of existing inventories of travel and of land use to provide predictions of future travel. The actual transportation planning process comprises, in fact, a sequence of seven steps. These are:[1]

1. Inventory (land use, population, travel, and transportation facilities)
2. Land-use forecast
3. Trip generation
4. Trip distribution
5. Modal split
6. Network assignment
7. Evaluation

These seven steps constitute what is conventionally known as the transportation-planning process.[2] The remainder of this chapter comprises a brief examination of these steps, preparatory to a more detailed discussion in the following chapters.

## Inventory

Basically, the inventory comprises the development of a data base for evaluating existing travel demand and existing transportation performance, and a basis for predicting demand and future system requirements. The actual inventory process is frequently the major effort in a transportation study. Essentially, however, the inventory stage can be summed up by the following paragraphs.

When the first transportation studies were conceived, methods for inventory were somewhat primitive, and comprised basically the measurement of volumes of travel on various parts of the highway network. Since then, the techniques of collecting data have improved considerably, and the scope of the data that have been collected is considerably greater than it used to be.

The inventory may be seen as comprising a number of separate steps. The first step is an inventory of the land uses in the urban area that is being studied. The second step is the organization and carrying out of a number of different inventory procedures designed to yield information about the way in which people currently travel, the number of trips they make, and the levels of use of various facilities. The third step of the inventory, which is carried out usually at the same time as the second and through the same medium, is that of collecting information about the population of the urban area. The information is that of the total population and various aspects of socioeconomic characteristics of that population. The fourth step comprises an inventory of the existing transportation systems, designed to determine the capacity of existing systems and their level of service characteristics. In the past, well over half of the cost of major studies has been devoted to the collection and processing of data.

Both because the survey is carried out as a sample survey and because the amount of data for an urban area is so vast, conventional transportation studies utilize some sort of spatial aggregation over the entire region for which the study is being made. This spatial aggregation usually takes the form of a hierarchy of areal units starting with the largest, which may be sectors or districts, then zones, and finally blocks. For each spatial unit the inventory data are aggregated. As far as possible, zone boundaries are chosen in such a way as to maintain the maximum possible homogeneity of each zone relative to socioeconomic characteristics, and also to attempt to represent coherent units in relation to the transportation system.

The actual zone structure that is arrived at exerts considerable influence on the accuracy and validity of later analyses. This is particularly so when those analyses employ zonal mean values as representative of the entire zonal population, and utilize a point centroid of a zone as an areal representation of that zone.

A second phase of this aggregation process is to construct a coded network. This is effectively an abstraction of the existing network of highways or transit routes into a graph of links and nodes. It *is not* usual that the coded network specifies every single link in the real-world system. It *is* usual, however, that the network will include all major links that are used by through traffic and all rail lines used, as well as all bus routes. It is also usual that the coded network for a major transportation study would comprise a hierarchy of highway facilities that could be classed as regional, feeder, distributor, and local. The parts of the network that provide purely a service or access facility would not normally be included for a regional or urban area study. However, it may be desirable to code networks to much finer detail in areas where intensive study will be carried out. Therefore, the exact extent of the hierarchy of facilities to be coded will depend very much upon the level, detail, and purpose of the analysis to be performed. The network coding procedure will also include specifications of either link travel times, or link travel costs, or link distances for each mode, together with terminal or intersection delays, and other level-of-service characteristics.

## Land-use Forecasts

The next stage of the urban transportation study is that of forecasting the future urban systems that the transportation system is to be designed to serve. This requires an estimation of the intensities and spatial distribution of population, employment, economic and social activity, land use, etc. The forecasts in this area are based usually upon known national trends in population, income, employment, and trends of distribution that are apparent within the urban area, utilizing both data collected in the land use and home interview section of the inventory, and also information from previous censuses of the population. In addition, some form of land-use models may be utilized to attempt to predict the probable changes in distribution and intensities of land uses within the urban area over the forecast time span. In most conventional studies in the past, this stage of the work has had little, if any, interaction or feedback with the transportation system, although more recent studies have begun to attempt to take this interaction into account.

## Trip Generation

Trip generation is conventionally the first of four models of travel demand that are used in a conventional transportation planning process. In a be-

havioral sense, trip generation may be regarded as the process that estimates the total number of trips being made or that models the decision
whether or not to make a trip. It is used to estimate the number of trips
generated and attracted by each areal unit, and these are set up as a function
of the socioeconomic and locational structure. In order to build models,
trips are normally categorized by purpose and mode. Other terms associated with trip generation include the concept of person trips and vehicle
trips, where the former are trips by each individual and the latter are vehicle
trips in a system where the vehicles may, of course, contain more than one
person; trip linking, which talks of the linking between various purposes of
trips; home-based and nonhome-based trips, which are trips with, respectively, one end of the trip at home or neither end at home; trip production
and trip attraction, which are the terms used for trips which emanate from
or are destined for a particular area.

At this point a digression is in order to consider the conventional way in
which trips are handled in a transportation study. As has just been mentioned, a number of terms are associated with trip making in trip generation. It is probably worthwhile to spend a few moments considering the
precise ways in which trips are defined. First, there are two categories of
trips in terms of their purposes: there are home-based and nonhome-based
trips. A *home-based trip* is any trip where one end of the trip is at home—
that is, it may have either started at home or ended at home. A trip is
essentially a one-way movement. Hence, a journey that involves leaving
home, going to a shopping center to visit stores and purchase goods, and
then returning home, consists, in fact, of two trips, the first trip being from
home to the shopping center, the second from the shopping center to the
home. On this basis, trips can be classified as home-based or nonhome-
based according to whether or not one end of a trip is at home. Some
modifications may be made to this concept in terms of trip linking in the
analysis stage. In recording trips, each specific trip is recorded individually. Consider the following journey of a housewife. She drives her husband
to the station, where he catches a train to go to work, then delivers the
children at school, subsequently drives to the store to do some shopping,
and finally returns home. This set of movements would be recorded as four
separate trips. The first trip would be from home to station with a purpose
to serve a passenger, the second would be from station to school, again with
a purpose to serve passengers, the third would be from school to shopping
center with the purpose of shopping, and the fourth would be purpose
home, which would be the trip returning from the shopping center to home.
However, since these trips are carried out as a sequence, trip linkage may
be utilized where the end of one trip is matched with the beginning of the
next trip.

The next concept, which has to be dealt with in the definition of trip making, concerns the ideas of origins, destinations, attractions, and generations or productions. Every trip has an origin and a destination. The origin is the place where the trip commences chronologically, and the destination is the place where the trip ends chronologically. In addition, each trip has a production end and an attraction end. However, production and attraction and origin and destination are not synonymous. Briefly, it can be summarized as follows: For a home-based trip, the zone of production is the home end of the trip; while the zone of attraction is the nonhome end of the trip. Thus, a trip from home to work and a trip from work to home will both have a production end which is home and an attraction end which is work. For nonhome-based trips, the production end is the origin and the attraction end is the destination (See Figure 4-1).

Returning now to trip generation, the estimation of the number of trips made from an areal unit is based on the observed relationships between trip making and characteristics of the unit of spatial aggregation, for example, the zone. Conventionally, the zonal characteristics that are used are entirely socioeconomic, land use, and population characteristics. On this basis, current relationships are produced between trip making and the zonal characteristics, and predictions made of future zonal characteristics, largely on the basis of the land-use forecast mentioned previously. An assumption is then made that the observed relationships at the present time between trip making and zonal characteristics will remain stable in the future, and future trip making is then predicted on the basis of the forecasts of future zonal characteristics.

**Trip Distribution**

This is the second, or sometimes third, travel-demand model that effectively attempts to model the way in which trips generated or attracted to zones are linked. In other words, each zone is taken one at a time, and a determination made of the zones to which its produced trips will be attracted. Distribution is made on the basis of a trade-off between the attractiveness of potential destination points and the costs or impedance of travel. A number of different models have been proposed that include, amongst the most prominent, the Fratar, gravity, and opportunity models. These models are all based on analogues or homomorphisms and operate at the aggregate interzonal level.

The models are set up in such a way that they contain unknowns that are a function of the specific area or region in which they are being applied, and of the transportation system in that region. In most cases, the transportation system and the area itself cannot be specified in the models in such a way that the relationships can be known regardless of the specific area of

|                | PRODUCTION | ATTRACTION  |
|----------------|------------|-------------|
| HOME – BASED   | HOME       | NON – HOME  |
| NON–HOME –BASED| ORIGIN     | DESTINATION |

**Figure 4-1.** Trip Categories.

application of the model. It, therefore, becomes necessary to calibrate the model for each specific application to a new urban area. The models are then calibrated for existing conditions, and this calibration is extrapolated into the future. Conventionally, there is little or no feedback between trip distribution and trip generation. In other words, trip generation produces the total trip productions and attractions that are used as the basis of trip distribution, but the effects of trip distribution do not normally have any effect in the modeling process on the actual trip productions and attractions.

**Modal Split**

This third, or sometimes second, model effectively attempts to distribute trips between the various modes available. Both historically and in terms of sophistication, modal split and trip distribution have not always appeared in the order shown here. In the earliest models, modal split occurred before trip distribution. Subsequently, however, the majority of model processes placed modal split after trip distribution. Attempts are made to allocate interzonal trips among the competing modes in terms of the levels of service, accessibility, and personal preference structure of the population. In the event that modal split occurs before distribution, conventionally the allocation is performed only in terms of characteristics of the zone that produces the trips, and possibly in terms of a general global-accessibility measure or level-of-service measure. In this approach, it is not possible to relate modal split to specific accessibilities or levels of service, because it is not yet known along which interzonal linkage the trip will be made. On the other hand, if trip distribution is performed before modal split, then the specific trip interchanges are known. This, then, allows the modal-split model to be constructed in terms of the specific modes, level of service, and accessibilities existing between each zone pair.

The models of modal split vary quite considerably in both their sophistication and computational structure. In computational structure, the models include simple cross-classification techniques, using percentage shares for each mode; regression analysis; diversion curves; and nonlinear mathematical curve-fitting procedures. However, in general, they are again calibrated for existing conditions and existing behavior and are then extrapolated into the future.

**Network Assignment**

The fourth and final travel forecasting model of the conventional planning process comprises an assignment, specific to each mode, of trips on the network of links and nodes. Separate assignments are made for each of the different travel modes. Conventionally, trips are assigned by route, based on minimum-impedance paths. Impedance is normally interpreted as time, and therefore the assignment process becomes that of attempting to allocate trips to a minimum-time path through the network between the zone of production and the zone of attraction. Again, as with modal split, a considerable variation in sophistication and computational structure is available in assignment models. The simplest assignment procedures attempt to assign all trips based on a single calculation of minimum-time paths throughout the whole network, or the times on the network that would be experienced under loads of less than saturation flows. This is called an uncapacitated assignment, and because all trips are assigned on the basis of a single calculation of minimum time paths, it is also termed as an all-or-nothing assignment.

Alternatively, instead of the simple uncapacitated assignment, a capacity-restrained assignment may be made. The capacity restraint is achieved by an iterative procedure, in which, at the end of one specific assignment process, the capacities and load volumes of traffic on each link are compared, and revised times are assigned to each link according to a predetermined rule of relationship between travel time, volume, and capacity. This form of capacity restraint can be incorporated on an all-or-nothing assignment. Alternatively, a further modification may be made whereby a diversion assignment is devised. The diversion assignment effectively attempts to load traffic onto the network with repeated calculations of volumes, capacity and trip time, in such a way that the minimum-time paths are continually being updated according to the traffic assigned on any particular route. This form of assignment is perhaps the most realistic of all, in terms of the actual real-life situation. It is also quite frequent that two separate assignments are made in any specific study, one for peak hour and one for the remainder of the time of the day. Each of these two assignments will use travel times based on the types of loading of the network that would be experienced at these times.

**Evaluation**

The final stage of the current conventional transportation-planning process involves the testing and evaluation of alternative networks in terms of both the traffic system performance and the environmental impact of each alternative. Most conventional studies have, however, employed only a partial evaluation process. This process has concentrated on the direct impacts only and has employed unidimensional evaluation criteria. The forms of impact that are considered are usually those which affect the user of the facility. It has only been within the last few years that any attention at all has been paid seriously to a consideration of the impact on nonusers and the environment in general. Judging by current trends of concern, it is probable that, in the future, a considerably greater emphasis will be placed upon the environmental effects and impacts of any transportation facility (e.g., see the Environmental Protection Act of 1970 and the Bureau of Public Roads Policy and Procedures Memorandum, 20-8, of 1970).

Little attention has been paid to questions of implementation, accessibility, and the specification of a full spectrum of consequences. The major emphasis has been on the development of a single final-state plan, based on the extrapolation of existing behavior and technology. No attempts have been made to determine a phasing in which this implementation of the final-state plan can be achieved, particularly with a built-in means of reassessing and revising the final-state plan during the course of implementation. There has also been little or no feedback to land-use and trip-generation phases from the final traffic system proposed, and little or no allowance made for technological innovation. The majority of plans considering a future of 20 to 50 years are based upon an assumption of the same mix of transportation modes and transportation characteristics that currently exist. In other words, they are based upon a highway system with conventional rail rapid transit, bus transit and railroad movements in the same form and with the same characteristics.

**Summary**

An outline of the urban transportation-planning (UTP) process has been presented here without any reference to inherent problems and shortcomings. A critical evaluation of each of the steps is provided at the end of each of the next seven chapters. A comprehensive, critical review of the entire process forms chapter 12 of this book, where the review process is based upon specific theoretical and operational characteristics and shortcomings identified in chapters 5 through 11.

A number of computer program packages of this process have been developed over the past few years. Initially, the United States government developed and provided two alternative packages, one known as the BPR package (developed and provided by the Bureau of Public Roads) and a second one known as the HUD Transit Planning Package (developed by the Department of Housing and Urban Development). In addition, several transportation consultant firms developed their own proprietary packages, where each package contained minor differences from any other one.

More recently, two new computer packages have been developed by the U.S. Department of Transportation to replace the BPR and HUD packages. Again, the emphasis of the two original packages have been retained, in that the new FHWA (Federal Highway Administration) package is more highway-oriented and the new UTPS package (UMTA Transit Planning System) is primarily transit-oriented. In principal, the process modeled in these computer programs is identical to the process outlined in this chapter. The primary changes from the original BPR and HUD packages lie in the sophistication of the computer programming and in the use of modern peripheral hardware, for example, the incorporation of interactive programming and displays, etc.

At the same time, transportation consultants have worked on increasing the sophistication of their respective program packages. These changes include some of those incorporated in the new FHWA and UTPS packages, as well as proprietary procedures for the estimation and calibration of individual models in the process.

In spite of all these programming efforts and changes, the basic seven-step process, outlined in this chapter, remains the backbone of the urban transportation-planning process. Furthermore, the specific model structures, which are described in the next few chapters, have also remained largely unchanged. The programming changes have mainly been to improve the efficiency of calibration techniques and the flexibility of application of these models. As a result, no attempt is made in this book to describe any one individual programming package.

# 5 Inventory

## Data Needs

A data base is a necessary input to the urban transportation- and land use-planning process and is made up of a number of separate parts.[1] First, there is an inventory of present transportation systems. These systems would include highways, transit facilities, terminals, control systems, etc., and the inventory relates to the supply of these facilities. Second, there is an inventory of present land uses, in which the types, locations, and intensities or densities of land uses are recorded. These two inventories provide a profile of the physical supply of facilities for and affecting urban area travel. The third element in a data base is an inventory of the levels of use of the transportation system.

The remainder of the data base that is required comprises first, a sampling of the desires for travel, and second, a sampling of the characteristics and desires relating to growth and land-use change. The first of these, the sampling of desires to travel, would be obtained by recording the origins and destinations of trips according to their mode of travel, their purpose, the time of day, for both passenger and goods movements. The characteristics and desires relating to growth and land-use change would include those of economic activity, employment, population, income, and car ownership. This information may also be enlarged upon by the use of attitudinal surveys of travel preferences, land and housing preferences.

The scope and form of the data have to be related to the use to which the data are to be put. First, data on the current usage of the transportation system and on the levels of activity relating to land use must be suitable for input into models selected for the various forecasting and evaluation stages of the process. This generates the need for prior knowledge of the models to be used and of the requirements of these models in terms of input data. This need clearly cannot be fulfilled except at extraordinary expense, unless these requirements are known when the survey is being planned. The size of the sample must be related both to the use of the data, and to the accuracy required. If trip data are to be stratified according to the categories into which the trip makers fall, for example, income, car ownership, size of family, etc., then it will be necessary to collect a large sample of travel data in order to be able to have adequate representation of travel behavior in each subcategory of the population. On the other hand, a small sample may be adequate if the objective is to provide updating information in a continuing study.

Finally, it is worth noting that the type of cooperation, necessary to achieve the foregoing data design requirements, mandates careful organization and staffing design for the transportation study. It is not possible to commence the design of the inventories prior to the appointment of staff to all the major functions of the study and, indeed, until after this staff has had the opportunity to study, evaluate, and select strategies for the different aspects of the study. Similarly, the organizational structure must be set up to ensure adequate interaction between the various study functions, so that all necessary inputs to stages, such as inventory, are assured.

## Data Collection

### Coding and Zoning

The first stage in the data collection procedure is to carry out a process of zoning of the total area to be covered by the survey, and a coding of the network that is to be used.[2] (It is assumed that the bounding of the study area will have been carried out in the initial study design.) The zoning procedure requires the division of the survey area into spatial units suitable as a basis for data collection, and later for aggregate analysis purposes. The designation of zone boundaries in this case should be done on the basis of selecting units that will be as nearly homogeneous as possible, and that represent natural run-off areas for travel patterns. As a guide to this type of selection of boundaries, zones should be selected such that they are circumscribed either by major transportation facilities that represent, in effect, a partial barrier to movement, in that not a great deal of movement is likely to occur across them but a considerable amount of movement onto them and along them; or by barriers to movement such as rivers. In certain cases, it may be desirable to set up two complete zoning patterns. The first of these would be the zoning pattern to be used in data collection, and would divide the area up into spatial units best suited to be treated as individual elements in a sampling process. This first zone system may comprise amalgamations of census enumeration areas, or other spatial units particularly suited to the available sampling frame. Such spatial units will rarely coincide with the requirements for data analysis for transportation and land use. Therefore, the second set of zones would comprise the zones to be used for analysis purposes. These zones would be determined on the basis of the transportation criteria outlined. Some examples are shown in Figures 5-1, 5-2, 5-3, and 5-4.

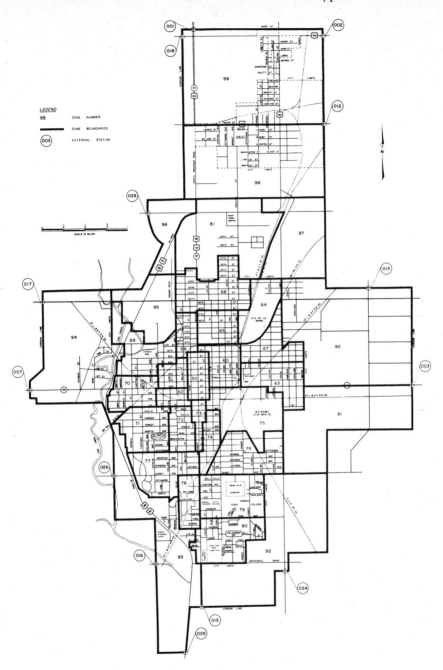

Source: *Traffic Assignment Manual*, U.S. Department of Commerce, June 1964.

**Figure 5-1.** Sample Zoning System for a Hypothetical City.

72

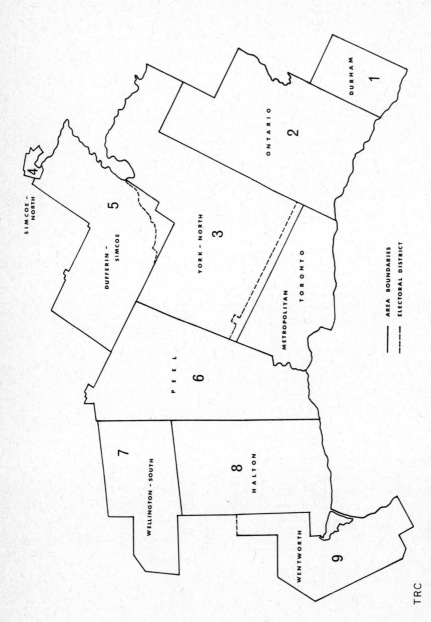

TRC

Source: MTARTS 1964 Home Interview Survey, March 1965.

**Figure 5-2.** Traffic Sector Boundaries for Metropolitan Toronto and Region Transportation Study.

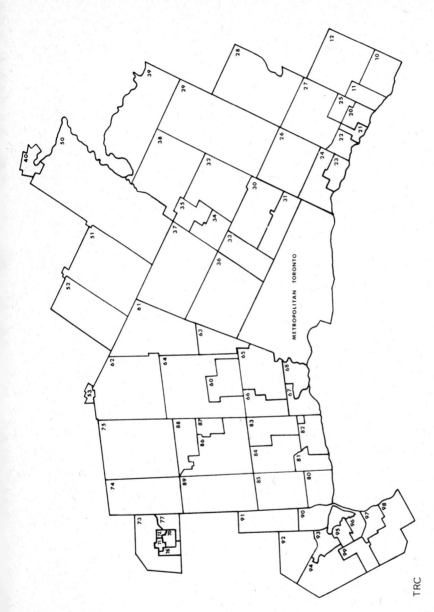

TRC

Source: MTARTS 1964 Home Interview Survey, March 1965.

**Figure 5-3.** Traffic District Boundaries for Metropolitan Toronto and Region Transportation Study.

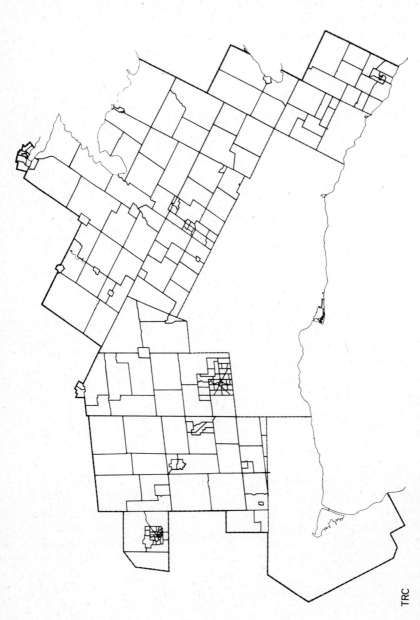

TRC

Source: MTARTS 1964 Home Interview Survey, March 1965.

**Figure 5-4.** Traffic Zones and Subdistricts for Metropolitan Toronto and Region Transportation Study.

In addition to the zoning of the area that is to be studied, it is also necessary to design a coding system for the network. Given that the study is to look at all forms of surface transportation, separate networks need to be identified for each of highway, bus, rail rapid transit, commuter railroad, etc. Each network is coded as a series of links, each of which begins and ends at a node. A link is a schematic representation of a section of right-of-way and nodes are defined as the intersections of three or more links. Links possess spatial and locational properties, such as length, direction, and capacity, while nodes possess no dimensions. Thus, intersection capacities, delays, etc. are normally assigned to the appropriate links and not to the nodes. In transit networks, nodes will also be defined at any point where access to the transit system is possible, for example, at stations on a fixed rail system and bus stops on a bus system.

In general, for an urban transportation study, coding of the entire street and highway network would not be attempted. First, it is improbable that the ensuing planning activities would be concerned with such a fine level of detail as to necessitate such network precision and, second, the magnitude of the coding task and its concommitant demands on computer capacity would be insufficiently productive to warrant such detail. Hence, for the highway network, it is necessary first to define categories of highways for which planning is envisaged and subsequently define a reduced or simplified network for coding. Such a procedure will generally exclude most residential and other access streets and will be concerned primarily with local feeder routes, intracity and intercity arterials, interstate highways, etc.

The aggregation to zones also introduces the need for the definition of an additional set of nodes, called "load nodes." These load nodes are the representation, for the networks, of the sources and sinks for trips. In other words, it is assumed that all trips made from a particular zone originate at its load node, and all trips made to the zone terminate at the load node. In order for trips to leave from and arrive at a load node, and in the absence of network links for local access streets, one or more "loading links" are created, connecting the load node into the network. These loading links are usually given the aggregative capacities of the local access roads and the mean access and egress times for the zone from the primary network. Loading nodes and links are required for both highway and transit networks.

Having identified a system of links and nodes, it remains to code the network for computer applications. The coding comprises the assignment of identifying numbers to the nodes, such that each node is uniquely identified. A link is then coded by using the numbers for the nodes at each end of the link, where the order of the node numbers indicates the directionality of the link (links are normally considered to be unidirectional). In addition to this, a large amount of additional information may be recorded at the same time as the network is coded. This information may include, for highways, such items as the length of the link, the zoned speed on the link, parking control, the type of area through which the link passes, the free-flow travel time, and the capacity. For transit networks, information may be recorded about the frequency and capacity of services, the number of stops, the type of service provided, etc. Finally, additional coding needs to be carried out to include, within the entire network, committed construction, and also, eventually, alternatives for improving the transportation system. An example of a highway network is given in Figure 5-5, and its coded arterial system is shown in Figure 5-6. A detail of the network, showing load nodes and loading links, is given in Figure 5-7.

*Supply Inventory*

The information required for the coding of the networks in a transportation study is usually obtained by means of an inventory of existing highway and transit facilities; in other words, an inventory of the supply of transportation facilities. This inventory is typically executed by a combination of physical measurement in the field, measurement on maps maintained by local authorities, and records of regulations, schedules, etc. Free-flow travel times are either computed on the basis of link length, intersection controls, lane widths, and presence or absence of parking; or are measured by the use of a vehicle equipped with a fifth wheel and instrumentation for recording times and distances as accurately as possible. In addition to these physical attributes of the networks, information is required on the traffic volumes for all of the links in the network. There are three basic ways to collect data on travel volumes on streets and highways. The type of data collection technique and the intensity of collection depends upon the importance of the street or highway, and upon the purpose of the traffic count. Major arterials and critical links in the highway network should usually be subjected to a full 24-hour count for at least one typical work day, probably utilizing full-scale counts of turning movements, etc. and using survey teams to conduct the counts. Minor streets may be covered by the use of moving-observer surveys or by the use of mechanical traffic counters. Second, at least one cordon will be defined around the transportation study area. One such cordon will coincide approximately with the study area boundaries, while internal cordons may be defined around such areas as the CBD. At each point where the cordon intersects a street or highway, cordon counts will be made. Generally, these will be conducted on a sample basis and for less than 24 hours. Their purpose is to provide volume measures of traffic going in and out of the cordoned area. Minor

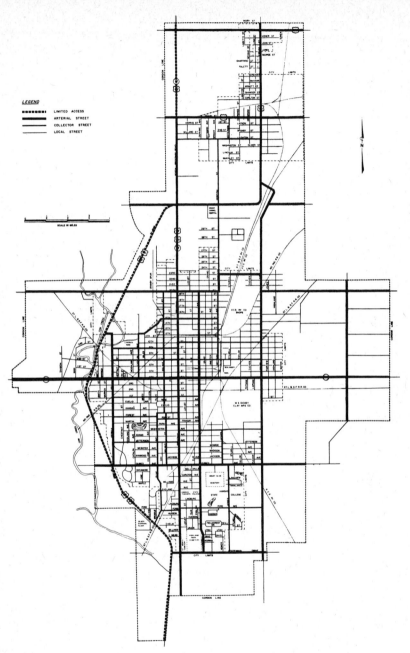

Source: *Traffic Assignment Manual*, U.S. Department of Commerce, June 1964.

**Figure 5-5.** Hypothetical Street System.

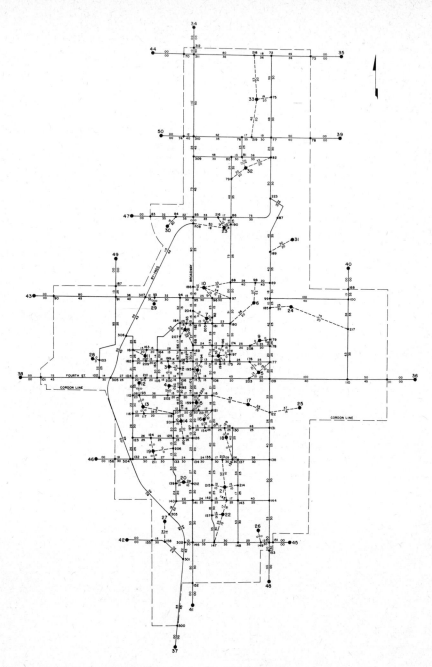

Source: *Traffic Assignment Manual*, U.S. Department of Commerce, June 1964.

**Figure 5-6.** Coded Arterial Network for the Hypothetical Street System of Figure 5-5.

79

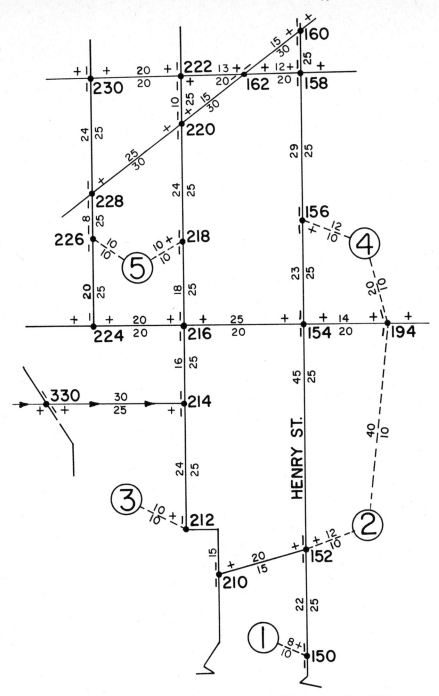

Source: *Traffic Assignment Manual*, U.S. Department of Commerce, June 1964.

**Figure 5-7.** Detail of Part of a Coded Network.

streets crossing the cordon may be surveyed using mechanical traffic counters, while more major streets and highways are likely to be surveyed using both counts and roadside interviews. Finally, screen lines will be defined to cross the study area, usually along natural or artificial barriers to movement, such as rivers, railroad lines, etc. As will be described later in this chapter, the screen lines are used to check data collected on personal travel movements, and are therefore surveyed in a similar fashion to a cordon. That is, each highway crossing a screen line will be subjected to at least 12-hour counts, often supplemented by sample interviews. Counting may be by mechanical counter, but is often by survey team, to record vehicle type and occupancy, as well as overall totals of vehicles.

These studies and counts will provide information about the level of usage of the highway system. In addition to this, similar information may be required of the transit network. This information may be obtained by a number of methods, such as on-vehicle counts, use of records of ticket receipts, and cordon interviews. Generally cordon and screen-line surveys will include counts of passengers in road-based public transport vehicles. In addition to this information, inventories are made of travel times, parking and accident rates on the highway network, and travel times on the public transport networks. This information is utilized at various stages of the planning process.

*Land-use Surveys*

The purpose of the land-use surveys is effectively to provide the other side of the supply picture affecting transportation. The surveys comprise an inventory of the types and intensities of land uses in the study area, based upon a trip-generating or trip-attracting typology. The classification of land uses is generally based, to a large extent, on one of the existing detailed land-use codes, but is aggregated to no more than about ten basic land-use types, in most instances. A typical set of land-use categories might be:

1. Residential
2. Retail
3. Commercial
4. Government and institutional
5. Light industrial
6. Heavy industrial
7. Transportation and utilities
8. Open space
9. Vacant land

Intensity measures for land uses will generally comprise floor area, employment, and population density.

Sources of data for land-use surveys generally comprise local zoning maps, Sanborn maps, and other local records and surveys of land use. Usually, however, it will be necessary to conduct some further inventories of land uses by field inspection, to provide both updates and checks on these existing sources. Generally, such field surveys are conducted on a small-sample basis. These surveys complete the supply picture for transportation and land use.

*Travel Inventories*

The final major inventory is of the travel desires and demands within the study area. This information is normally provided by a series of surveys. The type of survey to be carried out will depend to a large extent upon the total size of the area being surveyed. In metropolitan areas of less than 75,000 population, the U.S. Federal Highway Administration recommends the use of roadside interviews for this inventory. In larger metropolitan areas, it is more usually necessary to obtain origin and destination from home interviews.[3] In addition to this, the level of detail and breadth of travel information required will also influence the choice of type of survey to be carried out. In order to conduct a home-interview survey, it is necessary first to identify the total numbers of households in each zone within the study area. These households are then selected at random on the basis of some sampling procedure determined prior to this stage of the survey work. Each household selected for the sample is listed for interview. In present studies, it is usual that the interviewing procedure obtains details about all trips made by a sampled household on the day or week prior to the interview. In addition, information is collected upon various characteristics of the household, including the size of the household, household income, number of cars owned, number of licensed drivers, ages and occupations of household members, and the locations of their workplaces or schools. The interviewing procedure generally involves the use of teams of trained interviewers who will visit all of the selected addresses and interview members of the household, using predesigned survey forms and questioning procedures. An example of an interview questionnaire is given in Figure 5-8.

In addition to the household information obtained by interview, it is also necessary as mentioned previously, to make a study of travel entering and leaving the designated study area. To this end, stations are selected at points where highways and transit facilities cross the external cordon line. On highways, motorists are stopped at the interview stations and are

**1**
**HOUSEHOLD**
**REPORT**

Zone No.
Sample No.

## METROPOLITAN TORONTO AND REGION TRANSPORTATION STUDY
## TRANSPORTATION SURVEY 1964

**MEMBERS OF THE HOUSEHOLD are requested to complete this form.**

**YOUR ANSWERS WILL BE CONFIDENTIAL AND WILL BE USED FOR STATISTICAL PURPOSES ONLY. No name or signature is needed.**

A. How many persons live at this address? (Do not include visitors.)

B. How many are children under 5 years of age?

C. How many are servants living in, or roomers?

D. How many passenger cars are owned by persons at this address? (Include station wagons, jeeps)

E. How many company or leased cars are used and garaged here? (Include station wagons, jeeps)

F. How many trucks or vans are used and garaged here?

G. **List the persons 5 years of age and older who live at this address.** Include servants who live in or roomers. List visitors who live outside the survey area but are temporarily staying at this address.

| Person Identification Number | Person Identification (For example, father, mother, son-John, daughter-Mary) | Check (√) if Interviewed | Sex (√) M 1 / F 2 | Age Group (use code shown below) | Driver's Licence? (√) 1 Yes / 2 No | Did You Make Trips? (SEE FORM 3) (√) 1 Yes / 2 No / 3 Not known | Occupation What do you do? (clerk, machine operator, cook, agent, retired, housewife, student, unemployed, etc.) | Industry In what type of business or industry do you work? (car manufacturing, bakery, hotel, fire dep't, etc.) |
|---|---|---|---|---|---|---|---|---|
| 1 | Head of Household | | | | | | | |
| 2 | | | | | | | | |
| 3 | | | | | | | | |
| 4 | | | | | | | | |
| 5 | | | | | | | | |
| 6 | | | | | | | | |
| 7 | | | | | | | | |
| 8 | | | | | | | | |
| 9 | | | | | | | | |
| 10 | | | | | | | | |
| 11 | | | | | | | | |
| 98 | Visitor | | | | | | | |
| 99 | Visitor | | | | | | | |

| Age Groups Code | 5-10 | 11-15 | 16-20 | 21-25 | 26-35 | 36-45 | 46-55 | 56-65 | over 65 |
|---|---|---|---|---|---|---|---|---|---|
| | 1 | 2 | 3 | 4 | 5 | 6 | 7 | 8 | 9 |

Source: MTARTS 1964 Home Interview Survey, March 1965.

**Figure 5-8.** Example of the Layout of an Interview Survey Form.

FACTS

**Complete for HEAD OF THE HOUSEHOLD.**

**THE ANSWERS ARE COMPLETELY CONFIDENTIAL AND WILL BE USED FOR STATISTICAL PURPOSES ONLY. No Name or signature is needed.**

1. What type of residence do you occupy **now**? (Circle the code)

   Single detached ........................................................... 1

   Attached (semi-, row-, or maisonette) .......................... 2

   Duplex, 3, 4, 5, or 6 Plex ............................................ 3

   Apartment or residential hotel (6 or more apartments) ... 4

   Rooming house (10 or more rooms available as lodgings) ... 5

   Residence attached to business ..................................... 6

2. HOW IMPORTANT was **each** of the following reasons when you selected this place of residence:
   (Circle the degree of importance, one code number per line)

| | Very Important | | Important | | Not Important | | Did Not Apply |
|---|---|---|---|---|---|---|---|
| Good price or rent for residence | 1 | or | 2 | or | 3 | or | 4 |
| Neighbourhood | 1 | or | 2 | or | 3 | or | 4 |
| Easy to get to by road | 1 | or | 2 | or | 3 | or | 4 |
| Easy to get to by public transportation | 1 | or | 2 | or | 3 | or | 4 |
| Quality of schools | 1 | or | 2 | or | 3 | or | 4 |
| Near to schools | 1 | or | 2 | or | 3 | or | 4 |
| Near to parks and playgrounds | 1 | or | 2 | or | 3 | or | 4 |
| Near to work (Reasonable Travel Time) | 1 | or | 2 | or | 3 | or | 4 |
| Near to local shopping centre | 1 | or | 2 | or | 3 | or | 4 |
| Near to major shopping centre | 1 | or | 2 | or | 3 | or | 4 |
| Near to friends and family | 1 | or | 2 | or | 3 | or | 4 |
| Near to church | 1 | or | 2 | or | 3 | or | 4 |
| Other _____ (Please specify) | 1 | or | 2 | or | 3 | or | 4 |

3. How long have you lived at **this** address? _____ years _____ months

4. Where did you live **previously**? (address) _____
   Number, Street, Municipality, or Lot, Concession, Municipality (if unknown describe location)

5. Where do you work **now**? (address) _____
   Number, Street, Municipality, or Lot, Concession, Municipality (if unknown describe location)

6. How long have you worked at **this** address? _____ years _____ months

7. Where did you work **previously**? (address) _____
   Number, Street, Municipality, or Lot, Concession, Municipality (if unknown describe location)

8. Approximate Annual Household Income — combined wage and salary income of all members of the household (Circle the code)

| | | | | | |
|---|---|---|---|---|---|
| under $ 2,000 | 1 | $ 6,000 - $ 8,000 | 4 | $12,000 - $16,000 | 7 |
| $ 2,000 - $ 4,000 | 2 | $ 8,000 - $10,000 | 5 | $16,000 - $20,000 | 8 |
| $ 4,000 - $ 6,000 | 3 | $10,000 - $12,000 | 6 | over  $20,000 | 9 |

**Figure 5-8 (continued)**

**3**
**TRIP**
**REPORT**

**EACH PERSON 5 YEARS OF AGE AND OLDER REPORT ALL TRIPS FOR A 24-HOUR PERIOD BEGINNING 4 A.M. ON** ______

Members of household, servants who live in, roomers and visitors who live outside survey area, each complete a separate form. **If more than 6 trips use additional forms.**

**"TRIP"** is the one way travel from one point to another for a particular purpose. **Stop-overs** are regarded as the end of one trip and the beginning of another.

**Do not** include stops made for relatively **unimportant** purposes, for example, drop a letter in a mailbox, purchase gasoline, parking your automobile, transferring from one public transportation vehicle to another.

**Do not** report walking trips, except walking from Home to Work and from Work to Home.

Zone No. ______
Sample No. ______
Person No. ______

**Person Identification** ______
(Please use same identification as on Household Report 1)

For AUTO DRIVER Only

| Trip No. | I STARTED THIS TRIP AT: Number, Street, Municipality or Lot, Concession, Municipality (if unknown describe location) | Time: Hrs. | Time: Min. | Time: A.M. P.M. | Minutes walked at start of trip | I ENDED THIS TRIP AT: Number, Street, Municipality or Lot, Concession, Municipality (if unknown describe location) | Time: Hrs. | Time: Min. | Time: A.M. P.M. | Minutes walked at end of trip | TYPE OF PROPERTY at TRIP END Describe (store, school, factory, house, roadside, playground, etc.) | PURPOSE of TRIP (FROM / TO) Circle from and to purpose for each trip (see pamphlet) | METHOD of TRAVEL Circle one code per trip | For Passenger of Public Transit: Number of Transfers | No. Persons in Car include Driver | VEHICLE PARKING AT TRIP END: Type of Parking Circle one code per trip | Duration of Parking: Hrs. | Duration of Parking: Min. | Fee: $ | Fee: ¢ | Method of Payment Circle code |
|---|---|---|---|---|---|---|---|---|---|---|---|---|---|---|---|---|---|---|---|---|---|
| | | | | A.M.<br>-or-<br>P.M. | | | | | A.M.<br>-or-<br>P.M. | | | 1 Work 1<br>2 Personal business 2<br>3 Shopping 3<br>4 Social 4<br>5 Recreation 5<br>6 School 6<br>7 Serve passenger 7<br>8 Change travel method 8<br>9 Home 9 | Auto driver 1<br>Auto/Truck passenger 2<br>Taxi passenger 3<br>Public Transit (TTC, Gray Coach etc.) 4<br>Railway 5<br>School bus 6<br>Other 7<br>Walk between home-work 8 | | | Street free 1<br>Street meter 2<br>Lot free 3<br>Lot paid 4<br>Garage free 5<br>Garage paid 6<br>Service, Repair 7<br>Residential 8<br>Cruised 9 | | | | | Monthly 1<br>Daily 2<br>Duration of parking 3 |
| | | | | A.M.<br>-or-<br>P.M. | | | | | A.M.<br>-or-<br>P.M. | | | 1 Work 1<br>2 Personal business 2<br>3 Shopping 3<br>4 Social 4<br>5 Recreation 5<br>6 School 6<br>7 Serve passenger 7<br>8 Change travel method 8<br>9 Home 9 | Auto driver 1<br>Auto/Truck passenger 2<br>Taxi passenger 3<br>Public Transit (TTC, Gray Coach etc.) 4<br>Railway 5<br>School bus 6<br>Other 7<br>Walk between home-work 8 | | | Street free 1<br>Street meter 2<br>Lot free 3<br>Lot paid 4<br>Garage free 5<br>Garage paid 6<br>Service, Repair 7<br>Residential 8<br>Cruised 9 | | | | | Monthly 1<br>Daily 2<br>Duration of parking 3 |
| | | | | A.M.<br>-or-<br>P.M. | | | | | A.M.<br>-or-<br>P.M. | | | 1 Work 1<br>2 Personal business 2<br>3 Shopping 3<br>4 Social 4<br>5 Recreation 5<br>6 School 6<br>7 Serve passenger 7<br>8 Change travel method 8<br>9 Home 9 | Auto driver 1<br>Auto/Truck passenger 2<br>Taxi passenger 3<br>Public Transit (TTC, Gray Coach etc.) 4<br>Railway 5<br>School bus 6<br>Other 7<br>Walk between home-work 8 | | | Street free 1<br>Street meter 2<br>Lot free 3<br>Lot paid 4<br>Garage free 5<br>Garage paid 6<br>Service, Repair 7<br>Residential 8<br>Cruised 9 | | | | | Monthly 1<br>Daily 2<br>Duration of parking 3 |
| | | | | A.M.<br>-or-<br>P.M. | | | | | A.M.<br>-or-<br>P.M. | | | 1 Work 1<br>2 Personal business 2<br>3 Shopping 3<br>4 Social 4<br>5 Recreation 5<br>6 School 6<br>7 Serve passenger 7<br>8 Change travel method 8<br>9 Home 9 | Auto driver 1<br>Auto/Truck passenger 2<br>Taxi passenger 3<br>Public Transit (TTC, Gray Coach etc.) 4<br>Railway 5<br>School bus 6<br>Other 7<br>Walk between home-work 8 | | | Street free 1<br>Street meter 2<br>Lot free 3<br>Lot paid 4<br>Garage free 5<br>Garage paid 6<br>Service, Repair 7<br>Residential 8<br>Cruised 9 | | | | | Monthly 1<br>Daily 2<br>Duration of parking 3 |
| | | | | A.M.<br>-or-<br>P.M. | | | | | A.M.<br>-or-<br>P.M. | | | 1 Work 1<br>2 Personal business 2<br>3 Shopping 3<br>4 Social 4<br>5 Recreation 5<br>6 School 6<br>7 Serve passenger 7<br>8 Change travel method 8<br>9 Home 9 | Auto driver 1<br>Auto/Truck passenger 2<br>Taxi passenger 3<br>Public Transit (TTC, Gray Coach etc.) 4<br>Railway 5<br>School bus 6<br>Other 7<br>Walk between home-work 8 | | | Street free 1<br>Street meter 2<br>Lot free 3<br>Lot paid 4<br>Garage free 5<br>Garage paid 6<br>Service, Repair 7<br>Residential 8<br>Cruised 9 | | | | | Monthly 1<br>Daily 2<br>Duration of parking 3 |
| | | | | A.M.<br>-or-<br>P.M. | | | | | A.M.<br>-or-<br>P.M. | | | 1 Work 1<br>2 Personal business 2<br>3 Shopping 3<br>4 Social 4<br>5 Recreation 5<br>6 School 6<br>7 Serve passenger 7<br>8 Change travel method 8<br>9 Home 9 | Auto driver 1<br>Auto/Truck passenger 2<br>Taxi passenger 3<br>Public Transit (TTC, Gray Coach etc.) 4<br>Railway 5<br>School bus 6<br>Other 7<br>Walk between home-work 8 | | | Street free 1<br>Street meter 2<br>Lot free 3<br>Lot paid 4<br>Garage free 5<br>Garage paid 6<br>Service, Repair 7<br>Residential 8<br>Cruised 9 | | | | | Monthly 1<br>Daily 2<br>Duration of parking 3 |

**IF REPORT INCLUDES AT LEAST ONE WORK TRIP AS CAR DRIVER, BY PUBLIC TRANSIT OR BY RAILWAY SEE REVERSE SIDE**

**Figure 5-8 (continued)**

**TO WORK TRIP REPORT**

Sample No.
Person No.

Please complete either section I or section II for the trip made on the reverse side.

(Report for the first journey if more than one journey made "to work" during the day.)

## I
## FOR CAR DRIVERS ONLY
(Report only if you drive all the way to work)

**A. How important were the following reasons for using the car?**
(Circle one code number per line)

| | Very Important | | Important | | Not Important | | Did Not Apply |
|---|---|---|---|---|---|---|---|
| 1. Car necessary to do work (For example, salesman, doctor, etc.) | 1 | or | 2 | or | 3 | or | 4 |
| 2. Time to travel by car | 1 | or | 2 | or | 3 | or | 4 |
|    Time saved? _____ minutes | | | | | | | |
|    or Time lost? _____ minutes | | | | | | | |
| 3. Daily cost to travel by car (including parking cost) | 1 | or | 2 | or | 3 | or | 4 |
|    Money saved? _____ cents per day | | | | | | | |
|    or Money lost? _____ cents per day | | | | | | | |
| 4. Car more convenient | 1 | or | 2 | or | 3 | or | 4 |
| 5. Long walk to public transportation stops | 1 | or | 2 | or | 3 | or | 4 |
|    How long a walk at trip start? _____ minutes | | | | | | | |
|    How long a walk at trip end? _____ minutes | | | | | | | |
| 6. Long wait for public transportation at start | 1 | or | 2 | or | 3 | or | 4 |
|    How long a wait at trip start? _____ minutes | | | | | | | |
| 7. Too many transfers | 1 | or | 2 | or | 3 | or | 4 |
|    How many transfers? | | | | | | | |
| 8. Ride by public transportation uncomfortable | 1 | or | 2 | or | 3 | or | 4 |
| 9. Others _____ | 1 | or | 2 | or | 3 | or | 4 |
| (Please specify) | | | | | | | |

**B. Use attached road map to indicate your route of travel FROM HOME TO WORK**
(If "serve passenger" trip is a portion of journey to work, mark start and end of "serve passenger" trip with an S)

**C. Why was this route chosen rather than other routes?** (Circle one code number per line)

| | Yes | | No | | Did Not apply |
|---|---|---|---|---|---|
| 1. Shortest travel time | 1 | or | 2 | or | 3 |
| 2. Shortest travel distance | 1 | or | 2 | or | 3 |
| 3. Traffic is free flowing (least driving strain) | 1 | or | 2 | or | 3 |
| 4. Enjoy scenery of this route | 1 | or | 2 | or | 3 |
| 5. Necessary to serve passenger | 1 | or | 2 | or | 3 |
| 6. Others _____ | 1 | or | 2 | or | 3 |
| (Please specify) | | | | | |

## II
## FOR PUBLIC TRANSPORTATION PASSENGERS ONLY
(Report if any portion of journey to work made by public transit or railway)

**A. How important were the following reasons for using public transportation?**
(Circle one code number per line)

| | Very Important | | Important | | Not Important | | Did Not Apply |
|---|---|---|---|---|---|---|---|
| 1. Do not own a car | 1 | or | 2 | or | 3 | or | 4 |
| 2. Do not have driver's licence | 1 | or | 2 | or | 3 | or | 4 |
| 3. Car used by other persons | 1 | or | 2 | or | 3 | or | 4 |
| 4. Time to travel by public transportation | 1 | or | 2 | or | 3 | or | 4 |
|    Time saved? _____ minutes | | | | | | | |
|    or Time lost? _____ minutes | | | | | | | |
| 5. Daily cost to travel by public transportation | 1 | or | 2 | or | 3 | or | 4 |
|    Money saved? (including cost for parking) _____ cents per day | | | | | | | |
|    or Money lost? (including cost for parking) _____ cents per day | | | | | | | |
| 6. Safer than by car | 1 | or | 2 | or | 3 | or | 4 |
| 7. Public transportation more convenient | 1 | or | 2 | or | 3 | or | 4 |
| 8. Long walk from parking lot to work | 1 | or | 2 | or | 3 | or | 4 |
|    How long a walk _____ minutes | | | | | | | |
| 9. Others _____ | 1 | or | 2 | or | 3 | or | 4 |
| (Please specify) | | | | | | | |

**B. Use attached road map to indicate your route of travel FROM HOME TO WORK**
(If "change travel method" trip is a portion of journey to work, mark start and end of "change travel method" trip with a C)

**C. Why was this route chosen rather than other routes?** (Circle one code number per line)

| | Yes | | No | | Did Not Apply |
|---|---|---|---|---|---|
| 1. Shortest travel time | 1 | or | 2 | or | 3 |
| 2. Shortest travel distance | 1 | or | 2 | or | 3 |
| 3. Prefer to ride subway | 1 | or | 2 | or | 3 |
| 4. Seat available | 1 | or | 2 | or | 3 |
| 5. Fewest transfers | 1 | or | 2 | or | 3 |
| 6. Frequent service | 1 | or | 2 | or | 3 |
| 7. Scenery | 1 | or | 2 | or | 3 |
| 8. Others _____ | 1 | or | 2 | or | 3 |
| (Please specify) | | | | | |

**Figure 5-8 (continued)**

questioned as to their origin, destination and trip purpose. It is usual that this type of survey is a sample survey, where the size of the sample depends largely upon the traffic volume. In addition, the information may be obtained either from transit carriers or by interviewing at the stations or stops nearest to the cordon line on mass-transit facilities.

A further part of the travel data is that of truck and taxi trips, which are usually inventoried by interviewing commercial operators. Again, a sample is chosen and the size of the sample depends upon both the level of detail of subsequent analysis, and the total size of each of the truck and taxi operations in the study area. Frequently, truck and taxi trips are obtained by requesting operators to furnish their drivers with a log sheet for a complete week. They are requested to record on this log sheet information about the origins and destinations of each trip made, the number of people or quantity of goods and type of goods carried, together with other information determined to be pertinent to the study being undertaken.

The final studies usually undertaken at this time are those needed in order to allow the data from the sample surveys to be grossed-up to the entire metropolitan area. Clearly, the travel data needed for a transportation study are those pertaining to all households in the survey area, rather than those of the small sample (generally less than ten percent) actually surveyed. In order to make the necessary grossing-up, it is necessary to obtain some information that will allow checks to be made to determine the rates at which trips should be grossed-up to represent total trips in the area. The usual methods employed to do this comprise screen-line surveys together with a number of check traffic-volume counts. Along the screen line, a total ground-volume count of all traffic is taken, together with limited sample roadside interviewing to determine trip purpose, origin, and destination. These volumes are then checked against the origin and destination data obtained from home interviews, from truck and taxi studies, and possibly, also, from studies of mass-transit facilities. One of the reasons for carrying out such screen-line checks is that experience has shown that certain types of trips tend to be either underreported or overreported. This means that, to obtain the most accurate estimates of the total amount of travel in an urban area, it is necessary to expand data by different rates, according to different trip purposes. The precise expansion rates can be calculated by comparing the screen-line volumes with the volumes that would be obtained simply by direct expansion of origin and destination survey data according to the percentage sample used.

*Sampling Frames and Sample Size*

Before proceeding with a detailed description of the inventory procedure, it is appropriate to consider some details about sampling.[4]

Inventories, particularly of households, are generally carried out on a sample basis, that is, information collected only from a certain, usually small, proportion of all households in the geographic area being studied. There are generally at least two reasons why a sample is used. First, data on all households would be too time-consuming to collect and analyze, and would constitute more information than could reasonably be handled. Second, the collection and analysis of data on all households would be inordinately expensive in almost any size urban area. Thus, it becomes necessary to choose somehow a proportion of all households from which to collect the data.

The word "sample" implies two important things: A sample is a small proportion of a total population (e.g., households in a geographic area), and it is a representative proportion. In other words, the sample must be chosen in such a way that it represents the characteristics of the whole population and in the same proportions as they occur in the whole population.

If one were to go down to a sandy beach and pick up a handful of sand, one could be reasonably sure that the handful of sand would be representative of all the sand on the beach. Or, again, if one took a spoonful of instant coffee out of a jar of a popular brand, one would except that spoonful to be representative of the whole jar, or even of any jar of that brand and type. In both these cases, no attention need be paid to the selection of the sample. The reason for this is that the separate grains of sand on the beach are all similar, and all the grains of instant coffee are similar. In other words, a random selection of a small quantity from a homogeneous group of objects will be a representative sample.

However, if one were to take a teaspoonful out of the top of an unshaken bottle of oil and vinegar salad dressing, that spoonful would comprise almost all oil and practically no vinegar. Thus, it would not be representative of the contents of the bottle. If a representative sample is to be obtained, then a special procedure must be used to select that sample, when it is to be chosen from a heterogeneous population. This applies particularly to sampling human populations.

Thus, for human surveys, the first concern is with how to choose a sample that will be representative of the population under study. Before considering the details of choosing samples, a brief examination of the concept of a sample is in order. To illustrate what sampling means, consider Table 5-1, which is a record of the heights of 100 men. Certain specific figures can be determined from this table that describe the population of 100. First the mean (average) height is 5'7.66" and the median height is 5'8". A frequency table can be constructed, showing the frequency with which each height occurs, as shown in Table 5-2.

Now suppose that one wishes to choose a sample of 100 individuals, rather than measuring all 100 men. In any sample of ten, the mean and median heights should closely approximate those of the whole population,

**Table 5-1**
**Height Observations for 100 Individuals**

| Obs. No. | Height | Obs. No. | Height | Obs. No. | Height |
|---|---|---|---|---|---|
| 1 | 5'10" | 34 | 5' 8" | 67 | 5'10" |
| 2 | 5' 9" | 35 | 5' 7" | 68 | 5' 3" |
| 3 | 6' 0" | 36 | 5'11" | 69 | 5' 1" |
| 4 | 6' 0" | 37 | 5' 9" | 70 | 6' 1" |
| 5 | 5'11" | 38 | 5' 4" | 71 | 5' 8" |
| 6 | 5'10" | 39 | 5' 8" | 72 | 5' 5" |
| 7 | 5' 7" | 40 | 6' 1" | 73 | 5' 0" |
| 8 | 5' 5" | 41 | 5' 0" | 74 | 5' 2" |
| 9 | 6' 1" | 42 | 5' 6" | 75 | 5' 6" |
| 10 | 5' 4" | 43 | 5' 7" | 76 | 5' 3" |
| 11 | 5' 8" | 44 | 5'11" | 77 | 5' 1" |
| 12 | 5' 9" | 45 | 6' 0" | 78 | 5'11" |
| 13 | 5' 3" | 46 | 6' 1" | 79 | 6' 0" |
| 14 | 5' 7" | 47 | 5' 3" | 80 | 6' 3" |
| 15 | 6' 2" | 48 | 5' 5" | 81 | 4'10" |
| 16 | 6' 0" | 49 | 5' 8" | 82 | 5' 4" |
| 17 | 5'11" | 50 | 5'11" | 83 | 5' 8" |
| 18 | 5' 8" | 51 | 5' 9" | 84 | 5' 9" |
| 19 | 5' 7" | 52 | 5' 2" | 85 | 5'11" |
| 20 | 5' 1" | 53 | 5'10" | 86 | 5' 7" |
| 21 | 6' 0" | 54 | 5'10" | 87 | 5' 5" |
| 22 | 5' 9" | 55 | 4'11" | 88 | 6' 1" |
| 23 | 5' 4" | 56 | 5' 7" | 89 | 5' 2" |
| 24 | 5' 6" | 57 | 5' 8" | 90 | 5' 0" |
| 25 | 5'10" | 58 | 6' 0" | 91 | 5' 9" |
| 26 | 5' 5" | 59 | 6' 2" | 92 | 5' 7" |
| 27 | 5' 6" | 60 | 5' 9" | 93 | 5' 3" |
| 28 | 5' 3" | 61 | 5' 7" | 94 | 5' 4" |
| 29 | 6' 1" | 62 | 5' 8" | 95 | 6' 0" |
| 30 | 5'10" | 63 | 5' 5" | 96 | 5'11" |
| 31 | 6' 0" | 64 | 6' 0" | 97 | 5' 8" |
| 32 | 6' 3" | 65 | 5' 6" | 98 | 5'10" |
| 33 | 5' 5" | 66 | 5' 9" | 99 | 5' 3" |
|  |  |  |  | 100 | 5' 6" |

and the height distribution should be similar to Table 5-2. One could expect, in a sample of ten, the following distribution shown in Table 5-3. If the first ten were chosen, then the mean height would be 5'9.3", the median height 5'10" and the distribution as shown in Table 5-4. It is clear that there is an overrepresentation of the taller men in this sample. The median is higher, not lower, than the mean and there are too many individuals at the top end of Table 5-4 and not enough at the bottom end.

Suppose, now, that one chose the first five and the last five observations (i.e., numbers 1-5 and 96-100). In this case, the mean height is 5'9.2" and the median height is 5'10". These results are almost identical to the previous

**Table 5-2**
**Frequency Distribution of Heights**

| Frequency | Height | Frequency | Height |
|---|---|---|---|
| 1 | 4′10″ | 9 | 5′ 7″ |
| 1 | 4′11″ | 10 | 5′ 8″ |
| 3 | 5′ 0″ | 9 | 5′ 9″ |
| 3 | 5′ 1″ | 8 | 5′10″ |
| 3 | 5′ 2″ | 8 | 5′11″ |
| 7 | 5′ 3″ | 10 | 6′ 0″ |
| 5 | 5′ 4″ | 6 | 6′ 1″ |
| 7 | 5′ 5″ | 2 | 6′ 2″ |
| 6 | 5′ 6″ | 2 | 6′ 3″ |

**Table 5-3**
**Frequency Distribution of Heights for Ten Representative Individuals**

| Frequency | Height |
|---|---|
| 1 | 4′10″ to 5′ 2″ |
| 1 | 5′ 3″ to 5′ 4″ |
| 1 | 5′ 5″ to 5′ 6″ |
| 2 | 5′ 7″ to 5′ 8″ |
| 2 | 5′ 9″ to 5′10″ |
| 2 | 5′11″ to 6′ 0″ |
| 1 | 6′ 1″ to 6′ 3″ |

**Table 5-4**
**Frequency Distribution of Heights for the First Ten Individuals**

| Frequency | Height |
|---|---|
| 0 | 4′10″ to 5′ 2″ |
| 1 | 5′ 3″ to 5′ 4″ |
| 1 | 5′ 5″ to 5′ 6″ |
| 1 | 5′ 7″ to 5′ 8″ |
| 3 | 5′ 9″ to 5′10″ |
| 3 | 5′11″ to 6′ 0″ |
| 1 | 6′ 1″ to 6′ 3″ |

ones, but quite different from the true values. The distribution, shown in Table 5-5, is similarly biased.

This example should have served to demonstrate two things: First, it should have made clear what is meant by choosing a sample; and second it should have shown that sampling to yield a representative sample is not a simple process of haphazard selection. In fact, selecting a sample from dissimilar objects requires the use of specific sampling rules, which serve to guarantee, within certain known limits, a representative sample. These known limits are termed "sampling error," and this error can be determined for any of a number of different sampling procedures.

The basic principle of all sampling procedures is that of *random* selection. In this context, random does not mean haphazard. It is specifically defined by a number of statistical measures. In simple terms, selecting at random means that every member of the population from which the sample is selected has an equal probability of being chosen. To assist in choosing random samples, there are tables of random numbers[5] and most digital computers have programs that can generate random numbers.

To illustrate the use of simple random sampling, the earlier example can be used again. Using the RAND table,[6] page 263, line 13104, gives the following ten observations: numbers 65 8 62 50 96 77 36 95 54 93. Using this selection, the sample mean is 5'7.8" (compared with 5'7.66" true mean) and the sample median height is 5'8" (the same as that of the total population). The distribution of values is shown in Table 5-6. Although the distribution is not the same as that shown in Table 5-3, the distribution is more even than those obtained before, Table 5-4 and 5-5.

Provided that there is no ordering of members of the population in a list, choosing every tenth member for a ten percent sample would give similar results. Since Table 5-1 presents a random ordering of individuals, an approximately random sample could be chosen. If, in the above example, the population had been ordered by increasing height (in Table 5-1) then selecting every tenth member (say, numbers 2, 12, 22, etc.) would not produce a random sample.

Many variations on simple random sampling have been devised, designed to produce specific known characteristics. These procedures are described in any standard text on survey sampling[7] and are not described here.

In applying simple random sampling to human populations, for example, households, a list, or sampling frame of all elements in the population is needed first. For example, the sampling frame of households in an urban area could be the electricity company's address list. The random sample can then be chosen by selection from the list. Clearly, the completeness of the sampling frame will have far-reaching effects on the representativeness of the sample. If some addresses are not listed, they have zero probability

**Table 5-5**
**Frequency Distribution of Heights for the First Five and Last Five Individuals**

| Frequency | Height |
| --- | --- |
| 0 | 4'10" to 5' 2" |
| 1 | 5' 3" to 5' 4" |
| 1 | 5' 5" to 5' 6" |
| 1 | 5' 7" to 5' 8" |
| 3 | 5' 9" to 5'10" |
| 4 | 5'11" to 6' 0" |
| 0 | 6' 1" to 6' 3" |

**Table 5-6**
**Frequency Distribution of Heights for a Random Sample of Ten Individuals**

| Frequency | Height |
| --- | --- |
| 1 | 4'10" to 5' 2" |
| 1 | 5' 3" to 5' 4" |
| 2 | 5' 5" to 5' 6" |
| 1 | 5' 7" to 5' 8" |
| 1 | 5' 9" to 5'10" |
| 4 | 5'11" to 6' 0" |
| 0 | 6' 1" to 6' 3" |

of being selected and if some addresses are listed more than once, they have much too high a probability of being selected. In both cases, violations of the basic principle of random sampling occur. Such violations lead to *sample bias,* which should never be confused with sampling error. To avoid confusion, these two are defined as follows:

*Sample Bias.* This is the error introduced by "bad" sampling. It may be due to the use of an incomplete sampling frame, insufficient control of sampling, or lack of response from the chosen sample. Generally, bias cannot be calculated and therefore has an undetermined effect on the survey results. It should be absent from a good sample.

*Sampling Error.* This is the error introduced by the use of a sample to represent a population. There is always a sampling error in any sample. The size of the sampling error depends upon a number of factors, including the method of sampling and the sampling rate (e.g., ten percent sample rate means one tenth of the population is chosen for the sample). The sampling error can be calculated for any standard sampling method.

As is indicated by the above definition, sampling error can be determined for any sampling method. Details of formulae for sampling errors are included in most texts on survey-sampling procedures. As an example, the sampling error for a simple random sample is given by equation 5.1.

$$\varepsilon_\rho = \sqrt{pq/n} \qquad (5.1)$$

where $p$ = the proportion of the population that possesses some attribute

$\rho$ = the sample estimate of $p$

$\varepsilon_\rho$ = the sampling error of $\rho$

$n$ = the sample size

and $q = 1 - p$, the proportion of the population that does not possess the attribute

(If $p$, $q$ and $\rho$ are all expressed in percentages, the formula is unchanged.)

Suppose a survey of 50 households has been made to determine how many heads of household drive to work, and that the actual population proportion that drive to work is 30 percent. The sampling error is given by equation 5.2.

$$\varepsilon_\rho = \sqrt{\left[\frac{30 \cdot 70}{50}\right]} \qquad (5.2)$$

and the percentage sampling error is about 22 percent. Since $p$ and $q$ are, in fact, to be estimated from the sample, the sampling error can only be determined as an estimated error, based on estimates of $p$ and $q$. A similar procedure to the above one is used to estimate sampling errors for attributes which can be measured in quantities, for example, income, number of cars owned, etc.

One of the major uses to which the data will be put is that of allowing a calibration to be carried out of each of the models in the transportation-planning process. The calibration of models using statistical or analytical or other basically mathematical techniques requires a certain standard of sample data in order to be able to arrive at good approximations of the coefficients. The sample size is therefore, at least in part, predicated upon the types of models that are to be calibrated. The basic form of sampling that is used in most home-interview surveys is that of random sampling. In this case, as illustrated previously, the size of the sample has a considerable bearing upon the accuracy with which models can be calibrated. There are, at present, a number of differences of opinion as to the adequacy of small samples for calibrating most of the models in the transportation-planning process. As yet, no conclusive figures have been produced that indicate the minimum sample size necessary to allow adequate calibration of most of the more frequently used models.

Another type of sampling that may have application for transportation studies is that of cluster sampling. In cluster sampling, the total population to be sampled is divided up into a number of clusters, and the clusters are selected at random. The survey is then carried out on either all, or a large sample of the entities making up each of the selected clusters. This type of sampling has been tested in at least two cases—in Hamilton, Ontario and in Pittsburgh, Pennsylvania. In each case, it appeared that the data provided an adequate level of data for calibrating trip-generation equations. However, in the test in Pittsburgh, it did not appear that the cluster-sample data provided adequate information for full calibration of a trip-distribution model, nor adequate data on trip attractions. At present, it appears that there is still much unknown about ideal types and sizes of samples for calibration processes of the transportation-planning models.

*Tabulation and Checking*

After the survey work has been completed, it is necessary to tabulate and check the information recorded. A number of stages can be identified in the process necessary to enable the data collected to be adapted for use on a computer, and for the checking of the various processes of collecting and coding data. At the time when the various survey forms are designed, a comprehensive coding scheme has to be set up, resulting in a series of codes and specifications for the way in which the data collected on the various survey forms are to be transferred onto computer punched cards or magnetic tape. The various stages of collection of data, of coding and card punching are all subject to various sources of error. It is therefore necessary that in the stage where the coding is set up, a number of checks on the computer data are designed to locate inconsistencies and errors that may have occurred in the various stages of data collection, coding, and punching. In addition, tabulations are usually produced from the computerized data, which would provide further means of checking, both visually and from control totals. These control totals may be developed either directly from the survey forms or from supplementary sources, such as a recent census.

When full checks have been made of the basic data, the data can be assumed to be ready for use in the survey analysis phase. The first phase of the analysis usually comprises a study of present patterns of travel and land use, and the preparation of necessary maps, etc., detailing information of the present use of the transportation system and present characteristics of the study area that may affect transportation. This information usually forms volume 1 of a set of study reports. The data are then used in initial studies of trip generation, calibration of trip-distribution models, and other relationships that are based on present conditions. These models are examined in more detail in subsequent chapters. This phase of the study normally requires the setting up of the models to be used for the entire forecasting process.

Steps in developing urban-growth patterns follow next, utilizing data from economic and population studies, and analyses of information on residential mobility, changes in industrial location, retail growth in the past, etc. On the basis of the previous two steps, forecasts will be made of the demand for transportation by purpose, by mode, by time of day and by origin and destination for some future forecast year or years. The information is usually produced on the assumption that sufficient capacity on all modes will be provided to allow this level of demand to be satisfied. The modeling and forecasting steps usually make up volume 2 of the study report. The final stage in the use of the data will comprise the evaluation of various alternative plans for catering for the total demand or a part of the total demand. If total demand is not to be catered for, the evaluation process will also require the forecasting of the consequences on the metropolitan area of a forced reduction in the total amount of travel. The stages of work outlined in this fifth section are as yet very unstructured in the majority of studies, and a complete evaluation and specification of consequences has rarely been achieved. The material covered by this section usually comprises volume 3 of a study report.

In addition to this work and the work previously indicated in terms of collection of data, further parallel studies may be conducted to provide additional information for the forecasting and evaluation processes. This information may include studies of the economic status of various land uses, of growth in population, income, and related data on car ownership, and on employment. Further data may be gathered on the attitudes and travel preferences of people with respect to modes of travel, expenditure patterns, residential and housing preferences, and recreational desires. Finally, supplemental data may be gathered on public policies relating to financing, standards of service, land-use controls, and other constraints such as availability of water and sewage services, drainage and flooding, costs of land, and other data needed in land-use models. Information is also required to enable an evaluation to be made of the consequences of various transportation plans on the environment, and upon the social and economic life of communities through which the facilities will pass.

*Alternative Survey Techniques*

Although it is standard practice to obtain origin and destination data together with socioeconomic information about trip makers from home-interview surveys, a number of other alternative methods exist for collecting this information.[8] Among these are the use of the following techniques:

**Controlled Postcard Surveys.** Postcards are mailed to owners of registered vehicles, asking for records of all vehicle trips made on the day after receiving the card. A number of different alternative methods may be used to generate the sample for this method. This method suffers from several advantages and disadvantages. Included among these are that self-administered questionnaires of any form tend to return a lower response rate than interview-type surveys; trips reported from a postcard survey of this type generally show a better level of nonwork trips; the selection of the sample from owners of registered vehicles introduces a serious bias in terms of data on transit trips; and the actual sample yielded in terms of the returned questionnaires is subject to an uncontrollable bias.

**Home Questionnaire.** This method involves the use of questionnaires that are left in the home to be filled out by or on behalf of each family member over three years old. The completed questionnaires are collected by survey staff at a later stage. In general, the results of this type of questionnaire appear to be relatively comparable to those of a home interview; however, the reliability of some information, particularly that of an attitudinal nature or that which may be difficult for a person to provide unless prompted by a skilled interviewer, may render some of the data so collected to be of less use than that from an interview.

**The Telephone Survey.** This method is a possible cost-saving alternative to face-to-face home interviewing, and has been successfully used in a number of applications. It can also be used for studying Sunday peak-hour travel and is well adjusted to the use of precontact and the mailing out of trip cards, where the final telephone interview obtains information that has already been partially recorded by the interviewee. This method can be used to obtain a somewhat larger sample of trip making in the urban area than can the home-interview survey. However, the choice of the sample is again likely to lead to some bias, and the bias may be greater than that yielded by the conventional home-interview method.

**Driver-license Renewal Interview.** This technique takes a sample of licensed drivers drawn from persons appearing for license renewal. Interviews are then used to obtain data on trips made by the household on the previous day for each of those persons in the sample. Again, the sample that is used is biased in favor of auto ownership, and the total data is likely to lack very seriously in transit-trip reporting. It is also subject to inaccuracies due to either neglecting to renew at the correct time or to renewal of licenses in other locations. It is, however, a flexible system of sampling, which could be the basis for continuous sampling, and is a much more economical method than the standard home-interview system.

**External Cordon-parking Survey.** This type of survey is useful in smaller cities, of under about 75,000 population, where much of the travel is oriented to the central area. It involves an external cordon interview, with curb interviews being made also of all people parking or unparking in the central area. It does not provide information on origins or destinations of persons whose trips are inside the external cordon but who do not go to or from the central area.

**Vehicle-registration Number Recording and Matching.** This technique uses screen lines placed across a corridor or around an area. Each vehicle that crosses the screen line has the last four digits of the vehicle license number recorded. The numbers so recorded are matched by the computer, and the result is an origin-destination information set in terms of the point at which the vehicles cross the screen lines. If times are also recorded along with the vehicle licenses, then it is possible to obtain travel times as well. This study, however, does not provide a means of obtaining socioeconomic data about trip makers, is oriented only to car travel, and also does not give specific information as to the actual origin location and destination location of a trip.

**Other Methods of Sampling.** In the future, it is possible that various other methods of sampling may be used, which might include utilization of data from the census, the sampling of peak-hour trips only, sampling at destination as well as at home or instead of at home, and longitudinal sampling. Each of these techniques has some promise for future data collection.

*Limitations of Origin-Destination Studies*

The type of studies outlined as being those commonly used in the transportation-planning process are generally very expensive, and provide data for one weekday in one year only. They are, therefore, cross-sectional data at an extreme level. No method has yet been devised for keeping the survey up-to-date on a continuing basis. The survey reports also usually summarize total interzonal travel for a 24-hour day, with no published data on interzonal movements in the peak hour and by direction. Even if such data are available, the size of the sample is usually such that reliable estimation of movements between any pair of zones in the peak hour only is not possible. Beyond this, there are further limitations in the accuracy of reporting and in the accuracy of processing the data. In particular, multipurpose trips, linked trips, serve-passenger trips, the size of the zones, and other features of this type have considerable bearing upon the level of accuracy of the data.

# 6 Land-use Forecasting

## Elements of Urban and Regional Models

Transportation facilities constitute a land use. As a land use, transportation facilities clearly will have effects upon the levels of usage, intensity of activities, economic growth, and many other features of the remaining land uses in an urban or rural area. At the present time, few of these interactions are properly understood. For this reason, there are few models that specifically address the problems of interactions between transportation and land use. However, one of the model steps in the urban transportation-planning (UTP) process does permit the possibility of some rather fragmentary, interactive effects between land use and transportation. The model in question is that of trip generation, which does attempt to relate the usage of the system or the production of travel demand to factors describing land uses and their intensity of activity. Given the presence of this model in the transportation-planning process, it then becomes necessary that there exist models for land-use forecasts, which can also perform other tasks inherent within the transportation-planning process.

A number of modeling processes are required as inputs to the travel-forecasting element of the UTP process. Among these are the forecasting of future populations and their distribution within an urban area or regional context; the forecasting of land uses in terms of both their intensity and type of use, and the spatial distribution of land uses; and models of urban development and urban growth. It is not the intention of this book to provide an in-depth examination of all of these models. Detailed treatment may be found in other texts. However, it is appropriate to examine briefly some of the forms of models that may be used for these tasks.

In population forecasting there are several techniques that may be applied.[1] The first of these is often termed cohort survival and is based upon determining the number of births, the number of deaths, and the rates of net migration for an area. The forecasting of population for some future time is an extrapolation of existing trends of births, net migration, and deaths, which may be combined with the current population to yield an estimate of a future population based on past observed trends. Sources of information for this type of model, and also for most of the other population models, would be from past census work, in which information on net migration, birth rates, and death rates is almost always available. The basic

99

method used by the cohort-survival principle is to extrapolate the sum of births and net migration minus deaths as an entity, and to use the trend evinced by this total sum over a period of time. The second technique is to separate out the natural increase part of this, births minus deaths, and net migration, and treat these as two separate variables. A population forecast is then made on the basis of models, or trend analyses of these two separate entities. Basically, the types of models that are used could be labelled as follows: (1) aggregate trends, (2) step-down ratio, (3) center analysis, (4) economic base, and (5) interregional programming.[2]

The urban system and urban growth may be modeled on the basis of a number of theories. It is probably useful to look very briefly at the basic theories that are currently used. These theories all relate to some postulated pattern of growth of the urban area. The first of these might be termed the *concentric ring* theory, which postulates that the growth of an urban area occurs, or perhaps should be designed to occur, as a series of concentric rings, although variations exist on this whereby growth is seen to occur in sectors, or in rings around multiple nuclei within the urban area. As an extension to this, two elementary theories are employed, which refer to the population, or the density of population, or of land use in these concentric rings. The first of these rules is termed the *rank-size rule,* and postulates a mathematical relationship concerning the population within each concentric ring as being inversely proportional to the distance from the central businessdistrict (CBD) to the ring. The second of these is termed the *density-decay theory,* which theorizes that the density of use of land in these rings follows an exponential decay function based on distance from the CBD. Other theories that are commonly used include location theory, central-place theory, and market-area analysis, and theories of residential preference and location rent.[3]

In urban development models a number of problems exist and a number of possible solution methods are available. One of the most basic problems is that of specifying the system and identifying the constraints within which the model is to be built. The models require the development of some specific measures that allow identification of the structure of the urban system. In particular, it is necessary to identify the specific parcels of land or establishments that are to be used as a basic parameter in the models, which generates the problem of identifying the specific land uses and activities that are the most meaningful aggregations or abstractions of the system for modeling purposes. Models of urban development should, by their nature, be dynamic models. That is, they should be addressed to the problem of variations over a period of time. As a result, the solution methods that can be applied fall, generally, into one of two categories: The first category is that of a basic type of economic model, in which one is concerned with lagged variables. The alternative solution method is to use some form of iterative procedure. In both cases, some severe problems are encountered, in that convergence of the model calibration toward an equilibrium state is not guaranteed.

Finally, a major problem exists in structuring the models, in terms of the order in which it is assumed interactions take place in the urban structure. The major point is that of the precedence of residential location or industrial location. It is a question somewhat like that of the chicken and the egg, and is concerned basically with which comes first—residential development or industrial development. It is clear that any decision on one will tend to generate a new decision on the other. From the point of view of a forecasting model, it is important to establish which occurs before the other, since the correct identification of causality has already been defined (chapter 2) as a necessary requirement for forecasting.

## Land-use Models

The last type of model that exists within elementary urban systems modeling is the land-use model. There are a number of variations in land-use models, a few of which are examined here. The first of these types is based on an assumption of density saturation and uses a largely nonanalytical approach. The second type of model is a residential-succession model, which uses predictions of the incidence of conversion of rural or vacant land to residential use as the population of the study area increases, and then looks at the likely generated development of nonresidential land uses as a result of the residential growth. The next type comprises a form of hypothesized linear relationship between the amount of land use and various characteristics of those land uses, such as their intensity, their economic growth, etc. The final type of elementary land-use model is an acceptability model, which attempts to relate the growth of various land uses to changes in their accessibility, and changes in the total population of the study area.

The land-use model is used to determine the locations and intensities of land uses in the study area, as an input to the travel estimation and forecasting phases. It is postulated that land use is a function of the attractiveness of the location, in terms of its accessibility to other land uses and the availability of services and amenities. Development of land use is then constrained by budget limitations of the developer or purchaser, and by the zoning and other restrictions on the uses to which the land can be put. Ideally, aggregate land-use models should contain built-in constraints relating to land-use accounting. In other words, there should be a safeguard in the model against "overdevelopment" of the areal units, or zones, used for the model process. Over development occurs when the land-use model predicts more land being developed than is available in the zone at the maximum permitted density. It may also be desirable to consider establishment accounting, where limits can be identified on the number of establishments that can be built in a given zone. Finally, there is a concept of land-use succession that should be considered in any land-use model. This concept is concerned with the pattern of temporal changes that can take place for any specific parcel of land. For example, it may be postulated that vacant land can be developed into residential uses, which in turn can be redeveloped into commercial uses, etc. However, certain successions, for example, industrial to residential, may be postulated as implausible.

Many land-use models have been developed, some in connection with specific transportation studies and others outside that process altogether. Three models are described in this chapter, in order to provide the reader with examples of some of the types of land-use model that may be encountered.

### Chicago Area Transportation Study Model

The Chicago Area Transportation Study (CATS) land-use model[4] is basically a nonanalytical model that relies heavily on the judgement of the user of the model. The model is based upon three rules, determined from observation, and forming the only analytical element of the process. These rules are:

1. Land development decreases in intensity with increasing distance from the CBD.
2. Available land that is already in use declines with increasing distance from the CBD.
3. Proportional amounts of land devoted to different land uses are stable.

Initially, the model procedure requires that population forecasts be made for the study region. Following this, estimates are made of the residential development capacity of each zone in the study region. These capacities are determined partly by examining existing development plans of both private and public developers, and current land-use zoning restrictions or designations and partly by the application of the land-use intensity rule. The projected population growth, or change, is then allocated on a zone-by-zone basis.

Needs for space for residential services are calculated on a proportional basis, using presently observed rates of service and area to residential land area. These services are then allocated to the available land area in each zone. Finally, commercial and industrial land-use developments are allocated to the available land areas, where these are again determined on the basis of existing zoning and the density/intensity rules. Growth of these land uses is forecast for the region using the third rule, that the proportions of different land uses remain the same over the forecast period.

The zone-by-zone allocation procedure embodies a strict land-accounting rule that ensures that no zone can be allocated more development than its capacity. On the other hand, the model does not consider migratory patterns explicitly, nor does it embody any rules of land-use succession. It is a simple and quite effective model, which has proved to be of an equal order of accuracy to any other operational land-use model.[5]

## EMPIRIC Model

The EMPIRIC model was originally developed for use in the Boston Regional Planning Project by the Traffic Research Corporation, and has since been used in a number of other applications. The model has also undergone a continuing process of refinement, although this account is based on an early version of the model,[6] since newer accounts do not appear to have been published.

In the early version of the EMPIRIC model, five located variables are to be allocated: blue collar population, white collar population, retail and wholesale employment, manufacturing employment, and all other employment. The model predicts the changes in the subregional shares of each of these located variables, through the use of a set of five simultaneous, linear equations. It is postulated that the change in the subregional share of a specific located variable is a function of the changes in the other four located variables, and of the base year values and changes in a set of variables that describe the subregion. These latter variables include the residential and employment densities, accessibilities by auto and transit to different land-use types, and the water supply and sewage disposal qualities. They are called "locator" variables.

The models are of the form shown in Equation 6.1.

$$
\frac{R_{ik}^{(t+1)}}{\sum\limits_{k=1}^{K} R_{ik}^{(t+1)}} - \frac{R_{ik}^{(t)}}{\sum\limits_{k=1}^{K} R_{ik}^{(t)}} = \sum\limits_{\substack{j=1 \\ j \neq i}}^{N} a_{ij} \left[ \frac{R_{jk}^{(t+1)}}{\sum\limits_{k=1}^{K} R_{jk}^{(t+1)}} - \frac{R_{jk}^{(t)}}{\sum\limits_{k=1}^{K} R_{jk}^{(t)}} \right]
$$

$$
+ \sum\limits_{h=1}^{M-m} b_{ih} \left[ \frac{Z_{hk}^{(t+1)}}{\sum\limits_{k=1}^{K} Z_{hk}^{(t+1)}} - \frac{Z_{hk}^{(t)}}{\sum\limits_{k=1}^{K} Z_{hk}^{(t+1)}} \right]
$$

$$
+ \sum\limits_{h=M-m+1}^{M} b_{ih} \left[ \frac{1}{L} - \frac{Z_{hk}^{(t)}}{\sum\limits_{k=1}^{K} Z_{hk}^{(t)}} \right] \tag{6.1}
$$

There is one equation of this form for each of the five land uses. In the model, the $R_{ik}$ and $R_{jk}$ are the located variables of population and employment, while the $Z_{hk}$ are the locator variables. The superscripts, $t$ and $(t+1)$ refer to different time periods. $L$ is the number of subregions over which the model is applied, $K$ is the number of located variables and $M$ is the number of locator variables. The values $a_{ij}$ and $b_{ih}$ are coefficients, determined by simultaneous linear regression on two past time points. Subscript $i$ refers to a specific located variable, and $k$ is the subregion. All variables are, thus, expressed as shares of the regional totals and the model is formulated in terms of share changes over the forecast time period. Regional totals of all activities (located variable) are assumed to be externally forecast.

A large number of different variables have been formulated for the locator variables, $Z_{hk}$, with up to 22 formulated for one set of model tests.[7] Actual land uses are determined by multiplying subregional population and employment figures by the appropriate density figures. Again, the externally forecast regional population and employment figures are required to permit the forecasts of actual land use to be made. For further details of the model, the reader is referred to reports in other documents.[8]

Several comments on the model are in order here, however. First, the model does not embody a land-accounting procedure. It is theoretically possible, therefore, for a subregion to be overdeveloped, that is, allocated more activity than there is land available in the subregion for that activity. Second, like the CATS model, there is no land-use succession procedure and no account taken of market mechanisms in the form of land rents and assessments of the abilities of developers to pay for the land. On the other hand, the model represents a comparatively sophisticated attempt at a statistically-based land use model, which does not rely upon personal knowledge and judgement of the user. Also, the model provides a mechanism for interaction between land use and transportation through the presence of accessibilities among the locator variables.

## Herbert-Stevens Residential Model

The Herbert-Stevens model[9] is an attempt to develop a highly sophisticated land-use model and has added much to the understanding of land-use processes in urban areas. Unfortunately, a transportation study (the Penn-Jersey Transportation Study) is not an ideal environment for the development of an innovative tool such as this model, and it was initially deemed a failure for the study. It was not used in the study forecasting procedures, because it was not sufficiently well-developed in time for the study phases.

The model is based upon an analysis of the market demand for land and embodies land-use accounting procedures but not land-use succession ideas. The Residential Model is formulated as a linear programming problem, in which it is assumed that households attempt to maximize their site rent. Site rent is defined as the difference between the location budget of a household, that is, the amount a household is willing to spend on a house, services, associated travel, and the cost of the location of the household excluding the site cost. Households are aggregated, for the purposes of defining site rent, by groups based on incomes, patterns of consumption preferences, and daily movement patterns. The location of the household, in terms of its location costs, are defined by lot size, type and quality of structure, and available amenities. Finally, the model is applied on a district basis, where districts represent a convenient spatial unit for locating land uses in the study area. As a part of the computation of the cost of a specific location, destination-set accessibilities are calculated for each district.[10]

The model is designed to operate over discrete time periods (of, say, five years) to arrive at the forecasts for the planning horizon. At each stage of the operation, new values of the external inputs to the model are required, and policy changes may be implemented in the model. The model is applied to residential land-use forecasting only. The set of variables described above as constituting the basis for the computation of location cost—lot size, type and quality of structure, and amenities—are termed a "locational bundle." Thus, the external inputs to the model are:

1.  The amount of vacant land in each district that will be available, during the specified time period, for residential development
2.  The number of households in each socioeconomic group that will be looking for each type of locational bundle in the entire study area
3.  The location budget of each socioeconomic group of households seeking each locational bundle
4.  The cost of obtaining each locational bundle in each district, not including the site cost or rent

A discussion of the measurement problems for the variables listed here is presented later in this section. The linear programming formulation is shown in equations 6.2, through 6.5.

$$\text{Maximize} \quad Z = \sum_k \sum_i \sum_h x_{ih}^k (b_{ih} - c_{ih}^k) \tag{6.2}$$

$$\text{subject to} \quad \sum_h \sum_i s_{ih} x_{ih}^k \leq L^k \quad \text{for all } k \tag{6.3}$$

$$\sum_h \sum_k (-x_{ih}^k) = -N_i \quad \text{for all } i \tag{6.4}$$

$$x_{ih}^k \geq 0 \quad \text{for all } k \text{ and all } i \tag{6.5}$$

where    $k$ =   the $k$th district

$i$ =   the $i$th socioeconomic household group

$h$ =   the $h$th location bundle

$x_{ih}^k$ =   the number of households in a socioeconomic group $i$, choosing locational bundle $h$ in district $k$ during the time period under consideration

$b_{ih}$ =   the annual location budget for a household in socio-economic group $i$ for locational bundle $h$

$c_{ih}^k$ =   the annual cost of locational bundle $h$ in district $k$ for households in socioeconomic group $i$

$s_{ih}$ =   the acreage used for residential location by households of group $i$, choosing locational bundle $h$

$L^k$ =   the available acreage for residential development in district $k$

$N_i$ =   the total number of households in socioeconomic group $i$ to be located in the region in the specified time period

Thus, the model may be described as the maximization of the site rent for all households that are to be located in the time period, subject to the constraints that no more than the available residential land in a district may be used (equation 6.3), all households must be located (equation 6.4), and that the number of households in any group choosing any locational bundle in any district must be nonnegative (equation 6.5). The model is, therefore, a market-demand model, with strict land-accounting and implicit land-use succession, through the exogenous determination of land available for residential use. Population movement is not considered in the model, since it only allocates new residents to the available residential land. It should also be emphasized that the model is not an optimizing model. No attempt has been made to identify an objective function relating to the *optimum* distribution of residences in an area.

The identification of the variables that comprise the locational bundles and socioeconomic groups for subdividing the population can be handled fairly simply through standard procedures, for example, correlation analysis, factor analysis, etc. The problems arise, in the use of the model, when attempting to put values on the location budgets and location costs pertinent to specific groups, locational bundles and districts. Also, the forecasting of the variable $x_{ih}^k$ is troublesome, since population forecasting is generally insufficiently precise to be able to identify future new population by socioeconomic group. Hence, the model has proved somewhat difficult to operationalize in a standard transportation-study context.

In the idealized application of the procedure, the linear programming model allocates residential land uses only. This, in fact is achieved in two steps. The linear programming model, described here, estimates the number of households that will locate in a given district. The residential space used must then be calculated subsequently. In the same manner, it is intended that each of the manufacturing and the nonmanufacturing workforce be located by a linear programming model of similar form to the residential location model.[11] Subsequently, manufacturing and nonmanufacturing space consumption would be estimated. There does not appear to be any published reference to the use of this entire model set. The discussion of Ira S. Lowry[12] suggests that detailed models have only been developed for the residential model.

In summary, the Herbert-Stevens model, although not developed to an operational status, has provided many insights and advances in the area of land-use modeling. Chief among its disadvantages are the difficulties of placing values on two of its variables, the budget and location cost variables, and its extensive data demands.

### Land-use Models as Inputs to Travel Forecasting

It has been the intention of this chapter to outline the range of available land-use models, thereby indicating something of the state of the art. In broad terms, it must be concluded that the development of land-use models is not very advanced. This has important implications for the forecasting of travel in the UTP process. Land-use models provide the initial inputs to the travel-forecasting process. Hence, forecasting of travel can never be more accurate than the land-use forecasts upon which the travel forecast depends. No matter how sophisticated and accurate the travel forecasting models may become, the eventual product of the models cannot be improved beyond the capability of the land-use model.

There is no land-use model that embodies all the applicable land-use theories and constraints, that is, land-use accounting, land-use succession, population migration patterns, and the market mechanism of land-use change. The more complete models, such as the Herbert-Stevens model, have so far been found to be insufficiently operational. Land-use forecasting must therefore depend largely upon ad hoc procedures, such as the CATS model, or mathematical procedures such as the EMPIRIC model.

# 7      Trip Generation

## Introduction

Trip generation is the first phase in the travel-forecasting process. It involves the estimation of the total number of trips entering or leaving a parcel of land as a function of the socioeconomic, locational, and land-use characteristics of the parcel. It takes as input the predicted distributions of zonal population, employment, activities, and land uses for the design year and, by extrapolating base-year relationships between these distributions and zonal tripmaking, generates as output estimates of design-year trip productions and attractions. The underlying rationale for trip generation can be seen as comprising a number of factors. First, travel is an aspect of derived demand. The frequency and distribution of travel is a function of the distribution of activity and land use in an urban area. Second, it is assumed that the intensity of travel to or from a given zone is a function of the activities and land uses that are contained within that zone. It is then assumed that the intensity of travel can be estimated independent of the transportation service provided and independent of the set of opportunities available. This particular assumption is one that perhaps is most suspect of all those used in the trip-generation modeling process. Next, it is assumed that relationships between trip rates and zone characteristics may be assumed to remain stable over time. Finally, it is assumed that trip making and activity may be related by the specification of trip purpose. There is a heavy focus on trips to and from home, at least in part because these trips form a major part of total trip making in the urban area.

    Conventionally, in travel-demand analysis, there are two basic trip types: home-based trips and nonhome-based trips. There are also a number of trip purposes, usually classified into a set of about ten groups of purposes (see chapter 3). Since these various classifications of trips are made because the trips so categorized are considered to be based on different demand processes, it seems that a full classification of trips by purpose and type should be made before attempts are made to build models of trip generation. However, this will require an excessive number of models. Since each home-based model has one end at home (by definition), the other end of the trip has nine possible purposes. Therefore, nine trip-generation models are required for home-based trips. Similarly, by definition neither end of a nonhome-based trip is at home, so there are nine purposes possible at each end of the trip. There are thus 81 purpose-to-purpose combinations, thus needing 81 models. So far, 90 models are required. If further subdivisions are made by time of day, to morning peak, evening peak and the rest of the day, 270 models will be required.

It is clear that this type of detailed classification will yield a requirement for far more models than can be handled, let alone built. Thus, it is conventional to make much grosser classifications of trips. The standard subdivisions are into home-based work trips, other home-based trips, and nonhome-based trips. No subdivisions by time of day are used. Rather, it is assumed that the work/other split takes account of time-of-day variations. Since the output of these models will be the inputs to the remaining models of the process, the subdivisions used will dictate the maximum disaggregation that will be possible in any of the succeeding models. So far, trip generation has been discussed only from the aspect of trips by persons to various trip purposes, and supposedly largely by mass transit and auto. No consideration has been given to freight trips, etc. Thus, for nonresidential land uses, details are also required of the numbers of commercial vehicle trips attracted to and generated from such land uses. Finally, it is conventional to treat taxi trips as another separate category. Hence, there are usually two further models required, one for truck trips and one for taxi trips.

The first two models (home-based work and other home-based trips) are classified as *residential trip generation*, the third as *nonresidential trip generation*, and all three provide estimates of person trips. The last two models are concerned with estimates of vehicle trips. In the event that truck and taxi trips are a relatively small proportion of all trips, they may be combined, as person—not vehicle—trips, with nonhome-based trip generation.

## Residential Trip Generation

Conventional modeling of residential trip generation assumes that the propensity of a household to make trips is related to characteristics describing the socioeconomic status of the household and the neighborhood in which it is located. It is assumed that the propensity to make trips is not related to the transportation system. In addition, the trips that are considered in trip generation are those carried out by motorized vehicles only. Trips carried out solely by walking or by means such as bicycle are not included and are, therefore, assumed both to be constant and to have no interdependency with vehicular trips.

Residential trip generation models may be estimated in two ways. First, they may be estimated as zonal totals models. In this case, the input data for zonal residential trip-generation models will be in the form of zonal totals of various variables. Among the variables that have usually been considered are:

1. Car ownership
2. Family size
3. Number of persons five years old and over in the household
4. Length of residence
5. Family income
6. Number of persons 16 years old and over
7. Number of persons 16 years old and over who drive
8. Age of head of household
9. Distance from the central business district (CBD)
10. Stage in the family life cycle
11. Occupation of head of household
12. Type of house structure

*Estimation of Zonal Trip Generation*

Zonal trip generation will generally use means or totals of aggregated data for the input values. The use of zonal means is based on the assumption that they are representative of the households in the zone. For representativeness, two conditions are necessarily implied: First, it is implied that household values are distributed symmetrically around the zonal mean, which in turn implies normality or, at least symmetry of the distribution and centrality of the mean. Second, it is assumed that the between-zone variances are much larger than the within-zone variances, that is, that the households in a zone are homogeneous relative to households in other zones. These assumptions are critically reexamined later in the chapter.

Two basic methods are generally used to construct models of residential and nonresidential trip generation: cross-classification (or category analysis) and linear regression. Of these two, cross-classification is the simplest and makes the least assumptions about underlying distributions among the zones.

**Cross-classification.** This technique is known as cross-classification in North America and category analysis in Europe. Based on intuitive considerations, judgement, and simple data analysis, a set of parameters are chosen on which to base estimates of trip making. Each parameter, whether or not it originally represented some continuous measure, is split into a set of classes. Again, the technique can be used for zonal totals or trip rates. First, the procedure is described for zonal totals. On the basis of the zonal means, a zone is identified as falling into a particular class for each parameter. Having cross-classified all zones, a mean number of trips per zone is computed for each specific cross-classification. Forecasts are made of the changes in the parameters for each zone, and the new cell where the zone will locate in the forecast year is determined. The average number of trips per zone for that new cell is assigned to the zone as the forecast.

Alternatively, and more usually, the method is applied at the household level, that is, as a trip rate estimator. The procedure is the same as before, except that it is now households, rather than zones that are classified by the parameter categories and mean trip rates per household are entered into the matrix. Forecasts are of the future mix of households in each zone, from which zonal estimates of future trip making can then be derived. In either case, the mechanics of the process are very similar.

This method may be better understood by means of an example. Suppose that family size and auto ownership are the only variables being considered for purposes of trip generation analysis. Within each zone of the study area, information is recorded on the number of households in each category of family size and auto ownership, and the number of trips made by those households. The analysis might appear as shown in Table 7-1. Tables of this form are amassed for the entire study area and numbers of households and numbers of trips are summed for each cell of the matrix represented in Table 7-1. From these sums, an average number of trips per household is obtained and a cross-classification table arrived at as shown in Table 7-2. This completes what might be termed the calibration phase of the cross-classification analysis of trip generation. In order to use this technique to predict trip-generation rates, the following procedure is used: First for each zone the number of households in each cell of the matrix is predicted for the forecast year. For some zone, this might appear as shown in Table 7-3. The rates of trip making are then applied to each group of households. Thus, in family size 1 with no cars, the prediction would be:

$$23 \times 1.05 \text{ trips per household} = 24 \text{ trips}$$

for family size three with 1 car, the prediction would be:

$$79 \times 7.08 \text{ trips per household} = 559 \text{ trips}$$

and so forth.

By this simple procedure a new total number of trips may be predicted for each zone for the forecast year. There are a number of drawbacks to this method, a few of which are itemized below:

1. The variances between households or zones in a specific cell is totally suppressed.

**Table 7-1**
**Cross-classification of Households by Auto Ownership and Family Size**

| | Auto Ownership | | | | | |
|---|---|---|---|---|---|---|
| | 0 | | 1 | | 2+ | |
| Family Size | #HH | #Trips | #HH | #Trips | #HH | #Trips |
| 1 | 37,000 | 41,000 | 28,000 | 57,000 | 16,000 | 82,000 |
| 2 | 26,000 | 38,000 | 33,000 | 172,000 | 18,000 | 175,000 |
| 3 | 39,000 | 67,000 | 55,000 | 376,000 | 12,000 | 111,000 |
| 4 | 43,000 | 129,000 | 21,000 | 108,000 | 10,000 | 128,000 |
| 5+ | 31,000 | 163,000 | 17,000 | 165,000 | 7,000 | 131,000 |

**Table 7-2**
**Trip-rate Table for Cross-classification Method**

| | Auto Ownership | | |
|---|---|---|---|
| Family Size | 0 | 1 | 2+ |
| 1 | 1.05 | 2.69 | 4.01 |
| 2 | 1.47 | 5.22 | 6.86 |
| 3 | 7.08 | 7.08 | 9.38 |
| 4 | 3.17 | 7.67 | 12.11 |
| 5+ | 5.08 | 9.24 | 13.27 |

**Table 7-3**
**Forecast Households in Zone XXX, by Category**

| | Auto Ownership | | |
|---|---|---|---|
| Family Size | 0 | 1 | 2+ |
| 1 | 23 | 35 | 39 |
| 2 | 30 | 47 | 52 |
| 3 | 48 | 79 | 80 |
| 4 | 26 | 65 | 23 |
| 5+ | 21 | 28 | 18 |

2. The estimates of trip rates are dependent for their accuracy on the number of households or zones in each cell. Thus, there will be a complete inconsistency of accuracy of forecasts.
3. The method is sensitive to the grouping applied to each parameter.
4. Forecasts for households or zones that are located in the forecast year at the extremes of the matrix will be highly unreliable, because of the relatively low number of observations typically found there.
5. The addition of parameters increases geometrically the number of cell entries, and hence the number of households or zones needed to obtain a value of reasonable accuracy in every cell.
6. There are no readily available statistical measures to assess the goodness-of-fit or reliability of the method.
7. In zonal applications, forecasts are tied to the existing zone configurations.
8. In zonal applications variation in the size of zones will affect the accuracy.

**Linear Regression.** This technique is used somewhat more frequently than cross-classification. It comprises an attempt to construct a linear relationship between existing trip making and the various parameters already identified. There is an underlying assumption that this relationship represents a causal relationship that can be used for forecasting. The parameters are usually entered as zonal means, or totals that may be related respectively to households in a zone, or the zone as a whole. A typical linear regression equation for, say, home-based work trips might be of the form shown in equation 7.1.

$$T_i = 37.6 + 1.75H_i + 2.39C_i + 1.88W_i \qquad (7.1)$$

where    $T_i$ = the number of work trips produced by zone $i$

         $H_i$ = the number of households in zone $i$

         $C_i$ = the number of cars owned by households in zone $i$

and    $W_i$ = the number of workers resident in zone $i$

This model is an aggregate-totals model. The coefficients and constant term are found by calibration on the trip making at the base year, using standard linear regression[1] procedures and using the data from all zones in the study area. The coefficient estimates do, of course, take into account the variances and covariances among the zones, in contrast to the treatment of variances in cross-classification. On the other hand, linear regression imposes strict linearity assumptions on the relationship, while the cross-classification imposes no prior assumptions on the form of the relationship between trip making and the various zone or household characteristics.

For an aggregate-totals model, forecasts are required of the future values of each of the independent variables, $H_i$, $C_i$, and $W_i$, for each zone of the study area. These values are then used to obtain future estimates of $T_i$. The values of the constant and coefficients are assumed to remain unchanged over the forecast period. The future values of the independent variables are derived from the land-use model and associated urban-growth and economic-growth models.

In the case of aggregate-rates models, a typical home-based work trip generation model would be of the form shown in equation 7.2.

$$t_i = 0.734 + 2.622c_i + 1.793w_i \qquad (7.2)$$

where    $t_i$ = the number of trips produced by household $i$

            $c_i$ = the car ownership of household

            $w_i$ = the number of workers in household

The calibration is carried out, for the aggregate-rates model, by using either the data on all households in the study area or data comprising household averages in each zone of the study area. The latter procedure is generally more common, because of the zonal orientation of the travel-forecasting process. Forecasting is carried out in a similar manner to that for the aggregate-totals model, except that rates are now forecast that are to be multiplied by the forecast number of households in each zone.

In both the aggregate-totals and the aggregate-rates models, forecasting presents some serious statistical problems. Strictly speaking, a linear regression model may only be used for prediction for values within the range of observed combinations of values of all independent variables.[2] In general, forecast values of the independent variables in trip-generation models violate this requirement. It is also important to remember that the statistical goodness-of-fit measures available for linear regression are measures that relate to the calibration data only. They do not measure predictive or forecasting ability. High statistical significance of a trip-generation model is necessary but not sufficient for predictive validity. In addition to such significance, the model must be based on strong causal reasoning. This point will be discussed further a little later in this chapter. Suffice it to say that the existence of a high degree of significance in the final model is taken, erroneously, as an indication that a causal relationship has been determined.

Some recent analyses have been carried out on this approach to trip-generation modeling[3]. Included in the analysis have been investigations of the comparative accuracy of the use of aggregate totals as against aggregate rates for the parameters in conventional trip generation. The same level of aggregation is used and the same number of observations are therefore available for both methods. The aggregate totals are the totals for each zone of, say, cars owned, workers, etc; and the aggregate rates are the totals divided by the number of households in each zone.

From comparisons of the significance of the regressions, the size of $R^2$ and the computation of root mean square errors for several groups of the data, it was concluded that the aggregate-totals equations were generally superior. In interpreting these results some further points should first be noted about this type of trip-generation modeling. First, the use of an aggregate-totals model constrains the equation to the existing zone configurations, and is likely to exhibit relationships that are questionable in forecasting. For instance, most surveys have shown that trip-making is not linearly related to car ownership. The major increase in trips per household occurs with the acquisition of the first car. The addition of further cars does increase trip making, but to a lesser and lesser extent as the number of cars increases. In a situation where one-car families predominate, an aggregate-totals equation is likely to show cars per zone as an important variable. In such an aggregate-totals model, it can then be expected that identical increases in forecast trips will be predicted for a doubling of the cars in a zone from two different causes. This doubling may have occurred as a result of a doubling of the number of households in the zone, or from all the households acquiring a second car. A priori reasoning would suggest that the forecast resulting from the second occurrence would be a serious overestimate.

A further comparative property between aggregate totals and aggregate rates concerns the respective variances of the parameters over a survey area. The aggregate-totals parameters will have a total variance composed partly of the rate variance and partly of the zone-size variance. Of these two sources of variance, that due to zone size may often be much the greater. As a result of this, the use of a dependent variable, which is an aggregate total, in a model that contains independent variables which include a measure of zone variations, such as a number of households, or persons per zone, will yield a high $R^2$. In large measure, this $R^2$ will be due to an explanation of the variance due to zone-size variation. A model that is based on aggregate rates is likely to yield lower $R^2$ because the variance of both the independent variables are smaller, and the entire variance to be explained is due to rate variances alone, and not to zone-size variances. This may be illustrated by examining the results of regression runs on data from a small urban area, as shown in Tables 7-4 and 7-5.

It is clear, from an analysis of the correlation matrix and from conceptual considerations, that the totals variables must obtain their variance partly from natural variance from household to household, and partly from variance due to variations in zone size. It should be noted that the variance of households per zone is of the same order of magnitude as the variances of the trips, cars, and workers per zone.

**Table 7-4**
**Variances and Correlations for Sample Data**

| Variable | Standard Deviation | Variance | Simple Correlation with HH |
|---|---|---|---|
| Trips | 715.18 | 511,482.4234 | 0.921 |
| Households | 573.29 | 328,661.4241 | —— |
| Cars | 767.62 | 589,240.4644 | 0.848 |
| Workers | 660.56 | 436,339.5136 | 0.981 |
| Trip/HH | 0.2706 | 0.07322 | −0.292 |
| Cars/HH | 0.1406 | 0.01977 | −0.276 |
| Workers/HH | 0.3242 | 0.10512 | −0.304 |

**Table 7-5**
**Comparative Aggregate-totals and Aggregate-rates Models**

| Model | Trips = f(cars, worker, households) | Trips = f(cars/HH, workers/HH) |
|---|---|---|
| Regression S.S. | 9,572,298.447 | 1.093 |
| Residual S.S. | 145,784.503 | 0.299 |
| Statistics | $R^2 = 0.986$    $F = 350.190$ | $R^2 = 0.785$    $F = 31.056$ |
| Total S.S. | 9,718,082.950 | 1.392 |

Ideally, the variance of the totals of trips, cars, and workers should be reduced by the variance derived from the variation in zone size. Having done this, the regression on the variables trips/zone, cars/zone, and workers/zone, could be carried out, where the zone variance has been removed. This cannot be done within this problem structure, although an estimate of it could be obtained by "equating" zone sizes. This could be achieved by rezoning the area, or by computing rates for each zone and multiplying the rates by the mean zone size. Unfortunately, the original household files are no longer available for this analysis.

*Aggregation in Residential Trip Generation*

There are some very important reasons for using aggregate models and aggregate data, but also some important assumptions implicit in the application of aggregate models. In transportation studies sample data are gathered that are used to represent the entire population. This immediately suggests the use of aggregate data. In addition, to handle the entire data for an urban area at the disaggregate level would involve an inordinate expenditure on analysis and forecasting. Consequently, aggregation is necessary for analysis purposes.

However, aggregation requires three basic assumptions to hold:

1. That the zone sample mean is representative of the households in a zone, and that the zone sample mean is a reliable estimate of the population mean
2. That the zones are, to a large extent, homogeneous with respect to characteristics important in trip generation
3. That valid trip-generation relationships can be developed on the basis of zonal aggregates of household trip making and characteristics

G.M. McCarthy[4] investigated these basic assumptions and determined answers based, admittedly, on a small sample of zones from a single area. These answers are briefly as follows:

1. Zone sampling distributions are skewed, not normal, indicating that the zonal means are not the central values around which individual households are grouped. Thus, assumption 1 above does not appear to be upheld.
2. The within-zone variances of parameters associated with trip generation are large in relation to between-zone variances. In other words, these parameters exhibit a high degree of heterogeneity within zones. Assumption 2 above is also not upheld.

On the basis of these two findings, some doubt must surround the tenability of the third assumption. Thus, it appears that existing techniques of building trip-generation models at a zonal level are not satisfactory. McCarthy suggests some possible modifications that might improve the models, but there are some more fundamental questions that probably need to be posed. These questions are delayed until later in this book, when the whole question of aggregate and disaggregate models is taken up.

Before leaving this subject area, there is one final issue, raised by McCarthy, that should be mentioned. This is the problem of ecological fallacy. In building aggregate models, high $R^2$ values and $F$ values are obtained, erroneously, because of the aggregate data and the existence of aggregate-level correlations that are not helpful to a predictive model.

In developing household trip-generation equations from zonal averages, ecological correlations are being used to explain the trip-making behavior of individual households. Unfortunately, the incorrectness of such a procedure can be disguised in the results of the multiple regression equation because of ecological fallacies resulting from the use of aggregated data; the equation will appear to describe rather accurately the existing zonal trip-generation data. However, descriptiveness is only one criterion of model building. Sound statistical reasoning is also necessary if the resulting model or equation is to be truly predictive.[5]

### Introduction to Nonresidential Trip Generation

In the preceding sections, the various modeling aspects of residential trip generation were considerable. For the most part, this specific area of trip generation has traditionally been the most important, so far as the average transportation study is concerned. This is so because the number of home-based trips in most urban areas is around 80 percent to 90 percent[6] of total person trip making. As a result, it becomes very important to be able to model the residential trip generation. However, it is necessary to be able to model and estimate the numbers of trips made from nonresidential land uses, both to fill in the remaining 10 to 20 percent of person trip making in an urban area, and also to provide estimating procedures for specialized trip-generation calculations.

In general, the modeling of nonresidential trip generation has received considerably less attention than has modeling of residential trip generation. The techniques that have been used are generally somewhat less sophisticated than those used for residential trip generation, and revolve largely around the computation of average generation and attraction rates. Some minor attempts have been made to use multiple regression techniques to relate nonresidential trip making to various attributes of the land uses from which those trips are produced, or to which they are attracted. Before the actual modeling of nonresidential trip generation is considered, the purposes for which estimating equations for nonresidential trips are required should be addressed. Within the transportation-study format, the basic requirement of carrying out nonresidential trip generation is to provide a means of estimating the number of trip ends for nonresidential land uses. The basic residential trip-generation equations will give the number of trips that will originate from each residential area. This provides the number of productions of home-based trips. The task of the nonresidential trip generation here is to estimate the trip attractions for all nonresidential land uses, and also the trip productions for the same land uses. Thus, the nonresidential trip generation provides both the number of attractions of home-based trips and the number of attractions and productions of nonhome-based trips. It is clear that without nonresidential trip-generation estimates, the total travel demand estimation would not be able to proceed.

The second major use to which nonresidential trip generation is put is to determine the traffic consequences of the development of specific sites in an urban area. Here, the major requirement is to determine the total number of trips produced and attracted by a specific use of a site, developed to a specific intensity. In general, this requires the estimation of some mean rate of trip making, on the basis of some measure of size of the site.

In the earlier discussions of residential trip generation, the basic rationale of existing residential trip-generation models was determined as the postulate that trip making was related to the intensity of land use, and the socioeconomic characteristics of the units from which these trips originate. This same set of assumptions is extended to nonresidential trip making, and thus the nonresidential trips are assumed to be based upon the land-use and socioeconomic characteristics of the sites that are concerned.

There are two basic classes of trips of concern in nonresidential trip generation. These trip types are person trips and truck trips. Person trips refer to those trips that are made in order to allow a person to undertake some type of activity at the nonresidential site, or the trip of some person located at a nonresidential site and undertaking an activity at another site. Truck trips are those trips made to and from the nonresidential site for the purposes of delivery or collection of goods, services, etc. Within the person trips, three basic categories of trips are identified. These are trips by employees to work, trips by visitors, and nonhome-based trips. Trips by employees are basically trips to and from work, and will thus be related fairly directly to the number of employees at a particular site. The number of visitor trips will be related in part to the size of the location, and in part to its function. In considering a store or similar land use, the visitors would be all those people who come to that store for the purpose of obtaining goods or services; while visitors to industrial sites would include such people as potential or existing customers, and other persons not employed by that industry or not employed on that site, who come either to render some sort of service or, similarly, to purchase or deliver some sort of good. Nonhome-based trips from nonresidential land uses will largely be trips made by people employed at the site, who are traveling to other, nonresidential locations to carry out other trip purposes. These might include trips by employees to, perhaps, restaurants or similar facilities at lunch time, trips to go shopping or for other nonresidential purposes, either at lunch time or at some other break during the course of the day. Nonhome-based trips will, in part, be related to the size of the site in terms of its number of employees, and also in part to the type of land use. Finally, truck trips will be those trips made for the purposes of delivery and collection to the premises. If the site in question is a shopping area or a store, then the truck trips will largely be trips for delivering goods, and also, perhaps, to deliver purchased goods to the customers.

*Modeling Methodology*

The general method that is used for modeling nonresidential trip generation is the computation of aggregated rates of trip generation by various classifications. In general, the classifications that are used are those of the land-use type, and some measure of the total area or size of the specific site. The most frequently used classifications are:

1. Land-use types:
   a) Offices
   b) Industry
   c) Commerce
   d) Shops
   e) Education and health
   f) Public buildings
   g) Open space
   h) Transportation and utilities
   i) Vacant land

2. Classification:
   a) Trips per 10,000 square feet
   b) Trips per employee
   c) Employment intensity (employees per 10,000 square feet)

The general technique that is then used for the estimation of nonresidential trips comprises the categorization by the land use at the production or attraction end, followed by the computation of a rate based upon one of the three classification variables, above. These rates are derived from an aggregation either over the total survey area, or by a specific areal breakdown. Very infrequently, the areal breakdown is by CBD and non-CBD land uses. A further breakdown is sometimes made by stratifying trip making into peak and off-peak periods. This is used particularly for studies of small-area trip generation. The alternative approach, which is not used all that frequently, is to attempt to construct regression equations for each land use, relating the number of trips to one or more of the classification variables identified above, that is, employment, floor space, or employment density.[7] In general, it has been found that regression equations for estimating trip generation and attraction by nonresidential land uses are not more useful than a simple aggregated rate calculation. Rate calculations have been performed for most of the major transportation studies, although comparisons between study areas do not appear to have been documented.

One of the major problems that arises in attempting to use regression analysis is that, in general, the variables used as descriptors of the number of trips made are highly correlated with each other, and present almost as great difficulties of projection or future estimation as does the number of trips itself. It becomes somewhat more easy to use a simple rate computation for a particular type of land use, based mainly upon the floor-space estimation, where floor space is a value that may be reasonably forecast. In what little regression estimation has been carried out, it has also generally been found that the slope of the regression line is somewhat flat, although there is a large initial value of trips per plant regardless of the size of the plant.

More recently, some attempts have been made to produce new estimating equations for trips attracted to specific land uses. The major area of research of this type that has been explored has been that of attempting to estimate attractions to recreational uses. In this case, a large number of alternative variables are used to describe the attractions, based principally upon the attempt to typify a recreational use by the facilities available. In a study by I.I.T. Research Institute (IITRI),[8] a number of variables were used as descriptors of the recreational land use. These included, among others, the number of picnic tables, the number of campsites, the area of lakes, the acres of park intensively developed, etc. Attempts at building models based upon these characteristics appear statistically to be reasonably successful. Correlations of the order of 0.9 and above have been obtained by IITRI, but it is likely that, once again, there are problems underlying this type of modeling effort similar to those which were identified in the earlier discussions of residential trip generation.

*Freight Trip Generation*

The second area of nonresidential trip-generation modeling is concerned with freight trips. Almost all transportation studies have tended to neglect the analysis of freight trips. The typical approach to forecasting freight movements has been to express them as a percentage of person movements and assume that this percentage will remain constant over the forecast period. This approach has been justified on the basis of the relatively low proportion of trips that freight movements typically represent. It is also based partly on the fact that analytical efforts directed at freight movement estimation have been less successful than those efforts for person movements. Limited work has been done in developing both average freight movement rates and freight movement estimating equations[9] but only as elements of research efforts and not as an element of an operational transportation study.

*Summary of Nonresidential Trip Generation*

On the basis of the discussions here, it can be concluded that the estimation of nonresidential trip generation is largely an unexplored area. The work that has been done has concentrated principally upon determining numbers of trips per areal unit or per employee by land-use category. The estimation of these rates is extremely sensitive to the levels of aggregation of land-use types, and also to the levels of aggregation of the specific land uses in an urban area: that is, whether trips are aggregated for a particular type of land use over the entire metropolitan area, or over only segments of the metropolitan area. At best, these estimates are crude rates that are applied more or less globally to a specific land use. There is little or no attempt to determine a causal relationship that might underlie the trip-making behavior. Attempts to build regression models of nonresidential trip generation have largely been unsuccessful.

The uses to which these estimations of trip rates are put are both that of supplying estimates of trip attractions and nonresidential trip generations for use in the trip-generation phase of urban transportation-planning studies, and also for the computation of the traffic consequences of small-area developments. This latter is a use that must not be underestimated. Frequently, one finds that proposals to build a specific facility are accompanied by requests, either from a local government authority or from people who wish to oppose the development, to estimate the numbers of trips that will be made to and from the land use. This number is required, at least in part, to determine the capabilities of the local transportation network to accommodate the additional trips. At a small-scale level this use is very important, and the correct application of reliable rates would do much to prevent the provision of facilities that have a serious impact in overloading parts of a network.

Finally, it should be noted that similar concerns with aggregation and lack of causality, raised earlier in connection with residential trip generation, must be raised for nonresidential trip generation. With the generally lower level of sophistication achieved in nonresidential trip-generation modeling, concerns over ecological fallacies and regression assumptions are of less immediate concern. However, the standard approach to nonresidential trip generation can be characterized as effectively a simplistic cross-classification approach, in which the taxonomic variables are the type of land use and an intensity measure. The cross-classification is carried out at an extremely aggregate level, in which rates are computed only at the study area level for each land use. Thus, there is total suppression of inherent variances in trip-making rates within land uses. Problems of nonrepresentativeness of the sample measures and heterogeneity, this time within land uses, may cause as much trouble as for residential trip generation.

# 8 Trip Distribution

## Background

Trip distribution is frequently the second phase in the conventional travel-forecasting process, although on some occasions, it may appear as the third phase. The primary objective of this forecasting phase is to distribute the total numbers of trips originating in each zone among all the possible destination zones available. As input, it uses a set of zonal trip productions and attractions, and attempts to estimate the ways in which these productions and attractions will be linked. Mathematically, the problem is one of estimating flows on a directed zonal network. In practice, this is accomplished by the use of one of three classes of models:

1. Growth factor models
2. Gravity models
3. An intervening-opportunity model

Each is discussed in detail and comments are made on their respective theoretical bases.

In general it is assumed in trip distribution that there is an existing O-D table that defines the number of trips between the sets of origin zones, $i$, and destination zones, $j$. There is also an existing network of links and nodes defining the time, distance, or cost of travel between the zonal centroids for all origin zones $i$ and destination zones $j$. Additionally, estimates have been made of future zonal trip productions and attractions, $O_i$, and $A_j$, for each zone, produced by the trip-generation equations. An estimate has also been made of the future network travel impedances and it is then required to find, on the basis of these measurements, the future equilibrium flows $T_{ij}$ between the zones. The basic method that is used by all the models commences with a calibration phase, in which the model is set up to replicate the current pattern of travel, with an acceptable prespecified degree of error. The calibrated model is then used to extrapolate into the future by applying it to estimates of $P$, $A$, and the travel impedances for the design year. Within the basic rationale of trip distribution there is a set of conservation rules that should be met by any trip distribution model. These rules are as follows:

Attractions: $$\sum_i T_{ij} = A_j \qquad (8.1)$$

Productions: $\quad\quad\quad \displaystyle\sum_j T_{ij} = O_i$ $\hfill (8.2)$

Total Trips: $\quad\quad\quad \displaystyle\sum_i \sum_j T_{ij} = T = \sum_j A_j = \sum_i O_i$ $\hfill (8.3)$

In other words, these equations may be expressed as follows:

1. The sum of all trips between zones $i$ and $j$ for all origin zones is equal to the total number of attractions to zone $j$.
2. The sum of all trips between zone $i$ and $j$ for all destination zones $j$ is equal to the total number of trip productions from zone $i$.
3. The sum of all trips between zone $i$ and $j$ for all $i$ and all $j$ is equal to the total number of trips in the whole study area, which is equal in turn to the total number of attractions of all destination zones and the total number of productions of all origin zones.

   A further rule exists for trip distribution that states if two zones are combined into a single zone, then interzonal and intrazonal flows of trips should be unaffected. This can be shown in the following way:

If $\quad\quad\quad\quad\quad T_{ij}$ = flow before combination,

and $\quad\quad\quad\quad\quad T_{ij}^*$ = flow combination

then $\quad\quad\quad\quad\quad T_{ij}^* = T_{ij}$

where $i$ is formed by adding zones $a$ and $b$.

$$T_{ic}^* = T_{ia} + T_{ib} \tag{8.4}$$

$$T_{cj}^* = T_{aj} + T_{bj} \tag{8.5}$$

$$T_{cc}^* = T_{aa} + T_{bb} + T_{ab} + T_{ba} \tag{8.6}$$

There is of course, much more theory of the basic trip distribution models that could be developed. However, this would go beyond the scope of this present text. Instead, an outline of the basic model types is presented.


**Growth-factor Models**

The growth-factor models represent the simplest form of trip-distribution model, based on a simple expansion of existing interzonal trips by means of zonal growth factors. The models were originally developed for use in origin-destination studies conducted before the development of the comprehensive transportation-planning study. In these O-D studies, the only available data are of trip interchanges and total trip ends in the zones. Thus, the models are devised to use only this simple information. Growth-factor models are still used in current studies for the forecasting of those trips that have one or both ends outside the study area, since for such trips there is a lack of the detailed characterization of both origin and destination needed for more sophisticated models.

The development of growth-factor models can be traced through the consideration of four basic types of model, known respectively as the uniform-factor model, the average-factor model, the Fratar model,[1] and the Detroit model. In each case, the growth-factor models assume that future interzonal trip movements can be predicted by using some measures of the anticipated growth of trip making within the area being studied. It is assumed that either the interzonal trip transfers will be independent of changes in the network, or that no significant relative changes in network properties will occur over the forecast period. The primary differences between each of these techniques lie in the complexity with which the growth factors are applied, in terms of the assumptions of the interactance between the origin and destination zone.

In order to present the growth-factor models, it is necessary first to introduce the appropriate notation. The following notation is used:

$T_i^0 = \Sigma$ (present trip ends in zone $i$)

$T_i^* = \Sigma$ (forecast trip ends in zone $i$)

$T_i^k = \Sigma$ (computed trip ends in zone $i$ after the $k$th iteration)

$T_{ij}^0, T_{ij}^k =$ present and computed ($k$th iteration) trips between zones $i$ and $j$, in both directions

$T_{i \to j}^0, T_{i \to j}^k =$ present and computed ($k$th iteration) trips from zone $i$ to zone $j$

$F_i^0, F_i^k =$ initial and computed (after $k$th iteration) growth factors for zone $i$

$F^0, F^k =$ initial and computed (after $k$th iteration) regional (study area) growth factors

The growth factors are defined by equations 8.7, 8.8, and 8.9.

$$F_i^0 = T_i^*/T_i^0 \tag{8.7}$$

$$F_i^k = T_i^*/T_i^k \tag{8.8}$$

$$F^0 = \frac{\sum_i T_i^*}{\sum_i T_i^0} \tag{8.9}$$

The trip ends are defined by equations 8.10 and 8.11.

$$T_i^0 = \sum_j T_{ij}^0 \qquad i \neq j \tag{8.10}$$

$$T_i^k = \sum_j T_{ij}^k \qquad i \neq j \tag{8.11}$$

## Derivation and Calibration of Growth-factor Models

**The Uniform-factor Model.** The uniform-factor model applies a single growth factor to the entire area being studied, and estimates future vehicle trips or person trips between each zone pair, $i$ and $j$, by multiplying the existing interzonal movements by this global growth factor. The global growth factor is determined by summing total trips at the present time and total trips for the future, and dividing the total trips for the future by the total trips at present. Mathematically, the uniform factor model is shown in equation 8.12.

$$T_{ij}^* = T_{ij}^0 \, F^0 \tag{8.12}$$

It can be seen that the uniform-factor model does not obey the trip-conservation rules of equations 8.1 and 8.2, although it does obey the third rule, equation 8.3. As a result of the formulation of the model and its compliance with the third trip-conservation rule, there is also no way in which the first estimates of $T_{ij}^*$ can be refined through an iterative procedure.

These very basic problems with the uniform-factor model led to the development of more sophisticated growth-factor models and the abandonment of the use of the uniform-factor model.

**The Average-factor Model.** The average-factor model uses specific growth factors for each zone in the area being considered. In order to forecast the flow of trips from zone $i$ to zone $j$, the average of the growth factors of each of zone $i$ and $j$ is applied to the estimate of present trips between $i$ and $j$ to produce the forecast number. The growth factors are, in each case, determined as being the ratio of total future trips to total present trips for each zone being considered. When this process has been completed for each zone in terms of trips sent and received from all other zones, it will usually be found that the total number of trips for that particular zone will not agree with the original estimate of trips. In order to adjust this, an iterative procedure is applied, in which the entire allocation process is repeated until such time as the estimates are modified to give correct numbers of trip ends in each zone. The average-factor model may be written, mathematically, as shown in equations 8.13 and 8.14.

$$T_{ij}^1 = T_{ij}^0 (F_i^0 + F_j^0)/2 \quad \text{in iteration 1} \tag{8.13}$$

$$T_{ij}^k = T_{ij}^{k-1}(F_i^{k-1} + F_j^{k-1})/2 \qquad \text{in iteration } k \tag{8.14}$$

The method converges slowly to, usually, an unstable equilibrium. Because of the instability of the solution, it is usual to specify a closure criterion on the iterations, expressed in terms of limits to the value of $F_i^k$. Clearly, complete convergence occurs only when $F_i^k$ is unity for all zones, $i$. The closure criterion therefore takes the form of an a priori departure from unity. Typical closure criteria are:

$$0.95 \leq F_i^k \leq 1.05 \qquad \text{for all } i$$

or

$$0.99 \leq F_i^k \leq 1.01 \qquad \text{for all } i$$

Because of its slow convergence, the average-factor model has largely been replaced by either the Fratar or Detroit models.

**The Fratar Model.** The Fratar model represents a considerable improvement on the previous two methods and concomitantly brings with it an increase in the complexity of the computations required. The number of trips from zone $i$ to zone $j$ is assumed to be proportional to the present number of trips from zone $i$, modified by the growth factor of the zone to which those trips are attracted. The volume of trips from zone $i$ is determined by the growth factor of zone $i$. Thus, an equation is developed that relates the future number of trips from zone $i$ to zone $j$ as shown in equation 8.15.

$$T_{i \to j}^* = T_{i \to j}^0 F_i^0 F_j^0 \left[ \frac{\sum_{m=1}^{n} T_{im}^0}{\sum_{m=1}^{n} F_m^0 T_{im}^0} \right] \qquad (8.15)$$

The function in the brackets is denoted by equation 8.16.

$$L_i^0 = \frac{\sum_{m=1}^{n} T_{im}^0}{\sum_{m=1}^{n} F_m^0 T_{im}^0} \qquad (8.16)$$

This is the reciprocal of the average attracting force of all other zones. Equation 8.15 may thus be rewritten

$$T_{i \to j}^* = T_{i \to j}^0 F_i^0 F_j^0 L_i^0 \qquad (8.17)$$

Similarly, trips from $i$ to $j$ are given by equation 8.18.

$$T_{j \to i}^* = T_{j \to i}^0 F_i^0 F_j^0 L_j^0 \qquad (8.18)$$

The value of $T_{ij}^*$ is then the sum of equations 8.17 and 8.18, and is shown in equation 8.19, for the first iteration.

$$T_{ij}^1 = T_{ij}^0 F_i^0 F_j^0 \frac{L_i^0 + L_j^0}{2} \qquad (8.19)$$

where it is assumed that

$$T^0_{i \to j} = T^0_{j \to i} = T^0_{ij}/2$$

Again, the computed total trips for each zone, $T^*_i$, will not agree with the original total, so that a recycling process is necessary to balance trips. In subsequent iterations, the $L$ factors are redefined in terms of current estimates of trips and growth factors, as shown in equation 8.20.

$$L^k_i = \frac{\sum_{m=1}^{n} T^k_{im}}{\sum_{m=1}^{n} F^k_m T^k_{im}} \qquad (8.20)$$

The general iterative equation is then shown in equation 8.21.

$$T^k_{ij} = T^{k-1}_{ij} F^{k-1}_i F^{k-1}_j (L^{k-1}_i + L^{k-1}_j)/2 \qquad (8.21)$$

The Fratar model converges much more rapidly than the average-factor model, although an arbitrary closure criterion is still needed because of the instability of the iterative convergence. Similar closure criteria would be chosen to those discussed for the average-factor method. As was indicated earlier, however, in achieving more rapid convergence and a more realistic distribution rule, computational complexity has been increased. In general, however, it should be noted that the Fratar model has introduced a new concept into the growth-factor model, in the form of the $L$-factor. This factor modifies the trip making between zones by the relative attractiveness of other zones.

**The Detroit Model.** Finally, the Detroit model is an attempt to make the Fratar model computationally simpler. The basic simplification that is used in the Detroit model comprises the replacement of the $L_i$ term with a somewhat simpler formulation in which future trips from zone $i$ to zone $j$ are assumed to be proportional to the growth factor of zone $i$, modified by the growth factor of zone $j$, divided by an average growth factor for the entire region. Thus, the term $L_i$ is replaced simply with $1/F$.

$$T^1_{ij} = T^0_{ij} \frac{F^0_i F^0_j}{F^0} \qquad (8.22)$$

For the $k$th iteration, the Detroit model is shown in equation 8.23.

$$T^k_{ij} = T^{k-1}_{ij} \frac{F^{k-1}_i F^{k-1}_j}{F^{k-1}} \qquad (8.23)$$

The replacement of the $L$-factors by the regional growth factor (initially) is argued on the grounds that the $L$-factors are only slight variations from the regional growth factor. For example, the numerator in the $L$-factor is the total originating trips from a zone (equation (8.24)).

$$\sum_{m=1}^{n} T_{im}^0 = T_i^0 \qquad (8.24)$$

On the other hand, the denominator is similar to the total future trips, but is only identical when all zones have the same growth factor. The Detroit model effectively imposes this assumption for the purposes of evaluating a simplified $L$-factor. In the succeeding iterative solution, this simplification is modified.

Again, as in the case of each of the previous models, the sum of the trips from and to each zone will not agree with the original estimate obtained from the trip-generation process. It is therefore necessary to adjust the computations once again, in order to obtain as close a fit to the original trip-generation estimates as possible. Thus, an iterative procedure similar to that used in each of the other techniques is again applied, until the final estimates of total trips are sufficiently close to permit fulfillment of the chosen closure criterion.

*Example of the Use of Growth-factor Models*

To illustrate the basic alternatives that have been discussed, it is useful to look briefly at an example in which each of these models is applied to the same problem. Consider a four-zone system as shown in Figure 8-1.

**Uniform-factor Model.** The model requires, first, the computation of an overall growth factor, $F^0$.

$$F^0 = \frac{T^*}{T^0} = \frac{80 + 48 + 114 + 38}{40 + 32 + 38 + 38} = \frac{280}{148}$$

Hence, $F^0 = 1.89$. The computations for the model are shown in Table 8-1.

Comparing the values of $T_i^1$ with the forecast $T_i^*$, it is clear that considerable errors exist between the trip distribution and the original trip-generation forecasts. However, within the rounding tolerance introduced, all trips have been distributed. Hence, no iteration of the model is possible. The trip distribution is shown in Table 8-2.

**Average-factor Model.** The first iteration requires the computation of the values from equation 8.13 and is shown in Table 8-3. As with the uniform-factor model, it is again apparent that the total trip ends estimated in Table 8-3 do not agree with the predicted trip ends. It is notable, however, that with the exception of zone A, the estimated trip ends are closer to the predicted trip ends than those of the uniform-factor model, and the solution

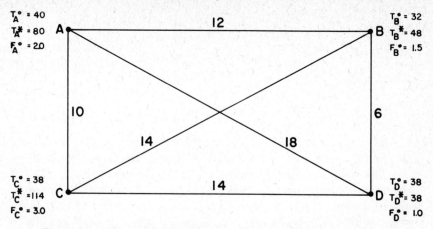

**Figure 8-1.** Example Problem for the Growth-factor Models.

**Table 8-1**
**Computations of the Uniform-factor Model**

| Zone | | | | | |
|---|---|---|---|---|---|
| $i$ | $j$ | $F^0$ | $T_{ij}^0$ | $T_{ij}^1$ | $T_i^1$ |
| A | B | 1.89 | (12) | 22.7 | |
| A | C | 1.89 | (10) | 18.9 | |
| A | D | 1.89 | (18) | 34.0 | 75.6 |
| B | C | 1.89 | (14) | 26.5 | |
| B | D | 1.89 | ( 6) | 11.3 | 60.5 |
| C | D | 1.89 | (14) | 26.5 | 71.9 |
| D | | | | | 71.8 |

**Table 8-2**
**Trip Interchanges for Uniform-factor Model**

| Zone | Zone | | | |
|---|---|---|---|---|
| | A | B | C | D |
| A | 0 | 23 | 19 | 34 |
| B | 23 | 0 | 27 | 11 |
| C | 19 | 27 | 0 | 27 |
| D | 34 | 11 | 27 | 0 |

can be refined by calculating new factors and iterating the calculations, as shown in Table 8-4. In this example, closure to within ± .05 of unity requires nine iterations, as shown in Table 8-5. Thus, in contrast to the uniform-factor model, the trip-conservation rules have approximately been adhered to. The final trip matrix is shown in Table 8-6. This matrix is noticeably different from the one obtained from the uniform-factor model, Table 8-2. Only the trip interchange between C and D is similar in both solutions. The inefficiency of the model is apparent from the fact that it required nine iterations to achieve a fairly inaccurate closure of the model.

**The Fratar Model.** In applying the Fratar model to the sampling problem, calculations must be made of the $L$-factors, before the first iteration can be made. This first iteration is shown in Table 8-7. The first thing to note here is that the trip-end estimates are much closer to the predicted values than even the second iteration of the average-factor model. The second iteration is shown in Table 8-8. In this example, the Fratar model meets the closure criterion on the third iteration—Table 8-9—in sharp contrast to the nine iterations required by the average-factor model. The final trip matrix is shown in Table 8-10. None of the trip interchanges differ from those of the average-factor model by more than one trip. Hence, the Fratar model provides a much more efficient solution procedure than the average-factor model, but with essentially the same resulting trip-interchange matrix.

**The Detroit Model.** The iterations of the Fratar model take substantially longer than those of the average-factor model, because of the necessity to calculate the $L$-factors. The Detroit model attempts to reduce the complexity of the Frator model, while retaining the efficiency of the iterative solution. The first iteration of the Detroit model is shown in Table 8-11. Again, the model is clearly more efficient on the first iteration than the average-factor model, but somewhat less efficient than the Fratar model, in that all estimates are less close to predicted trip-ends, with the exception of zone B. It is also notable that the model does not distribute all the trips in the region, as shown by the total trips of 260.4. On the other hand, the computations are much simpler than those of the Fratar model. The second and final (fourth) iterations are shown in Tables 8-12 and 8-13, respectively. The fourth iteration is almost identical to the third iteration of the Fratar model and satisfies the closure criterion being applied to this problem. The final trip-interchange matrix is shown in Table 8-14. It can be seen that this matrix is identical to the matrix obtained from the Fratar model (Table 8-10). It may therefore be concluded that the Detroit model provides the most efficient estimation procedure in that the computations are very simple and the iterations converge very rapidly.

**Table 8-3**
**First Iteration of the Average-factor Model**

| Zone | | | | | |
|---|---|---|---|---|---|
| $i$ | $j$ | $T_{ij}^1 = T_{ij}^0[F_j^0 + F_i^0]/2$ | $T_{ij}^1$ | $T_i^1$ | $F_i$ |
| A | B | 12(2.0 + 1.5)/2 | 21 | | |
| A | C | 10(2.0 + 3.0)/2 | 25 | | |
| A | D | 18(2.0 + 1.0)/2 | 27 | 73 | 1.095 |
| B | C | 14(1.5 + 3.0)/2 | 31.5 | | |
| B | D | 6(1.5 + 1.0)/2 | 7.5 | 60 | 0.80 |
| C | D | 14(3.0 + 1.0)/2 | 28 | 84.5 | 1.35 |
| D | | | | 62.5 | 0.608 |

**Table 8-4**
**Second Iteration of the Average-factor Model**

| Zone | | | | | |
|---|---|---|---|---|---|
| $i$ | $j$ | $T_{ij}^2 = T_{ij}^1[F_j^1 + F_i^1]/2$ | $T_{ij}^2$ | $T_i^2$ | $F_i^2$ |
| A | B | 21(1.095 + 0.80)/2 | 19.9 | | |
| A | C | 25(1.095 + 1.35)/2 | 30.6 | | |
| A | D | 27(1.095 + 0.608)/2 | 23.0 | 73.5 | 1.088 |
| B | C | 31.5(0.80 + 1.35)/2 | 33.9 | | |
| B | D | 7.5(0.80 + 0.608)/2 | 5.3 | 59.1 | 0.812 |
| C | D | 28(1.35 + 0.608)/2 | 27.4 | 91.9 | 1.242 |
| D | | | | 55.7 | 0.684 |

**Table 8-5**
**Ninth Iteration of the Average-factor Model**

| Zone | | | | | |
|---|---|---|---|---|---|
| $i$ | $j$ | $T_{ij}^9 = T_{ij}^8[F_i^8 + F_j^8]/2$ | $T_{ij}^9$ | $T_i^9$ | $F_i^9$ |
| A | B | 15.0(0.996 + 0.939)/2 | 14.5 | | |
| A | C | 50.6(0.996 + 1.052)/2 | 51.8 | | |
| A | D | 14.7(0.996 + 0.941)/2 | 14.2 | 80.5 | 0.994 |
| B | C | 34.1(0.939 + 1.052)/2 | 33.9 | | |
| B | D | 2.0(0.939 + 0.941)/2 | 1.9 | 50.3 | 0.954 |
| C | D | 23.7(1.052 + 0.941)/2 | 23 6 | 109.3 | 1.043 |
| D | | | | 39.7 | 0.957 |

**Table 8-6**
**Trip Interchange for Average-factor Model**

| | *Zone* | | | |
|---|---|---|---|---|
| *Zone* | *A* | *B* | *C* | *D* |
| A | 0 | 15 | 52 | 14 |
| B | 15 | 0 | 34 | 2 |
| C | 52 | 34 | 0 | 24 |
| D | 14 | 2 | 24 | 0 |

**Table 8-7**
**First Iteration of the Fratar Model**

| *Zone* $i$ | $j$ | $L_i^0$ | $T_{ij}^0$ | $F_i$ | $F_j$ | $(L_i + L_j)/2$ | $T_{ij}^1$ | $T_i^1$ | $F_i^1$ |
|---|---|---|---|---|---|---|---|---|---|
| A | B | 40/66 = 0.606 | 12 | 2.0 | 1.5 | $\left(\frac{40}{66} + \frac{32}{72}\right)/2$ | 18.9 | | |
| A | C | | 10 | 2.0 | 3.0 | $\left(\frac{40}{66} + \frac{38}{55}\right)/2$ | 38.9 | | |
| A | D | | 18 | 2.0 | 1.0 | $\left(\frac{40}{66} + \frac{38}{91}\right)/2$ | 18.4 | 76.2 | 1.05 |
| B | C | 32/72 = 0.445 | 14 | 1.5 | 3.0 | $\left(\frac{32}{72} + \frac{38}{55}\right)/2$ | 35.8 | | |
| B | D | | 6 | 1.5 | 1.0 | $\left(\frac{32}{72} + \frac{38}{91}\right)/2$ | 4.0 | 58.7 | 0.819 |
| C | D | 38/55 = 0.691 | 14 | 3.0 | 1.0 | $\left(\frac{38}{55} + \frac{38}{91}\right)/2$ | 23.2 | 97.9 | 1.140 |
| D | | 38/91 = 0.418 | | | | | | 45.6 | 0.834 |

# 136

## Table 8-8
### Second Iteration of the Fratar Model

| Zone i | j | $L_i^1$ | $T_{ij}^1$ | $F_i^1$ | $F_j^1$ | $(L_i^1 + L_j^1)/2$ | $T_{ij}^2$ | $T_{ij}^2$ | $F_i^2$ |
|---|---|---|---|---|---|---|---|---|---|
| A | B | 76.2/75.2 | 18.9 | 1.05 | 0.819 | $(1.014 + 0.917)/2$ | 15.7 | | |
| A | C | = 1.014 | 38.9 | 1.05 | 1.140 | $(1.014 + 1.094)/2$ | 49.1 | | |
| A | D | | 18.4 | 1.05 | 0.834 | $(1.014 + 0.930)/2$ | 15.7 | 80.3 | 0.996 |
| B | C | 58.7/64.0 = 0.917 | 35.8 | 0.819 | 1.140 | $(0.917 + 1.094)/2$ | 33.6 | | |
| B | D | 97.9/89.5 | 4.0 | 0.819 | 0.834 | $(0.917 + 0.930)/2$ | 2.5 | 51.8 | 0.927 |
| C | D | =1.094 45.6/49.0 | 23.2 | 1.140 | 0.834 | $(1.094 + 0.930)/2$ | 22.3 | 105.0 | 1.086 |
| D | | = 0.930 | | | | | | 40.5 | 0.938 |

## Table 8-9
### Third Iteration of the Fratar Model

| Zone i | j | $L_i^2$ | $T_{ij}^2$ | $F_i^2$ | $F_j^2$ | $(L_i^2 + L_j^2)/2$ | $T_{ij}^3$ | $T_i^3$ | $F_i^3$ |
|---|---|---|---|---|---|---|---|---|---|
| A | B | 80.3/82.6 = 0.972 | 15.7 | 0.996 | 0.927 | $(0.972 + 0.951)/2$ | 13.9 | | |
| A | C | | 49.1 | 0.996 | 1.086 | $(0.972 + 1.04)/2$ | 53.4 | | |
| A | D | | 15.7 | 0.996 | 0.938 | $(0.972 + 0.96)/2$ | 14.2 | 81.5 | 0.982 |
| B | C | 51.8/54.5 = 0.951 | 33.6 | 0.927 | 1.086 | $(0.951 + 1.04)/2$ | 33.7 | | |
| B | D | 10.5/10.1 | 2.5 | 0.927 | 0.938 | $(0.951 + 0.960)/2$ | 2.1 | 49.7 | 0.966 |
| C | D | = 1.040 40.5/42.2 | 22.3 | 1.086 | 0.938 | $(1.040 + 0.960)/2$ | 22.7 | 109.8 | 1.038 |
| D | | = 0.960 | | | | | | 39.0 | 0.974 |

**Table 8-10**
**Trip Interchanges for the Fratar Model**

|        |    | Zone |    |    |
|--------|------|------|------|------|
| Zone   | A    | B    | C    | D    |
| A      | 0    | 14   | 53   | 14   |
| B      | 14   | 0    | 34   | 2    |
| C      | 53   | 34   | 0    | 23   |
| D      | 14   | 2    | 23   | 0    |

**Table 8-11**
**First Iteration of the Detroit Model**

| Zone $i$ | $j$ | $T_{ij}^0$ | $F_i^0$ | $F_j^0/F^0$ | $T_{ij}^1$ | $T_i^1$ | $F_i^1$ | $F^1$ |
|------|-----|-----------|---------|-------------|-----------|---------|---------|-------|
| A | B | $12 \times 2.0 \times 1.5/1.89$ | | | 19.0 | | | |
| A | C | $10 \times 2.0 \times 3.0/1.89$ | | | 31.8 | | | |
| A | D | $18 \times 2.0 \times 1.0/1.89$ | | | 19.0 | 69.8 | 1.148 | |
| B | C | $14 \times 1.5 \times 3.0/1.89$ | | | 33.4 | | | |
| B | D | $6 \times 1.5 \times 1.0/1.89$ | | | 4.8 | 57.2 | 0.839 | |
| C | D | $14 \times 3.0 \times 1.0/1.89$ | | | 22.2 | 87.4 | 1.305 | |
| D | | | | | | 46.0 | 0.829 | 1.075 |
| Total | | | | | | 260.4 | | |

**Table 8-12**
**Second Iteration of the Detroit Model**

| Zone $i$ | $j$ | $T_{ij}^1$ | $F_i^1$ | $F_j^1/F^1$ | $T_{ij}^2$ | $T_i^2$ | $F_i^2$ | $F^2$ |
|------|-----|-----------|---------|-------------|-----------|---------|---------|-------|
| A | B | $19.0 \times 1.148 \times 0.839/1.075$ | | | 17.0 | | | |
| A | C | $31.8 \times 1.148 \times 1.305/1.075$ | | | 44.0 | | | |
| A | D | $19.0 \times 1.148 \times 0.829/1.075$ | | | 16.8 | 77.8 | 1.028 | |
| B | C | $33.4 \times 0.839 \times 1.305/1.075$ | | | 34.1 | | | |
| B | D | $4.8 \times 0.839 \times 0.829/1.075$ | | | 3.1 | 54.2 | 0.886 | |
| C | D | $22.2 \times 1.305 \times 0.829/1.075$ | | | 22.3 | 100.4 | 1.135 | |
| D | | | | | | 42.2 | 0.902 | 1.102 |
| Total | | | | | | 274.6 | | |

**Table 8-13**
**Fourth Iteration of the Detroit Model**

| Zone i | j | $T_{ij}^3$ | $F_i^3$ | $F_j^3/F^3$ | $T_{ij}^4$ | $T_i^4$ | $F_i^4$ | $F^4$ |
|---|---|---|---|---|---|---|---|---|
| A | B | 15.2 | × 0.989 × | 0.937/1.005 | 14.0 | | | |
| A | C | 50.4 | × 0.989 × | 1.070/1.005 | 52.9 | | | |
| A | D | 15.3 | × 0.989 × | 0.948/1.005 | 14.3 | 81.2 | 0.987 | |
| B | C | 33.7 | × 0.937 × | 1.070/1.005 | 33.7 | | | |
| B | D | 2.4 | × 0.937 × | 0.948/1.005 | 2.1 | 49.8 | 0.964 | |
| C | D | 22.4 | × 1.070 × | 0.948/1.005 | 22.6 | 109.2 | 1.042 | |
| C | | | | | | 39.0 | 0.976 | 1.003 |
| Total | | | | | | 279.2 | | |

**Table 8-14**
**Trip Interchanges for the Detroit Model**

| Zone | A | B | C | D |
|---|---|---|---|---|
| A | 0 | 14 | 53 | 14 |
| B | 14 | 0 | 34 | 2 |
| C | 53 | 34 | 0 | 23 |
| D | 14 | 2 | 23 | 0 |

*Summary of Growth-factor Models*

Growth factor models clearly represent a very simple process of distributing trips and are most suited to situations where a travel-time matrix is not available. They make only the assumption that future trips between each pair of zones will be proportional to the present number of trips between that pair of zones, and to some function of the growth factors of each of the two zones. There is therefore an implicit assumption in these models that the transportation system will have no measurable effect upon the distribution of trips within the area or, alternatively, that the transportation system will remain relatively stable over any forecast period. This assumption is implied by the fact that the distribution models contain no explicit term relating to any form of travel cost, travel time, or any other measure of travel impedance. Following on from this, a number of further properties of these growth-factor models may be noted. First, because the models assume no interdependence between trip distribution and the network, the models are essentially simple to operate.

The models work within a rigid spatial-unit framework. This means that the only ways in which existing boundaries may be changed is to recalculate growth factors completely and recalibrate the entire model. Thus, higher or lower levels of aggregation cannot be achieved readily using any of these techniques.

Since each of the models requires a growth factor for both the zones in a pair, it follows that any zone which has no trips at the base period will, consequently, have no trips in any forecast period, regardless of possible development. This comes about because the model requires growth factors that must, of course, be finite.

From the exercises carried out on the one example, it would appear that the models are all somewhat arbitrary in terms of the numbers of trips sent between any pair of zones. This arbitrariness is made greater by the fact that the iteration procedure is closed at a relatively arbitrary point, and that rounding errors, which rapidly become quite large as iterations proceed, can have a considerable influence upon the changes in numbers of trips sent between each pair of zones.

It is fairly clear from the examples worked through earlier, that the models tend to close more rapidly, in all cases, on zones with large initial interzonal movements and with relatively large growth factors. On the other hand, zones with small interzonal movements and small growth factors tend to be somewhat unstable in the iteration procedure.

The models all assume that a single growth factor can be obtained for each zone. Even if subdivision by land use is carried out, there is still an assumption that stable growth factors may be obtained for each land use within each zone. Such single-number growth factors are, in general, not easily obtained. The growth-factor models are clearly very dependent upon the accurate determination of such zonal growth factors, and the extent to which these growth factors are not stable, or exhibit a variance within a zone, will be reflected by a similar lack of accuracy in the growth-factor model forecasts.

Finally, it may be noted that the uniform- and average-factor models are no longer generally considered for use, while the Fratar and Detroit models may be applied to external trips and may also be useful in situations where a comprehensive data base does not exist. Of these two latter models, the Detroit model is computationally more efficient, although the availability of modern, high-speed computers would probably render the difference between the models insignificant.

## Gravity Model

*Derivation of the Gravity Model*

In this section, the Gravity model of trip distribution is derived from fundamental principles, and the various developments are traced, that have been proposed since the original model was developed.

The Gravity model is the commonest form of trip-distribution model, and is based on a loose analogy to Newton's Law of Gravitation, expounded in 1686.[2] This law states:

That there is a power of gravity pertaining to all bodies, proportional to the several quantities of matter which they contain, [and] the force of gravity towards the several equal particles of any body is inversely as the square of the distance of places from the particles.

Mathematically, this is shown in equation 8.25.

$$f_{12} = GM_1M_2/d_{12}^2 \qquad (8.25)$$

where $f_{12}$ = the force of attraction between bodies 1 and 2

$M_1$ = the mass of body 1

$M_2$ = the mass of body 2

$d_{12}$ = the distance between the bodies

and $G$ = the gravitational constant

The analogy to trip distribution was derived initially from a model of retail trade, proposed by William J. Reilly.[3]

Two cities attract retail trade from any intermediate town or city in the vicinity of the breaking point, approximately in direct proportion to the population of the two cities and in inverse proportion to the square of the distances of these cities from the intermediate town.[4]

Pallin[5] applied this analogy to traffic movements as shown in equation 8.26.

$$T_{ij} = KP_iP_j/(R_{ij})^n \qquad (8.26)$$

where $P_i$, $P_j$ = population of zones $i$ and $j$

$R_{ij}$ = distance between $i$ and $j$

$K$, $n$ = constants ($1 < n < 2$ usually)

$T_{ij}$ = one way movements from $i$ to $j$

The simple formulation of equation 8.26 has several major problems associated with it. The first of these is that the model cannot be consistently constrained to obey the trip-conservation rules. Application of the first trip-conservation rule is shown in equation 8.27.

$$\sum_j T_{ij} = KP_i \sum_j [P_j(R_{ij})^{-n}] = O_i \qquad (8.27)$$

Rearranging equation 8.27, the constant $K$ may be defined as shown in equation 8.28.

$$K = \frac{O_i}{P_i \sum_j [P_j (R_{ij})^{-n}]} \qquad (8.28)$$

Similarly, the second conservation rule may be applied, as shown in equation 8.29.

$$\sum_i T_{ij} = KP_j \sum_i [P_i(R_{ij})^{-n}] = A_j \qquad (8.29)$$

Hence, a second definition of $K$ is found, as shown in equation 8.30.

$$K = \frac{A_j}{P_j \sum_i [P_i(R_{ij})^{-n}]} \qquad (8.30)$$

It is therefore clear that the simple analogy will only hold when relatively restricted conditions exist, for example, that

$$\frac{A_j}{P_j} = \frac{O_j}{P_i} \quad \text{and} \quad \sum_j [P_j(R_{ij})^{-n}] = \sum_j [P_i(R_{ij})^{-n}]$$

Second, the number of trips made between two zones tends to be overestimated for densely populated areas and underestimated for lightly populated areas. Investigations of trip making have tended to indicate that the number of trips per household is higher in low-density areas and lower in high-density areas. Thus, trip making is not directly proportional to population, as implied by this simple formulation. Finally, it has been found in practice to be impossible to obtain a single value for the exponent, $n$, in the formula. Instead, it appears that the value should change for varying trip lengths, and possibly for other variations in trip characteristics.

In order to improve the gravity model in each of these three areas of concern, three major changes were made to the model structure. First, the single constant, $K$, was replaced by two sets of constants, one set associated with the production end of the trip and one with the attraction end. This ameliorates the problem of two conflicting values for $K$, when the trip-conservation rules are applied. Second, the populations of the two zones are replaced by the number of productions in the zone of production and the number of attractions in the zone of attraction. Third, the exponent form of the distance between the zones is replaced by a general function of distance (or travel time), where this function is to be determined from calibration. Hence, the gravity-model formulation of equation 8.26 is modified to that of equation 8.31.

$$T_{ij} = O_i A_j B_i C_j f(R_{ij}) \qquad (8.31)$$

where $\quad O_i = $ total trips produced by zone $i$

$\qquad A_j = $ total trips attracted by zone $j$

$\qquad R_{ij} = $ a measure of the spatial separation of zones $i$ and $j$

$\qquad B_i, C_j = $ constants associated with the production and attraction zones respectively

Equation 8.31 may be solved by using the trip-conservation rules as shown in the next few steps. The first trip-conservation rule is shown in equation 8.32.

$$\sum_j T_{ij} = O_i \qquad (8.32)$$

Summing the gravity model over all zones, $j$, produces equation 8.33.

$$O_i = O_i B_i \sum_j A_j C_j f(R_{ij}) \qquad (8.33)$$

The second trip-conservation rule is shown in equation 8.34.

$$\sum_i T_{ij} = A_j \qquad (8.34)$$

Similarly, summing the gravity model over all zones, $i$, equation 8.15 results.

$$A_j = C_j A_j \sum_i B_i O_i f(R_{ij}) \qquad (8.35)$$

The two equations, 8.33 and 8.35, may then be arranged to provide estimates of the constants, $B_i$ and $C_j$ as shown in equations 8.36 and 8.37, respectively.

$$B_i = \left[ \sum_j A_j C_j f(R_{ij}) \right]^{-1} \qquad (8.36)$$

$$C_j = \left[ \sum_i O_i B_i f(R_{ij}) \right]^{-1} \qquad (8.37)$$

For the purposes of calibration, there are now $n$ unknown values of $B_i$, $n$ unknown values of $C_j$, and an undefined function $f(R_{ij})$. For solution purposes, there is an $n \times n$ matrix of trip interchanges, which may be used to provide a set of estimates of these unknown values. In the event that $f(R_{ij})$ is an a priori undefined function, it will be necessary to determine a set of $n \times n$ discrete values of $f(R_{ij})$ from which a functional form may be inferred. However, this generates a situation in which there are $(n^2 + 2n)$ unknowns and only $n^2$ data points for calibration. Because of the relationships between the $B_i$ and $C_j$, it is not possible to develop a trial-and-error solution process that would allow the joint definition of these two sets of constants. Clearly, a unique statistical solution for the trip-distribution gravity model does not exist.

The conventional procedure adopted is to relax the second trip-conservation rule, by setting $C_j = 1$ for all $j$. Thus, equation 8.37 is removed and equation 8.36 is modified to equation 8.38.

$$B_i = \left[ \sum_j A_j \, f(R_{ij}) \right]^{-1} \qquad (8.38)$$

The effect of the relaxation of the second trip-conservation rule is to allow the trial-and-error solution for $f(R_{ij})$ to be obtained. There are still more unknowns than data points, but a convergent iterative solution can be obtained. There are $n \times n$ values of $f(R_{ij})$ to be found, together with $n$ values of $B_i$, which are unknown unless all the $f(R_{ij})$ are known. However, by proposing a set of trial values of the $f(R_{ij})$s the revised gravity model (equation 8.39) can be evaluated for all $T_{ij}$s.

$$T_{ij} = \frac{O_i A_j \, f(R_{ij})}{\sum_j A_j f(R_{ij})} \qquad (8.39)$$

Subsequently, the estimates of $f(R_{ij})$ are revised by comparison of the calculated and observed trip interchanges, and the calibration procedure is repeated using the new estimates of the $f(R_{ij})$s.

There are two alternative approaches that are generally taken to solving for $f(R_{ij})$. First, it may be proposed that the function is a single exponent. In this case, the solution proceeds by assigning a trial value to the exponent, calculating the $T_{ij}$s for each interzonal movement on the base-year data, using this trial exponent, and recomputing from these $T_{ij}$s, the $O_i$s, and $A_j$s. The $O_i$s and $A_j$s obtained from this first approximation are then compared with the real $O_i$s and $A_j$s. Since the constraint that the summation of the $T_{ij}$s over all destinations $j$ has been applied in the formulation of the model, the $O_i$s will always be more or less identical to those in the original data. However, the $A_j$s will not be. It will, therefore, be necessary to reiterate the model with a new approximation for the power function of $f(R_{ij})$, and obtain a new approximation of the exponent. The iteration process is then repeated until the estimates of the $A_j$s are sufficiently close to the observed

$A_j$s; and at this point, the solution for the exponent is assumed to be that which would be used for a forecasting model of trip distribution.

In general, attempts to calibrate the model in this form have not met with great success, since a satisfactory single value for the exponent cannot be determined which is stable over the whole urban area and which produces a meaningful trip distribution. As an alternative, a number of studies have used a travel-time factor, usually denoted $F(t)_{ij}$. It is assumed that a specific value of $F(t)_{ij}$ applies to each of a predetermined set of time intervals. Thus, a separate value is determined for each set of trips that occur within a specific time interval. Again, an iterative process is necessary to obtain the actual values of $F(t)_{ij}$. Conventionally, initial values are set at 1.0, and the model is evaluated to obtain estimates of the $T_{ij}$s between each pair of zones. The next iteration is obtained by adjusting the values of the $F(t)_{ij}$s to provide a closer fit to the observed data. The first iteration, as commonly used, is shown in equation 8.40.

$$T_{ij} = \frac{O_i A_j}{\sum_j A_j} \tag{8.40}$$

From this, the percentage of trips in each time interval can be determined. New travel time factors are then determined by the calculation of equation 8.41.

$$F_k^1 = F_k^0 \frac{OD\%}{GM\%} \tag{8.41}$$

where $F_k^1$ = the adjusted factor for time interval $k$

$F_k^0$ = the original factor for time interval $k$

$OD\%$ = the percent of observed trips in that time interval

$GM\%$ = the percent of trips predicted from the model in that time interval

This process is repeated until the adjusted factors differ by a predetermined amount from the original (previous) factors. This is a relatively arbitrary closure criterion, and may sometimes be replaced by the use of a statistical test, such as a Chi-square[6] test or a Kolmogorov-Smirnov[7] test. These latter two would test for a statistically significant difference in the distributions of trips among the time intervals between two succeeding iterations. When they become nonsignificant, the calibration process would be terminated.

The iteration process outlined above allows for the solution of the travel-time factors, based upon an attempt to fit the distribution of trips over travel time. There is go guarantee, within this fitting process, that the total number of trips attracted to each zone, the $A_j^f$s, estimated by the model will be equal to those found in the observed data. As a result of this, it is usual to find that the calibrated model does not replicate base-year data in the form of the total zonal trip attractions or at the detailed level of specific trip interchanges.

In order to handle the nonadherence to observed attractions, it is not uncommon to utilize a successive row- and column-factoring process, which is designed to reestimate the attraction and production totals. The calibration process yields a matrix of estimated values of the trip interchanges, $T_{ij}^e$, from which estimated row totals of $O_i^e$ and estimated column totals of $A_j^f$ are obtained. It is assumed that the relationship between the observed trip interchanges, $T_{ij}^0$, and the estimated trip interchanges, $T_{ij}^e$ is of the form shown in equation 8.42.

$$T_{ij}^0 = M_i N_i \, T_{ij}^e \qquad (8.42)$$

However, applying the trip-conservation rules (equations 8.32 and 8.34) to equation 8.42 permits the definition of $M_i$ and $N_i$ as shown in equations 8.43 and 8.44.

$$M_i = \frac{O_i^0}{\sum_j N_j T_{ij}^e} \qquad (8.43)$$

$$N_j = \frac{A_j^0}{\sum_i M_i T_{ij}^e} \qquad (8.44)$$

The values $M_i$ and $N_j$ may then be found by an iterative process of successive factoring the columns of the matrix by $A_j^0/A_j^e$ and the row by $O_i^0/O_i^e$. This process is equivalent to setting the $M_i$ initially to unity, for all zones, and estimating $N_j$, followed by substituting this trial value of $N_j$ into equation 8.43 and reestimating $M_i$. The process continues until the values of $M_i$ and $N_j$ do not change significantly on two successive iterations. The identical procedure is repeated on the forecast data, in order to replicate forecast zonal- productions and attractions from the trip-generation model.

It is also common practice to introduce a zone-to-zone adjustment factor to adjust further for the lack of fit between the observed and estimated trip interchanges. This adjustment factor is usually denoted $K_{ij}$. $K_{ij}$ is defined as a function of the socioeconomic characteristics of the producing and attracting zones, $i$ and $j$, which cause the trip interchange, $T_{ij}^0$, to be different from that estimated by the gravity model. Initially, it is assumed that these characteristics have no effect upon trip making. These adjustment factors are computed as the ratio of the original trip interchange between each zone pair to the trip interchange estimated by the gravity model, equation 8.45.

$$K_{ij} = T_{ij}^0/T_{ij}^e \qquad (8.45)$$

Although the adjustment factors, the $K_{ij}$, are intended to reflect the difference in socioeconomic characteristics between each zone pair, and the effect of these characteristics upon trip making, they do not do so explicitly. Therefore, the $K_{ij}$s that are computed to allow base-year data to be reproduced are retained as the $K_{ij}$s for a future forecast. This implies that either the socioeconomic characteristics have no further effect upon trip making after incorporation at the base year, or, alternatively, that every zone pair remains in the same socioeconomic status respective to all other zone pairs throughout the forecast period.

*Example Use of a Gravity Model*

At this point, it seems appropriate to introduce a simple example of the calibration and forecasting processes for the gravity model. The model used is of the standard form, presented in equation 8.39 and a set of discrete values of $f(R_{ij})$ are computed for five-minute time intervals. The example uses a simple four-zone system, for which the travel-time matrix is shown in Table 8-15 and the trip-interchange matrix in Table 8-16. The calibration of the model proceeds by defining a set of travel-time intervals and determining the resulting trip distribution. Initial values of the friction factors, $F_k^0$, are selected for each travel-time interval. These initial values are chosen as being unity in this example problem. Subsequently, the gravity model is estimated with these initial friction-factor values. The compilation of observed data and the first iteration calculations are shown in Table 8-17. The calculated trips in each travel-time interval do not match the observed trips, so the friction factors are adjusted by the procedure shown in equation 8.46.

$$F_k^1 = \frac{T_k^0}{T_k^1} F_k^0 \qquad (8.46)$$

The calculations of trips are then repeated by estimating trip interchanges by equation 8.47.

$$T_{ij}^1 = \frac{O_i A_j F_k^1}{\sum_j A_j F_k^1} \qquad (8.47)$$

where the $F_k^1$s are the appropriate ones for the travel time between the zone pair under consideration. The results of the next three iterations are shown in Table 8-18. It can be seen that, by the fourth iteration, the trip distribution is almost identical to that observed (Table 8-17), so that the model may now be considered to be calibrated. The trip-interchange matrix, for the

**Table 8-15**
**Example Travel-time Matrix (Minutes)**

| From Zone | To Zone | | | |
|---|---|---|---|---|
| | 1 | 2 | 3 | 4 |
| 1 | 5 | 16 | 13 | 18 |
| 2 | 16 | 7 | 20 | 12 |
| 3 | 13 | 20 | 2 | 9 |
| 4 | 18 | 12 | 9 | 3 |

**Table 8-16**
**Example Trip-interchange Matrix (Trips)**

| From Zone | To Zone | | | | $O_i$ |
|---|---|---|---|---|---|
| | 1 | 2 | 3 | 4 | |
| 1 | 250 | 125 | 375 | 75 | 825 |
| 2 | 100 | 400 | 50 | 225 | 775 |
| 3 | 205 | 60 | 225 | 420 | 910 |
| 4 | 155 | 215 | 320 | 175 | 865 |
| $A_j$ | 710 | 800 | 970 | 895 | 3,375 |

**Table 8-17**
**Observed Data and First Iteration for Example Gravity Model**

| Travel-time Interval | Zone Pairs in Interval | Observed Trips, $T_k^0$ | Initial Friction Factors, $F_k^0$ | Calculated Trips, $T_k^1$ |
|---|---|---|---|---|
| 0.1 - 5.0 | 11, 33, 44 | 650 | 1.0 | 664 |
| 5.1 - 10.0 | 22, 34, 43 | 1,140 | 1.0 | 674 |
| 10.1 - 15.0 | 13, 31, 24, 42 | 1,020 | 1.0 | 839 |
| 15.1 - 20.0 | 12, 21, 14, 41, 23, 32 | 565 | 1.0 | 1,198 |

final set of friction factors $F_k^3$, is shown in Table 8-19. Comparison with Table 8-16 reveals that no trip interchanges have been replicated, that all the row totals are exact, and that none of the column totals are replicated. The next step in the procedure is therefore to apply row- and column-factoring to adjust the column totals to match the observed attractions.

First, column-factoring is then carried out, using factors of $A_j^o/A_j^c$. This is followed by row-factoring, using $O_j^o/O_j^c$, and the whole process is repeated successively until the productions and attractions are replicas of the observed values. This process is shown in Tables 8-20, 8-21, and 8-22. Although row and column totals in Table 8-22 do not match those of Table 8-16 exactly, they are sufficiently close to be accepted as closure on the factoring process. It should be noted, however, that the individual trip interchanges still do not agree with the observed interchanges and have, in some cases, diverged further from the observed values (e.g., trips from zone 3 to zone 1, trips from zone 4 to zone 2, etc.). Unless $K$-factors are introduced for each trip interchange, Table 8-22 represents the final calibrated model results. To demonstrate further, the model is now used for forecasting, with the input information shown in Tables 8-23 and 8-24. Applying the final set of friction factors, $F_k^3$, and reassigning zone pairs to travel-time intervals as necessary, on the basis of Table 8-23, the forecast trip-interchange matrix shown in Table 8-25 is obtained. Again it can be seen that the attractions, $A_j$, do not match those predicted in Table 8-24. A process of alternate column- and row-factoring is applied, producing Table 8-26, after three iterations. Row and column totals in the final trip matrix (Table 8-26) agree with the predicted values to within less than one percent in all cases. Had $K$-factors been calculated at calibration, these would now be applied to the trip interchanges in Table 8-26, to provide estimates of the final forecast trip interchanges.

*Gravity Model Discussion*

At the start of this section, the implications and effects of some of the assumptions that have been made within the current formulation of a gravity model are considered. Also, some of the effects that may be anticipated as arising when the model is applied to real data, are discussed briefly.

The major area that is discussed here is the formulation of the travel-time factors. A significant amount of research has been carried out on the effects of varying assumptions on the travel-time factors and a number of findings can be put together from the literature. Returning to the earlier considerations of the gravity model, two alternative forms of travel-time factors were postulated. The first of these comprised the distance or time between each zone pair being raised to some power, normally a negative power. The second alternative that was discussed was the idea of using a separate friction factor for each time interval within the data being used. This latter set of friction factors effectively represents a discontinuous mathematical function.

**Table 8-18**
**Succeeding Three Iterations of the Gravity Model**

| Travel-time Interval | $F_k^1$ | $T_k^2$ | $F_k^2$ | $T_k^3$ | $F_k^3$ | $T_k^4$ |
|---|---|---|---|---|---|---|
| 0.1 - 5.0 | 0.979 | 646 | 0.985 | 651 | 0.983 | 650 |
| 5.1 - 10.0 | 1.691 | 1,067 | 1.807 | 1,128 | 1.826 | 1,138 |
| 10.1 - 15.0 | 1.216 | 1,057 | 1.173 | 1,025 | 1.167 | 1,021 |
| 15.1 - 20.0 | 0.472 | 605 | 0.441 | 571 | 0.436 | 565 |

**Table 8-19**
**Calibrated Trip-interchange Matrix**

| From Zone | To Zone | | | | |
|---|---|---|---|---|---|
| | 1 | 2 | 3 | 4 | $O_i$ |
| 1 | 224 | 112 | 364 | 125 | 825 |
| 2 | 74 | 350 | 101 | 250 | 775 |
| 3 | 200 | 84 | 231 | 395 | 910 |
| 4 | 70 | 207 | 393 | 195 | 865 |
| $A_j$ | 568 | 753 | 1,089 | 965 | 3,375 |
| Column Factors | 1.251 | 1.062 | 0.891 | 0.927 | |

**Table 8-20**
**Column-factored Trip-interchange Matrix**

| From Zone | To Zone | | | | | Row Factors |
|---|---|---|---|---|---|---|
| | 1 | 2 | 3 | 4 | $O_i$ | |
| 1 | 280 | 119 | 324 | 116 | 839 | 0.983 |
| 2 | 93 | 372 | 90 | 232 | 787 | 0.985 |
| 3 | 250 | 89 | 206 | 366 | 911 | 0.999 |
| 4 | 86 | 220 | 350 | 181 | 837 | 1.033 |
| $A_j$ | 709 | 800 | 970 | 895 | 3,374 | |

**Table 8-21**
**Row-factored Trip-interchange Matrix**

| From Zone | To Zone | | | | |
|---|---|---|---|---|---|
| | 1 | 2 | 3 | 4 | $O_i$ |
| 1 | 275 | 117 | 318 | 114 | 824 |
| 2 | 92 | 366 | 89 | 229 | 776 |
| 3 | 250 | 89 | 206 | 366 | 911 |
| 4 | 89 | 227 | 362 | 187 | 865 |
| $A_j$ | 706 | 799 | 975 | 896 | 3,376 |
| Column Factors | 1.006 | 1.001 | 0.995 | 0.999 | |

**Table 8-22**
**Column-factored (2nd) Trip-interchange Matrix**

| From Zone | To Zone | | | | |
|---|---|---|---|---|---|
| | 1 | 2 | 3 | 4 | $O_i$ |
| 1 | 277 | 117 | 316 | 114 | 824 |
| 2 | 93 | 366 | 89 | 229 | 777 |
| 3 | 252 | 89 | 205 | 366 | 912 |
| 4 | 90 | 227 | 360 | 187 | 864 |
| $A_j$ | 712 | 799 | 970 | 896 | 3,377 |

**Table 8-23**
**Forecast Travel-time Matrix**

| From Zone | To Zone | | | |
|---|---|---|---|---|
| | 1 | 2 | 3 | 4 |
| 1 | 6 | 18 | 15 | 20 |
| 2 | 18 | 8 | 19 | 14 |
| 3 | 15 | 19 | 3 | 10 |
| 4 | 20 | 14 | 10 | 5 |

**Table 8-24**
**Forecast Produced and Attracted Trips**

|  | Zone | | | |
|---|---|---|---|---|
|  | 1 | 2 | 3 | 4 |
| Productions | 950 | 1,000 | 1,350 | 1,210 |
| Attractions | 860 | 1,375 | 885 | 1,390 |

**Table 8-25**
**Forecast Trip-Interchange Matrix**

| From Zone | To Zone | | | | $O_i$ |
|---|---|---|---|---|---|
|  | 1 | 2 | 3 | 4 | |
| 1 | 392 | 150 | 258 | 151 | 951 |
| 2 | 77 | 513 | 79 | 331 | 1,000 |
| 3 | 270 | 162 | 234 | 684 | 1,350 |
| 4 | 91 | 391 | 394 | 333 | 1,209 |
| $A_j$ | 830 | 1,216 | 965 | 1,499 | 4,510 |
| Column Factors | 1.036 | 1.131 | 0.917 | 0.927 | |

**Table 8-26**
**Final Forecast Trip-interchange Matrix**

| From Zone | To Zone | | | | $O_i$ |
|---|---|---|---|---|---|
|  | 1 | 2 | 3 | 4 | |
| 1 | 403 | 171 | 235 | 139 | 948 |
| 2 | 77 | 565 | 69 | 294 | 1,005 |
| 3 | 287 | 190 | 220 | 649 | 1,346 |
| 4 | 94 | 449 | 361 | 308 | 1,212 |
| $A_j$ | 861 | 1,375 | 885 | 1,390 | 4,511 |

Considering the exponent form of travel-time factor, the size of the exponent chosen for the time or distance in the gravity-model formulation has a very pronounced effect upon the proposed rate of decay of trips as one moves away from the origin zone. Figure 8-2 illustrates the variation in the rate of decay as the exponent increases from 1 to 3. It can be seen from this figure that the rate of decay of trip making will decrease very much more rapidly as the exponent increases in size. However, even an exponent of 1 causes a fairly rapid decay as the time or distance of the trip increases. The main assumption that is being made by applying a single exponent of this form is that the decay of trip making with time or distance is of a regular mathematical form. In actual fact, observations of trip making are rarely as well-behaved as these curves would suggest. Figure 8-3 illustrates the typical form of decay with time, observed from a real transportation study.

A number of attempts have been made to fit various functional forms to the travel-time factor in the gravity model. Among the most recent attempts to do this is work carried out by Norman Ashford and Donald Covault.[8] This work comprised an attempt to fit curves of the Pearson system to the travel-time factors and found that curves from this system approximated closely empirically determined curves obtained from a number of specific surveys. These surveys included Cedar Rapids, Waterbury, Erie, New Orleans, Providence, Sioux Falls, Hartford, Fort Worth, Baltimore, and Los Angeles. From these data sources, home-based work trips and nonhome-based work trips were best modeled by Pearson Type I curves, while Pearson Type III curves appeared to be most appropriate for non-work home-based trips, in particular for shopping trips. Statistical relationships were also established between the parameters of the Pearson models and pertinent citywide variables. Among the variables that were found to be useful in determining the parameters of the Pearson models were the number of trips per car, the ratio of nonhome-based trips to all trips, total trips in the study area, nonhome-based trips per car, home-based work trips per thousand population, total trips per car, cars per person, and total trips per thousand population. Using statistical relationships based on these factors, good first approximations of the travel-time factors were obtained. It was recommended that the final curves should be obtained by an iterative procedure similar to that currently used for determining travel-time factors in more conventional gravity models. This particular piece of work is one of the latest in a series of research articles that have dealt, from time to time, with attempts at fitting some specific function to the travel-time factors in a gravity model.

Given these attempts, one may ask the question: Why be concerned with fitting a specific mathematical form to the travel-impedance function? This question can best be answered by looking briefly at the effects of using a travel-impedance factor of the form $F(t_{ij})$. Figure 8-3 illustrates the result of applying this form of travel-time factor to a gravity model. The basic

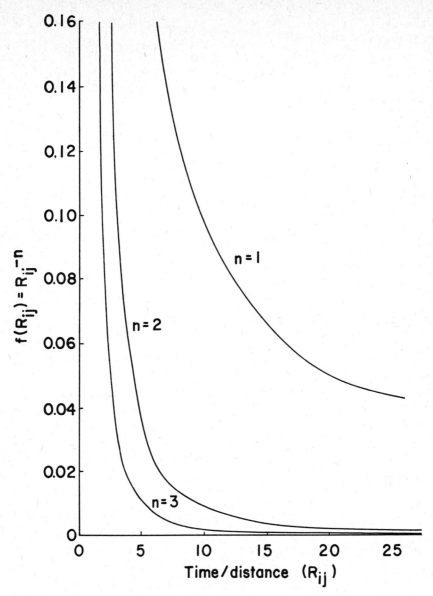

**Figure 8-2.** Variation of Rate of Decay with Exponent.

effect of this formulation is to provide a set of values of a travel-time factor that are implicit functions of travel time. These values are determined for discrete travel-time intervals. Thus, the only effect that transportation system changes can have is to move a zonal interchange from one travel-time interval to another. If the travel-time intervals are large, or the effects

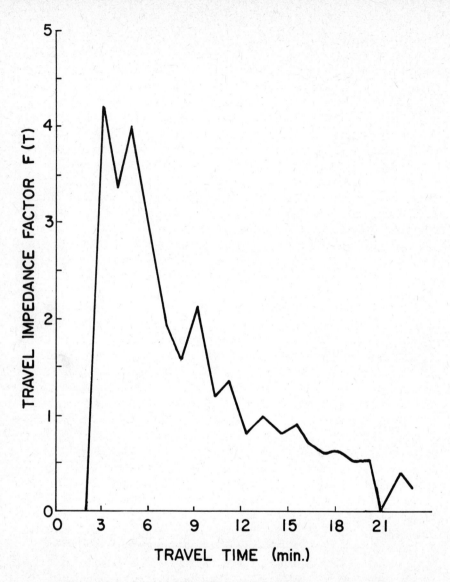

**Figure 8-3.** Typical Form of Rate of Decay with Travel Time.

of the transportation system change are small, the model may reflect no change in trip interchanges. Also, the model structure implies that travel times will be perceived in the same way in the forecast year as they are at present. These assumptions clearly indicate the desirability of obtaining an explicit function of travel times for the travel-time factor in the gravity model. They permit changes in the network to be reflected more accurately and responsively in changes in trip distribution.

155

The next concern with the gravity model is the effect of the calibration process upon the resulting model. It is fairly clear that the accuracy of the resulting model is going to be significantly affected by the degree of closure that is required for the model. The specific closure criterion that is normally applied to the calibration of the gravity model is to require two succeeding iterations to make only very small changes in the distribution of the percentage of the trips over the time intervals. Thus, the goodness-of-fit criterion is one applied only to the distribution of the frequency of trip making with trip length in terms of time. This does not relate directly to the accuracy with which the model reproduces specific interchanges in the observed data set, as was seen in the example. Also because the closure is judged on a total trip distribution by time interval, and because this distribution is one that exhibits a rapid decay, satisfactory closure will frequently be obtained when near trips are fitted well, at the expense of the longer trips. For instance, satisfactory closure may be defined to have occurred when the percent of trips in each interval is correct to within $\pm 1/2$ percent. However, the share of trips in perhaps as much as 1/3 of the time intervals may well be of the order of 1 percent or less. Clearly, under these circumstances, although the percent share of trips is correct throughout the entire distribution to within $\pm 1/2$ percent, the actual percent share at any one time interval could be out by as much as $\pm 100$ percent or more. Hence, there is clearly, a tendency for the gravity model to reproduce near trips more accurately than far trips. In fact, the model tends to go further than this, and it is frequently observed that the nature of the iteration procedure for the gravity model tends to overestimate near trips and underestimate far trips. While considering the process of calibration of the gravity model, it should also be noted that a trip distribution over travel time that is "badly behaved" tends to cause considerable difficulties in terms of achieving satisfactory closure. A badly behaved trip distribution is one in which the decay does not, under any circumstances, approximate some reasonably regular decay with time or distance. For instance, in a relatively small urban area, a major attractor within that urban area may cause a sudden upswing in the percent of trips at a fairly high time or distance from each origin zone. Such features as this will generally cause considerable problems in fitting a travel-time function, and frequently prevent the achievement of a satisfactory closure under any circumstances.

Another problem that arises in the gravity model relates to the travel-time matrices. It has already been noted that the gravity model requires as input a travel-time matrix for interzonal and intrazonal movements at the base year and a second travel-time matrix for the forecast year. When the model is applied directly after trip generation, the mix of travel by modes is not known. However, travel times between each zone pair are likely to differ significantly according to the mode of travel used. Hence, the definition of an appropriate travel-time matrix is unclear. Conventionally, because of the relatively large proportion of trips that are made by automobile (in the United States) and because all zone pairs are usually connected by highway but may not be by transit, automobile travel times are used for the matrix. The travel times used are also defined as the minimum travel times and are produced by the minimum-path algorithm of the network-assignment procedure.[9]

It might be supposed that the problem of what travel times to use could be solved by carrying out modal split before trip distribution. However, it will be seen[10] that this produces more severe problems in modal split than the problems already described in trip distribution. Thus, it must be borne in mind that trip distribution, carried out as the second step in the travel-forecasting process, will tend to misallocate all those trips that are made by modes other than automobile and that this misallocation may be more responsible for the mismatch of trip interchanges between observation and model calibration than socioeconomic differences between the zones.

Finally, it is pertinent to consider the effects of the constant $K_{ij}$. This constant is introduced in an attempt to cause each interzonal volume to be reproduced by the calibrated model with the base-year data. Thus, there is a specific value of $K_{ij}$ for each interzonal movement. It is suggested that this value represents some combination of socioeconomic values pertaining to the two zones being considered that have an effect upon trip making that is otherwise not reproduced by the gravity model. This theory or explanation of the value is reasonably plausible, but unfortunately introduces a further problem, in terms of the predictive use of the model. It is fairly clear that unless $K_{ij}$ can be related to specific social and economic characteristics, in some form of statistical or mathematical relationship, then the values of $K_{ij}$ obtained for each zone pair must be assumed to remain constant throughout the forecast period. However, it is clear that since social and economic parameters may be expected to change over any forecast period, this assumption is likely to introduce serious problems in the usefulness of the gravity model for prediction.

In spite of all the criticisms that have been leveled at the gravity model, it remains one of the most satisfactory trip-distribution models that is currently available. It is clear, however, that there is considerable room for further research on this model, which would include further research on the form of the travel-time factors, research on the evaluation of the $K_{ij}$s in such a form that they can be used predictively, and investigations and improvements in the calibration process.

*Prediction Errors in the Gravity Model*

For each model, one would, ideally, wish to determine both calibration and measurement errors. In the case of a typical gravity model, of the form shown in equation 8.48,

$$T_{ij} = B_i O_i C_j A_j F(t_{ij}) \qquad (8.48)$$

one cannot easily determine the calibration error because of the complexity and arbitrariness of the calibration process. It will therefore be assumed that $B_i$ and $C_j$ are known without error. It will also be assumed, for this example, that the friction factor, $F(t_{ij})$ is of the form shown in equation 8.49.

$$F(t_{ij}) = t_{ij}^{-2} \qquad (8.49)$$

Applying the measurement error formula, equation 2.28, from chapter 2, the errors in each of $O_i$, $A_j$ and $F(t_{ij})$ can be determined as shown in equations 8.50, 8.51, and 8.52.

$$f_{x_1} = \partial T_{ij}/\partial O_i = B_i C_j A_j \, (t_{ij})^{-2} \qquad (8.50)$$

$$f_{x_2} = \partial T_{ij}/\partial A_j = B_i C_j O_i \, (t_{ij})^{-2} \qquad (8.51)$$

$$f_{x_3} = \partial T_{ij}/\partial t_{ij} = -2\, B_i C_j O_i A_j \, (t_{ij})^{-3} \qquad (8.52)$$

Therefore, the total error in $T_{ij}$, due to measurement errors in $O_i$, $A_j$ and $t_{ij}$, is given by equation 8.53.

$$
\begin{aligned}
e_{T_{ij}}^2 = {} & A_i^2 B_j^2 (t_{ij})^{-6} \, [D_j^2 e_{0_i}^2 t_{ij}^2 + O_i^2 e_{D_j}^2 t_{ij}^2 + 40_i^2 D_j^2 e_{t_{ij}}^2] \\
& + A_i^2 B_j^2 [O_i D_j (t_{ij})^{-4} e_{0_i} e_{D_j} r_{OD} - 2 D_i^2 D_j (t_{ij})^{-5} e_{0_i} e_{t_{ij}} r_{Ot} \\
& - 2 O_i D_j^2 (t_{ij})^{-5} e_{D_j} e_{t_{ij}} r_{Dt}]
\end{aligned} \qquad (8.53)
$$

Now assume that

$$C_j = 1 \quad \text{and} \quad B_i = \left[ \sum_j A_j (t_{ij})^{-2} \right]^{-1}$$

To see the magnitude of this error, it is necessary to assume some arbitrary, but not unrealistic, values of the terms in equation 8.52. These values, for a zone are shown in Table 8-27. All three estimates are assumed to be subject to errors of $\pm 5$ percent; that is, $O_i = 2,000 \pm 100$, $A_j = 4,000 \pm 200$ and $t_{ij} = 20 \pm 1$. Then, the error equation (equation 8.53) may be evaluated to yield the values shown in equation 8.54.

$$e_{T_{ij}}^2 = 550 - 160 = 390 \qquad (8.54)$$

Then the prediction of $T_{ij}$ for this set of values is 200 and the prediction error is $\pm 9.85$ percent. Therefore, the prediction error in $T_{ij}$ is almost twice the measurement error in any of the variables. Again, it must be emphasized that this result is obtained only by assuming that $B_i$ and $C_j$ are known without error, while it might be expected that significant errors will

**Table 8-27**
**Sample Values for Error Calculation**

| Term | Value | Term | Value |
|------|-------|------|-------|
| $O_i$ | 2,000 | $r_{OD}$ | 0.2 |
| $D_j$ | 4,000 | $r_{Ot}$ | 0.2 |
| $t_{ij}$ | 20 | $r_{Dt}$ | 0.4 |
| $B_j$ | $(100)^{-1}$ | | |

exist in both terms. Hence, the total measurement error in $T_{ij}$ must be significantly larger than that found here.

### Intervening-opportunity Model

The intervening-opportunity model is a somewhat more sophisticated attempt at modeling trip distribution than either of the methods that have been considered so far. The concepts of the model are derived to a very large extent from work carried out in the area of population migration and intercity travel. The original formulation of the model is due to S.A. Stouffer,[11] and was applied to population migration. The model is shown in equations 8.55 and 8.56.

$$\delta P = K/V \qquad (8.55)$$

$$P = K \ln V + C_1 \qquad (8.56)$$

where $V$ = total number of opportunities within a radius $R$ from the town of origin

$P$ = number of migrants who find destinations within a radius $R$ from their starting place

Although this model is not directly applicable to traffic movements, it served as the basis for the establishment of the intervening-opportunity model in trip distribution. The formulation of the opportunity model for use in urban transportation is due largely to Morton Schneider.[12] The model that he proposed was first used extensively in a transportation study by the Chicago Area Transportation Study (CATS), and has since been used by several other transportation studies. The original concepts of the model are based to a large extent upon assumptions about the behavior of an individual in choosing possible destinations for a specific trip.

*Derivation of the Opportunity Model*

The model is conceptualized on the basis of two assumptions, or hypotheses, about human behavior. These are:

1.  Total travel time from a point is minimized, subject to the condition that every destination point has a stated probability of being accepted if it is considered.
2.  The probability of a destination being accepted, if it is considered, is a constant, independent of the order in which destinations are considered.

Consider an individual, at home, who decides that he needs certain groceries. It is assumed that he is equally likely to accept any grocery store, and that he considers grocery stores in terms of increasing travel time from his home, as shown in Figures 8-4 and 8-5. $G_1$, $G_2$, $G_3$, $G_4$, etc. represent the locations of grocery stores, ranked by distance from home. The probability that the individual will accept any one grocery store is $L$. This assumption implies that there are no differences in the quality, availability, price, etc. of the groceries needed, so that each grocery store is perceived as being equally acceptable as any other grocery store. On the other hand, the insertion in the assumptions of the phrase "if it is considered" provide the mechanism to exclude all destinations that are not, in this case, grocery stores. Thus, no probability of acceptance is defined here for drug stores, hardware stores, libraries, banks, etc. Assuming that the individual tries to minimize his travel time, the alternative destinations can be considered in travel-time order from home. In general, the probability of stopping at any one destination will be the probability that the destination is an acceptable one, multiplied by the probability that the individual has not already stopped at a preceding destination. The probability of accepting a destination is denoted $L$.

Considering the first grocery store in the example, the probability of acceptance is $L$ and the probability that the individual has not already stopped at a preceding grocery store is 1 (since there are no preceding grocery stores). Thus, the probability, $P_1$, that he stops at $G_1$ is given by equation 8.57.

$$P_1 = L \cdot 1 \qquad (8.57)$$

Now, considering the second grocery store, there is a probability $(1 - L)$ that the individual did not stop at the first store, and a probability $L$ that the second store is acceptable. Hence, the probability of stopping at the second store is given by equation 8.58.

$$P_2 = (1 - L)L \qquad (8.58)$$

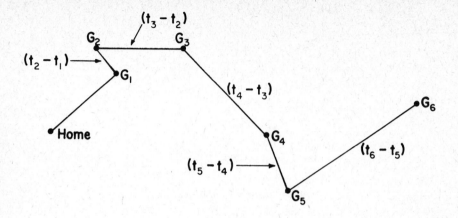

**Figure 8-4.** Distribution of Grocery Stores around a Hypothetical Home Location.

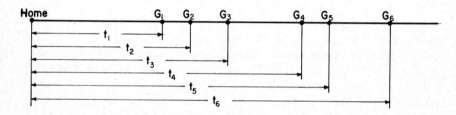

**Figure 8-5.** Representation of Grocery Stores, Ordered by Increasing Travel Time from Home.

Similarly, the probability that the individual does not stop at either the first or the second store is $(1 - L)(1 - L)$. The probability of accepting the third store is again $L$, so that the probability of stopping at the third store is $P_3$ (equation 8.59).

$$P_3 = (1 - L)(1 - L)L \qquad (8.59)$$

It can be seen, therefore, that a general expression can be put forward for the probability of stopping at the $k$th store, as shown in equation 8.60.

$$P_k = (1 - L)^{k-1}L \qquad (8.60)$$

Since the travel-forecasting process is an aggregate process, it is now necessary to extend this model formulation to aggregate zones. It is assumed that all opportunities in a zone exist at the zone centroid and that zone centroids are ordered by increasing travel time from each production-zone centroid.

Let  $i = $ origin zone

$j = $ $j$th destination in order of increasing travel time (or distance) from $i$ ($j = 1$ denotes the origin zone as the first destination)

$A_j = $ number of destination opportunities in the $j$th zone

$U_{j+1} = $ probability of traveling beyond zone $j$

$L = $ probability of accepting any destination opportunity

The probability of a trip ending in the first destination zone is $LA_1$. Hence, the probability of traveling beyond the first destination zone is given by equation 8.61.

$$U_2 = 1 - LA_1 \qquad (8.61)$$

Similarly, the probability of a trip going beyond zone 2 is shown in equation 8.62.

$$U_3 = U_2(1 - LA_2) \qquad (8.62)$$

These expressions may be generalized, for the $j$th zone, to equation 8.63.

$$U_{j+1} = U_j(1 - LA_j) \qquad (8.63)$$

Rearranging the general expression of equation 8.54, to express $L$, one may obtain equation 8.64.

$$-LA_j = \frac{U_{j+1} - U_j}{U_j} \qquad (8.64)$$

Let $V_j$ be the number of opportunities passed up to the $j$th zone. Then $A_j$ may be written as equation 8.65.

$$A_j = V_{j+1} - V_j \qquad (8.65)$$

Hence, equation 8.64 can be written in the form shown in equation 8.66.

$$-L(V_{j+1} - V_j) = \frac{U_{j+1} - U_j}{U_j} \qquad (8.66)$$

Thus, the probability of a trip terminating in zone $j$ is equal to the probability that the zone contains an acceptable destination, multiplied by the probability that a closer acceptable destination has not been found. Since these probabilities will vary continuously, if the zones are defined as being sufficiently small, equation 8.66 can be rewritten in terms of limiting small quantities as shown in equation 8.67.

$$-L\,dV = dU/U \qquad (8.67)$$

Let $P$ be the probability of a trip terminating in volume $V$, that is, $P = (1 - U)$ and $dU = -dP$. Then, equation 8.67 can be rewritten as equation 8.68 or 8.69.

$$(1 - P)L\,dV = dP \qquad (8.68)$$

Hence,

$$dP/(1 - P) = L\,dV \qquad (8.69)$$

Integrating equation 8.60, assuming that $L$ is constant, produces equation 8.70.

$$-\ln(1 - P) = LV + k \qquad (8.70)$$

where $k$ is a constant of integration. Rewriting equation 8.70 in exponential form, rearranging terms, and defining $K = e^k$, equation 8.71 results.

$$P = 1 - Ke^{-LV} \qquad (8.71)$$

The number of trips from zone $i$ which terminate in zone $j$ will be the probability of a trip from $i$ terminating in $j$, times the number of trips originating in $i$, equation 8.72.

$$T_{ij} = O_i(U_j - U_{j+1}) \qquad (8.72)$$

where $T_{ij}$ represents the one-way movement $T_{i \to j}$, and $O_i$ is the number of trips originating in zone $i$. Since $P = 1 - Ke^{-LV}$ (equation 8.71), then $U = Ke^{-LV}$. For the $j$th zone, $U_j$ may be written as shown in equations 8.73 and 8.74.

$$U_j = Ke^{-LV_j} \qquad (8.73)$$

$$U_{j+1} = Ke^{-LV_{j+1}} \qquad (8.74)$$

Hence, equation 8.72 may be written in terms of $L$ and $V$, as shown in equation 8.75.

$$T_{ij} = KO_i(e^{-LV_j} - e^{-LV_{j+1}}) \qquad (8.75)$$

The constant, $K$, may be evaluated by using the first trip-conservation rule. If there are $n$ zones, then application of the rule results in equation 8.76.

$$\sum_j T_{ij} = O_i K(1 - e^{-LV_n}) = O_i \qquad (8.76)$$

Hence, by rearranging equation 8.76, $K$ is defined as shown in equation 8.77.

$$K = \frac{1}{1 - e^{-LV_n}} \qquad (8.77)$$

Equation 8.75 can then be rewritten as equation 8.78, which is known as the forced intervening-opportunity model.[a]

$$T_{ij} = \frac{O_i\,(e^{-LV_j} - e^{-LV_{j+1}})}{(1 - e^{-LV_n})}$$  (8.78)

It should also be noted that all trips must be made. In other words, $U_1$ must be one. Thus, from equation 8.73, equation 8.79 is obtained for $U_1$, and substituting $V_0$ as zero yields equation 8.80.

$$U_1 = Ke^{LV_0}$$  (8.79)

$$1 = K$$  (8.80)

Substitution of equation 8.80 in equation 8.75 produces the Free Intervening-opportunity Model. Thus, it is clear that equation 8.77 only becomes internally consistent when $n$ becomes very large, so that equation 8.81 holds.

$$p \lim_{V_n \to \infty} e^{-LV_n} = 0$$  (8.81)

Hence, it can be stated, a priori, that the intervening-opportunity model will theoretically be unsatisfactory for study areas with small populations (e.g., less than 100,000 population).

In applying the model to an actual study area, it should be noted that $V_j$ has to be evaluated. $V_j$ was defined as the number of opportunities passed up to the $j$th zone. The number of opportunities is conventionally equated to the number of destinations in each of the zones passed up to the $j$th zone, equation 8.82.

$$V_j = \sum_{k=1}^{j-1} A_k$$  (8.82)

The application of the constraint $\Sigma_j T_{ij} = O_i$ is the first of the conservation rules for trip distribution. However, the opportunity model of equation 8.78 does not fulfill the second trip-conservation rule, shown in equation 8.83.

$$\sum_i T_{ij} = A_j$$  (8.83)

As in the case of the gravity model, an iterative balancing process may be applied to approximate this constraint. The balancing process again comprises alternate factoring of row elements by $A_j^0/A_j^e$ and column by $O_i^0/O_i^e$, where $O_i^0$ and $A_j^0$ are the required row and column totals.

---

[a] The terms "free" and "forced" denote that the forced intervening-opportunity model must distribute all trips within the study region. In contrast, the free intervening-opportunity model can theoretically distribute some trips to an infinite distance and will certainly distribute a significant number of trips outside the study region. The model, in this form, is thus not forced to distribute all trips within a finite, predefined region.

*Calibration Procedures*

First, consider equation 8.70. This equation represents the operation-alization, in mathematical terms, of the two hypotheses inherent in the derivation of the intervening-opportunity model of destination choice. It can also be seen that equation 8.70 is a simple linear relationship between the probability of acceptance of a destination, as shown in equation 8.70.

$$-\ln(1 - P) = LV + k \qquad (8.70)$$

where $L$ = the slope and $k$ is the intercept in a simple binary linear relationship, Figure 8-6. Clearly, the slope of the line in Figure 8-6 is $L$, and $L$ has the units (trip ends)$^{-1}$. It is clear that one of the calibration procedures that could be carried out would be to evaluate $P$ and $V$ in equation 8.70 for a series of time intervals from each origin zone, and use regression techniques to obtain the values of $L$ and $k$.[13] It is interesting to note, however, that this form of calibration does not appear to have been used in any application of the model. Such a procedure provides a simple calibration method, which does not require arbitrary iterative solutions and does not make a number of somewhat suspect assumptions, as do some of the other techniques of calibration. The problems that are likely to arise center around putting values on $P$ and the discrete nature of the values of $P$ and $V$, due to the consideration of zone centroids as the locations of origins and destinations. It should also be noted that the idea of multiple $L$-values arises from empirical plots of the form of Figure 8-7. These plots of $\ln(1 - P)$ against $V$ indicate the possibility that there should be at least 2, and maybe more, $L$-values, as shown in Figure 8-7. It seems reasonable to expect that for one zone the $L$ value may possibly change with distance or time. If this is the case, the evaluation of the $L$ values becomes only slightly more complex in the above rationale, requiring the determination of the approximate point at which one $L$-value ceases to be valid and the next one commences validity. It is then necessary to subdivide the values of $V$ and $\ln(1 - P)$ such that a set of data values is obtained for each separate $L$-value. This procedure, of course, raises problems of piecewise regression, in that minor changes in the location of the boundary may have a substantial influence on the $L$-values obtained.

A second calibration method[14] may also be derived from an examination of the fundamental equation of the opportunity model, equation 8.70. This is based on two new assumptions:

1. That trip-end density is assumed to be constant
2. That the time ranking of possible destinations can be replaced by a distance ranking without loss of accuracy

165

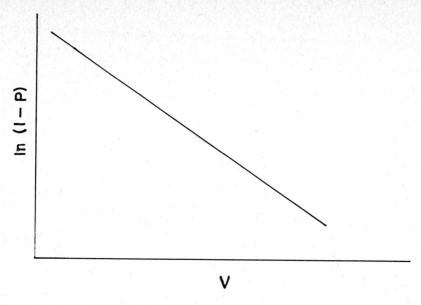

**Figure 8-6.** Relationship between *P* and *V* in the Intervening-opportunity Model.

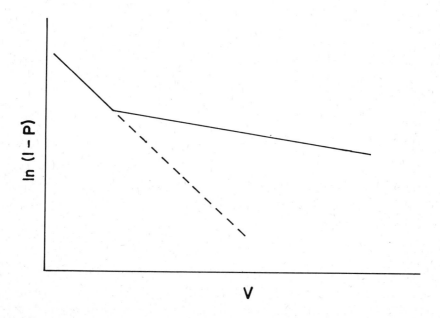

**Figure 8-7.** Multiple *L*-Values from the Relationship between *P* and *V*.

On the basis of these two assumptions, and using the fact that the opportunity model is based upon notions of probability, the concept of mathematical expectation may be applied to find the mean trip length, as shown in equation 8.84.

$$\bar{r} = E(d) = \int_a^b f(V)\,dP \qquad (8.84)$$

where   $d$ = distance

and   $f(V)$ = expression of distance in terms of $V$.

The value of $dP$ can be obtained in terms of $V$ by differentiating equation (8.71), to produce equation (8.85).

$$dP = Le^{-LV}dV \qquad (8.85)$$

Since a constant trip-end density and a ranking of destinations by distance is assumed, the origin can be considered to be at the center of a circular distribution of trip ends. Under this assumption, $V$ can be expressed in terms of the distance from the origin, as shown in equation 8.86.

$$V = \rho \pi d^2 \qquad (8.86)$$

Rearranging equation 8.86, $d$ may be expressed as a function of $V$ (equation 8.87).

$$d = (V/\rho \pi)^{1/2} \qquad (8.87)$$

Substituting equations 8.85 and 8.87 in equation 8.84 results in a new expression for the mean trip length, equation 8.88.

$$\bar{r} = \int_0^\infty \left(\frac{V}{\rho \pi}\right)^{1/2} Le^{-LV}dv \qquad (8.88)$$

Integrating and simplifying equation 8.88 yields equation 8.89.

$$\bar{r} = \frac{1}{2}\left(\frac{1}{\rho L}\right)^{1/2} \qquad (8.89)$$

Solving for $L$ in equation 8.89, provides equation 8.90.

$$L = 1/(4\rho \bar{r}^2) \qquad (8.90)$$

Dimensionally, $L$ again has the units of 1/trip ends, as determined before. The problems that relate to this calibration method are primarily those of defining $\rho$, the trip-end density, and the mean trip length $\bar{r}$. In particular, this method does not provide good results when trip-end densities are highly variable, or when the study region does not approximate a circular area. Similarly, the method runs into problems where multiple $L$-values are indicated, since the theoretical development does not allow such multiple values to exist.

In addition to these two calibration methods a number of further alternative calibration methods have been suggested.[15] The only one of these that is described here is the one that is most often used in practice for the opportunity-model calibration. This calibration method is an iterative calibration method, based upon the relationship between the mean distance of trips from an origin and the distribution of trips. Effectively, this process is based upon a discrete version of equation 8.84 considering trips from one origin zone 0, and using the evaluation of $K$, given in equation 8.77, and is shown in equation 8.91.

$$\bar{r}_0 = \frac{\sum_j d_{0j}(e^{-LV_j} - e^{-LV_{j+1}})}{1 - e^{-LV_n}} \tag{8.91}$$

where $\bar{r}_0$ = the mean trip length for origin zone 0 and $d_{0j}$ = the distance from zone 0 to zone $j$.

It is not possible to isolate the $L$ value on one side of equation (8.91), so an iterative procedure is necessary. The values $\bar{r}_0$ and $d_{0j}$ can be calculated for each zone pair, and $V_j$ can be determined by a summation of the $A_k$s for zones from 1 to $j$.

Multiplying both sides of equation 8.91 by $L/\bar{r}_0$, provides equation 8.92.

$$L = \frac{L \sum_j d_{0j}(e^{-LV_j} - e^{-LV_{j+1}})}{\bar{r}_0(1 - e^{-LV_n})} \tag{8.92}$$

Convergence will occur if Hildebrand's[16] rule holds true as shown in equation 8.93.

$$\left(\frac{dF(a)}{da}\right) < 1 \tag{8.93}$$

where $a$ = the true value of the parameter to be evaluated.

Using equation 8.90 to express $L$, adherence to Hildebrand's rule may be tested and is shown in equation 8.94.

$$\frac{dF(L)}{dL} = \frac{1}{4\bar{r}}\left(\frac{1}{\rho L}\right)^{1/2} \tag{8.94}$$

However, equation 8.89 may be rearranged to yield equation 8.95.

$$\frac{1}{2\bar{r}}\left(\frac{1}{\rho L}\right)^{1/2} = 1 \tag{8.95}$$

From this, it follows that Hildebrand's rule is adhered to, as is shown in equation 8.96.

$$\frac{dF(L)}{dL} = 0.5 \qquad (8.96)$$

Therefore, the iterative solution will converge, provided that equation 8.89 is approximately true.

Thus, iterative solution of equation 8.92 would yield, under the above conditions, a convergent solution for $L$. In general, $L$ is a value of the order of $10^{-4}$ to $10^{-5}$, and an initial value can be used to start the iterative process. A number of iterative procedures are available to develop solutions to equation 8.92, with the most efficient procedure being a hill-climbing linear programming method. In the procedure, trial values of $L$ are used to evaluate equation 8.92 and the two sides of the equation are compared. Adjustments are then made upwards or downwards in the value of $L$ until the two sides of the equation are approximately equal, or alternatively until 8.97 is approximately true.

$$\sum_j [d_{0j}(e^{-LV_j} - e^{-LV_{j+1}})] = \bar{r}_0(1 - e^{-LV_n}) \qquad (8.97)$$

It should be noted that, in this form of calibration, travel times may be substituted for travel distances without apparent harm to the model, itself. Such a substitution, however, is not legal according to the derivation process that leads to equation 8.97. Rather, it is a pragmatic relaxation of the second assumption introduced in this section, which may conceivably destroy the theoretical underpinning of the method. It is clearly possible, using the above calibration technique, to define multiple $L$ values on at least two alternative bases. In the first place, a separate $L$ value may be computed for each origin zone. This would be done by simply carrying out the calibration process on equation 8.92 for each zone separately. Alternatively, separate $L$ values may be determined for different ranges of trip lengths, as was done originally by CATS.[17] In that instance a subdivision into short trips, long residential trips, and long nonresidential trips was used. For each of these ranges of trips, a value of $\bar{r}_0$ was determined, and the calibration procedure carried out specifically for each trip length.

*Example Use of an Intervening-opportunity Model*

As with the previous two methods of trip distribution, the intervening-opportunity model can be illustrated by the use of a simple sample problem. In this case, the sample problem used is identical to the one used for the gravity model, although it should be borne in mind that the intervening-opportunity model is not well-suited to small urban areas and, hence, is not ideally used in such a small sample problem.

For the purposes of calculation, a single $L$-value is assumed, where that value is given by equation 8.98.

$$L = \frac{1}{\text{Number of Present Trips}} = \frac{1}{3375} = 2.963 \times 10^{-4} \quad (8.98)$$

It can be shown that this value satisfies equation (8.97) approximately, under the assumptions that each of the four zones is one square mile in area and that there is a constant travel speed on the network.

In order to test this "calibration" value for $L$, it is first necessary to rank the zones in increasing travel time from each zone as origin and compute the total opportunities contained between the origin and each ordered zone, as shown in Table 8-28. The intervening-opportunity model of equation 8.78 is applied with the assumed $L$-value and the data of Table 8-28.

$$T_{ij} = \frac{O_i\,(e^{-LV_j} - e^{-LV_{j+1}})}{(1 - e^{-LV_n})} \quad (8.78)$$

Some sample calculations are shown in Table 8-29. The final estimated trip-interchange matrix is shown in Table 8-30, together with the column factors for row- and column-factoring. The row- and column-factorings are each repeated twice to yield a final estimated trip-interchange matrix, Table 8-31. This table should be compared with the observed trip-interchange matrix, Table 8-16, and the calibrated gravity-model trip-interchange matrix, Table 8-22. From these it can be seen that, in most instances, the intervening-opportunity model has provided less accurate estimates of the trip interchanges than the gravity model. It can also be seen that the intervening-opportunity model has overestimated the trip volumes for longer travel times and underestimated for shorter travel times. Both of these results conform with a priori expectations.

To complete the example, the intervening-opportunity model is also used to forecast future trips, using the data from Tables 8-23 and 8-24. The $L$-value is retained as the same value used in calibration, that is, $2.963 \times 10^{-4}$. It should be noted that, although the forecast travel times are different from the base-year travel times, the ordering of the zones is not changed through the forecast period. The results of this use of the model are shown in Table 8-32, which also includes the first estimates of the column factors. After applying the process of row- and column-factoring, until no further changes occur, the final forecast trip-interchange matrix, Table 8-33, is obtained. This table should be compared with Table 8-26 for the gravity model. Again, the same pattern is revealed as was noted for the calibrated models. The intervening-opportunity model sends more trips to the further zones and fewer trips to the nearer zones than does the gravity model. As a result of the lack of change in the ordering of the zones, the intervening-opportunity model has also been unresponsive to the travel-time changes contained in Table 8-33.

**Table 8-28**
**Ordered Zones and Subtended Volumes for Sample Intervening-opportunity Model**

| Origin Zone | | | | | |
|---|---|---|---|---|---|
| | Order | 1 | 2 | 3 | 4 |
| 1 | $V_j$ | 710 | 1,680 | 2,480 | 3,375 |
| | Order | 2 | 4 | 1 | 3 |
| 2 | $V_j$ | 800 | 1,695 | 2,405 | 3,375 |
| | Order | 3 | 4 | 1 | 2 |
| 3 | $V_j$ | 790 | 1,865 | 2,575 | 3,375 |
| | Order | 4 | 3 | 2 | 1 |
| 4 | $V_j$ | 895 | 1,865 | 2,665 | 3,375 |

**Table 8-29**
**Sample Calculations for "Calibrated" Intervening-opportunity Model**

| Origin Zone | Distribution Zone j | $O_i$ | $(1 - e^{-LV_n})$ | $e^{-LV_j}$ | $e^{-LV_{j+1}}$ | $T^o_{ij}$ |
|---|---|---|---|---|---|---|
| 1 | 1 | 825 | 0.63212 | 1 | 0.81028 | 248 |
| 1 | 3 | 825 | 0.63212 | 0.81028 | 0.60788 | 264 |
| 2 | 2 | 775 | 0.63212 | 1 | 0.78896 | 259 |
| 2 | 1 | 775 | 0.63212 | 0.60518 | 0.49037 | 141 |
| 3 | 4 | 910 | 0.63212 | 0.75021 | 0.57546 | 252 |
| 4 | 3 | 865 | 0.63212 | 0.76706 | 0.57546 | 262 |

**Table 8-30**
**Estimated Trip-interchange Matrix for Intervening-opportunity Model**

| From Zone | To Zone | | | | |
|---|---|---|---|---|---|
| | 1 | 2 | 3 | 4 | $O_i$ |
| 1 | 248 | 167 | 264 | 146 | 825 |
| 2 | 141 | 259 | 150 | 225 | 775 |
| 3 | 157 | 142 | 360 | 251 | 910 |
| 4 | 118 | 166 | 262 | 319 | 865 |
| $A_j$ | 664 | 734 | 1,036 | 941 | 3,375 |
| Column Factors | 1.069 | 1.090 | 0.936 | 0.951 | |

**Table 8-31**
**Final Estimated Trip-interchange Matrix**

| From Zone | To Zone | | | | |
|---|---|---|---|---|---|
| | *1* | *2* | *3* | *4* | $O_i$ |
| 1 | 262 | 181 | 244 | 138 | 825 |
| 2 | 149 | 278 | 139 | 210 | 776 |
| 3 | 170 | 158 | 340 | 241 | 909 |
| 4 | 128 | 184 | 247 | 306 | 865 |
| $A_j$ | 709 | 801 | 970 | 895 | 3,375 |

**Table 8-32**
**Forecast Trip-interchange Matrix**

| From Zone | To Zone | | | | |
|---|---|---|---|---|---|
| | *1* | *2* | *3* | *4* | $O_i$ |
| 1 | 321 | 281 | 195 | 154 | 951 |
| 2 | 148 | 492 | 90 | 270 | 1,000 |
| 3 | 245 | 280 | 377 | 448 | 1,350 |
| 4 | 146 | 321 | 223 | 520 | 1,210 |
| $A_j$ | 860 | 1,374 | 885 | 1,392 | 4,511 |

**Table 8-33**
**Final Forecast Trip-interchange Matrix**

| From Zone | To Zone | | | | |
|---|---|---|---|---|---|
| | *1* | *2* | *3* | *4* | $O_i$ |
| 1 | 321 | 281 | 195 | 154 | 951 |
| 2 | 148 | 492 | 90 | 270 | 1,000 |
| 3 | 245 | 280 | 377 | 448 | 1,350 |
| 4 | 146 | 321 | 223 | 520 | 1,210 |
| $A_j$ | 860 | 1,374 | 885 | 1,392 | 4,511 |

## Discussion of the Intervening-opportunity Model

The intervening-opportunity model has, since its inception, been the subject of a large number of different papers and research tasks. Because of the number of these papers, it is not possible to embark upon a thorough discussion of the intervening-opportunity model within the confines of this book. However, a few of the salient points may be noted, that have arisen in the various investigations carried out, and some properties of the model may be noted.

First it can be seen that the intervening-opportunity model, in concept, is a somewhat more satisfying formulation of trip distribution than either the growth-factor models or the gravity model. It has a stronger conceptual base, and attempts to address the problem of individual behavior. In initial concept, the model is an isomorphism, although the resulting aggregate model is perhaps, more homomorphic. In general, the use to which it has been put suggests that it is no more inaccurate than the gravity model, and that both the gravity model and the intervening-opportunity model are generally more accurate and more policy-responsive than are any of the growth-factor models.

Second, like the gravity model, the intervening-opportunity model suffers in one important respect in its calibration process, in that the determination of a satisfactory calibration does not depend upon the ability of the model to replicate existing interzonal trip movements. In other words, it will, in general, satisfy conditions that the row and column totals of the trip matrix be replicated, but the fate of the individual cells in the matrix will largely be determined by the form of the model itself. Unlike the gravity model, there is no possibility in this model to put any form of $K$-factor into the model in order to attempt to balance existing trip interchanges from the model with those observed at the base year. Third, it has been noted, through various uses of the model, that even with the base-year data, the model has a tendency to overestimate trips where there are natural barriers, such as mountainous areas, or river crossings. This occurs because the model is sensitive only to the *ordering* of zones by time or distance and not to the *amount* of time or distance involved. Fourth, the existing process is cumbersome and somewhat arbitrary. This results from the fact that there is some difficulty in defining a satisfactory closure criterion for determining when calibration is complete. Fifth, the model is very sensitive to situations in which the assumptions of a uniform trip-end density do not hold. As would be expected, the general feature that one finds, if this assumption does not hold, is that the calibration process will not converge. The conditions for convergence are effectively a well-behaved decay of trips from any specific origin, and a relatively uniform density of possible trip-ends by distance from the specific location. Unfortunately, it is not uncommon to find that the central business district (CBD) of a metropolitan area represents a somewhat higher concentration of possible trip-ends than any other zones. As a result, the density of trip-ends will increase sharply for the CBD, thus destroying the well-behaved decay of trips and the uniform trip-end density assumption.

## General Summary

At this point, the principal methods of trip distribution that are used in conventional urban travel forecasting have been presented. All the techniques are aggregate models, based upon an aggregation of households to spatial units called zones. All of the models are inaccurate in performance, and have drawbacks that make the outputs from the models somewhat questionable under all circumstances. A number of general conclusions can be drawn at this point.

The growth-factor models do not take into account explicitly the effects of the transportation network upon trip distribution. As such they are unresponsive to possible transportation-network changes. However, they are generally the simplest of all the trip-distribution models, and require the least amount of effort to calibrate and apply them. It should be noted that, in contrast to the other two trip-distribution models, the growth-factor models cannot provide forecasts of intrazonal trips, that is, the diagonal of the trip-interchange matrix. Both the gravity model and the opportunity model take into account the effects of the network in some form. Both models can be calibrated on distance alone, and under these circumstances, their account of the transportation network is slight. Both of the models have a conceptually stronger basis than the growth-factor models, the opportunity model being superior in this respect to all the other trip-distribution models. However, the techniques of calibration of these models, and the methods of determining a satisfactory calibration, tend to lead to a situation in which the values that are to be forecast by the models—that is, the specific trip interchanges—do not figure in any way in the estimation of calibration accuracy. As a result, these trip interchanges become very much a function of the specific mathematical form of the model.

All of the models may be described as analytical, deterministic, aggregate, forward-seeking, cross-sectional, descriptive, unidirectional models. The gravity model is an analogue model, while the growth-factor models and the intervening-opportunity model are attempts at isomorphic models. It is clear that many of these attributes of the models make them unsuitable for the uses to which they are to be put, of providing forecasts of the future trip interchanges. It is clear that serious error propagation will occur in the use of these models, as was shown for example, in the gravity model.

# 9 Modal Split

## Purpose

The modeling stage termed modal split is concerned primarily with the attempt to assign person-trips to the various alternative modes available. In the most limited sense, it is concerned with splitting trips between automobiles and nonautomobile forms of transportation. In the early transportation studies this was its prime function and was required since the end-product of the studies was seen as a highway plan and it was therefore necessary to determine the number of trips in the whole urban area that would take place on the highway network. Now, in somewhat more comprehensive transportation studies, modal split is concerned with the allocation of trips to all available modes, specifically by each mode.

The basic rationale of modal split is the assumption that travelers, either individually or in groups, make rational choices between the available modes, based in part upon characteristics of those modes, and in part upon characteristics of the travelers. It is assumed that this evaluation is performed within the constraints imposed by the purpose and destination of their trip, and their attitudes towards alternative transportation system characteristics.

There are basically two types of modal-split model, their type being determined by the point in the modeling package where they are considered to operate. The first of these two types is the trip-end model, which precedes trip distribution, and has as its function the prediction of the split of total trips generated by each zone among the available modes. The trip-distribution phase, which follows the trip-end modal-split model, involves the construction of separate distribution models for each mode. The second form of modal-split model is the trip-interchange model, which follows the stage of trip distribution, and has as its function the splitting of specific zonal interchanges among available modes.

Unlike the other stages in the modeling process, there are no commonly accepted rationales or models of modal split that are frequently used in a variety of transportation studies. Instead, the general rule has been for specific modal-split models to be developed within the context of each major transportation study. In addition to models developed within transportation studies, a large amount of work has also proceeded in developing separate modal-split models. One of the reasons for this is that the attention paid to diversions of traffic between different modes has tended to become a more and more important area for study, with the resulting requirement of

175

an ability to model such diversions accurately. More than the modeling steps of trip generation, distribution, and assignment, modal-split models are frequently required for small-scale planning decisions, such as those that might be encountered in a large metropolitan area concerned with the overall planning and implementation of mass transit and highway transportation.

All modal-split models require the input of some socioeconomic measures generally derived from the urban-growth modeling stage. With the exception of the earliest few models, all modal-split models require a matrix of interzonal travel times by each mode. The matrices are generally produced by the path-finding algorithm of the network-assignment procedure (see chapter 10) and represent minimum travel times between each zone pair for each mode. Finally, the trip-end models require the input of a set of produced and attracted trips by zone, while the trip-interchange models require an interzonal trip matrix.

**Trip-end Models**

*General Description and Background*

In general, the trip-end models were typically among the first models to be developed, when urban transportation planning first began to become an accepted idea. They are computationally simple models and are concerned with the prediction of a total percentage of trips by each available mode emanating from a particular area. These models have several features in common. First, because they are not specific to trip interchanges, measures of the transportation system are necessarily gross measures for the entire area being studied. Thus, if one is considering a single zone within an urban transportation study area, transportation system measures used in modal split prior to trip distribution necessitate the computation of mean or average trip characteristics for travel from that zone to any other zone in the entire area. Hence, the amount to which these models use system characteristics is extremely limited and they rely much more heavily upon the relationships between the use of various travel modes and the social and economic characteristics of the people who will use the modes. Second, since the models are generally aggregate models, the measures of social and economic characteristics are means or medians for the spatial units of analysis, for example, the zones. These variables are also usually the same variables as those used in the trip-generation model preceding the trip-end modal-split model. Third, most of the trip-end modal-split models rely either upon regression analysis for their construction or upon analytical models similar to the gravity model of trip distribution. In all cases, the models appear to contain a mathematical statement of modal split.

The reasons for the development of trip-end modal-split models reside both in pragmatism and hypotheses of traveler behavior. The primary pragmatic reason has already been alluded to—that early urban transportation-planning (UTP) studies were concerned with highway planning. Hence, the earlier in the process that transit trips could be estimated and removed from further consideration, the more efficient would be the resulting highway travel-forecasting process. On the other hand, if the sequential travel-decision process has any basis in fact, it may be argued that a potential traveler, having decided to make a trip, will next decide by what mode he will travel. The decision on mode of travel will then define the set of available destinations from which he may choose, on the basis of whether or not he can reach those destinations by the selected mode of travel. Nothing in empirical research has, so far, negated this postulate.

In the following few pages, several specific trip-end modal-split models are described and compared. It is not possible within the confines of this text, to describe all such models, so a sample has been selected to provide some idea of the range of sophistication of available models.

### Adams' Model

The model that was developed by Warren T. Adams[1] represents one of the first modal-split models ever to be devised to attempt to predict the proportions of travel on different modes in an urban area. By and large, it was constructed before any of the major urban transportation studies had proceeded far enough to produce usable data sets. His principal source of data was origin-destination information collected in various cities in the United States over the period from 1948 to 1953. The model that he constructed was a model that would estimate, for any urban area, the sum total percentage of person-trips made by transit within the urban area. It is therefore an urban-area-specific model only, and is not a model that attempts to predict the specific modal split for each origin zone within an urban area. The model that he produced is basically a regression model, using the logarithms of a number of complex variables. These complex variables appear to have been generated by a long process of manipulation of available data, with a certain amount of a priori reasoning on the form and type of variables that should be included. There are a total of five composite terms in the final model: the population of the urban area, an economic factor, a transit-service factor, a land-use distribution factor, and the urbanized land area. With the exception of the first and last of these variables, the formulation of the factors is somewhat complex, and is not detailed here. The principal model that Adams developed[2] is shown in equation 9.1.

$$Y = -2.6466 + 3.7084 \ln P + 0.3912 \ln E$$
$$+ 2.3757 \ln T + 0.4918 \ln U - 0.9708 \ln M \qquad (9.1)$$

where  $Y$ = percentage of person trips on transit

$P$ = population over five years old (in 10,000s)

$T$ = transit-service factor

$E$ = economic factor

$U$ = land-use distribution factor

$M$ = urbanized land area in square miles

This model was based on data from 16 cities, for which the standard error of estimate was found to be 1.5 percent of person trips. The signs of the variables are intuitively acceptable. Transit ridership would generally be expected to increase with increasing population and increasing transit service. The land-use distribution factor comprises three measures that are basically measures of centralization, while the economic factor is inversely proportional to auto ownership and employment and directly proportional to population and number of dwelling units. Again, transit ridership would be expected to increase with increases in either of these variables. Finally, transit ridership would be expected to decrease with increasing urbanized land area, given that population has already been taken into account. In this case, increases in urbanized land area suggest decreases in population density and, hence, decreasing use of mass transit.

Subsequent to estimating the equation, Adams obtained data on an additional five cities, for which the estimated results were within the standard error of estimate previously computed for the 16 original cities. None of the cities used in the original calibration or the subsequent testing had rapid-transit facilities. Hence, the transit-service factor is essentially a bus-service factor. Tests carried out later by the Traffic Research Corporation showed that this model was generally very unsatisfactory for attempting to predict the levels of transit usage at an intracity level. This tends to bear out an already fairly well-established empiricism that aggregate models in general cannot be applied at finer levels of aggregation than that used for calibration.

## Chicago Area Transportation Study Model

The model developed in connection with the early stages of the Chicago Area Transportation Study (CATS) was another trip-end model.[3] The model was designed to accept the outputs of trip-generation models and provide separate estimates of transit trips to the CBD (central business district), other transit trips, and auto trips—the last two of which were then to be distributed throughout the study area, using the intervening-opportunity model. The study isolated some seven variables that appeared to have a significant effect upon mass-transit ridership, which were land use, the sex of the trip maker, the employment status of the trip maker, and the ability of the trip maker to drive. The findings relating to the use of these variables in modal-split forecasting varied among the three trip types identified earlier.

**CBD Trips.** It was concluded that the number of transit trips to the CBD would not change over the forecast period (1956 to 1980). This conclusion was based, in part, upon the expectation that several of the variables identified would remain unchanged over the forecast period (e.g., the distributions of sex and age) and, in part, upon forecasts of development in the CBD. It was also found that variations in the modal split with land use and density of development could be approximated by the distance from the CBD. Hence, CBD transit trips were forecast by using, first, a distance relationship with the percent of CBD trips on transit and, second, application of this percentage estimate for each zone to the zonal population. The percentage estimates were then reviewed by comparing the resulting forecasts with total present transit trips to the CBD and adjusting all percentages by a constant factor until the total number of forecast CBD transit trips equalled the total number of observed CBD transit trips. It should be noted that the percentage of CBD transit trips was assumed to be a percentage based on population and not on trip making.

**Other Transit Trips.** Forecasts of the distributions of sex, age, employment status, and driving ability were found to be little different from base-year values. Therefore, it was concluded that none of these variables would affect the forecasting of future transit trips for non-CBD destinations. The land-use and development-density variables were found to affect the number but not the percentage of transit trips, and their effects were found to be adequately taken care of in the trip-generation model. This left only automobile ownership as a candidate variable and this was, indeed, found to exert significant influence on transit use. The forecasting procedure was developed simply as a set of percentage rates of transit trips for different automobile-ownership households. These rates, found from the base-year data, are shown in Table 9-1 and were applied as forecasts on the assumption that there would be no change in the rates over the forecast period. The forecast procedure provided estimates of percentages of transit trips for each zone, which were converted to trip totals by subtracting the CBD trips from the total trip forecasts of the trip-generation model and applying the percentage to the resulting non-CBD trips.

**Table 9-1**
**Transit Trip Rates by Auto Ownership for**
**Chicago Area Transportation Study**

| Number of Cars per Household | Percent of Trips by Transit |
|:---:|:---:|
| 0 | 58 |
| 1 | 12 |
| 2 - 3 | 10 |

**Automobile Trips.** Since the base-year data and the trip-generation estimates were based upon vehicular trips only, the total number of automobile trips was determined as the balance remaining after subtraction of all transit trips.

*Pittsburgh Area Transportation Study Model*

A very similar procedure to that used by CATS was developed by the Pittsburgh Area Transportation Study (PATS) in their somewhat later study.[4] Again, the model was devised to predict the share of trips on transit for the whole urban area, and for each zone, prior to the distribution of trips between zone pairs. The total number of trips to be assigned to transit was subdivided into several specific groups, namely school transit trips, CBD transit trips, and other trips. In estimating CBD-oriented transit trips, a similar assumption was made to that used in the Chicago Area Transportation Study, that the number of trips to the CBD at the study time, 1958, would be the same in 1980. The difference between the assumptions is important. In Chicago it was assumed that the number of transit trips would remain unchanged, while the Pittsburgh study assumed that the *total* number of trips to the CBD would remain unchanged. On this basis, the model then had to predict how the CBD-oriented trips would be split between transit and automobile. It was established that three principal factors appeared to determine the level of transit usage: the auto ownership, the net residential density, and the distance from the CBD. Distance from the CBD was used to distinguish areas within walking distance of the CBD, since the fixed-fare feature of transit trips makes it particularly susceptible to competition from walking, for short trips.

The method of forecasting for 1980 was basically a cross-classification analysis, in which trips per thousand population by mass transit were computed for each combination of car ownership and net residential density. These rates were then used as the basis of forecasting, using expected levels of car ownership and net residential density for the forecast year of 1980. After cross-classification analysis had been completed, some further investigation was carried out of the variation in the percent of transit trips with the variables determined to have an effect upon transit ridership. Regression equations were derived for each of school transit trips and other transit trips, using the variables of percent transit trips and net residential density only. For the relationship for school transit trips, the regression equation related the log of the percent of the school transit trips to the log of the residential density and obtained a negative coefficient of correlation of approximately 0.75. The model is shown in equation 9.2.

ln (school transit trips/1,000) =

$$3.30 - 0.91 \ln \text{(residential density)} \tag{9.2}$$

The equations for other transit trips determined a relationship between percent transit trips, net residential density, and squared net residential density, stratified by car ownership, resulting in three separate equations as shown in equations 9.3, 9.4, and 9.5.

(other transit trips/1,000 noncar-owners) =

$$84.02 \text{ (residential density)} - 0.094 \text{ (residential density)}^2 \tag{9.3}$$

$r = 0.52$

Standard error of estimate = 68

(other transit trips/1,000 one-car-owners) =

$$3.04 + 3.20 \text{ (residential density)} - 0.026 \text{ (residential density)}^2 \tag{9.4}$$

$r = 0.75$

Standard error of estimate = 22

(other transit trips/1,000 owners of two or more cars) =

$$16.4 + 3.6 \text{ (residential density)} - 0.0334 \text{ (residential density)}^2 \tag{9.5}$$

$r = 0.83$

Standard error of estimate = 10

The correlation coefficients, $r$, are shown below each equation, together with the standard errors of estimate per 1,000 population.

*Erie Transportation Study*

Following in the steps of CATS and PATS studies, the Erie Transportation Study also attempted to build a trip-end modal-split model.[5] However, that is about as far as the similarity extends and the eventual model that was derived in the Erie study marks a significant change in the types of trip-end models being devised. The Erie study staff decided to estimate transit usage for work trips only, since 58 percent of all transit trips were for work purposes, while transit trips accounted for less than 4 percent of all person trips. Also, in the present trip-making situation, the total volumes generated on a network at peak period, particularly on transit systems, are the deciding factors in the design processes.

The major departure of this study from the models of CATS and PATS was the attempt to introduce into the modeling process a measure of the quality of transportation services for use in predicting the share of trips by mass transit. Since the trip-end models estimate total transit share of trips to all possible destinations from each origin, it is necessary to devise some measure of joint accessibilty to all other possible zones. Since the model being devised was one for work trips only, the accessibility was defined as an accessibility to employment. The accessibility defined is shown in equation 9.6.

$$Q_i^k = \sum_j E_j(F_{i \to j}^k) \qquad (9.6)$$

where   $Q_i^k$ = accesibility to employment of zone by mode $k$

$E_j$ = employment in zone $j$

$F_{i \to j}^k$ = travel-time friction factor from zone $i$ to zone $j$ by mode $k$

These accessibilities were calculated for each of transit and highway, and it was determined that the transit system in general provided a lower accessibility to employment than the highway system. An investigation of the ratio of transit accessibility to highway accessibility showed that, in the central area, this ratio was near to 0.4, but dropped to 0.1 in outlying areas. Percent transit usage was then determined by plotting existing levels of transit usage against the accessibility-to-employment ratio comprising a diversion curve. This relationship was used as the basis of forecasting. Future estimates of transit usage were based upon assumptions about the future highway transportation system and the future level-of-service provided by transit. Having determined the level of expected highway usage, this was converted to driver trips by factoring by auto occupancy where a relationship was determined between auto occupancy and auto ownership.

*Puget Sound Transportation Study Model*

The model developed in the Puget Sound Transportation Study[6] followed after the Erie study, in attempting to enter into the model a measure of accessibility to explain share of transit trips. The modeling process was devised to predict the transit share of trips for four home-based trip purposes—work, shopping, social recreation, and miscellaneous—on the basis of income and accessibility. Income level was entered as a stratification of households within each zone, and an accessibility was computed similar to that produced for the Erie study, equation 9.7.

$$Q_i = \sum_j A_j(F_{ij}) \tag{9.7}$$

where   $A_j$ = number of attractions in zone $j$

$Q_i$ and $F_{ij}$ are as for the Erie model

In this case, the accessibility is the denominator of the gravity model as developed for application in transportation studies. Using the accessibility defined in equation 9.7 for each of transit and highway, an accessibility ratio was then computed. Variations in the percentage of trips on transit with the accessibility ratio for each income group were then determined for each of the trip purposes, and plotted as diversion curves. An example of one of these is shown in Figure 9-1. These were initially used as the principal basis for forecasting future transit trips. Application of this model did not reproduce the existing transit-trip shares adequately, and a geographical bias was found to exist in the overestimation or underestimation of the transit share of trips. The addition of two further variables—average auto ownership and net population density—served to correct the bias obtained with the 1961 observed data. Both of these additional parameters were entered as a basis for stratification, in which auto ownership was stratified into three sections—low, medium, and high—and net residential density into ten groups. At this point, the total number of cells into which the data were split is 90, since stratification was accomplished using three auto ownership groups, ten net-residential-density groups, and three income groups. In addition to this, models were computed separately for each of the four home-based trip purposes being analyzed. It was found that the application of the transit-trip estimating procedure to the future generally resulted in the prediction of a larger number of attracted transit trips than forecast transit trip productions. Therefore, it became necessary to carry out a factoring process to factor forecast transit trip attraction rates to equal total trip productions.[7]

*Southeastern Wisconsin Region Planning Study*

This study has probably developed one of the last trip-end modal-split models to be developed, based on the areas of Milwaukee, Racine, and

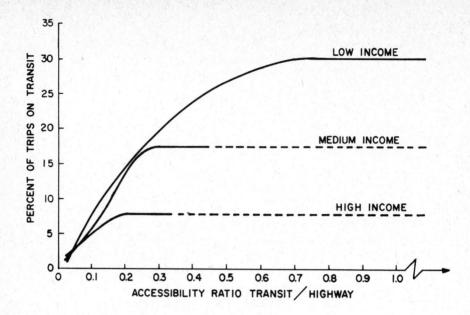

**Figure 9-1.** Puget Sound Diversion Curve.

Kenosha, Wisconsin.[8] The model represents a further modification or revision of the models of the Erie study and the Puget Sound study, again using a measure of accessibility, together with measures of net residential density and auto ownership. The formulation of the accessibility terms was again based upon the denominator of the gravity model, and the friction factor was defined here as being the inverse of the door-to-door travel time, raised to some power, which varies with the travel time. The ratio of auto and transit accessibilities was again defined as being the pertinent parameter to enter in the modal-split model. The other term used in the model was auto availability, which was defined as being the number of autos owned and garaged per household. For this variable, relationships were developed between it and the net density of an area, and further investigations carried out to determine whether or not the type of structure in which the household was located, the income, and residential density should be included as pertinent parameters. The results of the analysis suggested that, out of these variables, auto availability was the only independent variable needed to indicate trip-maker characteristics. Modal-split procedures were developed for five trip purposes—home-based work trips, home-based shopping trips, home-based other trips, nonhome-based trips, and home-based school trips. The estimation of transit trips for home-based school trips was carried out separately by a hand-fitting procedure, so that models were used for only four trip purposes. The final models were in the form of cross-classification tables comprising entries of the percent of transit trips made for each combination of accessibility ratio and average number of autos available per household for each purpose. Relationships of this form were developed for each of the four trip purposes and further stratified by urbanized area, using Milwaukee as one area, and Racine and Kenosha for the other. The cross-classification entries were derived from a three-dimensional curve-fitting procedure on auto availability and accessibility ratio. In general, the model produced was capable of replicating base-year data to a high degree of accuracy, this being of the order of 99.5 percent for the entire region and the model was therefore accepted as being a suitable one on which to base predictions. In general, it was found that the predictions only required extrapolation into one cell beyond that used in the base data. Extrapolation was carried out from the original plots of the variation in transit usage with each of the accessibility ratios and auto availability and subsequently estimating the entries for the cells. An example of the cross-classification tables produced is shown in Table 9-2.

*Critique and Summary*

Several transportation study trip-end modal-split models have now been described, without critical comments. It is appropriate to reexamine these models critically and evaluate them. Chronologically, the inclusion of measures of the transportation system has been a somewhat late development in the structure of these trip-end models. An in-depth reading of material available on the formulation of each of these models indicates that, to a very large extent, each model is constructed by examining the aggregate relationships exhibited by the specific study area at the time when the survey was undertaken. This is largely at the root of the lack of transferability of the models produced. It is clear that there has been little attempt to reason, on an a priori basis, the type and form of variables that should be included in a modal-split model, on the basis of a careful analysis of travel behavior. It is noteworthy that the developers of the early trip-end models assume that an accessibility measure was not necessary, in that they could see no probability that changes in the transit system would occur; or alternatively, that any changes that would occur would have little or no effect upon total transit ridership. In fact, the early models attempt to estimate transit captivity as a social and economic characteristic and implicitly assume that only captives will use transit. In the Pittsburgh area, it was observed that a large proportion of existing transit trips were, in fact, captive, and that apart from work trips, probably over 90 percent of all transit trips were carried out by people who had no alternative means of transportation. This was used as a justification for not incorporating

**Table 9-2**
**Modal Split Cross-classification Table—Milwaukee Home-based Shopping Trips**

| Accessibility Ratio | Average Auto Availability per Household | | | | | | | | | | |
|---|---|---|---|---|---|---|---|---|---|---|---|
| | 0.1 | 0.3 | 0.5 | 0.7 | 0.9 | 1.1 | 1.3 | 1.5 | 1.7 | 1.9 | 2.0 |
| 0.10 | 52.2 | 44.7 | 37.2 | 29.7 | 22.2 | 17.7 | 14.9 | 11.9 | | | |
| 5.00 | 52.0 | 44.5 | 37.0 | 29.5 | 22.0 | 14.8 | 12.0 | 9.0 | 6.0 | 4.1 | 0 |
| 25.00 | 49.1 | 41.6 | 34.1 | 26.6 | 19.1 | 10.2 | 7.4 | 4.4 | 1.4 | 0 | 0 |
| 170.00 | 44.5 | 37.0 | 29.5 | 22.0 | 14.5 | 5.5 | 2.7 | 0 | 0 | 0 | 0 |
| 650.00 | | 32.3 | 24.8 | 17.3 | 9.8 | 4.1 | 1.3 | 0 | 0 | 0 | 0 |
| 2,500.00 | | 29.9 | 22.4 | 14.9 | 7.4 | 2.6 | 0 | 0 | 0 | 0 | 0 |
| 4,000.00 | | | 20.9 | 13.4 | 5.9 | | 0 | 0 | 0 | | |
| 10,000.00 | | | 0 | 0 | 0 | | | | | | |

Source: Martin J. Fertal et al., *Modal Split: Documentation of Nine Methods for Estimating Transit Usage*, U.S. Department of Commerce, 1966, p. 62, fig. 28.

characteristics of the system in the models produced. One cannot fault the observations, but it does seem to be a short-sighted way of building models to make observations of the failure of the existing systems, but to ignore any possibilities of incorporating measures of the system that might change the acceptability of the system at some future time. Models of this form will, regardless of their justification, lead to a continuing degradation of transit services and discourage any attempt to inject capital and new expertise and technology into transit systems. The models, by nature, are unable to deal with estimations related to possible major changes in the transportation system.

In general, the models described here were found to be readily able to replicate base-year data to an adequate level of accuracy. However, the models still leave a considerable amount to be desired in their ability to produce acceptable forecasts. This is largely a result of the fact that the models are not based on sound reasoning of the actual processes that determine choice of mode of transportation. In general, the later models, which incorporated accessibility measures, were found to be insufficiently responsive to transit investments. This arises because the accessibility measures must necessarily be areawide and the effects of localized transit system changes become insignificant in such a formulation. Thus, potential improvements in the transit system are largely understated by the models, while decreases in transit usage resulting from increasing car ownership tend to dominate the forecasting process. Table 9-2 demonstrates this fairly clearly. A change of 0.2 in car ownership availability per household generally accounts for as much change in transit-use levels as two increments of the accessibility ratio. Assuming a constant level of automobile accessibility and zonal attractions, a fairly substantial transit service change would be necessary to change the accessibility ratio by two levels in this table.

It may also be noted, however, that almost all of the models that have been described relied basically upon some form of cross-classification analysis for their prediction process. Somewhat refreshingly, there has been a lack in the development of these models of misguided attempts to throw large quantities of data into a computer and allow it to churn them around and produce some form of probably spurious relationship, which would then be interpreted as a model.

**Trip-interchange Models**

The other principal type of modal split model is termed the trip-interchange model, because it seeks to split each trip-interchange volume between the available modes. It is therefore a modal split model that uses as input the specific trip interchanges produced by a trip-distribution model and provides output in terms of volume by mode for an assignment process. In general, the trip-interchange models have been developed more recently than the trip-end models.

The primary reason for the development of trip-interchange models is the relative unresponsiveness of the trip-end models to transit system changes, as discussed in the critique of the trip-end models. The primary cause of the unresponsiveness was identified as the gross accessibility measure used, which provided the only mechanism for incorporating transit system changes. It was seen that the only available procedure for improving the responsiveness of modal-split models was to change the location of the model in the travel-forecasting process, so that it could utilize more specific trip-making, and hence transportation system, information. The need to make such a change resulted from both the realization in the early 1960s that the automobile could not provide the sole solution to the urban transportation problems, and the new availability of federal funds for mass transit improvements at that time.

In order for modal-split models to be more responsive to transportation system changes, it was seen to be necessary to estimate modal split for individual zone pairs in the study area. Using such a strategy, the model would be able to relate transit ridership to specific level-of-service comparisons for every zone pair. Concomitantly, the sensitivity of the procedure to localized changes would improve. As a consequence of this change in rationale, starting in about 1960, a number of transportation studies started to develop trip-interchange models. Three of these models are examined here, in order to demonstrate the type of properties that these models have, the rationale on which they are based, and the general effectiveness of the models in terms of the task for which they are designed.

*Bay Area Transportation Study*

At about the turn of the decade, the San Francisco area[9] was investigating in depth the possibility of building a subway system, the system which is now known as BART (Bay Area Rapid Transit). The study included attempts to estimate the probable ridership of such a facility, in order to be able to determine various operating characteristics, such as the costs of running the system, and the fares that would be charged. As a result of this, a modal-split model was built to estimate the share of trips that the subway might be expected to obtain, by investigating each specific trip interchange.

A fairly large number of variables, of potential use in a modal-split model, were listed and curve fitting was carried out between each variable by itself and the existing measured transit share of trips, for each zonal interchange. As a result of this curve-fitting exercise, a number of the variables were rejected, leaving time ratio, a purpose split between work and other purposes, CBD and non-CBD orientation, and peak and off-peak as the only variables apparently significant in explaining transit share of the trips.

The curve-plotting process resulted in the identification of a particular shape of diversion curve, as shown in Figure 9-2, for which two alternative mathematical formulae were considered. These two formulae were the logit curve[10] and the Gompertz exponential curve. In comparing these two mathematical formulae, the investigators decided that the Gompertz exponential curve was the better of the two, since it approaches its asymptotes more rapidly than the logit curve does. Computations of correlation indices were carried out for each of the curves, and for those of greatest importance to rapid-transit travel estimates, such as peak-period work trips and CBD-oriented trips, the correlation indices were generally greater than 0.9.

*Washington-Toronto-Philadelphia Model*

Probably the most comprehensively developed model of modal-split to date is the one that was developed for the transportation studies in Washington, Toronto, and Philadelphia.[11] The model represents the first major attempt to hypothesize the decision process that may underlie modal split and to incorporate this process into a predictive model. The model uses five basic parameters:

1. Relative overall travel time of transit and auto
2. Relative overall travel cost of transit and auto
3. Relative excess travel time (out-of-vehicle time) of transit and auto
4. Income of the worker
5. Trip purpose

Each of the variables in this list that relate to the transportation system were formulated as ratios. The two overall factors, travel time and travel cost, were each expressed as ratios of the total door-to-door travel times and travel costs, respectively. In determining the costs for auto, costs for gas, oil, and lubrication, plus half of total parking costs, plus bridge tolls and any other highway tolls, were used as the basis of the one-way auto cost. The excess travel time was defined as the total time taken on each of transit and auto out of the vehicle together with the time spent moving in a vehicle not getting any closer to the desired destination, for example, time spent searching for a parking space.

Each of the remaining variables—income and trip purpose—were used as variables of stratification, trip purpose being stratified into work and

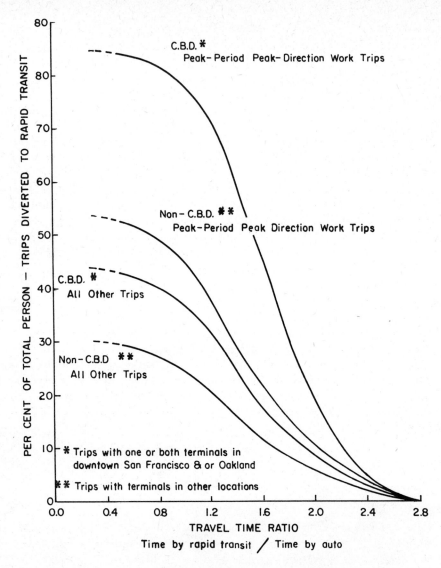

**Figure 9-2.** Bay Area Transportation Study Diversion Curves.

nonwork trips and income being stratified into five ranges. The process of analysis that was used by this study was that of the construction of diversion curves of use of transit against the time ratio for stratifications of the origin-destination trip volumes by the other four parameters. At this point, purpose was restricted to work, so that all subsequent analysis was conducted on work trips only. Cost ratios and excess-travel-time ratios were stratified into four ranges each. Thus a total of 80 separate diversion curves were fitted against time ratio, one curve for each possible combination of a range of cost ratio, excess-travel-time ratio, and income. At this point in the development of the model, the split in terms of modes was between auto and nonauto. Furthermore, the data were kept separate for each of the three locations: Washington, Toronto, and Philadelphia. Analyses were made of the accuracy of the models, in terms both of their expected errors and the correlations between time ratio and transit use. In general, the error analysis suggested that the models were predicting within a tolerable error range, and correlations were obtained between 0.86 and 1.00 for all diversion curves. The three different locations gave somewhat different ranges of cost ratios, time ratios and excess-travel-time ratios, so that it was hoped that it might be possible to combine the curves from the three cities in order to obtain diversion curves over the largest possible ranges of each of these variables, see Figure 9-3. In general, this process led to the extension, or extrapolation, of each of the diversion curves, since the differences between each of the curves were generally statistically insignificant at five percent but not at one percent. On the basis of these tests, the curves from the different cities were combined to give an extended range of validity for each of the parameters being used in the analysis.

As stated a little earlier, the analysis had so far been carried out using only a two-mode split. Another later refinement was to split the transit mode into its constituent submodes[12] and perform similar analyses on each of the submodes. On this basis, tests were again carried out to determine whether the diversion curves between auto and each separate submode were statistically significantly different. The results of these tests were that, in general, there was no significant difference. One should perhaps point out here that the division into submodes required the creation of four transit modes, along with auto, and therefore required the construction of four separate diversion curves for each category of cost ratio, excess-travel-time ratio, and income and purpose. Thus, a minimum of 320 separate diversion curves were to be constructed; and even though data were derived from three separate cities, the number of data points available for each curve has become small. The lack of a significant difference between curves for each of the separate submodes may well be due to the fact that the separate diversion curves have such wide confidence limits that an extremely large difference would be necessary between two curves for it to be statistically significant. Certainly, it appears that, in some instances, there were insufficient data for statistical testing.[13] It is interesting to note, on examining the curves produced, that once again a sigmoid ogive is the form hypothesized for the diversion curves. This is in agreement with the findings of the San Francisco Bay Area Study and may suggest the beginnings of a general hypothesis of modal split behavior.

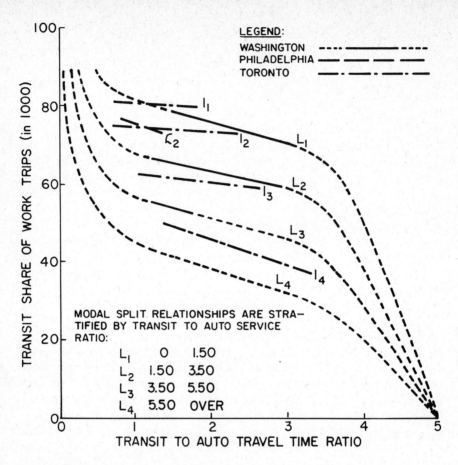

**Figure 9-3.** Example of Diversion Curves for the TRC Model.

The models produced in this exercise were subjected to fairly exhaustive sensitivity tests.[14] The findings of these tests are summarized in the following paragraphs.

The income factor was found to be adequately sensitive on a zonal basis, but had no apparent sensitivity on an areawide basis. The cost ratio was found to be sensitive over only a very limited range of values. The stratification of the cost ratio used in the model was such as to cause changes, beyond the very limited range, to be treated identically. Consequently, there was an inability of the model to reflect possible changes that were well outside the range of cost ratios encountered in the survey data. The excess-travel-time ratio was found to be highly sensitive over a whole range of realistic values, but was thought to be oversensitive in one respect. The excess-travel-time ratio involves the measurement of out-of-vehicle time, which can only be estimated very inaccurately. This time often amounts to less than five minutes. If excess time for transit is three minutes and for car is 1.5 minutes, the excess-travel-time ratio is 2. However, an error of 30 seconds in the measurement of either one of the excess times leads to a range of possible ratios from 1.5 to 3.0, while such an error in both excess times generates a range of possible true values from 1.25 to 3.5. In this respect, it was felt that the excess-travel-time ratio was somewhat overly sensitive to possible measurement errors.

The travel-time ratio was found to be reasonably sensitive over a wide range of predictions. However, it was found to be sensitive only to overall changes in times, and was insensitive to time changes from speed variations on just one given route.

In further pursuit of a full testing of the model, tests were made from the data of identical surveys carried out in Toronto in 1954 and 1964. An initial test was conducted by resubstituting the 1954 data into the model, .the results of which were that the predicted transit use was always within the range of daily volume fluctuation observed in 1954. Changes in the variables over the ten-year period were then fed into the model to provide predictions of the 1964 level of use of transit. The result was that the model predicted an overall increase in transit use of 66 percent in the peak periods. The actual increases in transit use from 1954 to 1964 were 73 percent in the morning peak and 55 percent in the evening peak, so that the 66 percent increase predicted by the model was probably very close to the average observed. Significance tests were carried out to test for significant differences between actual and predicted transit shares of trips at an intrazonal level. The results of these tests indicated that none of the predicted trip-interchange modal-split shares were significantly different from the actual measured values. In addition to this work, the model was also used to predict the patronage of the new Bloor-Danforth subway,[15] and the predictions of volumes at each specific station on the new line were generally predicted within five percent of the real volumes encountered on average during the first year of operation. Overall, the diversion of trips to the new subway line was predicted within two percent.

*Twin Cities Modal-split Model*

The Twin Cities modal-split model[16] was again developed in the early 1960s and was, again, an attempt to build a trip-interchange or postdistribution model. Attempts were made to include characteristics of the tripmaker, characteristics of the environment, and characteristics of the trip as pertinent variables in the model. The technique used, in this instance, was a simple regression approach, attempting to provide a linear relationship between the volume of trips on each mode for a specific interchange as a linear function of the set of three types of characteristics.

A total of nine variables were identified for analysis, which were:

1. Overall travel-time ratio
2. Median income of families and unrelated individuals
3. Housing units per net residential acre
4. Cars per housing unit
5. Accessibility to employment (ratio of transit to highway)
6. Nine-hour parking cost
7. Three-hour parking cost
8. Employment per gross acre
9. Accessibility to population

The models were developed for home-based trip purposes only, comprising home-based work, home-based school, and home-based other. For home-based work trips and home-based other trips, two models were developed which were deemed to be satisfactory, as shown in equations 9.8 and 9.9, together with the correlation coefficients for each model.

$$T_{ij}^{wt}/T_{ij}^{w} \times 100\% = 41.4 - 12.1 \text{ in (travel-time ratio)} - 4.4 \ln \text{ (income)}$$
$$+ 8.0 \ln \text{ (residential density)} + 1.3 \ln \text{ (employment density)}$$
$$+ 363.5 \text{ (9-hour parking cost)} \qquad (9.8)$$
$$r = 0.80$$

$$T_{ij}^{ot}/T_{ij}^{o} \times 100\% = 29.0 - 3.6 \ln \text{ (travel-time ratio)} - 3.2 \ln \text{ (income)}$$
$$+ 2.4 \ln \text{ (residential density)}$$
$$+ 285.2 \text{ (3-hour parking cost)} \qquad (9.9)$$
$$r = 0.79$$

where $T_{ij}^{wt}$ = number of work trips between zones $i$ and $j$ by transit

$T_{ij}^{w}$ = number of work trips between zones $i$ and $j$

$T_{ij}^{ot}$ = number of "other" trips between zones $i$ and $j$ by transit

$T_{ij}^{o}$ = number of "other" trips between zones $i$ and $j$

The apparent cutoff point for inclusion of a variable in these models was the 90 percent significance level, which is somewhat lower than is usually accepted. It is also noticeable that the variables included have fairly high intercorrelations, the results of which may be that the final model will tend to amass rather significant errors when used as a predictive model. In spite of the relatively low statistical performance of the variables and the high intercorrelations of the independent variables, the signs of the coefficients agree with a priori reasoning. Transit ridership is seen to decrease with increasing travel-time ratio (expressed as transit travel time divided by auto-travel time) and income, while it increases with increasing residential and employment densities and parking costs. It should be noted, however, that the models contain a serious inconsistency. The dependent variable is a percentage of transit trips that must lie between zero and 100 percent. However, the left-hand side of each model is theoretically unconstrained and may range from very large negative to very large positive values. Clearly, a sigmoid curve, of the type used by the San Francisco study and the Washington-Philadelphia-Toronto studies, would be more appropriate. Finally, it should be noted that not all the data were used for the model development. Low-volume trip interchanges were found to be "biased" and were excluded from the final calibration. Low-volume trip interchanges were defined as those comprising less than 250 trips (after expansion from the five percent sample).[17]

Testing of the models was carried out to establish whether or not they could replicate base-year data. It is not clear whether the data used for the test of base-year replication were, in fact, identical to that used for calibration. The comparison made at an interareal level, a higher level of aggregation than that used for calibration, was accepted as being sufficiently satisfactory and, clearly in this procedure, the properties of the regression procedure will not predetermine the accuracy results.

*Critique and Summary of Trip-interchange Models*

Once again, some critical evaluation of the models examined in this section is appropriate. In contrast to the trip-end models, the trip-interchange modal-split models described here have been developed on the basis of careful hypothesis formulation and appear to contain sufficient similarities to suggest that transferability might be possible. Indeed, in the work of Donald Hill and Hans von Cube,[18] a modal-split model has been developed for use in three different urban areas.

All of the models suggest a fairly optimistic outlook for mass transit, since they imply that increasing patronage is attainable by the provision of a sufficiently competitive level of service. This optimism may be rooted in the fact that four of the five urban areas dealt with in this section were already planning to provide improved transit service through the construction of new subway lines—BART, the Bloor-Danforth subway, the Lindenwold line in Philadelphia, and the Washington Metro.

Sceptically, one may suggest some elements of predetermination in modal-split modeling. The early trip-end models, as already discussed, indicated decreasing transit ridership and generally mandated the construction of more and better highway facilities, a conclusion generally being aimed for by the studies. In contrast, the trip-interchange models were mostly developed for studies in which the planning of a new transit facility was the primary concern and for which, increasing patronage levels are predicted.

Apart from the Twin Cities model, the trip-interchange models are all diversion-curve models. Only the Bay Area model provides a mathematical formulation for the diversion curves. Other diversion-curve models, including several not described here, rely on the use of graphical plots, or the reduction of the plots to cross-classification tables. Again, there is little use of the technique of linear regression in the development of these models.

Finally, it is notable that the trip-interchange modal-split models are consistent in their definition of competitiveness between automobile and transit. In all cases, as with the accessibility measures in the trip-end models, competitiveness is represented by a ratio. It does not appear, however, that this representation was based upon causal or empirical analysis and the concept has never been called into question within the transportation planning study. This question is dealt with more fully in chapter 16.

## Summary

Some of the comparative points between trip-end and trip-interchange models can be summarized by examining briefly the basic differences between these two types of models. The trip-end models gradually developed from being based simply on socioeconomic characteristics to being based upon these characteristics together with some indicators of the accessibility provided by the transportation system to all possible destinations in an urban area. In this development of modal-split models, it appears that it became clear that the trip-end models were unsatisfactory in that their ability to include and reflect changes in the transportation system was seriously below what might be expected or desired in the planning process. Furthermore, it seems rational to expect that the choice between alternative modes of transport, will depend upon various features of those competing modes. On these premises, the development of trip-interchange models appears to be a logical extension and improvement of the early modal-split models.

It may be noted, however, that the trip-end models and trip-interchange models still have one basic point in common: They are based on aggregate data, and fit within an aggregated model structure. In this respect, it may be expected that the models so devised will demonstrate ecological fallacies rather than true behavioral correlations, and that the relationships produced will tend to lack the validity over time that is a prerequisite of models required for forecasting.

Three basic techniques have been used in the development of these modal-split models, these being regression analysis, diversion curves, and cross-classification, or category analysis. In regression methods, several problems are encountered. In the first place, regression analysis aims at two almost incompatible goals, in terms of real-world problems. First, it aims to include enough variables to get an adequate explanation of the phenomenon to be modeled; and second, it aims to ensure that there are not so many colinear variables included that the errors in the regression variables become enormous. It is difficult to reach some compromise between these two aims, which rapidly become impossible to fulfill together when one considers the types of variables available, and appropriate for inclusion in a modal-split model. A second problem encountered in the use of regression analysis is that it is not usually possible to establish a one-way cause-and-effect relationship. As a result of this, it may be found that modal split is a function of car ownership, while car ownership may be a function of net residential density, income, and family size. The land-use planner, in attempting to estimate density, may also estimate a linear equation relating net residential density to income, family size, and labor-force participation rate. In general, these various modeling stages are carried on independently, and the estimates from one model are used as input to the next, and so forth. Effectively, this is a type of reduced-form solution of a set of simultaneous equations, where the reduced-form solution is valid only when simultaneous variation in the dependent variables is assumed not to occur. It is clear from this that the use of regression techniques in modal split will tend to generate the necessity for the development of a series of simultaneous equations, which should almost certainly be solved by a two-stage or three-stage least-squares technique.[19]

Two further complexities enter the picture in the use of regression techniques in these models: problems due to stratification or subdivision of the data base, and problems due to methods of judging the adequacy of the models. In the first of these, a common occurrence is that models are stratified on the basis of certain characteristics that affect or are assumed to affect modal split, but that cannot be built into the model as variables. Frequently, these include trip purpose, mode pairs, and also additional variables such as geographic location of zones, transit service index, etc. The addition of such stratifications to the process requires the generation of a large number of models on a relatively small data-base. As a result of this, the statistical reliability of each model produced and the resulting complexity of the prediction process, render the product extremely cumbersome and expensive to use, with a very questionable level of validity. The second problem is that the major tests that are available and used for judging the adequacy of the model are the correlation coefficient and $t$- and $F$-tests of significance. Frequently, it will occur that models which completely fulfill these statistical measures of adequacy are seriously inadequate for other reasons, particularly those based on the concepts and rationale of the modeling process.

The construction of diversion curves has been used in two different ways. In the first technique, a mathematical formulation approximating the observed plotted curve is used as the basis of providing a mathematical model. An analysis of this form was demonstrated by the Bay Area study, which used the Gompertz exponential curve. The other technique is to use the graphical representation directly, or through conversion into a cross-classification table. In this case, statistical measures of goodness-of-fit are largely unavailable, and problems of extrapolation are unexplored. It is interesting to note that those studies which used some form of curve plotting have tended in general to come up with some form of a sigmoid curve, or an approximation thereto, as being the form of the relationship between both transportation system and user characteristics and the share of trips by transit or auto. The last technique used is cross-classification, the problems of which have been discussed previously in connection with trip-generation models.[20]

Again, the models described in this chapter may be described in terms of the eight dimensions of models, previously outlined. In general, the modal-split models described here are aggregate, cross-sectional models. Because most of them estimate percentages of transit use, the models are more nearly probabilistic than deterministic. They are, however, unidirectional, forward-seeking models and are either analytical or statistical in structure. The early trip-end models are clearly homomorphic models, while the later trip-end models and the trip-interchange models are all isomorphic models. The trip-interchange models may also be considered to be predictive in form, while all the trip-end models tend to be descriptive models.

In summary, it would appear that the more recent modal-split models may be reasonably well-suited to the task of forecasting future transportation. Certainly, they are more suitable than any of the trip-generation and trip-distribution models described so far. It may perhaps be concluded that the lack of any standardized process for modal-split estimation has been advantageous in fostering considerably more research and development of modal-split procedures.

# 10 Network Assignment

## Introduction

Network assignment constitutes the final stage in the travel-forecasting process described in the preceding chapters. This step involves the assignment of the distributed volumes of trips, by mode, to individual network links. Among the choices or decisions that make up the entire trip-making decision process, it represents the choice of route.

The basis of network assignment assumes that a choice of route is a choice to minimize total travel time. It is, therefore, assumed that the total travel time on the path used will be less than or equal to the time on all paths not used for any given interzonal trip. It is also assumed that travel times over the routes that are used will be equal to or less than the travel times over all routes not used, with the exception of saturated routes. The application of trip assignment in this form assumes that the only costs which are variable with route are those costs associated with travel time, which in turn assumes present methods for charging for travel by road. It also assumes that each traveler is fully aware of all the alternative routes by which he might travel.

Network assignment, as such, is not to be regarded as a modeling process in the same sense in which trip generation, distribution, and modal split are modeling processes. Rather, network assignment is an attempt to determine a minimum time-path through a network, on the basis of which travel volumes are assigned to the network. The form of calculation that is carried out in network assignment requires the identification of the minimum-time paths for each interzonal trip movement, followed by an assignment of the interzonal volumes to those particular routes. According to the sophistication of the assignment procedure being used, an iterative process may then be used in which travel times are recalculated on the basis of the loaded network, new minimum-time paths calculated, and traffic reassigned on the basis of the loaded travel times. Such an iteration would be repeated until, hopefully, an equilibrium status is achieved.

## Minimum-path Algorithm

Before minimum-path algorithms are discussed, it is necessary to put forth some definitions of network technology. A *branch* or *link* is defined as a connection between two adjacent nodes. A *path* constitutes a series of adjacent links that can be traversed without covering any one link more than once. A *tree* is defined as a collection of connected branches or links. A number of additional definitions were presented in the appropriate context in chapter 5.

The basic component of the network assignment model is an algorithm to seek out the minimum-time paths or trees through the network. The basic algorithm that is usually used in these models is some version of E.F. Moore's[1] algorithm. The algorithm is a tree-building process that adds the shortest distance/time link in a network, connected to a node already in the tree, but where the link is not yet in the tree. The algorithm constitutes a basic dynamic programming solution.

This particular algorithm determines a minimum-route tree by considering successive closest nodes, starting out from a given origin node and building up a tree, or set of branches, representing the minimum path from that node to all other nodes. Thus, this algorithm starts at a specific node in the system, and then seeks out the closest node to the one that it is at, at the present time. The search procedure is then continued, to determine the next closest, and these nodes are recorded to make up a minimum-time-path tree.

Figures 10-1 and 10-2 and Table 10-1 illustrate the procedure prescribed by the minimum-path algorithm. Using the hypothetical network of Figure 10-1, minimum-time-path trees from node 1 to nodes 2 and 3 can be built by starting at node 1 and adding the shortest link from 1, which is clearly link (1-30) with a travel time of 2.0 minutes. When more than one node has the same travel time from the origin, the lowest numbered node is taken, and the process builds by considering cumulative times.

Since the intent is to build a tree that branches to each node only once, each link that joins a node into the system which has previously been reached by a shorter route is disregarded. Examining the resulting paths, a minimum-time-path of 16.0 minutes to zone 2 and of 21.0 minutes to zone 3 has been developed. At the same time, minimum-time-paths to every node in the network were produced. Figure 10-2 shows the minimum-time tree for zone 1.

The algorithm takes a considerable amount of time to compute for this very simple network, so it is fortunate that a computer algorithm has been developed for applying Moore's algorithm. There is, however, no need to spend time examining the computer version, since this is well-documented and the basic principle is identical to the process illustrated above.

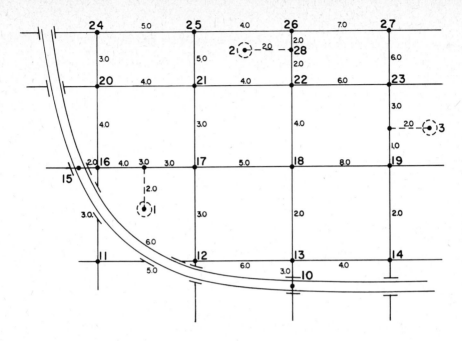

**Figure 10-1.** Hypothetical Transportation Network.

## Table 10-1
### Listing of Cumulative Travel Times among Links

| Link Added | Cumulative Travel Time | Link Added | Cumulative Travel Time |
|---|---|---|---|
| ( 1, 30) | 2.0 | X (18, 22) | 14.0 X erase |
| (30, 17) | 5.0 | (22, 28) | 14.0 |
| (30, 16) | 6.0 | X (13, 10) | 15.0 X erase |
| (17, 12) | 8.0 | (13, 14) | 16.0 |
| (16, 15) | 8.0 | (28,  2) | 16.0 |
| (17, 21) | 8.0 | (28, 26) | 16.0 |
| (16, 11) | 9.0 | X (26, 25) | 17.0 X erase |
| (17, 18) | 10.0 | (14, 19) | 18.0 |
| (16, 20) | 10.0 | X (18, 19) | 18.0 X erase |
| (18, 13) | 12.0 | (22, 23) | 18.0 |
| (21, 22) | 12.0 | X (24, 25) | 18.0 X erase |
| (20, 24) | 13.0 | (19, 29) | 19.0 |
| (21, 25) | 13.0 | (29,  3) | 21.0 |
| (15, 10) | 14.0 | X (23, 29) | 21.0 X erase |
| X (11, 12) | 14.0 X erase | (26, 27) | 23.0 |
| X (20, 21) | 14.0 X erase | X (23, 27) | 24.0 X erase |
| X (12, 13) | 14.0 X erase | | |

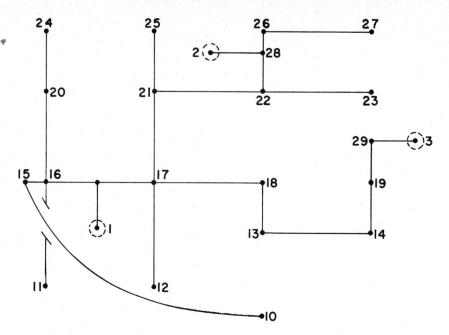

**Figure 10-2.** Minimum-time Paths Between Zones 1, 2, and 3.

## Highway-network Assignment

The basic requirements of data for running an assignment process are determined according to the sophistication of the assignment to be applied. This information (required for running the average assignment program) would include a comprehensive coding of the network, the locating and numbering of centroids of zones, and designation of access links from the zone centroids onto the network, and information on travel times, on parking, on design speeds, etc., for each link in the network. The assignment procedure would then give as output a total volume of vehicles or people on each link, together with turning movements at each node, travel costs and times for use in evaluation procedures, and vehicle-miles of travel at given levels of service on the network.

There are, basically, five general methods that are used in traffic assignment: all-or-nothing assignment with no capacity restraint; diversion-curve assignment with no capacity restraint; all-or-nothing assignment with capacity restraint; diversion and proportional assignment with capacity restraint; and incremental assignment with capacity restraint. Basically, assignment can be carried out either on 24-hour or peak-hour interzonal movements. Assignment by purpose or mode of travel is also possible.

## All-or-Nothing Assignments

Basically, an all-or-nothing assignment is one that loads all travelers between two points in a network onto the single minimum-time path connecting those two points. This is exactly what is meant by all-or-nothing. The simplest all-or-nothing assignments are uncapacitated assignments, which simply compute a single minimum-time path, based on free-flow traffic conditions through the network, and assign all traffic on the basis of these minimum-time paths. A number of alternative refinements of this process are possible.

The first refinement is one of introducing some idea of capacity restraint. This attempts to address the fact that once traffic is loaded onto the network, the original free-flow travel times will not generally be the appropriate travel times that the traffic will experience. As a result of this, some attempt is made to recompute travel times on the basis of the loaded network, and then reassign traffic on the basis of the new travel times. In order to apply this type of assignment, it then becomes necessary to carry out an iterative procedure, in which the travel times on each link on the network are computed at the end of each assignment, and used as the input to the tree-building process for the next assignment. The procedure continues until some sort of equilibrium is established in the system.

Capacity restraint can be made either a part of the computer program that carries out the assignment, or may be applied manually after obtaining the single unrestrained all-or-nothing assignment. The basis of most capacity-restraint techniques is the utilization of some form of capacity-restraint function, in the form of a volume-to-capacity ratio. A number of alternative formulations of a capacity-restraint equation are available. A brief look at one or two of these is presented below.

The Traffic Assignment Manual of the Bureau of Public Roads (BPR)[2] details a capacity-restraint function of the form shown in equation 10.1.

$$T = T_0\left[1 + 0.15 \left(\frac{\text{Volume}}{\text{Capacity}}\right)^4\right] \qquad (10.1)$$

where  $T_0$ = travel time on the link at zero volume

$T$ = assigned travel time for assigned volume on the link

This formula is derived from an S-shaped curve representing the rate of change of speed, relative to speed at practical capacity, against the increase of $V/C$ ratio.

An alternative function is that proposed by A.S. Rathnau[3] for use by the Chicago Area Transportation Study. This function is based on a similar curve, but is given by equation 10.2.

$$T = T_0 \, (2)^{V/C} \tag{10.2}$$

where    $T$ and $T_0$ are as before

and     $V$ = assigned volume

        $C$ = practical capacity

This relationship is somewhat more arbitrary than the BPR formula, since it represents only a very loose approximation to the empirical relationship between Volume/Capacity and speed.

     A rather more complex process has been proposed by the Road Research Laboratory (RRL),[4] which attempts to compute link times from the basic geometrics of the roadway, and the assigned volume. Five assumptions are made in deriving the formula:

1. Travel time on a link in any direction is affected only by the volume in that direction.
2. Journey-speed/flow and running-speed/flow relationships are linear and intersect at zero flow.
3. The rate of change of running speed with the flow $(dr/dg)$ in the same direction on a road of given total width is given by equation 10.3.

$$\frac{dr}{dg} = -\frac{2}{3(w - 6)} \tag{10.3}$$

     where    $w$ = average total pavement width.

4. There is an overriding maximum speed of 24 mph.
5. There is a minimum speed of 3 mph.

The RRL formula, based on these assumptions, is shown in equation 10.4.

$$j = R + \frac{2}{3(w - 6)} - q\left[\frac{R - J}{Q} + 3(w - 6)\right] \qquad 3 \le j \le 24 \tag{10.4}$$

where    $j$ = journey speed

        $q$ = flow in the same direction

        $w$ = average total pavement width

        $Q$ = observed flow level

        $J$ = corresponding observed journey speed at flow level $Q$

        $R$ = observed running speed at flow level $Q$

     This relationship has been found, in practice, to involve a large number of iterations for a satisfactory convergence, and work is still in progress to attempt to improve it.

Numerous other attempts have been made to determine the speed/volume relationships that should be used, but the ones reviewed here represent the basic principles quite adequately.

The basic attributes of an all-or-nothing capacity-restrained assignment have been presented now. However, the procedure identified so far contains at least one major fault. This fault arises from the fact that, as outlined here, the assignment process involves iterations within each of which a complete new assignment is computed. The result of this complete new assignment is the generation of an instability of loadings in the system, arising out of the fact that subsequent iterations for an overloaded link will tend to alternately overload one link and provide no load on another link, and reverse this in the next iteration. In general, the practice is to average the results of several iterative assignments of this type, and thus arrive at a final estimated system loading. An alternative to this procedure is to use either a random or partial loading assignment.

**Random Assignments.** The basic principle of the random assignment is the generation of several random orderings of the zone-to-zone movements to be assigned to a network. The assignment procedure is then undertaken by assigning a single zone pair at a time, and recomputing minimum-time paths after each zone pair has been loaded onto the network. By this means, each succeeding assignment takes into account the existence of traffic on certain parts of the network. Clearly, a single random assignment will have a result that is highly dependent upon the actual ordering of the assignment of zone-to-zone movements. Thus, it becomes necessary to make a series of assignments based on alternative random sequences, and again average the results that are obtained, in order to generate the most probable assignment of traffic to the total network.

**Partial Assignments.** The second refinement that is possible comprises a partial assignment process, in which a given percentage of all traffic movements are assigned at one time and minimum-time paths recomputed after that portion has been assigned, as the basis for the next identical proportion to be assigned. For instance, this assignment might proceed by a decision to load ten percent of all interzonal movements onto the network at one time. Thus, first the minimum-time paths are computed on the basis of zero flow throughout the network. On the basis of these minimum-time paths, the first ten percent of all the interzonal movements are assigned to the network. At the conclusion of this loading, minimum-time paths are recomputed, based upon the travel times on each link achieved with the first ten percent of traffic of the links. The second ten percent is then loaded onto the network, on the basis of the new minimum-time paths. This process is repeated until the entire interzonal movements have been assigned to the network. Since ordering of trips within each interzonal movement has, basically, no effect upon the assignment, this partial assignment results in a more acceptable initial answer than does a single random assignment.

These, then, represent the usual variations on the basic all-or-nothing assignment process, in varying degrees of sophistication. To summarize, basically an all-or-nothing assignment assigns all traffic to a minimum-time path through the network. In order to make this process somewhat more realistic, various modifications can be made. In the first instance, the assignment may be reiterated, with a capacity-restraint equation used that will change the travel times on each link in relation to the traffic assigned to the link. On the basis of a series of iterations, an assignment can be obtained that is responsive to the capacity limitations of the network. As further modifications, the assignment process may be undertaken as a sequential, randomly ordered loading process, in which each fresh interzonal movement is assigned to the network, taking into account traffic already assigned to the network; or a partial sequential assignment may be undertaken, in which the traffic between each pair of zones is assigned by a certain percentage at each step in an assignment process. Basically, these different modifications still have certain properties in common. They assume an all-or-nothing type of assignment, in which each trip is assumed to be undertaken on the minimum-time path through the network and they all assume that the only determinant of the choice of route is time.

*Diversion and Proportional Assignments*

The basic difference between all-or-nothing assignments and the diversion or proportional assignments is the fact that the latter two types of assignments try to assign traffic to more than one route between two points. The alternatives of a diversion or a proportional assignment indicate that either two routes or two or more routes are used for the assignment. However, the assignments performed by these means are basically very similar to the all-or-nothing assignment, in that they use a minimum-time path for the initiation of the procedure, and then find alternative paths at slightly greater times than the minimum for the other alternative routes. Thus, these assignments, like the all-or-nothing assignment, are founded principally upon an hypothesis that the basis of choice of route is a consideration of travel time only.

**Diversion Assignment.** In diversion assignment, the basic rationale comprises the determination of the minimum and next-shortest time paths through the network for every zone pair, and the assignment proceeds on the basis of a diversion curve that gives the percentage of traffic on the longer route as a function of the difference or ratio of travel times of the two available routes. The basic model is, therefore, somewhat similar to the concepts in the modal-split model developed by the Traffic Research Corporation.[5] Once again, as with the all-or-nothing assignment, some form of capacity restraint may be implemented, in order to ensure that the loads on each link are conformal with the capacity of the link, and that the travel times on which the minimum-time paths have been found are more or less realistic in terms of speed-flow relationships on each link.

**Proportional Assignment.** The other alternative, proportional assignment, comprises a further extension of the diversion assignment to a multiple set of routes. In general, this type of assignment has not been widely used, at least in part because of the complexity of building programs and models for it. It is usually necessary to attempt to build a mathematical model that will assign proportions of traffic among a number of alternative routes, as a function of the time differences or time ratios between those alternatives. Basically, the relationship will appear somewhat like a multimodal-split model, in which proportions of traffic are assigned to the alternative routes that have been computed in a manner that attempts to approximate that which is observed in practice. Again, the model is basically carrying out an assignment using the total travel time as the determinant of route choice. In this case, it becomes necessary to work out not only a minimum path, but a large number of additional paths, with the number being determined by the relative times, as dealt with in the model of proportional assignment. An example of a proportional assignment is one developed by the Traffic Research Corporation.[6] This model uses travel times to determine minimum paths between the zones. After carrying out an initial distribution of trips, using ideal travel times, the entire network is loaded on the basis of a minimum-time path, all-or-nothing assignment. At this point, the loads on the links in the network are checked, and travel times are adjusted according to a set of relationships between travel time and flow, and the speed on the link. A new set of routes is then generated, using the adjusted travel times; but unlike the capacity-restrained all-or-nothing assignment, the volumes between zones are split between the old routes and the new routes in inverse proportion to the travel times on the old route and the new route. On this basis, as many as four alternative routes may share a particular interzonal volume. The method is, however, extremely time consuming and expensive to use, and is subject to substantial variation in the output as a function of the loading sequence and of the somewhat arbitrary capacity functions.

A more recent sophistication of the assignment process was proposed by J.E. Burrell.[7] He proposes a capacity-restrained multiple route assignment that builds multiple routes between nodes, but not between zones (or load nodes). The process is carried out by assuming that people do not have an exact knowledge of the time for a trip, and uses instead a random distribution of link times about the "true" link time as the basis for minimum-path routing. All the travelers from one zone are assumed to have the same perception of link travel times (to reduce computational complexity), where these travel times are drawn at random from a normal distribution with mean of the "true" time and standard deviation of 20 percent of the actual link time. A set of minimum-time paths is then obtained for that zone to all other zones.

For the next zone, a new set of random link times is drawn and minimum-time paths computed. Capacity restraint is accomplished by the usual iterative technique, in which the minimum-time paths are again computed, using random variations around the actual link time. The degree of sophistication of this process is largely a function of the amount of time and money available for using the model. It is clearly possible to assign separate link times to every individual in the system and compute minimum-time paths for each person. This would clearly be inordinately expensive. However, any level of sophistication between this and zonal-link times is possible.

## Transit Assignment

The foregoing sections of this chapter have dealt primarily with assignment to highway networks. There has, however, been increasing interest in and development of techniques for transit assignments during the last decade or so. These developments have largely coincided with the change to trip-interchange modal-split models and incorporation of greater sensitivity of the modeling process to levels-of-service for transit.

The basic path-finding algorithm is the same for transit assignments as it is for highway assignments, and the options of all-or-nothing or multipath assignments also exist. It should be noted that relatively few urban areas have a sufficiently complex network to warrant multipath transit assignment. However, the network data, the requirements for network-coding, and the need for special "flags" in the network-coding are different from highway assignments.

The required data include the frequencies (headways) of vehicles on a route, the capacities of the vehicles, speed of travel along each link, and a route code. Nodes are defined at each boarding and alighting point. Variations occur in the treatment of lengths of right-of-way with more than one route traversing them. In some assignment procedures, each route, whether or not it uses the same right-of-way, is coded as a discrete set of links. In other procedures, common rights-of-way are treated as common links and the frequency on the link is the sum of the individual frequencies of the routes traversing the common links. Both treatments lead to some problems. Combination of all routes on a single link suggests misleadingly high frequency of service that is not maintained once the routes diverge. On the other hand, separation of the routes leads to serious difficulties in analyzing network loadings. These problems will be referred to again in later sections of this chapter.

In addition to the links representing the traveled way, two further sets of links must be coded. First, loading links are required connecting transit stops to the zone centroids. These links are coded with average appropriate access or egress times. For example, for a bus network, the times would be average zonal walking times to bus stops located in or near the zone. Second, connecting links are required between transit routes where interchanges may take place. This interchange is coded with any walking time that is appropriate and an average waiting time for transfer from one route to another. It is possible to add an interchange penalty, if so desired, to reflect the lower utility of interchanging compared with through-routing. In the event that discrete network coding of multiple routes is adopted, "flags" are needed in the network coding to indicate the route number being followed, in order to prevent indiscriminate shifting of travelers from one route to another, along the shared right-of-way. These signal values are somewhat similar to the incorporation of "turn-penalties" in highway-network assignments.

From this point, the procedure is very much the same as that used in highway-network assignments. The first step is to find the minimum-time paths through the network[8] in order to construct a set of minimum-time trees. If a multipath assignment is used, then the necessary number of paths are determined, starting with the minimum-time paths and then selecting subsequent longer paths for each origin zone. Trips are then allocated to the trees for each origin zone, as in the highway-network assignment. Problems arise at this point for dealing with road-based transit systems. In order to simulate actual travel speeds on the network, under forecast conditions, it is necessary to load transit vehicles and automobiles simultaneously on the common parts of the network. Techniques for doing this are still under development. Traditionally, buses have been assigned first and their road-space requirements calculated on each link. These requirements are subsequently subtracted from the capacities of the highway links, thus effectively giving buses a priority they do not, in practice, enjoy. This process also leads to the calculation of unrealistically low travel times for the buses, since they are effectively loaded onto the network under free-flow conditions. This problem can be partially resolved by iterating the two assignments, but no guarantee of convergence can be made. Finally, problems also arise in interfacing the various network assignments, where one mode may provide access to a second mode. For example, if a transit network for commuter railroads is defined, access to the stations may be by foot, automobile, or bus. Since the entire transportation-planning process is set up without explicit recognition of access and egress modes, the actual mix of such modes may not be known. In addition, even were the modes to be known, the interfacing of the different networks is not currently possible.

## Summary

In terms of the model dimensions discussed in chapter 2, network assignment models can be characterized as aggregate, cross-sectional, and unidirectional in nature. They are forward-seeking, homomorphic, and descriptive models. Their structure is that of simulation models.

In general, all the techniques discussed in this chapter have been based on assignment to a minimum-time path through a network. The assignments are founded upon the hypothesis that the basis of route choice is a consideration of travel time only.

The simpler all-or-nothing assignments generally show problems of instability and lack of realism, in that they do not replicate base-year volumes very accurately. Although the random and partial assignment techniques constitute certain refinements in the assignment procedure, they also introduce some artificiality into the process. For example, since travel times are increased after each random or partial assignment, traffic will be assigned at a wide range of different "speeds" on the network.

Diversion and proportional assignments take into account alternative routes to the minimum-time path. They assign traffic to more than one route between two points, but the definition of alternative routes is still time-based.

The techniques of transit assignment are quite similar in their basic approach and rationale. The characteristics of transit operation, however, add a considerable amount of complexity to the basic procedure.

The transportation planner's understanding of the underlying mechanisms of capacity constraint and route choice are still rather limited. Only gradual refinements and sophistications can be observed in this phase of the urban transportation-planning process.

# 11

## Transportation-plan
## Evaluation

### Introduction

The phases of the urban transportation-planning (UTP) process described in the preceding five chapters have led to the development of projected travel volumes on the transportation network for each of the relevant modes. These volumes will exceed the present capacities of certain segments of the transportation system. The transportation planner is faced with the responsibility of developing a number of alternative transportation plans capable of accommodating these future travel volumes. The formulation of such transportation plans has to be considered the final goal of the UTP process. These plans have to be evaluated in terms of their respective consequences in order to provide the basis for decision making. Examples of relevant consequences are considerations of pollution, energy consumption, modal shares, route diversions, and the attainment of specific levels of service.

This chapter addresses some questions and problems relating to the plan evaluation phase of the UTP process. The authors recognize that an in-depth coverage of this economic evaluation process would far exceed acceptable length limitations of this book. Consequently, this chapter only provides a rather cursory treatment of the relevant aspects of the plan evaluation phase in the UTP process.[1]

The evaluation process essentially attempts to answer the question: Is a plan worthwhile? A series of supplementary questions is triggered by this basic query, whose answers will ultimately be directed towards providing a solution to the basic problem about the worthwhileness of a proposed transportation plan.[2]

In order to indicate the worthwhileness of a plan, the basic question has to be answered as to whom the plan should be considered worthwhile. Principally, the question needs to be posed in terms of user or nonuser. Traditionally, most highway projects have been evaluated in terms of the users alone, which would typically imply the generation of suboptimal solutions. Today, planners are concerned to attempt to identify a full spectrum of consequences that include the users, nonusers, and the total environment. It is probable that considerable efforts will be made in the future to identify wider consequences than those presently identified.

Another question that needs to be answered is one concerned with

211

timing. In posing a question concerning the worthwhileness of a plan, it is also necessary to ask when it will be worthwhile. The majority of plans produced by the urban transportation-planning process are of sufficient size that it becomes necessary to consider them as taking effect after not less than, say, five to ten years, and to consider their worthwhileness in terms of their likely completion date. This also raises a whole series of further possibilities such as phased, or staged construction.

Finally, the length of the planning horizon for the plans to be evaluated has significant implication on the weighting of projects in terms of their relative merits. It probably is a reasonable assumption that planning will take place under conditions of uncertainty, irrespective of the sophistication of the planner's modeling tools. Essentially this uncertainty is caused by the fact that complete control over all the factors that constitute the planning environment, cannot be achieved. Principally, this level of uncertainty requires a certain degree of flexibility in the overall planning process. This also suggests that phasing or staging in plan implementation is necessary. Thus, plans should be carried out in such a way that allows for adjustments in plan or overall goals, as changes in the planning environment occur over time.

**Ideal Evaluation Scheme**

In order to be able to make a complete evaluation of a plan, or set of alternative plans, there are several necessary requirements. As was implied already, there is a necessity to define and enumerate a complete spectrum of consequences. It is then necessary to devise a means of measuring consequences in such terms that it is possible to either place weights on each consequence for a total evaluation, or be able to evaluate all consequences in a common dimension so that they are automatically weighted.

The concept of weighting immediately introduces a new problem. If it is necessary to devise external weightings on each consequence, this implies a significant potential for bias and ambiguity. The question of who has the right or the ability to determine the weights is immediately raised. It is a thorny problem, and little has been done so far to attempt to answer it satisfactorily. In general, the planner has an obligation to strive for objectivity in evaluation, but he will find that the requirements of the process are such as to leave him little alternative to a large measure of subjectivity.

The identification of the full spectrum of consequences is part of a larger requirement for comprehensiveness in the planning effort. At each stage in the process, the planner wishes to strive for a level of comprehensiveness. This does not mean that he is trying to plan everything, but rather that he wants to ensure that everything pertinent throughout the process is considered. It is also necessary that the process is comprehensible as well as comprehensive. If all the interactions and modeling processes underlying the comprehensive planning effort cannot be understood, then that effort becomes questionable. Thus, it may be necessary to determine a trade-off between comprehensiveness and comprehensibility.

The planning process is carried out in a state of uncertainty. The impact of uncertainty on the plans needs to be known. Given present modeling abilities, the impacts on the plans of the expected range of errors of the models should be determined. Ideally, this process should be taken further, to show the impact on any set of plans of future uncertainty, over and above that of the modeling tools themselves.

The overall evaluation system that is implied in what is considered here is likely to be complex. A further feature of the ideal evaluation system, possibly rather hard to conceive within the system defined in this section, is that it should be simple. The plans and the evaluation of each plan are necessary inputs to the total process; and it is at this point that the process principally moves into the domain of the political decision maker, and out of the hands of the systems expert. This requires that the output has a sufficient degree of simplicity that it can be handled by the decision maker.

The need for flexibility is clearly a further requirement of the ideal evaluation system. As a subset of this, it is also necessary to provide within the system the means to effect feedback and to take account of different opinions and attitudes. The feedback process is essentially a part of the original systems analysis formulation, and comprises a means wherewith to modify the original goals, objectives, or criteria on the basis of the evaluation phase of a previous run through the system. It is likely that, after an initial run through the planning process, the evaluation of the first set of alternative plans may suggest modifications that should be made in the form of added or changed objectives or criteria. It is possible that the evaluation could even cause a complete change of goals. For instance, the planner's goal for an urban area may be to cater for the level of travel demand in, say, 30 year's time, in such a way as to ensure that travel times are no greater then than they are now. A further goal may have been added of attaining this level of travel supply without imposing more than a pre-specified amount of adverse consequences on nonusers as a result of it. At the end of a first run through the planning process, it may be determined that the result of supplying this level of capacity for travel, by any alternative available, will generate a level of atmospheric and ground pollution that will pose a serious and consistent threat to health. This may suggest a modification of the original goals to place certain air and water pollution standards as a higher priority goal than catering for the level of travel demand of 30 year's time.

## Costs and Benefits

Effectively, the preceding discussion has identified the need to determine both the costs and the benefits of any investment plan. At this point, the nature of those costs and benefits should be considered. These may be identified from a number of viewpoints. The respective viewpoint will determine a different relevant set of costs and benefits. For the purposes of the present exposition, these costs and benefits are viewed from a broad public standpoint. The extensive and likely nontransportation impacts will not be considered in detail at this stage since the concern of this chapter is the examination of a present evaluation methodology rather than ideal, or possibly near-future, methodologies.

A number of costs can be identified:

1. Construction and land acquisition costs for the facility
2. Costs of relocation of residences and businesses, and other social costs
3. Maintenance, operation, and administration costs of the new facility
4. User travel costs
5. Accident costs
6. Terminal costs

Similarly, potential benefits could be among the following:

1. User travel benefits
2. Facility-associated nonuser benefits
3. Other nonuser benefits
4. Intergovernmental transfers

In general, the items listed above are the principal costs and benefits to be considered in conventional evaluation processes. The specific items under each heading and the methods for putting values on them could be discussed at some length, but such discussions would exceed the scope of this book.

The magnitude of the costs and benefits listed above is clearly a function of the scope of the relevant transportation plan and its associated transportation operation and facilities. The latter are, of course, based on the results of the demand modeling phases in the UTP process. The importance of that phase and the requirement for good estimates of future travel cannot be stressed too much.

## Alternative Evaluation Criteria

Economic evaluation requires a comparison of streams of costs and benefits over the life of a project. This fact puts further demands on the accuracy of the travel-forecasting procedure in that streams of costs and benefits cannot be computed unless reliable estimates exist of future travel on a year-by-year basis.

A number of possible evaluation criteria can be proposed that may partially lead toward an ideal evaluation system. A few of these are mentioned here.

*Least Costs*

This requires the choice of that plan that costs the least. The definition of costs in this criterion is the major determinant of the effectiveness of it. Cost can be defined simply as the total outlay to be made in carrying out the plan, in terms of construction, new equipment, etc. Under this criterion, a "do-nothing" alternative would clearly always be the best plan. Any extension beyond this requires the costing, or monetary evaluation, of many items affected by the plans, such as travel time and congestion. Extensions in this direction will generally lead to one of the later, more sophisticated methods.

*Maximum Benefit*

A second criterion could be that of determining the benefit to accrue from each plan, and choosing that one for which benefits are a maximum. The usual application of this criterion requires the evaluation of benefits in monetary units. It will largely ignore costs but will assess the total benefits from each plan, often in terms of users alone. It will generally have different results from the application of least-cost criteria.

*Least Harm*

This criterion is a somewhat negative one in that it starts out by presupposing that plans will result in harm to a number of people. Again, its application requires the evaluation of the amount of harm that would result from each plan, and thence the choice of that plan which minimizes harm. Customarily, the application of this method is based on the evaluation of harm in an economic sense, and therefore may approach the least-cost criterion.

Although these criteria are not mutually exclusive, application of them is generally in isolation from each other. The techniques of benefit-cost computations are an attempt to combine the first two criteria into a single evaluation process.

Most of the evaluation work that has been done in the past has been carried out in relation to highway projects only. Thus, much of the terminology associated with evaluation, of the more traditional forms at least, is based on highway applications.

## Basic Principles of Economic-evaluation Techniques

Economic-evaluation techniques are based upon an examination of the relationship between costs and benefits of alternative plans, projects, or strategies. A necessary prerequisite for the applicability of these evaluation techniques is that costs and benefits for the alternatives can be identified by a common measurement unit, usually comprising the appropriate monetary unit. The economic evaluation techniques are basically a comparison of the monetary benefits and costs of alternative projects.

The objective of these techniques is, first, to establish the economic feasibility of any given alternative, and second, to rank these alternatives in order of decreasing desirability. The first objective implies that for an alternative to be economically feasible, its benefits would have to be at least equal to costs, and preferably exceed them. A comparison between economically feasible alternatives is made in order to determine which alternative provides the greatest benefit relative to its cost.

Costs and benefits are incurred over a certain period, namely the life of the project. This implies that the computation of costs and benefits has to be based on some type of discount rate in order to determine the streams of costs and benefits over the project life. This computation also demands a travel-forecasting process that is capable of providing estimates of annual facility usage throughout the life of the project. In the absence of such a process, the computation of streams of costs and benefits has to be based upon heroic assumptions of growth patterns over the project life.

Another question that underlies these economic evaluation techniques is that of who incurs the costs of a project and to whom the benefits will go. In this context consideration has to be given as to whether costs and benefits relate to the private or the public sector. A further question arises, namely as to whether users of transportation facilities and services, or nonusers, or both are affected. In traditional highway evaluation strategies, the public sector viewpoint has usually been taken, but with costs and benefits restricted to those of the public agency providing the facility and the users of the facility. Only recently has this viewpoint been interpreted more broadly to include nonusers.

## Concept of Cost-effectiveness

There are two main shortcomings that can be identified from the preceding discussion of alternative evaluation criteria and the basic principles of economic-evaluation techniques. First, an explicit assumption is made that all costs and benefits can be measured in monetary equivalents. From an economist's viewpoint, this further limits costs and benefits to those that are reflected in the GNP. The second shortcoming is that standard economic-evaluation techniques only allow for user benefits and costs to enter into the computations. There is typically no provision for the inclusion of nonuser costs and benefits.

In terms of the first assumption, a considerable amount of work has been carried out from time to time on the evaluation of travel time.[3] This relatively simple-sounding concept generates some very serious problems. The economist would have it that only working-time trips be given a monetary value, since this is the only time that contributes, or has potential contribution, to the GNP. Working time may be evaluated as either wage rate, or the worth of the employee to his employer, which would be the wage rate plus an overhead. The evaluation of travel time that is consumed outside working hours is a much thornier problem.

The computation of monetary equivalents for other, nonmonetary, concomitant effects is subject to questions of validity, as well as questions of feasibility. In terms still of the users, how does one set about evaluating the strain of driving in heavy traffic? Is it even valid to consider that such a user disbenefit can be conceived of as a monetary measure? The problem is seriously compounded when it comes to a consideration of nonuser costs and benefits. The infeasibility and questionable validity of such valuation processes has led to the development of the cost-effectiveness approach. The basis of the approach is an attempt to measure the effectiveness of each alternative to achieve a set of prestated goals at minimum cost.[4] Thus, the goals can be set up in a diversity of dimensions applicable to the various concomitant effects to be considered, and comparisons made of achievement, or lack of it, of each alternative. This permits an evaluation of all the concomitant effects with no presuppositions of valuing the effects. This approach is not without problems, and is not widely adopted as yet in the planning field. However, it holds out promise as a feasible principle for a better evaluation than can be achieved with the greatest degree of sophistication of the standard economic-evaluation approaches typically applied in the conventional UTP process.

# 12 Critique of the Conventional Urban Transportation-planning Process

## Introduction

Chapters 6 through 10 have provided a description of the different modeling phases included in the standard urban transportation-planning process. Even the casual reader will have become aware of a number of serious implications resulting from the structure of these models, their underlying assumptions, and the lack of interaction among these models. The development of future research directions in urban transportation planning is very much a function of an awareness of presently existing shortcomings.

This chapter is intended to summarize the shortcomings of the conventional urban transportation-planning (UTP) process as it was presented in the earlier chapters of this book. The presentation proceeds from a review of the overall UTP process and the interactions among its different phases to the discussion of specific shortcomings of each of the stages in the travel demand modeling sequence. Finally, some changing interpretations of the UTP process and a brief preview of recent research activities are presented.

## Critique of the Transportation-planning Process

Criticism may be leveled at the planning process on a number of grounds. In the first place, the transportation-planning process as practiced currently is extremely cumbersome and very expensive. Second, it is inflexible, and it is static rather than dynamic. That is, it is based upon measurements and estimated relationships from a single point in time, with an assumption that these relationships and estimates will not change over time except as may be specified by extraneous changes in total population, in wealth, and in similar characteristics. Third, the process is aimed at preparing a single final-state plan. Fourth, the objectives of the process are not well defined. There are numerous arbitrary assumptions implicit in its structure.

A fifth criticism may be leveled that the current set of planning models represent something of a computational dinosaur. They are unresponsive and insensitive to many of the questions that the policy maker or the decision maker needs to ask. In many cases, the models are based on unreasonable simplifying assumptions, or are just simply unresponsive to certain aspects of the urban system to which they should be responsive. As a direct corollary to this, the set of planning models are also subject to substantial error variance and problems of error propagation. There is, generally, no statement of the desired accuracy of the ultimate output of the planning process, nor is there any indication of the penalty cost associated with a given level of output error. In fact, in the conventional output of a transportation study, little or no mention is generally made of any level of error associated with the estimation procedures. It is very rare, in fact, that any acknowledgment is made of the fact that any error variance even exists. In addition to this, the whole process is centered around a concept of attempting to produce a plan for transportation that will satisfy a particular demand. It is assumed that this demand may be predicted accurately, and it is assumed that the desirable end-product is to meet that predicted demand. Essentially, the whole process is forward-seeking, and attempts to satisfy a specific demand level. There is little or no allowance within the system for feedback between the various stages isolated in the study of the whole urban system. There is no acknowledgment made of the fact that a preferable way of proceeding may be to attempt to specify an end state or set of goals, and determine the way in which these goals might be met.

A further criticism is that little account is taken, in the planning process, of the potential contributions that technological innovation may make. To some extent, this lack of account may be considered to be reasonable, in that little is known presently of the technological innovations that may occur within the next 20 years and it is very difficult to determine from current development of innovations just what their possible contributions or impact might be. However, the form of planning is usually so rigid that no possible way is provided by which technological innovations could even be considered. In addition, the existing evaluation strategies take into account only a partial spectrum of consequences. These consequences are usually those that will affect the users of the system rather than the nonusers, and take little account of effects or wider impacts upon the environment as a whole, and particularly upon the whole spatial organization of an urban area. However, with recent changes in legislation, relating to the requirement to evaluate social and environmental consequences, the evaluation process is beginning to be expanded into these areas. Much progress yet remains to be achieved in this changing evaluation procedure. Finally, there is insufficient attention paid to the question of implementation. Much of the staged implementation that occurs is in direct response to budgetary and political constraints, and is not a consequence of a planned implementation strategy. There is, therefore, little if any flexibility built into the process.

**Interactions Among Modeling Phases**

The next concern should be to see how the travel demand models interact.

Conventionally, they are applied in a unidirectional manner, commencing with trip generation and ending with network assignment. In this form, it is assumed implicitly that the decision whether or not to make a trip is made first; that the decisions of where to end the trip, and the mode to use for the trip, are made second and third or third and second, respectively, according to whether or not the model is a trip-end or trip-interchange model; and, finally, a choice is made as to which route should be used. It is implied, furthermore, that the decision whether to make a trip will largely be unaffected by subsequent decisions as to where the trip might be satisfied, which mode might be used, and which route might be used. Because of the directionality of the model process, the entire decision to make a trip is really split into four sequential decisions, where the sequence of the decisions is extremely rigid. In practice, there is occasionally some provision made for a recycling of part of this process, in an attempt to introduce some multidirectionality of interactions.

When iterations are carried out, they usually concern the stages of trip distribution, modal split, and network assignment. All three of these stages conventionally include some measure of trip time within them. Where trip time is included explicitly in each model, it is possible to reiterate these three modeling steps by using the travel times that are output by trip assignment as fresh input to trip distribution and modal split, and then to reassign the adjusted modal volumes. This type of iteration can be repeated a number of times, until some sort of equilibrium is, perhaps, achieved. However, this iterative process is not guaranteed to converge, and frequently does not do so. Furthermore, the use of travel times as the connecting link pre-supposes that total travel demand, as calculated from trip generation, is unaffected by the travel times on the network. Thus, the process assumes a fixed or given level of demand and is concerned only with attempting to determine some equilibrium status of the system in terms of that given demand.

This consideration of interactions has led to a large amount of the current research in transportation-planning models. In general, this research is aimed at attempting to structure new models, or a complete new system of models, in which demand for travel is made sensitive to the system. Attempts are also made to make the entire process much more interactive, as well as attempting to make the models themselves more plausible, in the sense of the actual process being modeled.

**Critique of the Travel-demand Models**

In addition to the above criticisms concerning the interactions that are permitted within the typical modeling process, a number of other shortcomings of the models may be noted, as they are currently used. If each model is examined in turn, specific shortcomings can be identified within each model, which exist in addition to those general ones of the whole process that have just been identified. First, in trip generation, the trip-generation models currently used do not allow for total travel demand to be affected by the transportation system that is available for travel. As a result, a zone that has a particular set of characteristics would appear to generate the same amount of travel, regardless of the level of transportation service provided.

As trip generation stands, it would be somewhat difficult to incorporate measures of the system within it. This is because the trip-generation model only addresses the estimation of total travel demand, and therefore does not allow any specification of the particular transportation system links, which would allow an easy assessment of the accessibility of the zone. It would, therefore, be necessary to attempt to devise some sort of global-accessibility measure[1] that could be evaluated for any zone in terms of its spatial and transportation location, with respect to the remainder of the urban area. In addition to this, the trip-generation model does not address the problem of whether or not there are acceptable destinations available for trips; nor does it examine the possible trade-offs between making a trip to carry out a particular activity, or substituting some other activity that can be carried out within the home, thus not necessitating a trip at all. In general, it has been demonstrated that both residential and nonresidential trip-generation models can replicate present trip making reasonably well. However, a very considerable variance exists in the trip rates between individual land uses. These variations are considerably greater among nonresidential land uses than they are among residential land uses. In addition to this, the reporting of nonhome-based trips has sufficiently large errors that nonresidential trip-generation models, based on measured data, tend to be extremely inaccurate.

The three major trip-distribution models each contain certain faults or shortcomings of their own, which were mentioned as each of the three different basic methods was examined.

In general, three major problems that exist in all of the models may be summarized. The first major one is that the models are calibrated in such a way that the specific interzonal movements are not used as any form of a check on the model. In other words, the calibration procedure is carried out on row and column totals of the trip matrix, that is, on total zonal productions and attractions. As such, it is possible to find a model that appears to calibrate extremely well in terms of its ability to replicate existing total zonal productions and attractions, while being highly erroneous on the specific interzonal movements. In none of the three basic methods of trip distribution are both of the conservation conditions fulfilled. In fact, they are basically calibrated assuming only that the first conservation law is to be met, and some sort of factoring is required to attempt to enforce adherence to the second conservation equation. This factoring process makes the end result a somewhat suspect model. None of the three distribution models necessarily include travel time or any other system characteristic as an explicit variable. In the gravity model, the usual formulation does not permit travel time to be included as an explicit variable. Furthermore, an assumption has to be made for forecasting that the existing relationship between travel times and trip-making propensity will remain the same throughout the whole forecast period.

In modal-split models, experience with the aggregate models has tended to indicate that, although it may be possible to devise linear regression models that can replicate existing travel reasonably accurately, these models are extremely suspect as predictive tools. The reasons for this are mainly reasons common to all three of the models that have been discussed this far. In all cases, an assumption is made that relationships, which can be observed at the present time between various aspects of trip making and characteristics of zones and of the transportation system, are stable over time. There is no justification whatsoever for such an assumption; and the fact that it is not found to be possible to transfer these models either geographically or temporally suggests that the assumption is completely unfounded.

Network assignment may be criticized on a number of grounds. The most major of these, which has already been discussed, is the assumption that people select their route on the basis of minimizing total travel time, irrespective of any other factors. In addition to this, there are serious drawbacks inherent in the way in which the assignment process is applied. In particular, the final assignment is very sensitive to the way in which the network is loaded, including the sequence in which interzonal volumes are loaded onto the system, and is also very sensitive to the capacity-restraint assumptions.

Before leaving the existing travel forecasting models, it is pertinent to determine how far these models are demand models in the sense in which they were originally introduced in this book. Since the models are all calibrated using cross-sectional data, describing trips carried out, the models, in fact, are descriptive of current equilibrium between price-volume and demand. Thus, the models determine a profile of price-volume demand equilibrium points for different socioeconomic groups. This is shown in Figure 12-1, which assumes a single price-volume curve. The equilibrium points represent the known data, and the result of the model-building exercise is to determine a relationship that joins these points. If the assumption of a single price-volume curve is a reasonable assumption (which would be so generally for a single facility, but less likely for an urban network), then the so-called travel demand models have, in fact, defined the price-volume, not the demand curve. If the models are built for an urban area, it is probable that there are a number of price-volume curves as well as a number of demand curves. In this case, the travel demand models have again mapped the location of equilibrium points. In this instance, these do not lie on either a demand curve or a price-volume curve. Where a mathematical function has been built for the demand model, forecasting will generally comprise some form of extrapolation of the present model. It is clear that this extrapolation is not a forecast of either supply or demand, and is most unlikely to forecast a future equilibrium.

In conclusion, it may be stated that these so-called travel demand models are misnamed and do not define a demand schedule for travel. Furthermore, it is unlikely that they can provide accurate forecasts of future travel.

Although some time has been spent in criticizing all of these models, it should be borne in mind that no models have yet been put forward that can provide substantive improvements for urban-area travel forecasting. A fair amount of research has been conducted into the various parts of this total process; but so far, this has failed to come up with any radical departure from the set of four models that have been described here. It is, therefore, essential to remember that, in spite of all their shortcomings, these four basic models represent the best available travel-forecasting process, although they have many serious problems and many inherent errors. It may, therefore, be assumed that, until such time as some new operational model structure has been developed for transportation studies, this set of four basic models will generally continue to be applied; although modifications may be made from time to time in the precise form and application.

## Changing Interpretations

Not all of the criticisms and shortcomings indicated above apply to all urban transportation-planning studies. Many of these criticisms have been overcome in some of the more recent major studies. Among these, the Southeast Wisconsin Regional Planning Commission (SEWRPC) and the Bay Area Transportation Study Commission have each been much more concerned with several of the items that were mentioned in the previous section. The Southeast Wisconsin Regional Planning Commission set up a broad set of objectives within which seven transportation objectives were embedded. All of these objectives were couched in operational and measurable terms. In the Bay Area Transportation Study, the planning strategy that was adopted called for the development of a succession of plans of increasing levels of detail and that involved continuous interaction between the land-use and the network-planning phases. Similar strategies were also employed in the SEWRPC study.

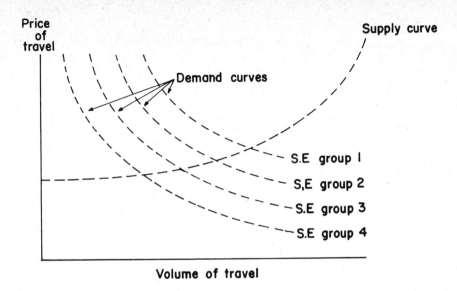

**Figure 12-1.** Profile of Supply-Demand Equilibrium Points for Four Socioeconomic Groups.

The existing process was criticized as having an end-product of a single inflexible plan. Currently, however, many of the ongoing studies have revised their basic rationale, and, as a result, have attempted to incorporate a new degree of flexibility in their planning. These are termed "continuing planning processes." As currently practiced, this involves a small degree of monitoring of the current situation in the urban system, and a continual updating of plans according to whether or not the state of the urban system corresponds with that originally predicted. At the same time, there is an increasing awareness of the necessity for short-range planning, and a number of studies are now placing considerable emphasis on such plans.

The criticisms leveled in the previous section make the entire urban transportation-planning process look rather bleak. However, it must be remembered that these criticisms are based on a comparison between the available process and some ideal point without any real knowledge of whether the ideal is attainable. Therefore, it must be remembered that the existing process, and the tools within it, represent the best that are available; and that the planning they permit shows a much greater awareness of interacting systems, allocation of scarce resources, and the long-term impacts of present decisions, than anything before in the transportation field.

It is possible to identify the functions that, ideally, would be incorporated within a continuing planning process:

1. Monitor changes in the urban system that influence the demand for

travel. Collect, maintain, and disseminate data, on a continuing basis, on the status of transportation facilities, travel, land use, and the distribution of activity. Also, update the basic planning data.

2. Project future travel demand and requirements for all modes, for both the long and the short range.
3. Reevaluate and modify the transportation system as required by continuing changes in the distribution of land use and activity.
4. Establish and maintain a capital improvement plan for transportation facilities.
5. Perform analyses leading to the final evaluation and implementation of proposed transportation plans.
6. Maintain a continuing current data base on the changing pattern of travel requirements and travel-generating activities within the study area.
7. Conduct specific studies of selected problem areas or specific transportation proposals.
8. Perform necessary research, as required, leading to the improvement of transportation planning techniques.

Many studies are now adopting some of these elements as a part of the continuing planning process. However, these attempts are still fragmented and incomplete.


**Recent Research**

In an attempt to overcome some of the shortcomings of the present model package, research has been conducted in at least two basic directions in an attempt to produce an improved package: The first of these attempts is centered around the use of conventional consumer-behavior theory from economics. This theory leads to the attempt to build what may be referred to as econometric models. These models are structured on the basis of making some assumptions about the elasticities and cross-elasticities of travel demand, with respect to the system and the user. In general, the econometric approach attempts to combine the processes of trip generation, mode choice, and distribution in one model. In these models, the dependent variable is usually the percent of trips between two zones by a particular mode, and the independent variables are an array of user and system attributes, usually raised to certain powers and in product form.

The second major thrust that is being made is basically an attempt at incremental improvements in the existing package. The first of these improvements is an incremental improvement of the existing aggregate models that is usually associated with the ongoing transportation studies. These improvements center around attempted refinements of the existing model procedures, in an attempt to generate somewhat more reliable and more plausible models. The future of such incremental improvements is, largely, only short range. They represent an attempt to make an immediate improvement on the basis of existing techniques of modeling. Examples of these types of improvements are the entropy-maximizing approach pioneered by Alan G. Wilson;[2] the use of so-called short-cut techniques[3] in the travel demand estimation process; and the UTPS[4] network programs in the transit planning area.

The third major thrust is an attempt to restructure the decision process and the models contained within it. In particular, this third thrust is concerned with an attempt to start off the modeling process at the most disaggregate level possible, in the hopes that such a disaggregate analysis will provide both more plausible behavioral models, and a better basis for aggregating data. Most of the attempts that have been made in this field, at the moment, have been concerned with attempting to predict mode choice. In this area, considerable attempts have been made to derive some form of probability models of travel-mode choice. These models have used a number of statistical curve-fitting techniques, apart from regression. In each case, the attempt is to obtain a probability of an individual using any of the available modes for a particular trip. Attempts are currently being made to see how this approach may be extended to the rest of the modeling procedure, with the end aim of attempting to build the entire package in terms of probability models, which address the problem in a much more behaviorally satisfying fashion, and with built-in interactions between each of the basic models.

In general, this appears to be a fairly promising approach to be taken, although current research has not progressed far enough to demonstrate conclusively whether or not this approach is likely to yield a feasible and better alternative to the existing set of models. One of the basic justifications that may be put forward for these models is that they are based upon an attempt to model people's behavior, and as such, are likely inherently to contain a validity for prediction not attained by the existing set of models, which are purely associative. This section constitutes only a brief preview of the content in the following chapters. These chapters will look at recent alternative research approaches in the travel-demand modeling area in some detail.

# 13 Direct Traffic-estimation Method

## Background

The technique of direct traffic estimation is an attempt to obtain traffic volumes on a network link by a single estimating process after trip generation. This method is somewhat disassociated from individual or aggregate behavior of trip makers. It concentrates on the links in a transportation network and estimates traffic volumes on these links as a function of the potential traffic generation of the region under consideration for each link as well as the availability of parallel links to accommodate this traffic. The analysis of each link proceeds independently of the analysis of other links.

The term direct traffic-estimation method should not be confused with the term direct travel-demand model. The latter refers to a completely different class and philosophy of modeling and is based on theories of consumer choice and preference. Another term used for direct travel-demand models is econometric models. The theory of econometric models constitutes the subject matter of chapter 15 in this book.

The basic rationale underlying the method, as well as the technique itself, was developed by Morton Schneider.[1] It grew out of the necessity or desirability of obtaining future traffic estimates for selected links or a subset of a complete urban-transportation network in cases where a full network assignment was unnecessary or too expensive. Much of the theoretical and applied work related to this method was performed under the auspices of the Tri-State Transportation Commission[2] whose transportation-planning responsibility encompasses the largest metropolitan area in the world. Tri-State considered Morton Schneider's theoretical developments promising for use in the analysis of future traffic volumes in smaller sections of the Tri-State area, eliminating the need for the application of the sequential phases in the conventional urban transportation-planning (UTP) process.

The basic analysis unit in the direct traffic-estimation method is the network link, and any desirable subset of the applicable transportation network can be scrutinized. The theoretical basis for this method is derived from a generalization of the gravity model in order to represent the relationship between transportation accessibility and land development. Schneider developed an accessibility function that is directly related to the trip generation at only one end of the trip and inversely related to a measure of land development, which, in a sense, represents the trip attraction at the other end of the trip.

### Derivation of the Direct Traffic-estimation Method

The basic method can be described as follows: Assuming that every piece of the earth's surface has some supply of trip-ends per day, and that the number of trips between two points is proportional to the number of origin trip-ends, the number of destination trip-ends, and is a function of the separation between the two points, then the number of trips between $i$ and $j$ can be represented as shown in equation 13.1.

$$V_{ij} = \frac{V_i F_{ij} V_j}{I'_i} \tag{13.1}$$

where $V_{ij}$ = Trips between $i$ and $j$

$V_i$ = Trips generated at $i$

$V_j$ = Trips attracted to $j$

$F_{ij}$ = Separation function between $i$ and $j$

$I'_i = \Sigma_j F_{ij} V_j$, an accessibility function

Equation 13.1 represents a generalized form of the gravity model. If $V_j$ is replaced by $R_j$, where $R_j$ is not associated with the trip attractions, but is defined as a function of the land development at $i$, then direct computation of traffic volumes on link $i - j$ can be achieved based on trip-generation information only. This is shown in equation 13.2.

$$V_{ij} = \frac{V_i R_j F_{ij}}{I_i} \tag{13.2}$$

where $R_j$ = undefined quantity, which replaces the usual trips attracted at $j$ term, $V_j$

$$I_i = \sum_j R_j F_{ij} = \int F \, dR$$

Assuming that origin trip-ends and destination trip-ends are equal during a given time period, it can be assumed that trip interchanges between $i$ and $j$ are symmetric in both directions. This assumption gives rise to equation 13.3.

$$\frac{V_i F_{ij} R_j}{I_i} = \frac{V_j F_{ji} R_i}{I_j} \tag{13.3}$$

The symmetry assumption also leads to the assumption that $F_{ij} = F_{ji}$, such that equation 13.3 simplifies to equations 13.4 and 13.5.

$$\frac{V_i R_j}{I_i} = \frac{V_j R_i}{I_j} \tag{13.4}$$

$$\frac{V_i}{I_i R_i} = \frac{V_j}{I_j R_j} \tag{13.5}$$

This can only hold for all pairs of points if both sides of the equation are separately equal to some constant, $a$. Thus, these equations can be generalized by rewriting equation 13.5 as shown in equation 13.6.

$$V/R = aI \tag{13.6}$$

If fine partitioning of an area is meaningful, this relationship can be written in terms of limiting small quantities as in equations 13.7 and 13.8.

$$dV/dR = aI \tag{13.7}$$

$$dV = aI\,dR \tag{13.8}$$

The trip density at a point, $V$, divided by $R$ is proportional to $I$. This implies that $I$ can be defined in terms of only one trip-end or point. $I$ may therefore be defined as the accessibility of a point that generates trip density $V$, modified by the characteristic $R$ of that same point.

The undefined quantity $R$ provides $I$ with a physical meaning as a variable, which in turn will give meaning to $R$. This is consistent with the relationship between them, shown in equation 13.9.

$$I = \int F\,dR \tag{13.9}$$

The specific definition of $R$ depends on a more specific definition of $F$:

Schneider's concept of a "destinationless" trip distribution/assignment process requires some additional conceptual clarifications. Schneider postulates that the two end points of a trip cannot be affected by the way in which the minimum-cost path between them is defined. Trip generation is exogenous to the distribution/assignment process. This implies that trip-ends are chosen independently of the path between them, but with knowledge of the existence of that path. Trip-ends are then defined as independent departures from the minimum path. In this context, trips are defined as those portions of the "travel trajectory" that lie on the minimum paths.[3]

Since different minimum paths are perceived by different travelers between given trip ends, the concept of a generalized cost function is introduced to take this fact into account. The accessibility function, $I$, should depend on the cost that each of the travelers perceives when making a trip to the trip end in question. Equation 13.10 defines the generalized cost function in terms of $F$, which is related to $I$, as was shown earlier.

$$F = e^{-(k_1 t + k_2 c)} \qquad (13.10)$$

The exponent is the generalized-cost function expressed as a linear, additive combination of travel time ($t$) and travel cost ($c$), $k_1$ and $k_2$ are trip-length coefficients. Substituting equation 13.10 into equation 13.9 results in equation 13.11.

$$I = \int e^{-(k_1 t + k_2 c)} \, dR \qquad (13.11)$$

Equation 13.11 defines the access to a trip-end point as the integral of a minimum-cost function taken over an area surrounding that point. It is clear that the integration is taken over the area's $R$ values. This contrasts quite strongly with the conventional accounting of origins and destinations. Origins and destinations of specific trips or groups of trips are only implicitly included in the access function.

The generalized-cost function is set up so that different coefficient $k$s will produce different minimum paths, dependent on individuals' different perceptions of costs. These different paths can be portions of the same network, or they may be segments of separate but overlapping networks, such that each network could represent a different travel model. Parallel links in the same network can also be considered as competing modes if they represent different cost characteristics.

A definition of $R$ remains to be developed. Schneider[4] accomplishes this by rewriting equation 13.6 into the form of equation 13.12.

$$R = a(V/I) \qquad (13.12)$$

This equation states that $R$ is proportional to trip density over access. Assuming that trip density is an effect and not a cause, this implies that an increase in trips can result only if either accessibility, $I$, is increased, or if $R$ is increased. Schneider intuitively suggests that the only other attractor of trips to an area, besides accessibility, is the amount and potential of development of that area. According to that reasoning a relationship between accessibility and land development was provided. Both terms lead to an increase in trip density. Accessibility and land development are inter-related as shown in equation 13.11. Increases in one lead to increases in the other, until an equilibrium is reached where trip generation per unit amount of land development has stabilized. Schneider[5] has suggested that the desirability of the land area under consideration for human activities could constitute a guideline for identifying practicable measures of $R$.

In applications of the direct traffic-estimation method, the study area is divided into a grid with reference coordinates. The different modal transportation networks are coded in terms of the coordinate system. Each grid square is then divided into quadrants, with the transportation node closest to each quadrant recorded. The minimum-cost path through the network is then determined from each node to the link under study. Finally, the cost between each corner of every grid square and the origin node of its minimum path is also computed. As a result, minimum-path trees will have been developed for each of the two nodes on the link under study.

This process provides the information necessary to integrate the cost function of equation 13.11. Values for $I$ are calculated for each of the trees. The trees are referred to as the two main, or north and south, domains of the particular link. These domains are defined in the following way: "The world" is divided into two main domains by a line representing the division between all points that might be reached by traveling in one direction on the link and all points which might be reached by traveling in the opposite direction. The prime domains are then those areas within the main domains that contribute traffic uniquely on a minimum-path basis, to the link in question. The $I$ values are computed by means of equation 13.13.

$$I = \sum_i f(C_{ni} + C_{ai}) T_i \qquad (13.13)$$

where $C_{ni} =$ the network cost of the minimum-cost path associated with the $i$th grid square

$C_{ai} =$ the approach cost from the $i$th grid square to its closest network node

$T_i =$ the number of trip ends in the $i$th grid square

Equation 13.13 provides a potential candidate for a cost function. It should be pointed out, though, that the exact form of the cost function used will develop as part of the calibration of the model. $T_i$, the trip-end density, is used as a surrogate variable for the land-development differential, $dR$, that was developed in the theoretical derivation.

The direct traffic-estimation is a direct function of the accessibility functions of the north and south domains, $I_n$ and $I_s$. The traffic volume $Q$ on a specific link can be expressed as the average of $I_n$ and $I_s$ multiplied by twice the proportion of the total represented by each of the domains. This is shown in equation 13.14.

$$Q = \frac{1}{2}(I_n + I_s)\left(\frac{2I_n}{I_n + I_s}\right)\left(\frac{2I_s}{I_n + I_s}\right) \qquad (13.14)$$

The first of the factors in equation 13.14 represents the accessibility of the link under study. The other two factors are necessary to balance this accessibility for its proportion in the north and south domains. In the case of perfectly balanced accessibility between north and south domains (i.e., given a homogeneous land area and no pronounced directionality of travel patterns), the accessibility function for the north and south domains would be equal, resulting in equation 13.15.

$$Q = I_n = I_s \qquad (13.15)$$

Only in the case of natural barriers can it be assumed that all trips between the north and the south domain traverse the link under study. A competitive factor ought to be specified that takes into account the existence of other competitive links between the two domains. This is accomplished by defining the domain boundary as the separator of the north and south minimum-path trees; calculating north and south minimum-path trees for those links intersecting the domain boundary; defining that portion of the north and south minimum-path trees, for the link under study, which are not in the minimum-path trees for the competing links as the prime domain; and finally defining the competitive factor as the average sum of the accessibilities of the north and south domains that are in the prime domain. Equation 13.16 shows the competitive factor.

$$\text{Competitive Factor} = \frac{1}{2}\left(\frac{I_n'}{I_n} + \frac{I_s'}{I_s}\right) \tag{13.16}$$

where $I_n'$, $I_s'$ are the accessibilities of north and south prime domains respectively

Multiplying equations 13.14 and 13.16 and simplifying gives rise to equation 13.17, which represents the generalized formula for the traffic volume on the link under study.

$$Q = \frac{I_n I_s' + I_s I_n'}{I_n + I_s} \tag{13.17}$$

Equation 13.17 indicates that the traffic volume on a link can be calculated directly on the basis of information about trip density and link costs of the surrounding area of the trip ends under consideration.


**Summary**

In summary, the following observations can be made with respect to the direct traffic-estimation method.

1. The direct traffic-estimation process is based on a sophistication of the gravity model, in which $F = \exp[-(k_1 t + k_2 c)]$, and $A_j$ is replaced by $R_j$, a more complex function of attractiveness.

2. Assignment to all links in a network, regardless of mode, is made simultaneously with trip distribution.

3. Specific trip interchanges are never evaluated, and the process works on the basis of the $P$s and $A$s from the trip-generation phase.

4. Specific assignments of movements to modes, and combinations of modes are also not explicit, and there is no clear guarantee that the combinations of modes and modal shares will replicate base data.

5. The individual trip maker is not considered, the network link is the focal point.

6. The determination of appropriate cost measures has remained un-solved.

   Because of the simplifications and compounding of the modeling process, the direct traffic-estimation (DTE) method cannot be expected necessarily to replicate base-year conditions. However, use of the method in the Tri-State area has suggested that it generally does replicate link volumes reasonably accurately. Since the end-product desired in a total transportation-planning process, as currently conceived, is link volumes, this method appears to be very useful. In terms of understanding the travel-demand process, and providing a basis for formulating and evaluating various policy alternatives that may have effects such as changing modal shares, diverting trip ends, etc., the DTE method appears to be very deficient.

# 14 Spatial-distribution Model Theory

## Background

In the development of various new approaches to travel forecasting, one of the incremental approaches is that of applying entropy theory to travel behavior. The rationale behind this approach comprises two facets. First, there is an attempt to investigate whether or not a sound theoretical basis can be found for the gravity model of trip distribution and to determine whether this model form is a unique model form or is closely related to any other trip-distribution model. Second, by investigating such a theoretical basis, there is an attempt to provide an improved understanding of the variable structures in the gravity model, for example, the friction factor, and to determine whether the model structure can be extended to other model phases of the travel-forecasting procedure.

The underlying theoretical structure used is that of entropy, as developed in several different disciplines, for example, thermodynamics, information theory, and statistical mechanics. In general, entropy is classified as one of the state variables, together with temperature, pressure, and volume.[1] In thermodynamics, entropy provides a relationship between energy and absolute temperature. It is postulated that any physical system, if left to itself, will disperse the useable energy while its entropy increases. For example, consider two bottles, each containing a different gas. If the two bottles are opened and placed together (so that the gases can pass freely between the bottles) and left alone, the two gases will eventually become thoroughly mixed. In so doing, entropy is maximized. Or, again, consider a pot full of water on a fire. The burning of the fire releases energy that boils the water and converts some of it to steam. Heat (energy) is also given to the atmosphere. Once the fire burns out, all its energy has been transferred to the water, steam, pot, and surroundings, but none is lost. However, if the steam is allowed to escape into the atmosphere and the remaining water is left to cool, none of that energy is reuseable. It still exists, but has been changed into nonuseable energy. The entropy of the system has, however, been increased. From this, *entropy* is defined as a state of the system that measures the disorder of a closed system. In other words, as the physical system is left to itself to disperse its energy, it degenerates into a state of disorder. The greater the disorder, the lower is the remaining usable energy, but the greater is the entropy of the system. In statistical mechanics, entropy is related to the probability of a state of a system and is defined by equation 14.1.

$$S = k \ln P + c \qquad (14.1)$$

where $\quad S =$ entropy

$\qquad P =$ probability of a state of the system

and $\quad k, c =$ constants

From this, it follows that the most probable state of a system (in statistical mechanics) is that state in which entropy is maximized.

Finally, in information theory, entropy is defined as a measure of the uncertainty of knowledge of a system. In this case, entropy is defined by equation 14.2.

$$S = -\sum p \ln p \qquad (14.2)$$

where $\quad p =$ the probability of a particular state

From all these definitions of entropy, the primary concept of interest to transportation planning is the definition of a state of the system. A specific (observed) distribution of trips in a region could be defined as a state of the transportation system. By defining that the observed state is, ipso facto, the most probable one, it follows that the maximization of entropy will define that state. Through this mechanism, a model of trip distribution can be defined and the procedure subsequently extended to describe any other state of the system, for example, mode usage, route usage, etc.

On the other hand, one may also consider that travel in a region represents a disordered system. If transportation were frictionless (i.e., had no costs associated with it, in terms of monetary cost, time, energy, resources, etc.) then travel patterns, at the regional level, would most probably be totally disorganized (i.e., randomized). Hence, entropy of the system would be maximized. Friction in the system requires energy (in its broadest sense) in order to be overcome, and this expenditure of energy reduces the entropy. Under the most extreme conditions of friction to movement, the system would become highly organized, with an urban structure that obviated the need to travel, and for which entropy would be minimized. Thus, entropy can be postulated as being somewhat equivalent to mobility. The determination of the maximum entropy state of the transportation system could then be equated with a state in which travelers maximize mobility within the constraint of existing friction to movement.

**Derivation of the Gravity Model**

To set up a general theory of the gravity model, consider three basic constraint equations, equations 14.3, 14.4, and 14.5, two of which are already familiar, but the third of which is a new one comprising a cost constraint.

$$\sum_i T_{ij} = A_j \qquad (14.3)$$

$$\sum_j T_{ij} = O_i \qquad (14.4)$$

$$\sum_i \sum_j T_{ij} c_{ij} = C \qquad (14.5)$$

where $O_i$, $A_j$, and $T_{ij}$ are as defined previously (chapter 8) and $c_{ij}$ is the total cost of making a trip from zone $i$ to zone $j$. The cost constraint assumes that there is a total cost budget for travel, $C$, for a region, which cannot be exceeded, but which will be totally spent. (A more relaxed formulation might use $\Sigma_i \Sigma_j T_{ij} c_{ij} \leq C$, where, simply, the total budget may not be exceeded.)

Then, let $T$ be the total number of trips made in the region, leading to equation 14.6.

$$T = \sum_i O_i = \sum_j A_j \qquad (14.6)$$

The basic rationale of the method is the assumption that "the probability of the distribution $\{T_{ij}\}$ occurring is proportional to the number of states of the system which give rise to this distribution, and which satisfy the constraints."[2] The symbol $\{T_{ij}\}$ is used to represent a specific matrix of trip interchanges, $T_{ij}$, that is, the observed trip-interchange matrix. In transportation-planning applications, there is generally no interest in who the individual travelers are who make up a specific trip interchange. Therefore, the number of distinct arrangements of individuals that can give rise to a specific trip-interchange matrix will be the number of combinations of individuals, not the number of permutations, since different permutations relate only to changes in the individuals in a specific trip bundle. Representing the number of distinct arrangements that can give rise to a trip-interchange matrix $\{T_{ij}\}_k$ as $w_k(T_{ij})$, that number is defined in equation 14.7.

$$w_k(T_{ij}) = (T!) \Big/ \left( \prod_{ij} T_{ij}! \right) \qquad (14.7)$$

Then the total number of possible states of the system, $W$, is given by equation 14.8.

$$W = \sum_k w_k(T_{ij}) \qquad (14.8)$$

The maximum value of $w_k(T_{ij})$ turns out to dominate other terms to such an extent that the trip-interchange matrix $\{T_{ij}\}$, which gives rise to the maximum, is overwhelmingly the most probable distribution, and hence the trip-distribution model will be found by determining the set of $T_{ij}$s that maximizes $w_k(T_{ij})$, subject to the constraints given in equations 14.3, 14.4, and 14.5. This set can be found by using the method of Lagrange multipliers, differentiating and determining the maximum. Defining a Lagrangian, $M$, in terms of $w_k(T_{ij})$ and the constraints, produces equation 14.9.

$$M = \ln w + \sum_i \lambda_i \left( O_i - \sum_j T_{ij} \right)$$
$$+ \sum_j \lambda_j \left( A_j - \sum_i T_{ij} \right) + \beta \left( C - \sum_i \sum_j T_{ij} c_{ij} \right) \qquad (14.9)$$

where $\lambda_i$, $\lambda_j$, $\beta$ are Lagrange multipliers and $w$ is used to represent $w_k(T_{ij})$ for the trip-interchange matrix being sought.

As is frequently the case, it is easier here to maximize $\ln w$ than $w$. The reason here is that the differential of a function of the form $(T!)/(\Pi_{ij}T_{ij}!)$ is very complex, while there is an approximation due to Stirling[3] for $\ln N!$ which allows easier differentiation. This is shown in the next two equations (14.10 and 14.11), where it is assumed that $N$ is a large number.

$$\ln N! = N \ln N - N$$

$$\frac{\partial \ln N!}{\partial N} = \ln N \qquad (14.11)$$

Applying equation 14.11 to 14.9 yields equation 14.12.

$$\frac{\partial M}{\partial T_{ij}} = -\ln T_{ij} - \lambda_i - \lambda_j - \beta c_{ij} \qquad (14.12)$$

Setting $\partial M/\partial T_{ij} = 0$, we find a maximum for $M$ occurs under the conditions specified in equation 14.13 or 14.14.

$$\ln T_{ij} = -\lambda_i - \lambda_j - \beta c_{ij} \qquad (14.13)$$

$$T_{ij} = \exp\left[-\lambda_i - \lambda_j - \beta c_{ij}\right] \qquad (14.14)$$

Returning to the constraint equations, 14.3 and 14.4, these may be applied to equation 14.14 to define the Lagrangian multipliers, $\lambda_i$ and $\lambda_j$, as shown in the next four equations.

$$O_i = \sum_j \exp\left[-\lambda_i - \lambda_j - \beta c_{ij}\right] \qquad (14.15)$$

$$O_i = \exp(-\lambda_i) \sum_j \exp\left[-\lambda_j - \beta c_{ij}\right] \qquad (14.16)$$

$$\exp(-\lambda_i) = O_i \Big/ \left[\sum_j \exp(-\lambda_j - \beta c_{ij})\right] \qquad (14.17)$$

$$\exp(-\lambda_j) = A_j \Big/ \left[\sum_i \exp(-\lambda_i - \beta c_{ij})\right] \qquad (14.18)$$

If $\exp(-\lambda_i)/O_i$ is written as $B_i$ and $\exp(-\lambda_j)/A_j$ as $C_j$, equation 14.14 may be rewritten in the form shown in equation 14.19, which is the gravity model in its usual form.

$$T_{ij} = B_i O_i C_j A_j \exp(-\beta c_{ij}) \tag{14.19}$$

This derivation has also led to the determination of the form of the friction factor, as shown in equation 14.20.

$$F(t)_{ij} = \exp(-\beta c_{ij}) \tag{14.20}$$

It should also be noted that the solution has not required a knowledge of $C$, the total travel-cost budget, since this has dropped out of the equation.

A number of additional interpretations and properties may be deduced from this formulation of the gravity model.[4] First, a very logical deduction may be made from the friction factor and its relationship to $C$, the travel-cost budget. The larger the size of $\beta$, the smaller is the average distance traveled (assuming the usual positive correlation between $c_{ij}$ and distance). Similarly, the larger the value of $C$, the smaller must be $\beta$ and the larger will be the average distance traveled.

Second, the form of changes in $T_{ij}$ that result from changes in the $O_i$s and $A_j$s may be examined. From this, it may be deduced that the constants $B_i$ and $C_j$, can be interpreted as accessibility-competition measures, associated with the origin and destination ends of the trip, respectively. It may also be deduced that the constraints, in total, are all that prevent the entire set of $T_{ij}$s from being equal. In other words, the three constraint equations jointly define the friction of travel, without which entropy would reach an absolute maximum.

Finally, it is interesting to determine the sharpness of the maximum. In order to determine this, it can be shown[5] that the change in $\ln w(T_{ij})$ is given by equation 14.21.

$$d[\ln w(T_{ij})] = -\frac{1}{2}\sum_i \sum_j p^2 T_{ij} \tag{14.21}$$

where $p$ is the proportionate change in each $T_{ij}$ away from the value it has in the most probable distribution. To make this expression more usable, one may consider the $T_{ij}$s to be grouped into $N$ size groups, in which the $n$th group has $S_n$ elements in it, then equation 14.21 can be rewritten as equation 14.22.

$$d[\ln w(T_{ij})] = -\frac{1}{2}p^2 \sum_n S_n T_n \tag{14.22}$$

Using this equation, it can be determined how sharp the maximum is. The negative sign of this equation implies that, as $p$ becomes very small, the change in $\ln w(T_{ij})$ approaches unity. This, in turn, implies a very sharp maximum. Using an example from Alan G. Wilson,[6] assume a large urban area with 1,000 zones. There will be one million trip interchanges in such an area, and it will be assumed that 100,000 of these are empty. Of the remaining 900,000, it will be assumed that there are 1,000 with trip interchanges of 10,000 trips, 10,000 with 1,000 trips, 100,000 with 100 trips, and 789,000 with 10 trips. Estimating the value of equation 14.22 with $p$ assumed to be $10^{-3}$ yields the values shown in equation 14.23.

$$d \ln w = -(1/2)10^{-6}(10^7 + 10^7 + 10^7 + 7.89 \times 10^6) = -18.95 \quad (14.23)$$

Thus, a change of one thousandth in each trip interchange causes a minute change of $5.89 \times 10^{-9}$ in $w$. However, considering a change of one ten-thousandth of each trip interchange (i.e., $p = 10^{-4}$) yields equation 14.24.

$$d \ln w = -(1/2) \times 10^{-8} \times 37.89 \times 10^6 = -18.95 \times 10^{-2} \quad (14.24)$$

In this case, the change in $w$ is $8.4 \times 10^{-1}$. A much greater increment in the change of $d \ln w$ occurs for a further change in $p$. Hence, the maximum is extremely sharply peaked at the most probable distribution and changes of as little as one trip per trip interchange in a large urban area will generate a massive change in the value of $\ln w$.

## Derivation of the Intervening-opportunity Model

The same derivation can also be modified to produce the familiar intervening-opportunity model. Let $U_{ij}$ be the probability that a traveler will continue beyond the $j$th zone (ranked by $c_{ij}$) from zone $i$. Then the total number of trips continuing beyond the $j$th zone, from zone $i$, is given by equation 14.25.

$$S_{ij} = O_i U_{ij} \quad (14.25)$$

Then, the number of trips terminating in the $j$th zone is shown in equation 14.26.

$$T_{ij} = S_{ij-1} - S_{ij} \quad (14.26)$$

Thus, the $S_{ij}$ variables define a new system as a possible alternative to $T_{ij}$, and the derivation may be set up to maximize $w(S_{ij})$, where $w(S_{ij})$ is given by equation 14.27.

$$w(S_{ij}) = \frac{S!}{\prod_{ij} S_{ij}!} \quad (14.27)$$

Before solving this, the new constraints that are operating here must be determined. These will not be the same as equations 14.3, 14.4, and 14.5. However, the first constraint can be determined by observing that the number of trips proceeding beyond the $j$th zone, $S_{ij}$, cannot be more than the total number of trips that originated in $i$. Hence, the first constraint becomes equation 14.28.

$$S_{ij} \leq O_i \qquad (14.28)$$

This may be expanded to the entire study area by summing over $j$, equation 14.29.

$$\sum_j S_{ij} = k_i' O_i \qquad (14.29)$$

where $1 \leq k_i' \leq N$, and $N$ is the total number of zones. The analogous cost constraint to equation 14.5 can be determined by considering the basic premise of the opportunity model: that the number of trips between $i$ and $j$ is determined by the number of opportunities at $j$, and varies inversely as the number of intervening opportunities. So, trips beyond zone $j$ will incur greater costs than those that ended in zones up to and including zone $j$. If the number of opportunities passed ($V_j$) so far is taken as a measure of the cost of passing them, then the minimum cost for trips beyond $j$ is $V_j S_{ij}$, where $V_j$ is given by equation 14.30.

$$V_j = \sum_{n=1}^{j} A_n \qquad (14.30)$$

If this cost is summed over all $j$ and over all origin zones, $i$, then a function that behaves like a cost function is obtained, equation 14.31.

$$\sum_i \sum_j V_{ij} S_{ij} = C \qquad (14.31)$$

However, the definition of $S_{ij}$ also produces equation 14.32.

$$S_{ij} = \sum_{n=j+1}^{N} T_{in} \qquad (14.32)$$

Substituting equation 14.32 in equation 14.31 and using equation 14.30 to define the $V_{ij}$, it can be seen that the coefficient of $T_{in}$ in equation 14.31 is $(j-1)A_1 + (j-2)A_2 + \ldots + A_{j-1}$, which gives some further insights into the form of the cost constraint.

Returning to the principal problem, $w(S_{ij})$ is to be maximized subject to the constraints of equations 14.29 and 14.31. This is the analogous situation to that of deriving the gravity model. The function to be maximized is shown in equation 14.33.

$$F = \ln w - L\left(\sum_i \sum_j V_{ij} S_{ij} - C\right) - \sum_i \lambda_i \left(\sum_j S_{ij} - k_i' O_i\right) \qquad (14.33)$$

where $L$ and $\lambda_i$ are Lagrangian multipliers. On differentiating this function, the most probable distribution occurs in the situation shown in equation 14.34.

$$-\ln S_{ij} - LV_j - \lambda_i = 0 \qquad (14.34)$$

From this, $S_{ij}$ may be defined (equation 14.35).

$$S_{ij} = \exp[-LV_j - \lambda_i] \qquad (14.35)$$

From this, $\lambda_i$ can be defined by substituting first from equation 14.29, yielding equation 14.36.

$$\exp(-\lambda_i) = \frac{k_i' O_i}{\sum_j \exp(-LV_j)} \qquad (14.36)$$

Letting $k_i = \exp(-\lambda_i)/O_i$, equation 14.36 can be simplified to equation 14.37.

$$S_{ij} = k_i O_i \exp(-LV_j) \qquad (14.37)$$

The trip distribution model is required to define $T_{ij}$ and not $S_{ij}$. However, these two are related as shown by equation 14.26. Hence, equation 14.37 can be used to define $T_{ij}$ as shown in equation 14.38.

$$T_{ij} = k_i O_i [\exp(-LV_{j-1}) - \exp(-LV_j)] \qquad (14.38)$$

which is the familiar form of the basic intervening-opportunity model.

The intervening-opportunity model has thus been derived from the same starting point as the gravity model, that is, the entropy-maximization procedure. However, this is done at the expense of assuming a rather strange cost constraint, in which the number of opportunities passed is used as a measure of cost. This suggests that, from a maximum-entropy viewpoint, the conclusions of conceptual appeal of the two trip-distribution models should be reversed. In this case, the gravity model is more conceptually satisfying, while the intervening-opportunity model requires a dubious assumption. In addition, the entropy-maximization process has not defined the constant $k_i$ and the model does not obey the basic trip-conservation rules.

## Generalization of the Gravity Model

Returning again to the gravity model version of this theoretical development, a more general model can be put forward. The model may be made more realistic by introducing some stratification:[7] by person type, and availability of travel modes. To do this, the notation must be extended.

Let   $T_{ij}^{kn}$ = trips between $i$ and $j$ by mode $k$ and person type $n$

$O_i^n$ = the number of origins at $i$ of people of type $n$

$M(n)$ = the set of modes available to type $n$ people.

(E.g., type $n$ could be car-owner or noncar-owner, and these will define $M(n)$, assuming that all $i-j$ pairs have the same set of modes available. If this assumption is not true, then $M(n)$ can be redefined as $M_{ij}(n)$.)

Since standard trip generation associates person types with the production end of the trip, but only land-use types with the attraction end, only $O_i$ is identified as being associated with person type $n$. Similarly, it will be found that the origin and destination constraints, $B_i$ and $C_j$, will be defined as $B_i^n$ and $C_j$. Finally, it should be noted that $\Sigma_{k \in M(n)}$ refers to summation over all modes in the set $M(n)$.

The constraint equations, 14.3, 14.4 and 14.5 can now be rewritten in terms of the newly defined variables. The first equation, 14.3, becomes equation 14.39.

$$\sum_i \sum_n \sum_{k \in M(n)} T_{ij}^{kn} = A_j \qquad (14.39)$$

and the second equation becomes equation 14.40.

$$\sum_j \sum_{k \in M(n)} T_{ij}^{kn} = O_i^n \qquad (14.40)$$

If it is hypothesized that each different person type has a different *per capita* expenditure on travel, and thus a different cost constraint, then the budget constraint becomes equation 14.41.

$$\sum_i \sum_j \sum_{k \in M(n)} T_{ij}^{kn} c_{ij}^k = C^{(n)} \qquad (14.41)$$

The procedure is now to maximize the function shown in equation 14.42 subject to the constraints of equations 14.39, 14.40, and 14.41, using the method of Lagrange multipliers.

$$\text{Maximand} = \ln \frac{T!}{\prod_i \prod_j \prod_{k \in M(n)} T_{ij}^{kn}!} \qquad (14.42)$$

The result is shown in equation 14.43.

$$T_{ij}^{kn} = B_i^n C_j O_i^n A_j \exp(-\beta^n c_{ij}^k) \qquad (14.43)$$

The constants, $B_i^n$ and $C_j$ are defined in equations 14.44 and 14.45,

$$B_i^n = \left[ \sum_j \sum_{k \in M(n)} C_j A_j \exp(-\beta^n c_{ij}^k) \right]^{-1} \qquad (14.44)$$

$$C_j = \left[ \sum_i \sum_n \sum_{k \in M(n)} B_i^n O_i^n \exp(-\beta^n c_{ij}^k) \right]^{-1} \qquad (14.45)$$

Equation 14.43 now represents a generalized linked set of gravity models for all $k$ modes and for person types $n$. The set is linked through the $C_j$s, which are functions of all $k$s and all the $n$s.

One may now make various simplifications of equation 14.43 by re-combining some of the categories. For instance, if the only person type used is that of car-ownership status, one may aggregate over $n$ to obtain the equation for the entire population of car-owners. The result is shown in equation 14.46, where the * represents a new parameter from aggregation.

$$T_{ij}^{k*} = B_i^* C_j O_i^* A_j \exp(-\beta^* c_{ij}^k) \tag{14.46}$$

Also, under this situation, the constants are redefined as shown in equations 14.47 and 14.48.

$$B_i^* = \left[ \sum_j \sum_k C_j A_j \exp(-\beta^* c_{ij}^k) \right]^{-1} \tag{14.47}$$

$$C_j = \left[ \sum_i \sum_k B_i^* O_i^* \exp(-\beta^* c_{ij}^k) \right]^{-1} \tag{14.48}$$

Note that if one were now to sum over all $k$, the original gravity model result would be obtained.

Alternatively, it might be useful to investigate a single-mode situation, or a model for trip interchange by person type. To obtain this, equation 14.43 is summed over all $k$, as shown in equation (14.49).

$$T_{ij}^{*n} = B_i^n C_j O_i^n A_j \sum_{k \in M(n)} \exp(-\beta^n c_{ij}^k) \tag{14.49}$$

The constants are defined in equations 14.50 and 14.51.

$$B_i^n = \left[ \sum_j C_j A_j \sum_{k \in M(n)} \exp(-\beta^n c_{ij}^k) \right]^{-1} \tag{14.50}$$

$$C_j = \left[ \sum_i \sum_n B_i^n O_i^n \sum_{k \in M(n)} \exp(-\beta^n c_{ij}^k) \right]^{-1} \tag{14.51}$$

Now, if each person type $n$ perceives a nonmodal-specific cost of traveling between $i$ and $j$, denoted $c_{ij}^n$, a new version of equation 14.49 could be developed. In such a case, the summation over the available modes is replaced by a single term, $\exp(-\beta^n c_{ij}^n)$, and the model becomes equation 14.52.

$$T_{ij}^{*n} = B_i^n O_i^n C_j A_j \exp(-\beta^n c_{ij}^n) \tag{14.52}$$

This time, the constants again take a new definition, equations 14.53 and 14.54.

$$B_i^n = \left[ \sum_j C_j A_j \exp(-\beta^n c_{ij}^n) \right]^{-1} \tag{14.53}$$

$$C_j = \left[ \sum_i \sum_n B_i^n O_i^n \exp(-\beta^n c_{ij}^n) \right]^{-1} \tag{14.54}$$

## Modal-split Models

There is another property of this basic theory that is worth exploring at this point: the use of the theory to devise a modal-split model. Several alternative forms may be developed based upon different assumptions about knowledge of trip ends, modes, etc.[8] Only one of these forms will be examined here, since this will be referred to again in chapter 16. Suppose that $T_{ij}^k$, $O_i^k$ and $D_j^k$ are the proportions of each of $T_{ij}$, $O_i$, and $D_j$ carried by mode $k$ in a multimodal situation. The original constraint equations, 14.3, 14.4, and 14.5 now have to be modified to equations 14.55, 14.56, and 14.57.

$$\sum_i \sum_k T_{ij}^k = A_j \tag{14.55}$$

$$\sum_j \sum_k T_{ij}^k = O_i \tag{14.56}$$

$$\sum_i \sum_j \sum_k T_{ij}^k c_{ij}^k = C \tag{14.57}$$

The maximand is now given by equation 14.58.

$$w(T_{ij}^k) = \frac{T!}{\prod_i \prod_j \prod_k T_{ij}^k!} \tag{14.58}$$

No knowledge is assumed of trip-end modal split in equations 14.55, 14.56, and 14.57, since these constraints only require total trips over all modes in the constraint equations. Using Lagrange multipliers as before, and solving for the maximum, equation 14.59 results.

$$T_{ij}^k = \exp(-\lambda_i - \lambda_j - \beta c_{ij}^k) \tag{14.59}$$

Setting $B_i = \exp(-\lambda_i)/O_i$ and $C_j = \exp(-\lambda_j)/A_j$, as before, equation 14.59 can be simplified to equation 14.60.

$$T_{ij}^k = B_i C_j O_i A_j \exp(-\beta c_{ij}^k) \tag{14.60}$$

However, $T_{ij}$ can be written as a summation over all modes, of equation 14.60, (equation 14.61).

$$T_{ij} = \sum_k T_{ij}^k = B_i C_j O_i A_j \sum_k \exp(-\beta c_{ij}^k) \tag{14.61}$$

Thus, the modal-split proportions can be expressed as equation 14.62.

$$\frac{T_{ij}^k}{T_{ij}} = \frac{\exp(-\beta c_{ij}^k)}{\sum_k \exp(-\beta c_{ij}^k)} \tag{14.62}$$

Two things may be noted about equation 14.62 at this point. On an aggregate level, the left-hand side of the equation, $T_{ij}^k/T_{ij}$, is the a priori probability of travelers between zones $i$ and $j$ using mode $k$. Similarly, it can be seen that, in a two-mode case, equation 14.62 can be written as equation 14.63.

$$\frac{T_{ij}^1}{T_{ij}} = \frac{\exp(-\beta c_{ij}^1)}{\exp(-\beta c_{ij}^1) + \exp(-\beta c_{ij}^2)} \qquad (14.63)$$

This equation is discussed further in chapter 16.

Similarly, one can modify this modal-split model by considering the generalized model of equation 14.43. It is simpler to examine first the model produced by the modal-distribution model, equation 14.46. The proportion of trips by mode $k$ will be given by equation 14.64.

$$\frac{T_{ij}^{k*}}{T_{ij}^{**}} = \frac{\exp(-\beta^* c_{ij}^k)}{\sum_{k'} \exp(-\beta^* c_{ij}^{k'})} \qquad (14.64)$$

This can be rewritten as equation 14.65.

$$\frac{T_{ij}^{k*}}{T_{ij}^{**}} = \frac{1}{1 + \sum_{k' \neq k} \exp[-\beta^*(c_{ij}^{k'} - c_{ij}^k)]} \qquad (14.65)$$

This is a logit model for a situation in which an unspecified number of modes exist. This model is referred to again later.

A modal-split model can also be formed for each person type by using equation 14.43 directly. By the same argument as above, equation 14.66 results.

$$\frac{T_{ij}^{kn}}{T_{ij}^{*n}} = \frac{\exp(-\beta^n c_{ij}^k)}{\sum_{k' \in M(n)} \exp(-\beta^n c_{ij}^{k'})} \qquad (14.66)$$

This model has some interesting implications that are also discussed later.


**Implications of the Theories**

First, referring back to equations 14.41 and the trip-end constraints 14.39 and 14.40, it is clear that $C^{(n)}$ must exceed some minimum value, in order that a value of $T_{ij}^{kn}$ can exist that meets the trip-end constraints. As $\beta^n$, in equation 14.43, tends to infinity, $T_{ij}^{kn}$ becomes very small and hence $\Sigma_{ijk} T_{ij}^{kn} c_{ij}^k$ tends to a minimum. This minimum value must therefore be the minimum value of $C^{(n)}$. To achieve finite values of $\beta^n$ by calibration demonstrates a value of $C^{(n)}$ larger than the minimum. This implies that people will travel more than the minimum distance, and are also prepared to travel by more expensive modes. (Remember that the cost, $c_{ij}^k$, is a generalized cost, including, at minimum, travel cost and travel time.)

In modal split, it may therefore be inferred that large values of $\beta^n$ indicate considerable sensitivity to travel cost and will tend to result in most people choosing the minimum-cost mode. Similarly, low values of $\beta^n$ show low price discrimination, or a relatively cost-inelastic situation. It is interesting to note that these interpretations on $\beta^n$ are also conformal with the assumptions of economic consumer behavior.

The values, $\beta^n$, also play an important role in trip distribution. They determine average trip length and, thus, the sensitivity of people to trip length. If $\beta^n$ is small, $C^{(n)}$ is large and so also is average trip length ($\bar{c}^k$).

A number of further implications can be drawn from these models, but are not expanded upon here. However, the approach may be extended to yield route-choice models, which are examined briefly.

## Route-choice Models

The extension to route-choice models is achieved by defining a $c_{ij}^k$ for each route, $\gamma_{ij}^r$, and applying a similar methodology to define $S_{ij}^{rn}/S_{ij}^{*n}$, where $S_{ij}^{rn}$ is the number of trips between $i$ and $j$ by persons of type $n$ on the $r$th route. Two alternative route-split mechanisms are considered: one in which mode and route split are combined in one operation; and the other in which mode choices are considered to occur first, followed by within-mode route splits.

The first alternative yields a model of the form of equation 14.67.

$$\frac{S_{ij}^{rn}}{S_{ij}^{*n}} = \frac{\exp(-\mu^n \gamma_{ij}^r)}{\sum\limits_{r' \in M_{ij}(n)} \exp(-\mu^n \gamma_{ij}^{r'})} \tag{14.67}$$

The second alternative yields two models, the first of which is mode split (equation 14.68).

$$\frac{T_{ij}^{kn}}{T_{ij}^{*n}} = \frac{\exp(-\lambda^n C_{ij}^k)}{\sum\limits_{k' \in M(n)} \exp(-\lambda^n C_{ij}^{k'})} \tag{14.68}$$

Then the route split within modes is given by equation 14.69.

$$\frac{S_{ij}^{rn}}{T_{ij}^{kn}} = \frac{\exp(-\mu^n \gamma_{ij}^r)}{\sum\limits_{r' \in R_{ij}(k)} \exp(-\mu^n \gamma_{ij}^{r'})} \tag{14.69}$$

where $R_{ij}(k)$ is the set of routes between $i$ and $j$ by mode $k$.

After examining these alternative mechanisms, and considering an example, it may be concluded that, a priori, the second mechanism appears to be preferable to the first. The reason for this is the fact that, in considering a new route, the first mechanism causes a change in a mode different from the one affected by the new route, while the second mechanism does not do this. In other words, a change in a specific route of a specific mode will change all $S_{ij}^m/S_{ij}^{*m}$ in equation 14.67, regardless of the mode or route. Thus, the addition of a new bus route will change all route allocations by automobile and rapid transit. It is admittedly true that many of these changes may be small, but they exist nonetheless, and are conceptually improper. In the second formulation, a route addition for the bus will only affect modal split for the trip interchanges affected. In turn, this route change will also affect only those routes between the zones where it occurs. This is conceptually more satisfying.

**Critique and Summary of the Entropy Approach**

The entire approach discussed here is in the form of an analogy. It has provided new insights into the structure of existing trip-distribution models and has been an instrument for developing new models of modal split and route split. As will be seen subsequently, the model forms developed in these latter two areas are also conformal with those developed from a markedly different theoretical structure. The models described here have also introduced the concept of a generalized cost[9] into transportation thinking. This generalized cost, $c_{ij}^{kn}$, is a compound of all resource outlays required in executing a trip. The presence of the generalized cost in all the models developed is conformal with notions of separability of choices.[10] Again, this emphasizes the robustness of the theory. It is also worth noting that this approach has not been restricted to academic research, but has been applied in at least one major transportation study.[11]

A number of criticisms may be leveled at the approach, however. First, being an analogy, the approach does not contribute much in the way of conceptual or behavioral development, per se. A number of arguments have been raised[12] that the use of utility maximization from consumer economics provides a sounder behavioral and conceptual basis to travel forecasting and may also be used to develop a gravity-form of trip-distribution model. Questions may be raised, also, as to why there should be such concern with demonstrating possible theoretical premises for the gravity model of trip distribution. The primary gain that has been achieved is in the definition of the friction factor as an exponentiated generalized cost. It has not been demonstrated that this definition reduces the errors in the conventional gravity model and, indeed, its effects may be overwhelmed by the need still to carry out a doubly-constrained iterative solution process to evaluate the model constants. The development of mode- and route-split procedures from the gravity model does not, in fact, require the gravity model as a basis. As will be seen later there are more conceptually satisfying approaches that yield identical model forms.

Hence, one may perhaps question the importance of the controversy between utility-maximization and entropy-maximization approaches to the gravity model. Indeed, it appears from the literature that proponents of each approach can muster as many arguments against the other approach as for their own.[13]

One of the original purposes of the approach does have some merit, however. This was to show that, despite outward appearances, there is a generic similarity between the gravity and intervening-opportunity models of trip distribution. Thus, reasons for preferring the intervening-opportunity model to the gravity model on conceptual grounds were exposed as being unfounded. Instead, it was found that the intervening-opportunity model, in its aggregate form, may be less conceptually appealing than the gravity model.

In summary, the entropy-maximization approach has contributed an improved distinction between two competing trip-distribution models—the gravity model and the intervening-opportunity model. It has also provided a concept of generalized cost, which has made possible an improved definition of the friction factor (travel impedance) term of the gravity model. Finally, the approach has led to the development of a set of nonunique specifications of mode-split and route-split models, also based on the generalized cost. On the basis of these improvements, the approach may be considered as having contributed to improved understanding and formulation of travel-forecasting models. However, the entropy-maximizing approach cannot be considered to be a major breakthrough in the development of travel-forecasting procedures, or a basic new theory of travel behavior.

# 15

**The Theory of Econometric Models**

## Introduction

Another major new area of theory in the development of travel demand models is based firmly in applications of economics to travel. There are two fundamental hypotheses put forward in this approach, one of which may be considered as being fundamental to, but not previously recognized in, any travel-demand modeling; while the other is fundamental to this approach only. The first of these hypotheses is that of "abstract modes." This effectively states that demand for travel by a mode is not dependent on the name of the mode, but on the characteristics that describe the level of service that each mode offers. Thus, demand is not for travel by bus, auto, train, etc., but is for travel by a mode that offers certain levels of service in terms of travel times, travel costs, frequency, safety, comfort, etc.

The general concept, in an economic sense of the consumer-choice independence from product names or labels, was developed by Kelvin J. Lancaster.[1] He stated that

The chief technical novelty lies in breaking away from the traditional approach that goods are the direct objects of utility and, instead, supposing that it is the properties or characteristics of the goods from which utility is derived. . . . Utility or preference orderings are assumed to rank collections of characteristics and only rank collections of goods indirectly through the characteristics that they possess.[2]

In the present modeling atmosphere, this may not seem to be a very startling hypothesis. However, when it was first put forward in about 1965-66, it was a very new concept and had not become very largely accepted in modeling mode choice.

The second basic hypothesis of this type of modeling concerns the theoretical basis for the construction of the model. The model to be built is a compound model, covering the total demand for travel between a pair of points by each available mode. The initial model form of the Baumol-Quandt model[3] is hypothesized as an adaptation of the gravity-model form. Later developments of this model form have been based specifically on assumptions about the direct-elasticities and cross-elasticities of demand with respect to each parameter in the model. The initial form of the Baumol-Quandt model, and also later developments, have generally assumed a constant elasticity of demand for travel by each mode with respect

253

to the various parameters. These two basic hypotheses can be summarized as follows: Demand for travel utilizes a demand for abstract modal types, that is, the characteristics that make up a level-of-service specification for a mode. The form of a model for travel demand by mode and $i-j$ pair can be determined by considering the direct- and cross-elasticities of demand.

Each specific model that has been proposed then goes on to develop several additional assumptions to specify more completely the actual function to be expected. Before looking at these specific developments, it is possible to develop some generalized statements of the modeling technique.[4] Two specific types of models can be developed here: the conductivity-demand model and the competition product-form demand model.

*Conductivity Model*

The first conductivity model can be put forward in the following way:

Let $a_k$ = a mode-specific conductivity parameter (mode $k$)

$V_{kijl}$ = the $l$th variable describing level of service on mode $k$ between origin $i$ and destination $j$

and $b_{kl}$ = a mode-specific parameter associated with the $l$th level of service variable of mode $k$

Then, the conductivity, or description of the ease of travel between two points by a specific mode, can be defined as in equation 15.1.

$$C_{kij} = a_k \prod_l (V_{kijl})^{b_{kl}} \tag{15.1}$$

The demand for travel will also be determined by the characteristics of the origin and destination, and mode-independent measures of the disutility of travel in general. Defining the trip-making propensity of the $i-j$ pair as $K_{ij}$, $K_{ij}$ can be expressed as in equation 15.2.

$$K_{ij} = c \prod_n (O_{in})^{d_n} \prod_m (D_{jm})^{e_m} \prod_p (W_{ijp})^{f_p} \tag{15.2}$$

where $c$ = a mode-independent parameter

$d_n, e_m, f_p$ = mode-independent parameters associated with the variables $O_{in}, D_{jm}, W_{ijp}$, respectively

$O_{in}$ = the $n$th variable describing the trip-generating propensity of origin $i$

$D_{jm}$ = the $m$th variable describing the trip-attracting propensity of destination $j$

and $\quad W_{ijp} =$ the $p$th variable describing mode-independent travel disutility between $i$ and $j$

Then, using the basic gravity-model formulation, the total trips between origin $i$ and destination $j$ can be determined as the product of the trip-making propensity of the $i-j$ pair and the sum of the travel conductivities by each mode, which is presented in equation 15.3.

$$T_{ij} = K_{ij} \sum_q [C_{qij}]^g \qquad (15.3)$$

where $g$ is a mode-independent parameter.

The product form of equations 15.1 and 15.2 is based partly on the gravity-model concept and partly on the fact that the assumption is being made that each mode has a constant elasticity of demand with each level-of-service variable. The elasticity of demand for a mode with respect to one of the characteristics of that mode is defined in equation 15.4.

$$e_x = \frac{\partial D}{\partial x} \cdot \frac{x}{D} \qquad (15.4)$$

where $\quad e_x =$ the direct-elasticity with respect to the variable $x$

$x =$ the level-of-service variable

and $\quad D =$ demand

Equation 15.5 presents the general form of the demand model.

$$D = ax^b \qquad (15.5)$$

Taking logs and partial derivatives produces equations 15.6, 15.7, and 15.8.

$$\ln D = \ln a + b \ln x \qquad (15.6)$$

$$\frac{\partial D}{D} = b \frac{\partial x}{x} \qquad (15.7)$$

$$\frac{\partial D}{\partial x} \cdot \frac{x}{D} = b = \text{constant} \qquad (15.8)$$

Hence, with respect to the conductivity, it can be seen that the model is a constant-elasticity model. To illustrate this, consider a conductivity comprising three variables: time, $t$; cost, $c$; and frequency, $f$. This is shown in equation 15.9.

$$C_{kij} = a_k (t_{kij})^{b_{kt}} (c_{kij})^{b_{kc}} (f_{kij})^{b_{kf}} \qquad (15.9)$$

Proceeding as shown in equations 15.6 and 15.7, equation 15.10 arises for $t_{kij}$, and similarly for $c_{kij}$ and $f_{kij}$.

$$\frac{\partial C_{kij}}{C_{kij}} = b_{kt} \frac{\partial t_{kij}}{t_{kij}} \tag{15.10}$$

Now the demand for trips between $i$ and $j$ by each mode is to be determined separately. This modeling approach makes the assumption that each mode's share is in proportion to the ratio of the conductivity of that mode to the sum of the conductivities of all the modes. This assumption is expressed in equation 15.11.

$$T_{ijk} = T_{ij} \frac{C_{kij}}{\sum_{l} C_{lij}} \tag{15.11}$$

This, then, is the conductivity model in general terms. Some specific forms of this model are considered later in this chapter.

### Modal-competition Product-form Model

The modal-competition product-form model uses similar variables, but differs from the conductivity model in two basic ways. First, the model uses only a single operator, namely multiplication, to express the modal shares of trips between each $i-j$ pair. Second, the model assumes that the trips by one mode are related, multiplicatively, to the disutility, or level-of-service variables of competing modes. Thus, the model develops as shown in equation 15.12.

$$T_{ijk} = a_k \prod_n (O_{in})^{b_{kn}} \prod_m (D_{jm})^{c_{km}} \prod_q \prod_l (V_{qijl})^{d_{kql}} \tag{15.12}$$

It is worth noting that in this case, the trip-production and attraction measures are raised to mode-dependent powers, and that the level-of-service variables have exponents dependent both on the mode of interest in each case and all the modes in the system.

The model is still a constant-elasticity model, and still resembles the basic gravity-model form. In fact, both of the model forms that were just developed are special cases of one generalization. The basic difference between the two forms is clearly in the way in which the modes are seen to compete.

At this point, the general treatment of this theory is supplemented by specifics of certain model developments based on this theory. A discussion of four specific models is presented below: the Baumol-Quandt model, the McLynn model, the Kraft-SARC model, and the Talvitie model.

## Baumol-Quandt Model

The original model was developed by Richard Quandt and William Baumol for the Office of High Speed Ground Transportation, in connection with the Northeast Corridor Project.[5] The model is developed basically at an intercity level, to describe movements within a corridor, such as the Boston-Washington corridor on the East Coast of the United States. The model is based, loosely, on an attempt to use the gravity-model approach to describe and predict travel demand by mode and $O-D$ pair. The argument is then used that direct-elasticities of demand with respect to each abstract modal characteristic will be constant. Thus, these characteristics enter as multiplicative terms, each raised by an exponent, which exponents have to be evaluated as part of the calibration process.

It now becomes necessary to determine the variables that should be included in the model. There are two categories of variables to be used: characteristics of the nodes, $i$ and $j$; and characteristics of the travel modes between $i$ and $j$. Quandt and Baumol propose three variables as descriptors of the nodes. Referring to equation 15.2 of the conductivity model, it can be seen that

$$O_{i1} = P_i = \text{population of node } i$$

$$O_{i2} = Y_i = \text{mean (or median) income for node } i$$

$$O_{i3} = M_i = \text{institutional character index for zone } i$$

The $D_{jm}$s are identical to the $O_{in}$s with the exception, of course, that they apply to the node $j$. The variables describing the travel modes also number three. Referring to the conductivity equation, 15.1,

$$V_{kij1} = H_{kij} = \text{travel time for the } k\text{th mode}$$

$$V_{kij2} = C_{kij} = \text{travel cost for the } k\text{th mode}$$

$$V_{kij3} = D_{kij} = \text{departure frequency of the } k\text{th mode}$$

Finally, the $W_{ijp}$ variable in equation 15.2 is the number of modes serving $i$ and $j$, denoted $N_{ij}$.

The Baumol-Quandt model is a conductivity model, with certain special features. Equation 15.13 shows its formulation.

$$T_{kij} = \alpha_0 P_i^{\alpha_1} P_j^{\alpha_2} Y_i^{\alpha_3} Y_j^{\alpha_4} M_i^{\alpha_5} M_j^{\alpha_6} N_{ij}^{\alpha_7} f_1(H) f_2(C) f_3(D) \quad (15.13)$$

The general form of the conductivity model can be expressed as equation 15.14.

$$T_{kij} = \frac{c \prod_n (O_{in})^{d_n} \prod_m (D_{jm})^{e_m} \prod_p (W_{ijp})^{f_p} \sum_q [C_{lij}]^g C_{qij}}{\sum_q [C_{qij}]} \qquad (15.14)$$

$C_{qij}$ is defined by equation 15.15 in general.

$$C_{qij} = a_q \prod_l (V_{qijl})^{b_{ql}} \qquad (15.15)$$

Equations 15.13 and 15.14 are identical when $a_l = 1$ for all $q$, $c = \alpha_0$ and where $\Sigma_q [C_{qij}]^g C_{kij}/\Sigma_q [C_{qij}]$ is replaced by $f_1(H) f_2(C) f_3(D)$. Next these functions of the mode characteristics need to be examined. Quandt and Baumol hypothesize that these functions must represent a measure of relativeness of the mode characteristics. They specify that this relativeness should be expressed by comparing each mode characteristic to the best available between the $i-j$ pair. Each characteristic is then expressed as a value relative to the best, thus defining variables $H^r_{kij}$, $C^r_{kij}$, and $D^r_{kij}$. In addition, the "best" values of each of $H_{kij}$, $C_{kij}$, and $D_{kij}$, denoted $H^b_{kij}$, $C^b_{kij}$, and $D^b_{kij}$, are entered as further components, effectively, of $\Pi_p(W_{ijp})^{f_p}$. Then, the relativeness of each mode characteristic is expressed as the ratio of the value for the mode in question to the "best" value on any mode. An example of this procedure is examined below. In the meantime, it should be noted that the model has changed to the form presented in equation 15.16.

$$T_{kij} = \alpha_0 P_i^{\alpha_1} P_j^{\alpha_2} Y_i^{\alpha_3} Y_j^{\alpha_4} M_i^{\alpha_5} M_j^{\alpha_6} N_{ij}^{\alpha_7} (H^b_{ij})^{\beta_0} \qquad (15.16)$$
$$(C^b_{ij})^{\gamma_0} (D^b_{ij})^{\delta_0} (H^r_{kij})^{\beta_1} (C^r_{kij})^{\gamma_1} (D^r_{kij})^{\delta_1}$$

This now shows certain additional specifications to the general model. First, in equation 15.14, it is clear that $g = 1$. Second, it is also obvious that the $b_{ql}$ in equation 15.15 are no longer mode-specific, and could be denoted $b_l$ only.

The question of the relative mode characteristics is considered in the following example. Consider a city pair where the values shown in Table 15-1 pertain. The "best" travel time is 55 minutes, the "best" travel cost is $3.50, and the "best" frequency is 16 departures per day. Note that the "best" value of each characteristic is taken independently of the other characteristics, and that the entire exercise is mode-independent. The values of the relative mode characteristics would now be expressed as shown in Table 15-2.

In the original paper and, more explicitly, in a paper by Richard E. Quandt and Kan H. Young,[6] a number of alternative variations of this general model form are put forward. These are not dealt with here. Certain properties of the parameters that might be expected should be noted before leaving this specific form of model. Referring to equation 15.16, it should be expected a priori that $\alpha_0$ through $\alpha_6$ will all be positive. The various travel disutility measures, times and costs principally, may be expected to have

**Table 15-1**
**Hypothetical Mode Characteristics for a City Pair**

| Mode | Travel Time | Travel Cost | Departure Frequency |
|------|-------------|-------------|---------------------|
| 1 | 55 | 35.00 | 12 |
| 2 | 70 | 8.50 | 10 |
| 3 | 90 | 3.50 | 16 |
| 4 | 80 | 5.75 | —— |

**Table 15-2**
**Hypothetical Relative Mode Characteristics from Table 15-1**

| Mode | $H^r_{kij}$ | $C^r_{kij}$ | $D^r_{kij}$ |
|------|------|------|------|
| 1 | 1.0 | 10.0 | 0.75 |
| 2 | 1.27 | 2.43 | 0.625 |
| 3 | 1.64 | 1.00 | 1.00 |
| 4 | 1.45 | 1.64 | — |

negative exponents, with the exception of frequency. The "best" values, which enter as $i-j$ descriptors, will be expected to have negative exponents, since the greater the travel disutility, the fewer trips between $i$ and $j$ will be expected. (Again, frequency of departure should be excepted, since this is a variable that is desirable to have as large as possible to give least disutility.) Likewise, the share of a specific mode will decrease as its characteristics increase relative to the "best" (decrease, in the case of departure frequency).

The final variable in the model, $N_{ij}$, is a little less obvious, a priori. Given that it is a measure of supply, and supply generally reflects demand, a positive exponent might be anticipated. This would occur, since the greater the number of modes, the more travel presumably takes place between the $i-j$ pair concerned. However, this is not useful for predictive purposes. First, it would be found that an increase of modes would apparently have the likelihood of increasing the travel between $i$ and $j$ by all modes. Second, the model would be overly sensitive to the definition of a mode. It can clearly become possible to make gross underestimates or overestimates in the future, according to present definition of a mode. If each separate operator of a carrier is defined as a mode (e.g., each railroad company, each airline company, etc.) then the exponent of $N_{ij}$ will be small, and the model will predict effectively the patronage of each operator. Predicting to the future, when a single new mode is introduced, presumably with one operator, may cause an underestimation of its effect on the market. Similarly, the estimation might go the other way if modes were defined much more parsimoniously.

Finally, one or two further properties of this model are of interest with respect to prediction in a situation where a new mode is added. In adding a new mode, two basic alternatives are possible: The new mode will not better the "best" existing mode in relation to any of the system characteristics included in the model; or it may have at least one characteristic that now becomes the "best." Under the first alternative, the model for each mode will experience an increase in the value of $N_{ij}$. However, since the "best" system characteristics remain unchanged, no other changes will occur for the existing modes. This means that travel on *all* existing modes will increase as a result of the new mode being introduced. Also, of course, the new mode will, itself, generate a demand. Therefore, the addition of the new mode will cause an increase in total demand, which will probably be large.

If at least one of the characteristics of the new mode is better than an existing "best," then the situation is less clear-cut. Certainly the new mode can be expected to generate a substantial patronage. However, the amount of demand it will divert from existing modes, if any, will depend upon the amount by which the existing "best" has been bettered, and on the importance of that characteristic in the prediction of $T_{kij}$. It is clearly possible to find that, if the increase in $N_{ij}^{\alpha_7}$, together with the effect of a smaller "best" value for one of the $V_{ijl}^b$s, is greater then the effect of a reduction in demand due to a change in $V_{ijl}^r$, then existing modes may actually obtain increased patronage as a result of the introduction of the new mode. Again, the effect of adding a new mode is an increase in total travel demand between $i$ and $j$. This will be dealt with further, later in this chapter.

The model shown here represents the original form of the Baumol-Quandt model. Subsequently, some of the criticisms that can be levelled against this particular model were considered by the authors and resulted in modified versions of the original model.[7]

*Prediction Errors in the Baumol-Quandt Model*

The model form to be evaluated in terms of its prediction error is presented in equation 15.17.

$$T_{kij} = \alpha_0 P_i^{\alpha_1} \ P_j^{\alpha_2} \ Y_i^{\alpha_3} \ Y_j^{\alpha_4} \ M_i^{\alpha_5} \ M_j^{\alpha_6} \ N_{ij}^{\alpha_7} \ (H_{ij}^b)^{\beta_0}$$

$$(H_{ij}^r)^{\beta_1} (C_{ij}^b)^{\gamma_0} (C_{ij}^r)^{\gamma_1} (D_{ij}^b)^{\delta_0} (D_{ij}^r)^{\delta_1} \tag{15.17}$$

Clearly, the prediction error of $T_{kij}$, ,$e_k$, will be a long and complex expression, since there are 13 separate items subject to error in this model. The form of the partial differentials is shown in equations 15.18 and 15.19.

$$\frac{\partial T_{kij}}{\partial P_i} = \alpha_1 \alpha_0 P_i^{\alpha_1-1} P_j^{\alpha_2} Y_i^{\alpha_3} Y_j^{\alpha_4} M_i^{\alpha_5} M_j^{\alpha_6} N_{ij}^{\alpha_7} (H_{ij}^b)^{\beta_0} (H_{ij}^r)^{\beta_1}$$

$$(C_{ij}^b)^{\gamma_0} (C_{ij}^r)^{\gamma_1} (D_{ij}^b)^{\delta_0} (D_{ij}^r)^{\delta_1} \tag{15.18}$$

$$\frac{\partial T_{jik}}{\partial P_i} = \frac{\alpha_1}{P_i} T_{kij} \tag{15.19}$$

After determining the set of partial differentials the total error of prediction for the model can be represented by equation 15.20.

$$e_k^2 = (T_{kij})^2 \left[ \frac{\alpha_1^2}{P_i^2} e_{P_i}^2 + \frac{\alpha_2^2}{P_j^2} e_{P_j}^2 + \frac{\alpha_3^2}{Y_i^2} e_{Y_i}^2 + \ldots \right]$$

$$+ (T_{kij})^2 \left[ \frac{\alpha_1 \alpha_2}{P_i P_j} e_{P_i} e_{P_j} r_{P_i P_j} + \ldots \right] \tag{15.20}$$

The first square bracket will contain 13 terms, but the second will contain 156 terms. This clearly makes equation 15.20 prohibitive to evaluate in this book. It is clear that the prediction error is proportional to the value of $T_{kij}$, so that $e_k/T_{kij}$ will be a constant percentage for any value of $T_{kij}$, assuming that all other errors are not dependent on the size of the parameters. It can also be seen that the errors will become rapidly larger as more variables are added, particularly if relatively high correlations exist between some of the parameters.

Finally, a brief look is provided at the effects of measurement error on regression estimates of the exponents for the estimation procedure used by Quandt and Baumol. Equation 15.21 shows a simple model form used here for illustrative purposes.

$$y = ax^b \tag{15.21}$$

Logarithmic transformation results in equations 15.22 and 15.23.

$$\ln y = \ln a + b \ln x \tag{15.22}$$

$$V = A \pm bU \tag{15.23}$$

where $V = \ln y$ and $U = \ln x$

The resulting measurement errors for $V$ and $U$ are given by equations 15.24 and 15.25.

$$e_V = \pm e_y/y \tag{15.24}$$

$$e_U = \pm e_x/x \tag{15.25}$$

These errors can then be used to determine the errors in the estimate of $b$. Hence, by extrapolation of this treatment to the multivariate case, the total prediction errors for the Baumol-Quandt model could be determined.

## McLynn Model

The McLynn model was also developed as part of the Northeast Corridor Project.[8] Again, it is an inter-city model, but it is specifically concerned with modal split alone. That is, it assumes a demand between an $i-j$ pair and allocates this demand among alternative available modes. The given demand is assumed to be generated by a gravity-model formulation, where the number of trips between zones $i$ and $j$ is assumed as in equation 15.26 (using the notation from the first section of this chapter).

$$T_{ij} = K_{ij} \sum_q [C_{qij}]^g \qquad (15.26)$$

This model formulation is referred to a little later in this section.

In the examination of the derivation of the McLynn model, the entire mathematical derivation is not given here, but the basis for it is set up and the final model that results is given. The McLynn model is based on a set of assumptions, which can be summarized in the following way:

1. It is assumed that no mode can be assigned a negative share of the market. This is expressed in equation 15.27.

$$0 \le T_{kij} \le 1 \qquad (15.27)$$

The $T_{kij}$s are expressed as fractions of the total demand.

2. Similarly, it is assumed that total demand must be completely allocated among available modes, as shown in equation 15.28.

$$\sum_k T_{kij} = 1 \qquad (15.28)$$

3. It is assumed that each modal share is a strictly monotone decreasing function of each transportation variable describing that mode, $V_{kijl}$.

4. It is assumed that all modes represent real options of travel. However, it is assumed that no mode has an assured minimum market (i.e., $T_{kij} = 0$ is possible); that any mode can theoretically cater to the entire demand (i.e., $T_{kij} = 1$ is also possible); and that any pair of modes can divide the whole market without either going to zero (i.e., $T_{1ij} + T_{2ij} = 1$ without either $T_{1ij} = 0$ or $T_{2ij} = 0$).

5. It is assumed that the model will have real and continuous second derivatives, as presented in equation 15.29.

$$\frac{\partial^2 T_{kij}}{\partial V_{mijl} \, \partial V_{nijt}} = \frac{\partial^2 T_{kij}}{\partial V_{nijt} \, \partial V_{mijl}} \qquad (15.29)$$

6. Assumptions 1 and 3 together ensure that each mode will have negative demand-elasticity with respect to its own system characteristics. It is now assumed, further, that the cross-elasticity of demand for a mode with respect to the characteristics of any other mode will be nonnegative, as is expressed in equations 15.30 and 15.31.

$$\frac{V_{kijl}}{T_{kij}} \frac{\partial T_{kij}}{\partial V_{kijl}} < 0 \tag{15.30}$$

$$\frac{V_{mijl}}{T_{kij}} \frac{\partial T_{kij}}{\partial V_{mijl}} \geq 0 \qquad k \neq m \tag{15.31}$$

7. Contrary to the argument developed in the introduction to this chapter, it is assumed that all direct- and cross-elasticities can be expressed as linear functions of all the modal shares. A constant elasticity assumption, in this case, can be shown to have no nontrivial solutions, as shown in equation 15.32.

$$\frac{V_{mijl}}{T_{kij}} \frac{\partial T_{kij}}{\partial V_{mijl}} = \sum_p \beta'_{kijlmp} T_{pij} + \gamma_{kijlm} \tag{15.32}$$

(A constant elasticity would require $\beta'_{kijlmp} = 0$.)

These are the basic assumptions that lie behind the development of the McLynn model. Two principal features of this should be noted. In the first place, no model form is prespecified. Instead, a set of assumptions are itemized with the task of building a model that will satisfy these assumptions. Second, the principal assumptions are either logical constraints, or assumptions about demand elasticities, based on consumer theory.

Since the concern here is with a given $T_{ij}$, it will simplify the notation if the $ij$s are dropped from all subscripts, bearing in mind that the relationships are interchange-specific. Thus, assumptions 1 through 7 can be rewritten in mathematical form as presented in equations 15.33 through 15.38.

$$0 \leq T_k \leq 1 \tag{15.33}$$

$$\sum_k T_k = 1 \tag{15.34}$$

Assumptions 3 and 4 do not have mathematical expressions.

$$\frac{\partial^2 T_k}{\partial V_{ml} \partial V_{nt}} = \frac{\partial^2 T_k}{\partial V_{nt} \partial V_{ml}} \tag{15.35}$$

$$\frac{V_{kl}}{T_k} \frac{\partial T_k}{\partial V_{kl}} < 0 \tag{15.36}$$

$$\frac{V_{ml}}{T_k} \frac{\partial T_k}{\partial V_{ml}} \geq 0 \qquad k \neq m \tag{15.37}$$

$$\frac{V_{ml}}{T_k} \frac{\partial T_k}{\partial V_{ml}} = \sum_p \beta'_{klmp} T_p + \gamma_{klm} \tag{15.38}$$

For convenience, it is desirable to remove the constant term from equation 15.38. This can be done by substituting for $\beta'_{klmp}$ as shown in equations 15.39, 15.40, and 15.41.

$$\beta'_{klmp} = \beta_{klmp} - \gamma_{klm} \tag{15.39}$$

$$\frac{V_{ml}}{T_k} \frac{\partial T_k}{\partial V_{ml}} = \sum_p (\beta_{klmp} - \gamma_{klm}) T_p + \gamma_{klm} \tag{15.40}$$

$$\frac{V_{ml}}{T_k} \frac{\partial T_k}{\partial V_{ml}} = \sum_p \beta_{klmp} T_p - \gamma_{klm} \sum_p T_p + \gamma_{klm} \tag{15.41}$$

However, equation 15.34 specifies that $\sum_p T_p = 1$. Hence, equation 15.41 can be rewritten as equation 15.42.

$$\frac{V_{ml}}{T_k} \frac{\partial T_k}{\partial V_{ml}} = \sum_p \beta_{klmp} T_p \tag{15.42}$$

The second assumption also implies that the partial differentials of $\sum_k T_k$, with respect to each $V_{ml}$, are all zero, as shown in equation 15.43.

$$\frac{\partial \left( \sum_k T_k \right)}{\partial V_{ml}} = 0 \quad \text{for any } m \text{ and } l \tag{15.43}$$

Using equations 15.42 and 15.43, the nontrivial solution to the set of assumptions 1 through 7 can be developed as presented in equations 15.44 and 15.45.

$$\frac{\partial \left( \sum_k T_k \right)}{\partial V_{ml}} = \sum_k \frac{\partial T_k}{\partial V_{ml}} = 0 \tag{15.44}$$

$$\sum_k \frac{T_k}{V_{ml}} \sum_p \beta_{klmp} T_p = 0 \tag{15.45}$$

From equation 15.45, it can be established that as a result of assumption 4, $\beta_{lmkk}$ and $\beta_{lmkp}$ are as shown in equations 15.46 and 15.47, respectively.

$$\beta_{lmkk} = 0 \tag{15.46}$$

$$\beta_{lmkp} = -\beta_{lmpk} \tag{15.47}$$

However, assumption 6 leads to $\beta_{lmkq} \geq 0$ and $\beta_{lmqk} \geq 0$. For these to hold along with equation 15.47, $\beta_{lmkp}$ has to equal 0, where $m$, $k$, and $p$ are all distinct. Thus, the only nonzero values of $\beta_{lmkp}$ will be those of the form:

$$\beta_{lmmp} \quad \text{or} \quad \beta_{lmpm} \quad p \neq m$$

By considering a simple two-mode case, McLynn develops the form of the models that predict $T_1$ and $T_2$ and satisfy these various constraints. Before embarking on this, however, McLynn makes the following statements.

The special case of the model in which all the $(\beta_{lmkp})$'s are equal to zero can be considered at this point. This possibility is ruled out by the assumption that the (direct-) elasticities of each mode are negative. It follows then that $(\beta_{lmmp})$ must be nonzero for some value of $p$.[9]

It appears, however, that McLynn overlooked the fact that the constant-elasticity formulation would specify that the $\beta'_{lmmp}$s are zero, not the $\beta_{lmmp}$s. Thus, this statement does not support the contention that a constant-elasticity solution is necessarily trivial.

By developing the simple, two-mode case, McLynn is able to put forward a general model of the form as represented by equation 15.48.

$$T_k = \frac{\alpha_k \prod\limits_{m,l} V_{ml}^{b_{mlk}}}{\sum\limits_{n} \alpha_n \prod\limits_{m,l} V_{ml}^{b_{mln}}} \qquad (15.48)$$

Bearing in mind that this is a modal-split model, the total-demand model could be written as in equation 15.49.

$$T_{kij} = \frac{K_{ij} \sum\limits_{n} [C_{nij}]^g C_{kij}}{\sum\limits_{n} [C_{nij}]} \qquad (15.49)$$

$C_{nij}$ is defined as in equation 15.50.

$$C_{nij} = \alpha_n \prod\limits_{m,l} V_{ml}^{b_{mln}} \qquad (15.50)$$

Equation 15.26 can be used to generate the total demand. In this case, it can also be seen that the McLynn model is a special case of the conductivity model, in which the $\Pi_p(W_{ijp})^{y_p}$ is unity (since there would be no term of this form in the gravity model). It only needs to be added here that the biggest problem that has been met with in using this model is finding a satisfactory demand model. The simple gravity formulation is not entirely suitable, and leads to some problems that are discussed at the conclusion of this chapter.

## Kraft-SARC Model

The Kraft-SARC model[10] is an attempt to provide a logical and predictively valid structure for estimating demand by mode. The approach is not confined to either intercity or intracity trips, but is considered as a general travel-demand approach. However, in the original form (developed by the Systems Analysis and Research Corporation—SARC), it was again an intercity model developed for the Northeast Corridor (NEC) Project.

The Kraft-SARC model is, like the McLynn model, based upon several assumptions or hypotheses. These assumptions may be itemized as follows:

1. It is assumed that the direct-elasticities of demand for a mode with respect to its own characteristics will be nonpositive.
2. It is assumed that the cross-elasticities of demand for a mode with respect to characteristics of other modes will be nonnegative.
3. It is assumed that the demand curve, expressing the relation between demand and total "price" (where "price" does not refer to money cost alone) is hyperbolic. This implies a relationship as expressed in equation 15.51.

$$T_{kij} = K \prod_m (X_{mij})^{\alpha m} \tag{15.51}$$

4. Travel demand by mode is assumed to be determined by the following characteristics:
   a) Characteristics describing the level of service offered by the mode in question
   b) Characteristics describing the level of service offered by the other available modes
   c) Characteristics of the traveler that may be associated with his travel choices
   d) Characteristics that describe the propensity of a zone, $j$, to attract trips

On the basis of these four assumptions, a model of the form expressed in equation 15.51 is hypothesized.

$$T_{kij} = \alpha_k \prod_m (O_{im})^{b km} \prod_n (D_{jn})^{c kn} \prod_q \prod_l (V_{qijl})^{d ql} \tag{15.52}$$

This model is clearly the modal-competition product form. Since each $d_{kl}$ will be negative, and each $d_{ql}(q \neq k)$ will be positive, then assuming a negative value for all $d_{ql}$s, equation 15.42 can be rewritten as equation 15.53.

$$T_{kij} = \frac{\alpha_k \prod_m (O_{im})^{b km} \prod_n (D_{jn})^{c kn} \prod_l (V_{kijl})^{d kl}}{\prod_{q(\neq k)} \prod_l (V_{qijl})^{d ql}} \tag{15.53}$$

It is also clear that this model is a constant-elasticity model.

Kraft suggests an explicit model of the form shown in equation 15.54.

$$T_{kij} = \alpha_k (Y_i)^{\beta_1} (P_i)^{\beta_2} (E_j)^{\beta_3} \prod_l (V_{kijl})^{\delta_{kl}} \prod_{q(\neq k)} \prod_l (V_{qijl})^{\gamma_{ql}} \quad (15.54)$$

where $Y_i$ and $P_i$ are median income and population for node $i$, $E_j$ is an employment measure for node $j$, and the other variables are as previously defined.

The formulation as put forward here is much less restricted and specific than the Baumol-Quandt and McLynn models. Kraft also indicates that other forms of the model may be desirable to use different concepts of demand elasticities, some of which are mentioned in his paper.[11] Gerald Kraft and Martin Wohl later modified the model for use in the intraurban case of travel-demand modeling.[12]

## Talvitie Model

The final example of an econometric travel-demand model is a model developed by Antti P. Talvitie.[13] This model is concerned with travel-demand model estimation for downtown work trips. Talvitie attempted to predict directly zone-to-zone work trips by mode. Similar to the Baumol-Quandt and Kraft-SARC models, it simultaneously predicts trip generation, trip distribution, and modal split. The Talvitie model postulates that the number of interzonal work trips is dependent on travel time and cost, on size and socioeconomic characteristics of the labor force in each origin zone, and on the number of jobs in the destination zone.

The Talvitie model is based on the Kraft-SARC model in that it extends that model to a three-mode situation (auto, bus, and rail) and is, therefore, a modal-competition product-form model. Equation 15.55 presents the functional form of the Talvitie model.

$$T_{kij} = F\{L_{kij}, SE_i, SE_j\} \quad (15.55)$$

where    $T_{kij}$ = the number of round trip work trips from zone $i$ to zone $j$ via mode $k$

           $L_{kij}$ = vector of level-of-service characteristics for mode $k$ operating between zone $i$ and zone $j$

           $SE_i$ = a vector of the socioeconomic characteristics for travelers from zone $i$

           $SE_j$ = a vector of socioeconomic characteristics for the destination zone $j$

Talvitie introduces a number of elasticity constraints in order to arrive at structurally valid travel demand models. Equations 15.56 and 15.57 show the elasticity constraints for the bus model.

$$\frac{\partial T_{bij}}{\partial L_{kij}} \frac{L_{kij}}{T_{bij}} \leq 0 \quad \text{for} \quad k = \text{bus} \tag{15.56}$$

where $b = $ bus

$$\frac{\partial T_{bij}}{\partial L_{kij}} \frac{L_{kij}}{T_{bij}} \geq 0 \quad \text{for} \quad k = \text{auto or rail} \tag{15.57}$$

For the rail model the same elasticity constraints hold that are presented in equation 15.56 and 15.57, except that the bus mode is replaced by the rail mode. In addition to the constraints that the direct demand elasticities be less than or equal to zero, and the cross-elasticities be greater than or equal to zero, a further constraint is introduced. The latter postulates that the elasticity of demand with respect to zone size variables be equal to one. Equation 15.58 represents an example of the specific form of the Talvitie model.

$$V^k = e^a e^{b_1 OT^a} e^{b_2 IT^a} e^{b_3 OT^b} e^{b_4 IT^b} e^{b_5 OT^r} e^{b_6 IT^r} e^{b_7 RC^a}$$

$$e^{b_8 OC^a} e^{b_9 AC^b} e^{b_{10} F^b} e^{b_{11} AC^r} e^{b_{12} F^r} e^{b_{13} I} e^{b_{14} CC}$$

$$e^{b_{15} L} e^{b_{16} E} (OT^a)^{C_1} (IT^a)^{C_2} (OT^b)^{C_3} (IT^b)^{C_4} (OT^r)^{C_5}$$

$$(IT^r)^{C_6} (RC^a)^{C_7} (OC^a)^{C_8} (AC^b)^{C_9} (F^b)^{C_{10}} (AC^r)^{C_{11}}$$

$$(F^r)^{C_{12}} I^{C_{13}} CC^{C_{14}} L^{C_{15}} E^{C_{16}} \tag{15.58}$$

where
$V^k = $ the travel volume by mode $k$ between two zones

$OT^a, OT^b, OT^r = $ out-of-vehicle travel times by auto, bus, and rail, respectively, between the two zones

$IT^a, IT^b, IT^r = $ in-vehicle travel times by auto, bus, and rail, respectively between the two zones

$RC^a = $ the running (operating) cost of the auto

$OC^a = $ the out-of-pocket auto cost

$AC^b, AC^r = $ the access costs for bus and rail, respectively

$F^b, F^r = $ the fares on bus and rail, respectively

$I = $ the income of the origin zone

$CC = $ the number of cars per person in the origin zone

$L = $ the labor force in the origin zone

$E = $ the employment ratio in the destination zone

$$a = \text{a constant}$$

$$b_1, b_2, \ldots, b_{16} = \text{coefficients (elasticities and cross-elasticities of demand) found by constrained elasticities and least squares}$$

$$c_1, c_2, \ldots, c_{16} = \text{exponents (elasticities and cross-elasticities of demand) found by constrained least squares}$$

The Talvitie model does not present a major digression from the Kraft-SARC model. Its difference and contribution lies in the fact that it deals with intracity work trips, that it attempts to extend the former model to a three-mode case, and that Talvitie conducted a number of predictive and structural accuracy tests with his models in relation to traditional transit models. He shows that his econometric model is superior in predictive accuracy, in that it has both a lower percent mean error and lower variation of the error than the traditional model.

**Summary**

In general, all four of these techniques represent an attempt to use economic consumer-behavior theory as the basis of a travel-demand model. All four models, implicitly or explicitly, end up using assumptions about the form and signs of the elasticities of demand with characteristics that may determine that demand. The basic difference between the conductivity models and the modal-competition product-form models lies in the assumptions concerning cross-elasticities. An assumption of constant cross-elasticities leads to the modal-competition product-form, while a more complex form of cross-elasticity leads to the conductivity form.

Having placed the gravity-form demand model in the McLynn model, all four models have in common the simultaneous prediction of generation, distribution, and modal split, and can easily be extended to add route assignment to this set. They thus represent an attempt to circumvent the traditional sequential modeling approach. All the models are based also on an "abstract mode" concept, where demand for travel modes is assumed to be related to the level of service each mode offers, and not related to the "name" of the mode. Furthermore, there is an implicit assumption that the demand for each travel mode is related, not only to the level of service of that mode, but to the levels of service of all the other modes competing in the market.

However, there are two major problems that are encountered in this approach. One of these is a major theoretical problem, the other is an operational problem. The theoretical problem results from the fact that none of these approaches takes into account the idea that travel is a derived demand. All three models are based simply on the application of demand theory to travel. Thus, given a certain level of improvement in the levels of service offered by all the modes, total travel demand would be predicted to rise substantially without any reference to what that demand would be servicing. This consideration prompts the brief consideration of each of the variables contained in the models. (It should be added that the demand-prediction part of the McLynn model, developed later in the NEC Project, contained the variables median income, population with income over $10,000 per household, and employment as the pertinent socioeconomic variables.) Demand is assumed to have a constant elasticity with each of these variables, and their effects in the model are multiplicative. However, although superficially this behavior does not seem unreasonable, deeper analysis suggests that it has a number of defects. Trip making may indeed have a constant elasticity with population, but if the spatial area of each node is fixed, increasing population implies increasing residential density. Past studies tend to indicate that trip making per person or household decreases as residential density rises. Similarly, trip making increases at a decreasing rate as income increases. Finally, as was already noted, trip making will apparently increase as the levels of service of the modes improve, regardless of the trip attractions or productions per se. No account is taken of the competition between nontravel activities and activities involving travel, nor of the demand for activities.

The second major problem arises from the calibration process. At present, all four models are calibrated by using linear regression on the transformed models. In other words, the models are expressed in log form, as shown in equation 15.59.

$$\ln T_{kij} = \ln \alpha_k + \sum_m d_m \ln O_{im} + \sum_n e_n \ln D_{jn}$$

$$+ \sum_p f_p \ln W_{ijp} + \sum_q \sum_l b_{mlq} \ln V_{mlq} \qquad (15.59)$$

The values of $\ln \alpha_k$, $d_m$s, $e_n$s, $f_p$s, and $b_{mlq}$s are estimated by applying least squares regression to equation 15.59, using a sample set of data. Because of the transformation process used, this form of estimation presents considerable problems when the variable to be predicted is $T_{kij}$, and not $\ln T_{kij}$. Serious problems of measurement errors and independent-variable collinearities also raise calibration problems.

In general, in spite of the plausibility of the basic model theories, current applications have not been conspicuously successful. Use of the Kraft-SARC and Baumol-Quandt models in the NEC Project yielded forecasts that were considered to be implausible. The McLynn model was more successful, and was adopted as the modal-split model. However, serious problems were encountered in devising a demand-estimating model, and without the same drawbacks as the former two models. No comments of this nature can be made about the Talvitie model, since it has not been used in any application.

# 16 Behavioral Travel-demand Models

## General

The last area of developmental work that is considered in this book is one that has been termed "the disaggregate, behavioral, probabilistic modeling of travel demand," a terminology that is discussed further below. Currently, it is widely held by researchers that this approach has the greatest likelihood of providing the basis for a totally new and more policy-responsive travel-forecasting procedure. At present, however, there has been little work that has progressed to the point of operation in typical transportation-planning situations. Thus, most of what is described here is the theory and empirical research undertaken so far.

As mentioned above, the approach has been described as being disaggregate, behavioral, and probabilistic. Apart from the last adjective, this description is not literally correct, but it serves to highlight the differences between this approach and the others that have been described so far in this book. The models are described as being disaggregate because the basic unit of observation for modal calibration is the individual traveler and not a traffic zone, as in conventional transportation planning. It must be stressed, however, that the models are aggregate in the sense that a single set of parameters is sought to describe a group of the population. The models are described as being behavioral for two reasons: First, much of the theoretical underpinning of the approach is founded in two disciplines dealing with behavior—the economics of consumer behavior, and the psychology of choice behavior. Second, the models have been constructed empirically upon the basis of hypotheses concerning the identification of decision variables in travel-choice situations. Finally, the models are probabilistic, since they assign a probability to each possible outcome of a particular travel decision for a specific traveler, or potential traveler.

Thus, the models developed from this approach are markedly different from those developed in the preceding chapters of this book. It is hoped that these differences will serve to overcome or remove many of the shortcomings of the more conventional approaches, without concomitantly introducing an entirely new set of problems into the travel-forecasting process.

Work on this approach commenced at the beginning of the 1960s[1] and proceeded relatively slowly into the latter part of the decade.[2] Since then, work in the area has accelerated markedly, as a result of the growing disenchantment with conventional travel-forecasting procedures and the realization that this new approach may hold the potential to replace the conventional procedures. Most of the developmental work has been concerned with one travel choice only, namely that of modal split, or mode choice. Research and development to extend the approach to other travel choices has occurred only within the last two or three years. Reasons for the selection of mode choice and the relative slowness of developments in other choices are described later in this chapter.

**Theoretical Structure**

In this section, a number of facets of the theory of this modeling approach are explored. Most of the theory has, in fact, been formalized only recently. This is not to say that the early models were not based upon any theoretical statements, but is rather an observation that the theory was not formalized as such until some empirical insights had been gained. The earliest statements of theory were in the form of a few broad hypotheses, which formed the basis of the emprical model-building efforts. Subsequently, some major efforts have been made to reconstruct these hypotheses into a comprehensive theory, which may also assist in the tackling of certain residual problems not handled by the early models.

*Early Statement of Hypotheses*

The earliest developments of the behavioral demand-modeling approach were founded on relatively simple postulates of behavior. These postulates stated first that individuals make travel choices on the basis of the comparison of alternative levels of service provided by the transportation system and the activity system, modified by characteristics of the individual. Second, it is asserted that decision making of individuals is to be modeled by the use of probabilities of choice, wherein these probabilities must conform to the basic rules of probability as shown in equations 16.1 and 16.2.

$$0 \le p_k^i \le 1 \qquad \text{for all } i \text{ and } k \qquad (16.1)$$

$$\sum_{k=1}^{n_i} p_k^i = 1 \qquad \text{for all } i \qquad (16.2)$$

where $p_k^i$ = the probability of individual $i$ choosing the alternative $k$

and $n_i$ = the entire set of available alternatives for individual $i$

This probability is assigned on the basis of the consideration by the individual of the choice environment, modified by relevant characteristics of the individual. This assumption is, in fact, consistent with modern theories of human discrimination and choice. Placed in the context of travel demand, the assumption effectively states that an individual will make the decisions or choices, implicit in making a trip to a specific destination by a specific mode and route, with a probability determined by trip considerations and his own scaling of the effectiveness of alternatives for that trip purpose. The psychologist asserts that, in essence, every human decision is probabilistic since there is a minimum variance in discrimination and there are dynamic changes in preference. This is an extremely important concept, since it leads to two conclusions of considerable importance in attempting to construct models on this basis. These conclusions are:

1. That the number of variables required to predict probability of choice is finite and asymptotically approaches the limit of human discrimination
2. That as a set of alternative choices becomes equivalent in subjective characteristics, the probability of choice approaches a limit of $1/n$, where $n$ is the number of alternatives

This statement of hypotheses does not lead directly to any specific model structure, in mathematical terms, but does provide a broad framework in which choice models can be constructed. Subsequent work has lead to the development of more precise statements of theory, as will be seen in the next two sections of this chapter.

*Psychological Theory of Traveler Behavior*

As noted in the preceding section, the view of the psychologist, or psychometrician is that human decisions are probabilistic in nature, but are based upon an evaluation of utilities. These utilities for each alternative provide a basis for estimating the probabilities of choice for each alternative. The psychological approach to the theory of travel behavior is formalized through the application of Luce's axiom of the Independence of Irrelevant Alternatives.[3] In this approach, it is assumed that any alternative $j$ has a utility $U_{ij}$, comprising attributes of the alternative, $X_j$, modified in some manner by the attributes of the individual, $S_i$, as shown in equation 16.3.

$$U_{ij} = U(X_j, S_i) \qquad (16.3)$$

The individual is assumed to assess his utilities of each alternative and subsequently to draw weighted lots to determine his choice. Thus, the individual is assumed to have an exact and "measurable"[a] utility, but is

---

[a] The assumption that the utility is measurable itself implies a number of assumptions about utility and the availability of techniques of measurement.

uncertain of his choice even after assessing the utilities. Clearly, an individual will have a higher probability of accepting an alternative with a higher utility than any other alternative. In other words, there is assumed to be a direct correlation between probability of choice and utility. Given that the utility is assumed to be exact and measurable, this approach may be termed a *strict utility model*. Since it is asserted that there is a direct correlation between the probabilities of choice and the utilities, it seems reasonable to postulate that a ratio of probabilities can be expressed as a ratio of utilities (equation 16.4).

$$\frac{P_a^i}{P_b^i} = \frac{U(X_a, S_i)}{U(X_b, S_i)} \tag{16.4}$$

where  $P_a^i$ and $P_b^i$ =  the probabilities of individual $i$ choosing alternatives $a$ and $b$, respectively

and        $U(X,S)$ = as defined previously

Luce's axiom can be used to test the acceptability, or validity, of this postulate. The axiom of the Independence of Irrelevant Alternatives states that the relative odds of choosing one alternative over another (where both alternatives have a nonzero probability of choice) is unaffected by the presence or absence of any additional alternatives in the set. This may be written mathematically as equation 16.5.

$$\frac{P^i(a|a,b)}{P^i(b|a,b)} = \frac{P^i(a|a,b,c,\ldots)}{P^i(b|a,b,c,\ldots)} = \frac{U(X_a, S_i)}{U(X_b, S_i)} \tag{16.5}$$

Thus, the axiom substantiates the assertion of equation 16.4 and goes further. It states that the ratio of probabilities is defined *completely* by the ratio of the utilities of the two alternatives being considered *and no others*.

In order to proceed further, it is necessary to define a functional form for the utility. Without loss of generality, the functional form may be assumed to be exponential, as shown in equation 16.6.

$$U(X_a, S_i) = \exp\left[V(X_a, S_i)\right] \tag{16.6}$$

If it is further assumed that $V(X_a, S_i)$ is linear in the $X_a$s, then this equation provides a classical convex utility curve in which there is a diminishing marginal return for improvements in the attributes of the alternative $X_a$. Hence, this assumption appears to be a reasonable one in terms of utility theory. Under these assumptions, equation 16.4 can be stated as shown in equation 16.7.

$$\frac{P_a^i}{P_b^i} = \frac{\exp[V(X_a, S_i)]}{\exp[V(X_b, S_i)]} \tag{16.7}$$

If there are only two alternatives in the set of alternatives available, then application of the probability rule (equation 16.2) leads to the definition of either probability, as shown in equation 16.8, and 16.9.

$$P_a^i = \frac{\exp[V(X_a, S_i)]}{\exp[V(X_b, S_i)] + \exp[V(X_a, S_i)]} \tag{16.8}$$

$$P_b^i = \frac{\exp[V(X_b, S_i)]}{\exp[V(X_a, S_i)] + \exp[V(X_b, S_i)]} \tag{16.9}$$

Given an assumption of linearity in the $X$s, these equations may be simplified by dividing throughout by either $\exp[V(X_a, S_i)]$ or $\exp[V(X_b, S_i)]$. Such a procedure (dividing by $\exp[V(X_b, S_i)]$) yields equations 16.10 and 16.11, in place of equations 16.8 and 16.9.

$$P_a^i = \frac{\exp[V(X_a - X_b, S_i)]}{1 + \exp[V(X_a - X_b, S_i)]} \tag{16.10}$$

$$P_b^i = \frac{1}{1 + \exp[V(X_a - X_b, S_i)]} \tag{16.11}$$

These equations define the standard binary logit[4] model.

Alternatively, if it is assumed that there are $M$ alternatives available to individual $i$, then the probability of the choice of alternative $j$ from the set $M$ is given by equation 16.12.

$$P_j^i = \frac{\exp[V(X_j, S_i)]}{\sum\limits_{k=1}^{M} \exp[V(X_k, S_i)]} \tag{16.12}$$

This equation is the standard multiple-logit[5] model.

Thus, the application of Luce's axiom with some fairly broad utility assumptions has provided a specification of a model structure for a disaggregate behavioral travel-demand model. However, the significance of this theoretical development is not limited just to the provision of a model structure. Some further insights are also offered, and a new problem is posed.

The standard logit formulation assumes linearity of the exponent function, as was postulated in demonstrating that equations 16.8 and 16.9 were the binary logit model. However, it is clear that the linearity assumption cannot extend to the characteristics of the traveler since these characteristics will then disappear from the probability definition. This is an important insight, the significance of which will become more apparent in subsequent sections of this chapter.

The second insight provided by this derivation is that a linearity assumption leads to the definition of differences in characteristics of alternatives as the comparative mechanism in human decision making. Similarly, a product-form assumption would lead to ratios of characteristics. However, the linearity assumption appears to be by far the most usual one.

The problem introduced by this theoretical development is the definition of an alternative. Throughout the theory, distinct alternatives are assumed, but classification of alternatives is not a part of the theory. Clearly, inappropriate definitions of the alternatives could lead to erroneous probability definitions. An example is in order to illustrate this. Suppose an individual wishes to purchase a car. For simplicity, it will be assumed that the individual has, initially, only two choices, namely, between make and model A and make and model B. Now suppose that the relative odds of him choosing A over B are 1.5, as shown in equation 16.13.

$$\frac{P_A^i}{P_B^i} = \frac{U(X_A, S_i)}{U(X_b, S_i)} = 1.5 \qquad (16.13)$$

Since A and B are the only alternatives, it follows that $P_A^i = 0.6$ and $P_B^i = 0.4$. Now a second car of make and model B is introduced into the choice set, where the original car was green and the new one is blue. If this additional car is introduced as a third alternative, then the axiom states that equation 16.13 remains unchanged. However, assuming that the individual is indifferent between the blue and green cars of model B, two new relative probabilities are defined. Denoting the blue car as option C, equations 16.14 and 16.15 now result.

$$\frac{P_B^i}{P_C^i} = \frac{U(X_B, S_i)}{U(X_C, S_i)} = 1 \qquad (16.14)$$

$$\frac{P_A^i}{P_C^i} = \frac{U(X_A, S_i)}{U(X_C, S_i)} = 1.5 \qquad (16.15)$$

These equations together with equation 16.13, now define the probabilities as $P_A^i = 0.428$, $P_B^i = 0.286$, and $P_C^i = 0.286$. Unfortunately, since it was stated that the individual was indifferent between the two different colored cars, the expected result would have been $P_A^i = 0.6$, $P_B^i = 0.2$, and $P_C^i = 0.2$.

It is clear that much care must be taken in defining what constitutes an alternative. However, the theory provides no insights into this definitional problem.

### Economic Theory of Traveler Behavior

The fundamental difference between the psychologists's approach and the economist's approach is that the economist postulates individuals as being deterministic utility-maximizers, while the psychologist asserts that individuals make probabilistic choices based upon utility assessment. The economic theory[6] is founded on an assumption that each individual receives utility $U_k^i$. This utility comprises two elements. The first element is common to some definable subgroup of the population (e.g., those individuals with a given income, etc.). The second element is an individual amount of utility, shared with no other individual. The utility is defined in equation 16.16.

$$U_a^i = U'(X_a, S_i) + \varepsilon(X_a', S_i) \qquad (16.16)$$

where $\quad U'(X_a, S_i) = $ the common utility of alternative $a$ for individual $i$, with socioeconomic characteristics, $S_i$

and $\quad \varepsilon(X_a', S_i) = $ the individual utility of alternative $a$ for individual $i$, with socioeconomic characteristics, $S_i$

It should be noted that the set of characteristics of the alternative is specified differently in each of the two elements of utility. As will be seen later, $X_a$ and $X_a'$ are assumed to be mutually exclusive.

As stated before, the individual traveler is assumed to be a deterministic utility-maximizer. Thus, he will choose that alternative, $k$, which has the maximum utility, $U_k^i$. However, the individual element of utility cannot be observed by the analyst. Therefore, it is necessary for the analyst to assign a probability to any individual decision, as shown in equation 16.17.

$$P_k^i = Pr\{U'(X_k, S_i) + \varepsilon(X_k', S_i) > U'(X_j, S_i) + \varepsilon(X_j', S_i)\}$$

$$j = 1, \ldots, M \qquad j \neq k \qquad (16.17)$$

where $\quad P_k^i = $ the probability that individual $i$ will choose alternative $k$

and $\quad Pr\{\ \} = $ "probability that"

It is assumed that, over the population, the $\varepsilon(X_j', S_i)$ are randomly distributed. Thus, this model (equation 16.17) may be termed the *random utility model*, in contrast to the psychologist's strict utility model. Simplifying the notation by writing $U'(X_k, S_i)$ as $U'_{ki}$, $\varepsilon(X_k', S_i)$ as $\varepsilon_{ki}$, and so forth, equation 16.17 can be rearranged and written as equation 16.18.

$$P_k^i = Pr\{\varepsilon_{ki} + U'_{ki} - U'_{ji} > \varepsilon_{ji}\} \qquad (16.18)$$

$$j = 1, \ldots, M \qquad j \neq k$$

In order to develop a model structure from equation 16.18, it is necessary to make certain assumptions about the random components of utility, $\varepsilon_{ki}$ and $\varepsilon_{ji}$. First, it is assumed that the random components of utility are independent across the set of alternatives, $M$. This clearly, implies that the attributes $X_k'$, $X_j'$ must be specific to each mode and cannot be common attributes. Second, a distributional assumption must be made for the $\varepsilon_{ki}$s. Clearly, a number of distributional assumptions are possible. The obvious one would be to select a normal distribution. However, it does not appear to be possible to generate a model structure from an assumption of normality. The simplest structural solution to equation 16.18 is found by assuming that the distribution of the $\varepsilon_{ki}$s is a Weibull, which is a skewed distribution that can be almost normalized by taking logarithms. The Weibull is given by equation 16.19.

$$Pr\{\varepsilon(X',S_i) \geq \varepsilon^*\} = \exp(-e^{-\varepsilon^*}) \tag{16.19}$$

The problem is now to determine a structural solution to equation 16.18.[7] Rearranging equation 16.18, yields equation 16.20.

$$P_k^i = Pr\{\varepsilon_{ij} > \varepsilon_{ki} + U'_{ki} - U'_{ji}\} \tag{16.20}$$

$$j = 1, \ldots, M \qquad j \neq k$$

In this equation, the terms to the right of the inequality may be replaced by $\varepsilon^*$, thus yielding equation 16.21.

$$P_k^i = Pr\{\varepsilon_{ji} > \varepsilon^*\} \tag{16.21}$$

$$j = 1, \ldots, M \qquad j \neq k$$

For any given value of $j$, say $m$, the distribution of the probability has been defined by the Weibull. Thus, the distribution function of the $\varepsilon_{ji}$ may be written as shown in equation 16.22.

$$F(\varepsilon_{ji}) = \exp\left\{-\sum_{j=1}^{M} e^{-\varepsilon^*}\right\} \tag{16.22}$$

Equation 16.22 is true only if the $\varepsilon_{ji}$ values are independent across all alternatives $j$. From the distribution function one can define the density function of $\varepsilon_{ji}$ and hence define the probability that alternative $k$ has a greater utility than any other alternative. The density function for a particular $\varepsilon$ value, $\varepsilon_{ki}$, is shown in equation 16.23.

$$\frac{\partial F(\varepsilon_{ji})}{\partial \varepsilon_{ik}} = e^{-\varepsilon_{ki}} \exp\left\{-\sum_{j=1}^{M} e^{-\varepsilon_{ji}}\right\} \tag{16.23}$$

More usefully, the density function can be defined for the value $\varepsilon^*$, which is composed of $\varepsilon_{ki}$, together with the difference between the common utilities of alternative $k$ and some other alternative $j$. Equation 16.20 may then be written as equations 16.24 and 16.25.

$$P_k^i = Pr\{\varepsilon_{ki} = \varepsilon^*; \varepsilon_1,\varepsilon_2, \ldots, \varepsilon_M > \varepsilon^*\} \tag{16.24}$$

$$P_1^i = F_1\{\varepsilon^*, \varepsilon^* + U'_{1i} - U'_{2i}, \varepsilon^* + U'_{1i} - U'_{3i}, \ldots,$$
$$\varepsilon^* + U_{1i} - U'_{Mi}\} \tag{16.25}$$

where $F_1\{\ \}$ = the probability density function

and $k = 1$

The probability of choosing alternative 1 is found by integrating the probability density function over all possible values of $\varepsilon^*$, as shown in equations 16.26 and 16.27.

$$P_1^i = \int_{-\infty}^{\infty} F_i\{\varepsilon^*, \varepsilon^* + U'_{1j} - U'_{2i}, \ldots, \varepsilon^* + U'_{1i} - U'_{Mi}\}d\varepsilon^* \qquad (16.26)$$

$$P_1^i = \int_{-\infty}^{\infty} e^{-\varepsilon^*} \exp\left\{ -\sum_{j=1}^{M} e^{-\varepsilon^*} + U'_{1i} - U'_{ji}\right\} \qquad (16.27)$$

This integral (equation 16.27) can be evaluated by partitioning the elements inside the bracket, as shown in equation 16.28.

$$P_1^i = \int_{-\infty}^{\infty} e^{-\varepsilon^*} \exp\left\{ -e^{-\varepsilon^*}\left( \sum_{j=1}^{M} \exp(U'_{1j} - U'_{ji})\right)\right\}d\varepsilon^* \qquad (16.28)$$

Replacing $e^{-\varepsilon^*}$ by $t$, equation 16.29 can be rewritten as equation 16.29.

$$P_1^i = \int_{0}^{\infty} \exp\left\{ -t\left( \sum_{j=1}^{M} \exp(U'_{1i} - U'_{ji})\right)\right\}dt \qquad (16.29)$$

This integral can be evaluated by noting that, for this integration, the summation term is a constant. The integration is therefore given by equation 16.30.

$$P_1^i = \frac{1}{\displaystyle\sum_{j=1}^{M} \exp-(U'_{1i} - U'_{ji})} = \frac{\exp(U'_{1i})}{\displaystyle\sum_{j} \exp(U'_{ji})} \qquad (16.30)$$

Hence, the random utility model produces, by using a Weibull distributional assumption, equation 16.31, in the general case.

$$P_k^i = \frac{\exp\{U'(X_k, S_i)\}}{\displaystyle\sum_{j} \exp\{U'(X_j, S_i)\}} \qquad (16.31)$$

The same model form has resulted from these assumptions as was determined for the strict utility model, namely the multiple-logit model. Again, some of the same insights are offered by this theoretical derivation as were offered by the strict utility model. For example, it becomes clear from this approach also that, if the $X_k$s in $V'_{ki}$ are linearly additive, the individual's characteristics, $S_i$, cannot be linearly additive. Similarly, structural implications of linear or product-form expressions for the utility,

$V'_{ki}$, lead to the same implications for measures of comparativeness for the characteristics of the alternatives.

However, an important new insight is provided by this derivation. The strict utility model left the definition of an alternative unspecified. The random utility model has now provided a specification of an alternative through the term $\varepsilon_{ki}$. A necessary assumption to arrive at equation 16.31 is that the $\varepsilon_{ki}$ terms are independent across the set of alternatives. This was seen to imply that the $X'_k$ must be unique characteristics of the alternative $k$. Thus, in the example discussed in relation to the strict utility model, the two cars of different colors, but the same make, model, etc. are not two distinct alternatives according to the random utility model. The distinction between the two cars was stated only as color. But both cars possess color. Even if one were to extend the argument ad absurdum, and describe the distinguishing characteristics as "greenness" or "blueness," both cars can be said to have some degree of either "greenness" or "blueness." If, however, one car has air-conditioning and the other does not, the two cars become alternatives. Of course, the car of make and model A is not a distinct alternative unless it has some specific characteristic that is not possessed by the other two cars (e.g., radial tires, etc.) or the possession of a specific make, styling, or proprietary feature is a characteristic of importance in the choice. Hence, the random utility model has provided resolution of the problem that arises in applying Luce's Axiom of the Independence of Irrelevant Alternatives.

One final point should be stressed here. In both of the derivations presented here, the assumption of an exponent-form utility and the assumption, in the random utility model, of a Weibull distribution are clearly nonunique assumptions. Thus, the derivations should not be construed as showing that the multiple-logit model is the unique structural form for these choice models, but rather that it is the one that results from some relatively nonrestrictive assumptions. It is also apparently the only readily tractable structural form that can be derived. Coincidentally, the multiple-logit model has highly acceptable elasticity properties, further strengthening the adoption of the derivation assumptions as being reasonable. These properties are discussed in the next section.

*Elasticity Properties of Multiple-logit Models*

A general logit model may be written as equation 16.32.

$$P^i_k = \frac{\exp[G_i(X_k)]}{\sum_j \exp[G_i(X_j)]} \tag{16.32}$$

It is assumed that $G_i(X_j)$ is a linear function of the vector of characteristics of the alternative $j$. Since it has been established that the characteristics of the individual, $S_i$, cannot be linearly additive in the function, it will be assumed that these characteristics enter the utility function through the vector of coefficients of the $X_j$s. The function $G_i(X_j)$ may therefore be written as equation 16.33.

$$G_i(X_j) = a_0^i + \sum_{t=1}^{T} a_t^i X_{jt} \qquad (16.33)$$

where    $T$ = the number of characteristics in the common utility of alternative $j$

and    $a_t^i$ = the coefficients of the characteristics $X_{jt}$

The direct-elasticity of demand for alternative $k$ with respect to characteristics $X_{ks}$ of that alternative is given by equation 16.34.

$$\varepsilon_{kks}^i = a_s^i X_{ks} (1 - P_k^i) \qquad (16.34)$$

In words, equation 16.34 states that the direct-elasticity ($\varepsilon_{kks}^i$) of demand for alternative $k$ with respect to attribute $s$ is proportional to the amount of the attribute possessed by alternative $k$ ($X_{ks}$), to the weight or importance of that attribute in the utility function ($a_s^i$), and to the share of the market that alternative $k$ has not yet obtained ($1 - P_k^i$). The first two dependencies of the direct elasticity appear to be intuitively reasonable, that is, that the elasticity is a function of both the importance and amount of an attribute. The final dependency modifies the strength of the direct elasticity by the market share of the alternative. The larger the market share, the smaller will be the direct-elasticity of demand, all other things being equal. Again, this is an intuitively reasonable statement of elasticity and is conformal with concepts of consumer behavior in economics.

In a similar manner, the cross-elasticities of demand may be expressed as a function of the model parameters. Thus, the cross-elasticity of demand for alternative $k$ with respect to attribute $s$ of alternative $m$ is given by equation 16.35.

$$\varepsilon_{kms}^i = -a_s^i X_{ms} P_m^i \qquad (16.35)$$

In words, the cross-elasticity of demand for alternative $k$ with attribute $s$ of alternative $m$ is proportional to the amount of the attribute possessed by alternative $m$, negatively proportional to the weight of the attribute, and proportional to the market-share of alternative $m$. Again, this elasticity definition is intuitively acceptable. For example, when alternative $m$ has a very small share of the market, the cross-elasticity of demand for alternative $k$ will be reduced substantially by any change in an attribute of alternative $m$, and vice versa.

Moreover, assuming that a positive coefficient is associated with any attribute for which increasing values enhance the utility of the alternative, the signs of the two elasticities are correct. Thus, increases in the amount of attribute $s$ possessed by alternative $k$ will generate increases in the demand for $k$, while increases in the attribute $s$ possessed by any other alternative, $m$, will decrease the demand for alternative $k$. Therefore, it may be asserted that the multiple-logit model is an intuitively and theoretically acceptable model structure for a choice model, regardless of whether the choice model is derived from a strict utility approach or a random utility approach.

## Model Structures

At this point, the alternative theoretical positions have provided a plausible mathematical structure for a choice model, that is, the multiple-logit model. The development of the theories to this point has required no definition of the choice context and, indeed, the entire theoretical development presented here could apply, in general, to any choice situation involving consumer goods. It now becomes important to consider some specific implications relating to travel choices.

In chapter 3 the economic basis of the consideration of travel was explored and it was asserted that, in effect, travel is not demanded for its own sake. Rather, individuals have a demand for an activity and the travel necessary to permit that activity to be accessed. Therefore, the theoretical derivations presented in this section must be interpreted as referring to the choice of both an activity and travel. This also implies that the utilities defined in the derivations will be joint utilities of travel and the activity. Potentially, this leads to an unfortunately complicated model structure in which it would appear that one must model, simultaneously, all possible travel-activity combinations. In other words, the multiple-choice logit model would appear to have to be constructed so that the denominator embraces all possible travel and activity options. This would clearly be an impossible task.

The axiom of the Independence of Irrelevant Alternatives has important implications relative to this structural problem. The independence axiom states that the relative odds of choosing one alternative over another are constant, no matter what the choice context is. It also results in a statement that the probability of choosing a particular alternative is proportional to the strict utility of that alternative. These statements lead to two important properties of choice models. First, a new alternative can be introduced without changing the relative odds of choosing any pair of preexisting alternatives. This has important transportation implications, as will be seen later. Also the random utility theory provides a useful basis for defining what constitutes a new alternative. Second, these statements lead to the notion of separability of choices.[8] The separability notion is of some considerable importance. Without it, all possible consumer choices would have to be considered—and modeled—simultaneously. The notion permits travel choices to be considered separately from all other choices (including such choices as home location, car ownership, etc.) and permits the separation of travel choices from each other as well.

It is clear that the conventional travel-demand models, described earlier, are based, unknowingly, on the separability notion. However, the separability of choices requires that the strict utilities be preserved through all choices. It is clear that the conventional models do not adhere to this condition.[9] The use of the separability property to permit the definition of sequential travel choices requires, in fact, that the strict utilities are maintained through all the choices. In turn, as will be discussed later, this implies that the models of the specific travel choices must be estimated in the reverse sequence from that in which the choices are seen to be made. Again, the conventional process violates this requirement.

Given the broad implications of the separability of choices, it is possible to define three categories of model structures for a complex choice, such as a travel choice. Before describing these structures, it is important to recognize that the structures have only limited behavioral implications. If it is analytically convenient to define sequential models, this does not necessarily require the assumption that individuals actually make sequential decisions. However, it will be seen that there are limited behavioral implications of the structures.

The first type of structure is an independent structure. In this case, a behavioral assumption is made that there is no dependence of one choice on another. Using the traditional urban transportion-planning (UTP) model structure, translated to an individual basis, the structure is illustrated in the following sentences. Suppose that an individual is considered to make four decisions: the frequency of the trip ($f$); the destination ($d$); the mode of travel ($m$); and the route ($r$). (Other decision groupings could be proposed; these are exemplary only.) The independence assumption implies that the choice of mode has no effect on the choice of route, or of destination, for example. It also implies total separability of the attributes for each choice. In other words, it requires the assumption of four independent sets of attributes $X_f$, $X_d$, $X_m$, and $X_r$. This assumption also implies an additive utility function of the form shown in equation 16.36.

$$U^i_{fdmr} = U(X_f, S_i) + U(X_d, S_i) + U(X_m, S_i) + U(X_r, S_i) \qquad (16.36)$$

The independence assumption leads to the set of conditional probabilities of choice defined in equations 16.37, 16.38, 16.39, and 16.40.

$$P^i(f) = F_f\{U(X_f, S_i)\} \qquad (16.37)$$

$$P^i(d) = F_d\{U(X_d, S_i)\} \qquad (16.38)$$

$$P^i(m) = F_m\{U(X_m, S_i)\} \tag{16.39}$$

$$P_i(r) = F_r\{U(X_r, S_i)\} \tag{16.40}$$

The sets of characteristics $X_f$, $X_d$, $X_m$, and $X_r$ are, as previously stated, independent across the choices. The demand model, which would provide the probability estimate of a trip being made with specific frequency $f_k$, to destination $d_k$, by mode $m_k$, and route $r_k$ would be given by equation 16.41.

$$P^i(f_k, d_k, m_k, r_k) = P^i(f)_k \, P^i(d)_k \, P^i(m)_k \, P^i(r)_k \tag{16.41}$$

The implications of this independent model are clearly unacceptable for a travel-demand model. The characteristics that define conditional probabilities for the various travel choices are not independent and mutually exclusive, as required for this structure.

The second type of structure is a recursive, sequential model structure. This may be viewed

. . . either as a simplifying assumption (this will require a sensitivity analysis of the partitioning scheme to determine how the results are affected) or as truly representing a sequential, or conditional, decision-making process.[10]

Adopting the standard sequential assumption of the trip-interchange type would lead to an additive utility function of the form shown in equation 16.42.

$$U^i_{fdmr} = U(X_f, S_i) + U(X_{d|f}, S_i) + U(X_{m|df}, S_i) + U(X_{r|mdf}, S_i) \tag{16.42}$$

where $\quad U(X_{d|f}, S_i) =$ the utility of destination $d$, given trip frequency $f$

$\qquad U(X_{m|df}, S_i) =$ the utility of mode $m$, given destination $d$ and trip frequency $f$

and $\qquad U(X_{r|mdf}, S_i) =$ the utility of route $r$, given mode $m$, destination $d$ and trip frequency $f$

These utilities lead to the set of choice probabilities of equations 16.43, 16.44, 16.45, and 16.46.

$$P^i(f) = F_f\{U(X_f, S_i)\} \tag{16.43}$$

$$P^i(d|f) = F_d\{U(X_{fd}, S_i)\} \tag{16.44}$$

$$P^i(m|df) = F_m\{U(X_{fdm}, S_i)\} \tag{16.45}$$

$$P^i(r|mdf) = F_r\{U(X_{fdmr}, S_i)\} \tag{16.46}$$

In this case, the characteristics are clearly dependent across all choices and the probability of a specific trip being made is given, again, by the product of the conditional probabilities, as shown in equation 16.47.

$$P_i(f_k, d_k, m_k, r_k) = P^i(f)_k \, P^i(d|f)_k \, P^i(m|df)_k \, P_i(r|mdf)_k \tag{16.47}$$

In this recursive structure, the strict utilities must be estimated and preserved through the entire sequential structure. Hence, as mentioned earlier, the estimation process must begin with the latest decision (route choice, in this instance) and proceed back to the earliest (frequency), preserving relative weights of the individual attributes in each earlier model. It is clear that the partitioning and sequencing of choices will, therefore, affect the estimation of strict utilities.[11] In particular the decision on which choice is last will have a considerable influence on the estimated models. If the decisions are sequential in reality, then it is mandatory that the correct sequence be determined. If sequential models are an analytical convenience, then sensitivity testing of the sequential assumptions is necessary. Clearly, the recursive, sequential structure is analytically convenient since it permits a considerable simplification of the choice sets for the modeling. In the example, route choice only needs to be considered for the set of routes for given mode, destination, and trip frequency, rather than for all possible routes in the system.

It can be seen that the conventional approach to travel forecasting constitutes an attempt at developing a recursive, sequential model system. It breaks down, however, because the models are estimated from earliest to latest and thus prevent the reservation of strict utilities. This is reflected both in the calibration of the models and in the structure.

The third model structure is a simultaneous one. In this case, it is assumed that the decisions are not multiple, but single and that the resulting single travel decision is based upon characteristics of the form $X_{fdmr}$. The utility is, therefore, given in equation 16.48.

$$U^i_{fdmr} = U(X_{fdmr}, S_i) \qquad (16.48)$$

Similarly, the demand is estimated directly from a single simultaneous model of the form shown in equation 16.49.

$$P^i(F, D, M, R) = F\{U(X_{fdmr}, S_i)\} \qquad (16.49)$$

This model necessitates, for the evaluation of a specific probability, the definition and estimation of all alternative travel choices for a given potential traveler. Clearly, this leads to a very complex model in which there are likely to be serious estimation problems. However, if the underlying decision is simultaneous, or has an unstable sequential pattern, this model is likely to yield the best estimates of the strict utilities and will not be subject to order problems of the type discussed for the recursive, sequential model.

In terms of travel behavior, the theoretical construction of a simultaneous structure appears to be the optimal one. Failing this, a recursive, sequential structure may be reasonably acceptable, if problems of order can be handled satisfactorily. An independent structure appears to be totally implausible.

Finally, it should be noted that the discussion of structure has been based upon behavioral theory and is concerned with defining a model structure for calibration. The way in which a resulting model set is used for forecasting or prediction may be totally independent of the calibration structure. Thus, having estimated a set of recursive, sequential models, they may be combined subsequently to produce, in effect, a simultaneous demand estimation (often termed "direct-demand estimation"). Alternatively, models may be combined or reordered as may be appropriate, without violating any of the basic precepts of structure discussed here.

*Summary of Theory*

In the preceding subsections, the theoretical structure of behavioral-demand models has been explored. From this, it has been found that two alternative theoretical hypotheses—strict utility and random utility, drawn from psychology and economics, respectively—lead, under certain assumptions, to an identical model structure: the multiple-choice logit model. The model structure is found to be appropriate for any choice situation and is not necessarily restricted to travel choices.

A number of insights were gained from the theoretical structures, including implications of the form of the relative measures of characteristics of the alternatives, the mechanism of entry of the socioeconomic characteristics in the choice model, and the definition of what constitutes an alternative. In addition, elasticity properties of the multiple-logit model were examined and found to agree with a priori expectations.

Finally, questions of the structure of demand models have been explored. Three alternative modeling structures have been defined—independent choices; recursive, sequential choices; and a simultaneous choice. Of these, the simultaneous choice model appears to be most appropriate for travel-demand modeling, but also presents the most difficult modeling situation. The recursive, sequential model is seen as a reasonable alternative to the simultaneous model of travel demand, while the independent choices model is seen to be inapplicable to travel demand.

## Calibration Techniques

The theoretical developments outlined in the previous section are relatively recent, and form an a posteriori theory for a modeling approach that had existed for some years in empirical form. The majority of the pioneering model-building was conducted without the insights of the theories. Thus, an early question that had to be addressed in the empirical development of behavioral models was that of the mathematical calibration technique to be used for these models. An early position that was taken was that linear regression[12] was largely inappropriate as a curve-fitting mechanism, because of the requirements of a probabilistic model. This position has been reexamined more recently[13] and found to be acceptable. Nevertheless, it is worthwhile to examine the question of the appropriateness of linear regression here. In addition to this method, three other curve-fitting procedures have been used for constructing probabilistic, behavioral demand models. Each one of these three—discriminant analysis, probit analysis, and logit analysis—is outlined here.

*Linear Regression*

The use of linear regression for building choice models of travel demand can be proposed in two forms: First, a linear probability model, of the form shown in equation 16.50 could be proposed.

$$p_k^i = a_0^i + a_1^i X'_{1k} + a_2^i X'_{2k} + \ldots + a_t^i X'_{tk} \qquad (16.50)$$

It is assumed that the coefficients, $a_s^i$, are specific to socioeconomic groups of the population and that the values $X'_{sk}$ are relative characteristics of alternative $k$. Such a model can clearly be fitted by standard linear regression techniques, assuming that both the dependent variable $p_k^i$, and the set of independent variables, $X_{sk}$, can be observed. Two principal problems arise from this model, however. First, the values of $p_k^i$ must be limited to the range of zero to one. However, the values of the $X_{sk}$ are theoretically unlimited, so that inconsistent values could be generated for the dependent variable, particularly under conditions of improvement or deterioration of alternative $k$.

Second, probabilities cannot be observed. Observed data for a disaggregate model will comprise information on which alternative was chosen by a particular individual. In the aggregate case, the observations will be of numbers of people making a specific choice. Representing the individual choices by a binary code (e.g., assigning a zero if a particular alternative is not chosen and a one if it is), the regression is between a dichotomous dependent variable and a set of continuous independent variables. This leads to a violation of the random, normal assumption on the error term of the regression, producing instead a binary distribution. Under these circumstances, although coefficient estimates can be obtained for the model, no goodness-of-fit statistics can be generated (since these rely on the normality of the error term) and it is not clear that the estimated coefficients will be best, linear, unbiased estimates or even maximum likelihood estimates.

The alternative use of regression would be to estimate a linearized form of the logit model, which is probably restricted to the binary case. The binary logit model can be arranged into the form of equation 16.51.

$$\frac{p_k^i}{1 - p_k^i} = \exp(G^i(X_k)) \qquad (16.51)$$

This model form can be made linear by taking natural logarithms of both sides of the model (equation 16.52) assuming that $G^i(X_k)$ is a linear function in $X_k$.

$$\ln\left(\frac{p_k^i}{1 - p_k^i}\right) = b_0^i + b_1^i X_{k1}' + b_2^i X_{k2}' + \ldots + b_t^i X_{kt}' \qquad (16.52)$$

This transformed model removes the first objection to the simple linear model, that the dependent and independent variables are inconsistently limited. However, it still remains impossible to observe probabilities of choice, so the dependent variable cannot be evaluated correctly for observed choice data. Thus, the second objection still holds, that estimated coefficients will not be best, linear, unbiased estimates nor maximum likelihood estimates. Also, no goodness-of-fit measures may be derived for this model. Even if they could be, the goodness-of-fit statistics would be applicable only to the transformed model, equation 16.52, and not to the original model, equation 16.51. Thus, a priori computations of probabilities from grouped data do not provide a satisfactory remedy for this situation.

In summary, it may be concluded that linear regression is not an acceptable curve-fitting procedure for building behavioral choice models. This unacceptability extends not only to a simple linear construct (which is also theoretically inappropriate), but also to the estimation of a logit model by log transformation.

*Discriminant Analysis*

One of the earliest nonlinear techniques to be considered for building choice models is discriminant analysis.[14] The technique was originally developed as a classification procedure for taxonomic problems.[15] As such, the technique is based upon the assumption that there exists in a population two or more distinct subgroups that can be distinguished by means of a discriminating function. The subgroups are assumed to be normally distributed and homoscedastic with respect to that function, as shown in Figure 16-1. The method is not described in this book, but descriptions may be found in several references.[16]

In application, the procedure is intended to be used for classification only. Supposing a binary situation exists, a discriminant function can be formulated as shown in equation 16.53.

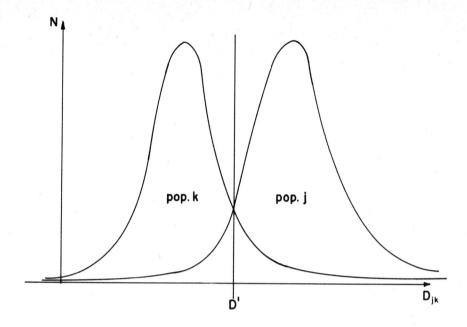

**Figure 16-1.** Assumed Distribution Pattern for Discriminant Analysis.

$$D^i_{jk} = c^i_0 + c^i_1(X_{j1},X_{k1}) + c^i_2(X_{j2},X_{k2}) + \ldots + c^i_t(X_{jt},X_{kt}) \quad (16.53)$$

where  $D^i_{jk}$ = the discriminant function for alternatives $j$ and $k$ and individual $i$

and  $(X_{js},X_{ks})$ = a relative function of the $s$th attribute of alternatives $j$ and $k$.

The discriminant function is applied by using the assigning rule shown in equation 16.54.

$$I^i_{jk} = \begin{cases} 1 & \text{if } D^i_{jk} > D' \\ 0 & \text{if } D^i_{jk} \leq D' \end{cases} \quad (16.54)$$

where  $I^i_{jk}$ = the subgroup to which individual $i$ belongs, such that

$I^i_{jk}$ = 1 if the individual is in subgroup $j$

and  $I^i_{jk}$ = 0 for subgroup $k$

and  $D'$ = the threshold value of the discriminant function

In this form, the discriminant function is not useful for the behavioral-choice model. However, the discriminant function can be transformed into a probabilistic-assigning rule by observing the relative frequency with which a specific value of $D^i_{jk}$ occurs in one of the two subgroups. By suitable transformation of the discriminant function to a term $d^i_{jk}$, a probabilistic rule of the form shown in equation 16.55, can be derived.

$$p^i_j = \frac{\exp(d^i_{jk})}{1 + \exp(d^i_{jk})} \qquad (16.55)$$

This is again the logit model, in binary form in this instance.

The discriminant model possesses certain goodness-of-fit measures, such as an $F$-statistic for the overall fit of the model and $t$-statistics for the individual coefficients. However, coefficient estimates do not represent maximum likelihood estimates for the model of equation 16.55. In fact, it must be noted that the goal of the fitting procedure is to maximize the separation between the subgroups in the population. This goal does not appear to be one that is easily interpreted into a statement of fit to an hypothesized relationship such as equation 16.55. Furthermore, the assigning rule violates certain assumptions of the original calibration procedure, principally that the technique is to be designed in order to classify each individual observation into one subgroup, where it is assumed that all individuals belong exclusively to one subgroup.

Empirical tests of discriminant analysis[17] seem to confirm that the technique may be incorrect. In comparison with estimates from probit and logit analysis, relative coefficient values are markedly different and uniform goodness-of-fit statistics have been found to be significantly inferior for discriminant analysis than for the other two techniques. Therefore, it does not appear to be appropriate to use discriminant analysis as a technique for building behavioral-choice models.

*Probit Analysis*

Like discriminant analysis, probit analysis[18] was also developed in bioassay. In this case, however, it is assumed that members of a population are subjected to a stimulus that generates a normally distributed response pattern over the range of values of the stimulus. Thus, if the stimulus is the relative utility of one alternative over another, the choice response of one alternative is assumed to be normally distributed over the range of relative utility. The choice-response distribution is, however, of less interest than the cumulative choice-response distribution, for which any ordinate gives the probability of an individual having responded by that value of the stimulus; see Figure 16-2.

The probit model is shown in equation 16.56.

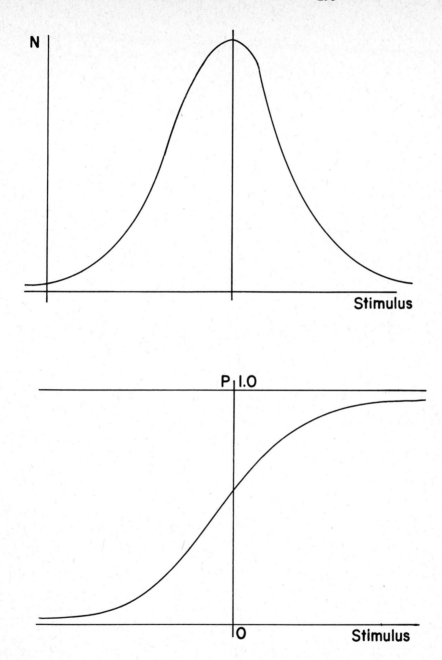

**Figure 16-2.** Frequency Response and Cumulative Response Curves for Probit Analysis.

$$p_k^i = \frac{1}{\sqrt{2\pi}} \int_{-\infty}^{Y_k^i} \exp(-1/2\,t^2)\,dt \qquad (16.56)$$

where    $Y_k^i$ = the stimulus, expressed as a linear function of the relative attributes of alternative $k$

and    $t$ = a dummy parameter for a normal distribution with zero mean and unit standard deviation

The coefficients in the linear function are determined by an iterative likelihood-maximization procedure. The only assumptions that need to be made are that the frequency-response distribution is normal (or can be normalized by a suitable transformation of the value $Y_k^i$) and that responses of individuals to the stimulus are independent of all other individuals. This, of course, implies that each individual makes up his own mind and is not influenced by the decisions of other members of the population.

The maximum-likelihood estimation of the model also produces goodness-of-fit statistics, such as $t$-statistics for the coefficients and a $\chi^2$-statistic for assessing the entire model. Normality tests can also be made to ensure that the underlying assumption of the procedure is upheld.

The principal objection to the probit model is the difficulty of estimating probabilities for population members. As can be seen from equation 16.56, this involves a two-stage procedure. In the first stage, the value of $Y_k^i$ is estimated for the specific set of attribute values of alternative $k$, relative to some other alternative, say $j$. Then, in the second stage, the integral of the normal curve must be evaluated. This requires either using a table of the area under the normal curve or a computer program that evaluates the integral by a stepped approximation process. In comparisons with the logit model,[19] the probit model was found to perform almost identically. However, its more complex formulation detracts from its usefulness. Also, there is no available multiple-choice extension of the probit model. Thus, its use is restricted to binary-choice situations.

### Logit Analysis

Unlike the preceding methods, logit analysis is simply the statement of a model structure without the specification of any distributional assumptions. The model may be specified as either a binary choice, equation 16.57, or a multiple choice, equation 16.58.

$$p_k^i = \frac{\exp(G^i(X_{jk}))}{1 + \exp(G^i(X_{jk}))} \qquad (16.57)$$

$$p_k^i = \frac{\exp(G^i(X_k))}{\sum_j \exp(G^i(X_j))} \qquad (16.58)$$

In the binary case, the terms $X_{jk}$ are assumed to be relative measures of the attributes of alternative $k$ against alternative $j$, while the terms $X_k$ in the multiple-choice model are absolute attribute measures. The form of the binary logit curve is shown in Figure 16-3, where it is seen to be very similar to the cumulative normal curve of probit analysis.

The calibration process is again an iterative maximum-likelihood procedure, based upon the assumption of independence of individual choices. The process is, in fact, almost identical to that used for probit analysis, the only difference being in the assumed model structure, equation 16.57 or 16.58, as opposed to equation 16.56. The same goodness-of-fit statistics are also produced.

Apart from the work of Stanley L. Warner,[20] using nonlinear regression to estimate the logit model, this technique was, chronologically, the last one to be tried for behavioral travel-demand models and also the one that fits the theories developed in the earlier part of this chapter. It is also of interest to note that the logit curve was one of the candidate curves considered by the staff of the San Francisco Bay Area Transportation Study[21] in the early 1960s for the modal-split model of that study. The curve appears again as the modal-split model of the entropy-maximizing approach.[22] Hence there appears to be considerable empirical and theoretical support for the adoption of the logit model as the primary structural form for behavioral travel-demand models.

The specific form of the logit model that has, at present, been adopted for behavioral travel-demand models is a binary- or multiple-choice model in which the $G^i(X_k)$ term is expressed as a linear function of attributes of alternative $k$. In general, as was discussed earlier in this chapter,[23] the linear form also implies that any attribute of two alternatives is compared as a difference. This contrasts sharply with the modal-split models discussed in chapter 9, which invariably assumed ratios.

*Prediction Errors in the Logit Model*

It appears that the logit model may possibly break all of the rules of model construction, relating to errors in the model, described in chapter 2. In fact, this is not the case, as is shown in this section.

Consider a simple binary-logit model of the form shown in equation 16.59.

$$p = \frac{e^{a+bx}}{1 + e^{a+bx}} \tag{16.59}$$

In order to determine the measurement error, the first differential with respect to $x$ is needed. This is given by equation 16.60.

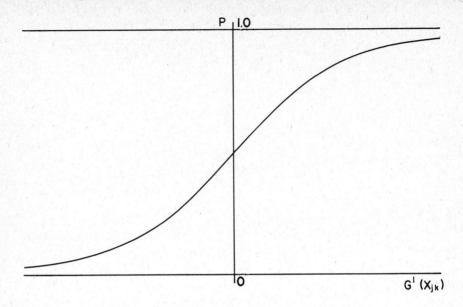

**Figure 16-3.** Form of the Binary Logit Curve.

$$\frac{dp}{dx} = \frac{bp}{1 + e^{a+bx}} \qquad (16.60)$$

Using equation 2.28 from chapter 2, the squared measurement error is shown in equation 16.61.

$$e_p^2 = \frac{b^2 p^2 e_x^2}{(1 + e^{a+bx})^2} \qquad (16.61)$$

Suppose now that the following values are those found for the calibrated logit model of equation 16.59.

$$a = 0.2$$

$$b = 0.01$$

$$x = 5$$

$$e_x = 0.25$$

Inserting these values in equation 16.61 yields equation 16.62.

$$e_p = \frac{bpe_x}{1 + e^{a+bx}} = \frac{0.01 \cdot 0.25 \cdot 0.562}{1 + e^{0.25}} = 0.000615 \qquad (16.62)$$

The relative error is given by equation 16.63.

$$e_p/p \ = \ \pm \ \frac{0.000615}{0.562} \ = \ \pm \ 0.00109 \ = \ \pm \ 0.11\% \qquad (16.63)$$

In this case, an actual reduction in both the proportional and absolute errors in the model occurs. However, the error in $x$ was chosen in an arbitrary fashion. To be more realistic, consider an actual functional form for $x$, where $x$ is derived as a difference between two values, $y$ and $z$. Suppose $y$ and $z$ each have errors of $\pm 5$, and are given as 40 and 30, respectively. Then, assuming a low correlation of 0.2 for $r_{yz}$, the squared measurement error of $x$ is given by equation 16.64.

$$e_x^2 \ = \ e_y^2 + e_z^2 + e_y e_z r_{yz} \ = \ 25 + 25 + 5 \ = \ 55 \qquad (16.64)$$

Hence, the measurement error in $x$ is approximately $\pm 7.5$. Substituting this, with the previous values, into equation 16.62, yields equation 16.65.

$$e_p \ = \ \frac{0.01 \cdot 7.5 \cdot 0.575}{2.350} \ = \ 0.01835 \qquad (16.65)$$

The relative error is $\pm 0.32$ percent, which is still a very small error compared with the very large error in $x$ of $\pm 150$ percent. Thus, it appears that the binary logit model has the property of reducing the measurement errors of the original variables used in the model. This is a most desirable property and strengthens the claim that logit analysis is the most useful procedure for building travel-choice models.

## Historical Development

Behavioral travel-demand models represent a relatively recent development in travel-forecasting procedures. So far, in this chapter, no clear definition has been advanced for what constitutes a behavioral model as opposed to a nonbehavioral model. In the broadest terms, a behavioral travel-demand model could be defined as one that is based upon hypotheses of human behavior. Using this broad definition, many of the conventional travel-forecasting models could be considered to be behavioral, for example, the intervening-opportunity model, etc. Similarly, the models of Quandt and Baumol,[24] McLynn,[25] etc., are founded on consumer behavior theories, and thus qualify also as behavioral travel-demand models. However, for the purposes of this chapter, the interpretation of what constitutes a behavioral travel-demand model is to be narrower. The specific models of interest here are those that led to the statements of theory outlined earlier in this chapter. These models are disaggregate in nature. This is not to say that models must be disaggregate to be behavioral, but rather an observation of the specific subgroup of behavioral models that have provided the basis for potentially major improvements in travel-forecasting procedures.

### Developments Through Mode Choice

All of the early attempts to build disaggregate, behavioral models focused upon the choice of travel mode for the modeling research. Further, most exercises concentrated upon mode choices for the work trip. There are a number of reasons for this narrow focus, many of which are still relevant for current research.

First, the choice of travel mode is one of the most easily defined choices in the travel-decision process. Modes of travel can be identified by name with little ambiguity for either researcher or surveyed traveler. This ease of identification and lack of ambiguity does not extend to choices such as route, destination, etc. Second, at the time that most of the disaggregate, behavioral research began, modal-split models were among the most unsatisfactory models in the travel-forecasting process. For all other steps of the process, reasonably standardized procedures were available that needed only local calibration. Every transportation study, however, defined its own modal-split model and no transferrability or standardization existed. It was therefore, a goal of the early research to attempt to provide a standardized procedure.

Third, mode choice was seen as one of the most policy-relevant steps in the travel-forecasting process. At the time of the genesis of this research, as is still the case, one of the major transportation concerns was beginning to be recognized as that of attempting to persuade more automobile users to choose public transportation. Whether such a goal is pursued in the interests of reducing congestion, air pollution, urban noise, or energy consumption matters little. The goal remains the same from a modeling viewpoint. Existing mode-choice models were recognized as being unequal to this task and the research was, therefore, aimed at producing models that would be sensitive to testing or defining policies that might effect desirable modal shifts.

Fourth, the most critical travel volumes, from a planning point of view are those that occur in peak traffic flow periods. In urban areas, peak flows are generally associated with the trip to and from work. Hence, concentration on work-trip mode choices appeared to be indicated in terms of tackling a relevant subset of the problem. Finally, the habitual and repetitive nature of the work trip suggests that knowledge of actual levels of service offered by the various modes of travel would be greater for each individual traveler than would be the case for less repetitive trips. Conversely, it could be argued that the repetitive nature of the trip may imply that choices of mode are not exercised on the work trip, but that modal usage is a matter of habit. Clearly, these two positions may be argued at length, but the researchers have generally maintained that the former effect of increased knowledge of alternatives outweighs any detractions of the habitual nature of the trip.

Pragmatically, one may summarize these various positions by stating that if the disaggregate, behavioral approach cannot be made to work for the choice of mode for the work trip, it is unlikely to be workable for any travel decision. On the other hand, if the approach does work for this special case, it would suggest that it is worthwhile investing the time and effort in attempting to expand the approach to other travel decisions. To date, the conclusions reached are, indeed, that the approach appears to work well for work-trip mode choice so that alternative extensions appear to be warranted.

*Summary of Disaggregate Mode-choice Research*

The earliest instance of research into disaggregate, mode-choice models was published in 1962 by Warner[26] who used household files from the Chicago Area Transportation Study to develop a set of three mode-choice models for both work and nonwork trips. Two basic mathematical techniques were used, the first being discriminant analysis and the second a nonlinear regression fit of a logit model. Transportation system variables were limited to travel time and travel cost, both expressed as ratios. Five socioeconomic variables were used as additive terms in the linear functions. The assigning rule for discriminant analysis that Warner found to be most effective was the one described earlier in this chapter, and Warner found no significant differences between deriving this rule from the discriminant function or calibrating it directly by nonlinear regression. (It should be noted that neither of these procedures is likely to produce maximum-likelihood estimates of the coefficients in the actual model structure used for estimation purposes.)

As an illustration of Warner's work, two models are presented here, both for the work-trip choice between train (commuter railroad) and automobile. The first model is the probabilistic assigning model derived from discriminant analysis and is shown in equation 16.66.

$$p_t = \frac{e^{L(X,N)}}{1 + e^{L(X,N)}} \tag{16.66}$$

The linear function, $L(X,N)$, was found to be given by equation 16.67.

$$L(X,N) = -9.28 + 1.78c + 1.46t + 0.30i_1' - 0.63i_2'$$
$$- 1.21z - 1.81s \tag{16.67}$$

where     $c$ = the log of the cost ratio (mode 2 : mode 1)

$t$ = the log of the time ratio

$i_1'$ = the log of the ratio of household income to adults in the household if mode 1 is more expensive than mode 2

$i_2'$ = the same as $i_1'$ but for the occasion on which mode 2 (auto) is more expensive than mode 1

$z$ = compound measure of household size, income and auto ownership

$s$ = 0 if the trip maker is male and 1 if female

The second model is that obtained by estimating a relationship of the form of equation 16.66 by regression. Distinguishing the regression model from the discriminant model by replacing the linear function with $L(X,R)$, the regression model for work-trip choices between automobile and commuter railroad is given by equation 16.68.

$$L(X,R) = -8.24 + 1.46c + 1.54t + 0.22i_1' - 0.57i_2'$$

$$- 1.07z - 1.47s \tag{16.68}$$

The symbols are the same as before. In large measure, it can be seen that the coefficients of the two models (equations 16.67 and 16.68) differ by little.

Following this work, whose significance was not recognized for some time, there appears to have been something of a hiatus in disaggregate, mode-choice work until a number of pioneering efforts were published in the period 1967 through 1969.[27] All of these research efforts had certain elements in common. They were each based on the collection of a body of data specifically designed for the research work; each expressed relative measures of travel times as differences; and each used binary-choice models, with automobile driver usually constituting one of the alternatives. Beyond this, some significant differences emerge between the three modeling efforts. Each model was based on a different mathematical calibration procedure: David A. Quarmby used discriminant analysis, Thomas E. Lisco used probit analysis, and Peter R. Stopher used regression and, subsequently, logit analysis. Quarmby and Lisco each used socioeconomic variables as linear additive terms in the model function, while Stopher stratified the data by socioeconomic variables. Stopher and Lisco each used total travel time and travel cost, while Quarmby used the work of the Traffic Research Corporation[28] and defined total travel time, excess travel time (see chapter 9), and travel cost.

Comparable examples of the three models cannot be given, since modal mixes and monetary units are different in each case. The model developed by Quarmby for car-bus work-trip choices is given in equation 16.69.

$$Z_b = 0.461 + 0.0556\Delta T + 0.0966\Delta ET + 0.0911\Delta C$$
$$- 0.535I - 0.0333A_1 + 0.620A_2 + 0.323A_3 \qquad (16.69)$$

where $Z_b$ = the discriminant function for bus (the $L(X,N)$ of Warner's model)

$\Delta T$ = the travel-time difference

$\Delta ET$ = the excess travel-time difference

$\Delta C$ = the travel-cost difference

$I$ = the income

$A_1$ = a car-competition factor

$A_2$ = a dummy variable indicating car captivity

$A_3$ = a dummy variable indicating that the employer owns the car

The relevant statistical measures may be found in the original reports of Quarmby's work.[29] The discriminant function, scaled appropriately, becomes the exponent of $e$ in a model of the form of equation 16.66.

Lisco,[30] using probit analysis, produced the calibrated model shown in equation 16.70 for work-trip choices between automobile and rapid transit.

$$Y = 1.379 - 0.084\Delta T + 0.012\Delta C - 0.234D_1 + 1.262D_2$$
$$+ 1.999I + 0.648S + 0.068A \qquad (16.70)$$

where $Y$ = the probit, or upper limit of integration of the normal curve

$\Delta T, \Delta C$ are as defined for Quarmby's model

$D_1, D_2$ = family structure dummy variables

$I$ = the income of the household

$A$ = the traveler's age

$S$ = the traveler's sex

This model was constructed by using an estimated auto operating cost of 6¢ per mile. Again, the statistical measures for the model are reported in the original documentation.

Finally, the linear model calibrated by Stopher[31] for auto-transit work-trip choices is shown in equation 16.71.

$$p_c = 0.331 + 0.0076\Delta C + 0.00529\Delta T \qquad (16.71)$$

The symbols are the same as used before and the coefficients are evaluated at the mean income of the sample used. This model was subsequently transformed to a logit model, where the linear function, $G(X)$, is shown in equation 16.72.

$$G(x) = 0.701 + 0.031\Delta C + 0.0216\Delta T \qquad (16.72)$$

These three models led to a rapidly increasing body of research, concerned with many aspects of incremental research on the models. It is not possible, within the confines of this book, to summarize each one of these subsequent efforts. However, a number of significant aspects can be highlighted.

Following closely upon the three models just described, Charles A. Lave[32] attempted a refinement of Lisco's probit model in which he added an interactive income and travel time variable and also added a dummy variable to represent comfort differences between the available modes. Robert G. McGillivray[33] used the discriminant model of Quarmby, but replaced the difference measurements with ratios. The results of both of these exercises, while adding further knowledge about the decision-making process, were inconclusive in terms of directing subsequent research. Following these efforts, a number of further studies were undertaken to investigate specific refinements in model structure. These are described in the next section of this chapter.

In the early developments of this modeling approach, it was suggested that implied values of travel time could be inferred from the coefficients of travel costs and travel times. Although serious theoretical and empirical problems have subsequently been identified in relation to this use of the models,[34] this usage generated a number of additional modeling efforts, which concomitantly advanced the state of the art of disaggregate, behavioral models. Among this work were two major efforts in value-of-time and mode-choice modeling by Francois X. de Donnea[35] and David A. Hensher.[36] Both of these efforts were concerned with the development of a utility theory of travel, and travel-time values and both developed models of mode choice for urban work trips. The work of de Donnea is notable in that it used data from several cities, collected for more conventional aggregate travel forecasting, yet produced successful disaggregate models. As an example, the selected logit model for Rotterdam,[37] for choices of the heads of households between auto and transit, is shown in equation 16.73.

$$G(X) = 1.0816 - 0.00274I\Delta T \qquad (16.73)$$

where $G(X)$ = the exponent of the logit model

and $I, \Delta T$ are as defined previously

Hensher examined a number of alternative formulations of travel times and travel costs and also improved the estimation of travel-time values through the inquiry of amounts of time or cost changes that would induce a modal shift. The "best-fit" model determined by Hensher is reported as a binary logit model of choice between car and train for work trips (equation 16.74).

$$G(X) = 0.254 - 0.00997 \, \Delta IT - 0.0283 \Delta WT$$

$$- 0.0149 \Delta TT - 0.271 \Delta C \qquad (16.74)$$

where $\Delta IT$ = the difference in in-vehicle time

$\Delta WT$ = the difference in waiting time

$\Delta TT$ = the difference in transfer time

and $\Delta C$ = the cost difference

Both the United States and United Kingdom governments commissioned a series of studies into travel-time values, all of which used some form of disaggregate choice models. In the United States the principal work was done by Stanford Research Institute[38] using route-choice models between toll and nontoll roads. The models were formulated as a type of binary-logit model. In the United Kingdom, a number of different studies were commissioned, with the largest single effort being undertaken by the Local Government Operational Research Unit (LGORU).[39] The initial work of the LGORU followed closely on the work of Quarmby and used discriminant analysis as the model-calibration technique. Subsequently, models have been developed using logit calibrations directly. Again, as with deDonnea's work, the LGORU work ranged over a large number of different cities and sought to explore similarities and differences between the different cities.

As has been noted throughout this section, all of the models described so far have been binary models of mode choice. Relatively few attempts have been made so far to develop and test multiple-choice models. One of the reasons for this lack of attempts, was, initially, the lack of computer programs to permit multiple-choice models to be calibrated. After such programs began to appear, some prototypical models were developed with some success.[40] These models developed for airport access trips in the Capital Region by Paul R. Rassam et al. and for application in San Diego, were reasonably successful in application. The question still remains as to whether the increased complexity of the multiple-choice model is worthwhile compared with the relative simplicity of the binary model. This question seems especially relevant for mode-choice models, but declines in relevance as one considers the broader issues of simultaneous models or a set of recursive, sequential models for the entire travel-decision process.

The final area of development of mode-choice models has been for intercity travel. The principal efforts, in this area, have been concerned primarily with the valuation of travel time. Three major research efforts have been conducted in this area by Peter L. Watson,[41] Shalom Reichman,[42] and Reuben Gronau.[43] Not suprisingly, the findings of this research have tended to be rather different from those of the urban-oriented work. In particular, important variables and variable structures are different, with a tendency for variables, such as travel time, to be expressed as a difference relative to average value. Also, there appears to be less consistency in both the models and the calibration techniques.

*Other Extensions*

Given the apparent success of the mode-choice models, outlined briefly above, there have been a number of extensions proposed and researched during the last four or five years. Many of these extensions are still under active research and not all have been publicized through journal articles, etc. However, some attempt is made here to outline the type of work that is being undertaken in extending efforts to a wider front than work-trip mode choice.

The first major extension is embodied in a research project conducted for the U.S. Department of Transportation by Charles River Associates.[44] In this project, two major extensions were made in the empirical development of behavioral travel-demand models. First, the project extended the approach to shopping trips. Second, models were developed for a number of other choices, besides mode choice. At the same time, another important departure from conventional travel-forecasting was proposed, that different trip purposes may have different decision sets associated with them. Thus, the work trip was considered as comprising only the mode-choice decision, while the shopping trip was built up from four decisions—frequency, destination, time of day, and mode of travel. This research was one of the earliest to utilize the concepts embodied in the independence axiom and to observe the necessity to preserve strict utilities through the models in a recursive, sequential set. The models were all built using logit techniques. The set of shopping choice models is shown in equations 16.75, 16.76, 16.77, and 16.78.

$$G(X,M) = -6.77 + 0.374WT - 0.654\Delta IT - 4.11\Delta C + 2.24A \qquad (16.75)$$

where $G(X,M) =$ the logit exponent for the mode-choice model

$WT =$ the transit walking time

$\Delta IT$ = the in-vehicle travel-time difference (including transit transfer and wait time)

$\Delta C$ = cost difference

and $A$ = a car-competition factor.

$$G(X,T) = 0.843 - 2.07(\hat{p}_o - \hat{p}_m) - 0.710P \qquad (16.76)$$

where $G(X,T)$ = the logit exponent for the time-of-day choice

$\hat{p}_o, \hat{p}_m$ = inclusive prices of travel, defined from the cost and time elements of equation 16.75 for off-peak and peak, respectively

and $P$ = the number of preschool children in the household

$$G(X,D) = -1.06\,(\hat{p}_i - \hat{p}_j) + 0.844\Delta E \qquad (16.77)$$

where $G(X,D)$ = the logit exponent for choice of destination $i$

$\hat{p}_i, \hat{p}_j$ = the inclusive prices of the alternative destination $i$ and $j$ ($j$ being the base alternative)

$\Delta E$ = the difference in shopping opportunities between $k$ and $j$ ( = retail employment in each zone)

$$G(X,F) = -1.72\,\hat{p} + 3.90\,\hat{E} \qquad (16.78)$$

where $G(X,F)$ = the logit exponent for the trip-frequency choice

$\hat{p}$ = the inclusive price of making a trip

$\hat{E}$ = the number of shopping opportunities obtained by making a trip

The models are listed here in order of estimation (latest decision to earliest decision and the preservation of strict utilities can been seen in the sequence of models.

More recently, Moshe E. Ben-Akiva,[45] and Antti P. Talvitie and Peter S. Liou[46] have examined the question of recursive against simultaneous model structures. Ben-Akiva examined destination and mode choices modeled simultaneously and in the two alternative sequential directions, concluding that, indeed, the order of sequential models has a significant bearing on the model calibration while also finding that a simultaneous model could be constructed. In contrast, Talvitie and Liou used access and line-haul mode choices and concluded that simultaneous models could not be built successfully. On balance, it must be concluded that the evidence for simultaneous or recursive, sequential models is inconclusive as yet and may depend upon the specific modeling situation, and the specification problems of the models.[47]

Another extension into other trip purposes has been attempted by Stein Hansen, Staffan Algers and Goran Tegner[48] in connection with the development of a land-use and transportation-planning procedure for Stockholm. Again, logit analysis is the technique being used and one of the results of the research is to define different model structures for different trip purposes. Additional research has also been concerned with the development of destination-choice models,[49] per se. Most of the current work in this area has focused on shopping trips and is concerned with the identification of destination characteristics using scaling methods discussed in the next section. Modeling efforts in this area have used both multiple-choice logit models and adaptations of Markov models. At this point, no concrete findings have been obtained, although many promising leads have been uncovered and are being followed, at the time of writing.

It is somewhat difficult to define a precise and unambiguous differentiation between modeling progress and structural issues. However, the foregoing research can largely be described as representing more in the direction of modeling progress than research into structural issues. This second area of work is the subject of the next major section of this chapter, although it may be argued that some elements of the present section belong under structural issues and vice versa.


## Structural Issues

Over the period of development of behavioral travel-demand models, a number of structural issues have been raised and subjected to research. In comparing the situation relating to these models with the conventional travel-forecasting procedures, some important differences must be borne in mind. Many of the issues being raised in relation to the behavioral models are equally valid to raise with respect to the conventional procedures. However, the pressures of ongoing transportation studies and the pragmatic needs of the decision makers have largely militated against detailed research into these issues. Second, the behavioral models have been proposed and are being developed while an existing forecasting procedure can continue to be used. During the developmental stages, there were no alternatives to the now-conventional travel-forecasting procedures. Thus, the environment for research is radically different for the behavioral approach than it was for the original development of the conventional travel-forecasting procedures.

In the remainder of this section, a number of these issues are discussed briefly, and results of research summarized. Again, it is impossible for this material to be exhaustively complete, but it is hoped that coverage of the major issues has been achieved.

*Measurement of Level-of-Service Variables*

It is pertinent to raise several distinct issues under this heading, all of them relating principally to aspects of the measurement of travel times and travel costs. Included among these are the mechanism for obtaining values of travel times and travel costs, the formulation of the comparative measures among alternatives (specifically travel modes), and the allied issue of whether a difference formulation should be scaled by the amount of time or cost involved in the trip.

Three distinct values of travel times and travel costs can be identified,[50] namely perceived, reported, and measured values. The perceived values are those values actually perceived by the individual traveler. The reported values are those values the individual reports when questioned about his trip, while the measured values are those that would be obtained by averaging a sufficient number of engineering measurements of travel times and travel costs. In general, these three values will be quite different from each other. Whether there are definable, mathematical relationships between the three is a matter for conjecture. Limited research into this question has been inconclusive, so far.

In a behavioral sense, it is clear that perceived values are those upon which individual decisions are made. Regardless of whether perception agrees with "scientific" fact or measurement, both psychologists and economists agree that perceived values of variables are the decision values.[51] There are two primary reasons why reported values will not agree with perceived values. First, some travelers may be unaware of travel times and travel costs of their alternatives, since their choices may be based on other concerns. In this case, there are no perceived values and the values reported will be the result of a stimulus (the survey) to place a value on each element of the trip. Second, many survey respondents may feel a need to appear logical in the eyes of the person conducting the survey. As a result they may lie, consciously or unconsciously, by trying to make their choice appear more favorable than it is (e.g., an auto driver may deflate his *perception* of his auto travel time and inflate his *perception* of his alternative bus travel time, in *reporting* these values). Third, it appears to be plausible to hypothesize that some people may have very accurate perceptions of the amounts of time and cost involved, but measured in some psychologically perceived units that are not minutes and cents (or whatever monetary unit is appropriate). Thus, the reported values may represent an individual's best attempts to translate his perceptions into standard measurement.

Thus, it may be concluded that, although perceived values are clearly the most appropriate for modeling choices, they are probably impossible to determine. Furthermore, it may be argued that perceived values cannot be predicted or forecast. Hence, predictive and forecasting models may be able to use only measured values. This appears to be the only basis on which the use of measured values can be justified.

The present position that is adopted on this issue appears to be based upon certain assumptions about the interrelationships among these different values. In essence, these assumptions may be summarized as saying that all three values are either linear transforms of, or random distributions around each other. Hence, a good explanatory model should be based upon reported values (where, nevertheless, respondents are given the minimal opportunity to distort perceived values), while forecasting and prediction with these models should use measured values. This is an interim position, while further research is awaited.

In terms of the mathematical representation of travel times and travel costs, the development of the theory has provided some needed insights. Empirical research, however, still has its place. Quarmby[52] initially explored the alternatives of ratios, differences, and logs-of-ratios to express the comparative assesment of times and costs. The same options were subjected to further tests by John O. Lavender.[53] The conclusions of both studies are in agreement. Ratios are considerably inferior in replicating behavior, while differences and logs of ratios are, on balance, indistinguishable. Since the log of a ratio of travel times can also be expressed as the difference in the logs of the travel times, this finding does not necessarily conflict with the theory.

A further alternative formulation is to express the difference divided by the average value, for example, difference in travel times divided by the average travel time. In intraurban work, this formulation has been found to be inferior to the simple difference, in limited test data,[54] while it has been found to be superior in interurban applications.[55] This empirical result seems to be intuitively reasonable. The use of differences of system variables is a behavioral statement that people react to the amount of time or money that is either saved by using one alternative, or must be expended in using the other. However, as the total outlay of cost or time for a trip becomes greater (e.g., interurban as opposed to intraurban), the sensitivity to an absolute difference decreases.

*Disaggregation of Travel Times*

Another issue of specification in behavioral travel-demand models relates to the specific methods of including travel times in models. This issue was initially raised by Quarmby,[56] who used both overall travel time and excess travel time in his model. Subsequently, several researchers have attempted to use highly disaggregate travel times, in an attempt to improve the specification of the models.[57] This disaggregation is based upon the hypothesis that travel time spent in different ways is assessed, or weighted, differently by travelers. In particular, time that involves the expenditure of energy or effort is considered more onerous than time spent sitting or standing in a vehicle.

Most of the studies that have utilized disaggregated times have been able to substantiate the hypothesis of differential weighting. However, several difficulties arise in utilizing disaggregated elements of travel time. First, the most heavily weighted times are, generally, both the shortest and concomitantly the least accurately reported travel times in a trip. Hence, the models become subject to much greater inaccuracies. Second, it is considerably more difficult to obtain disaggregated travel time data on alternatives that are not usually used. This is purely a matter of knowledge or retention of information on the part of the respondent. Thus, comparison of values in a model becomes difficult and may result in decreased accuracy of the coefficients for these travel time elements. Third, prediction and forecasting of the disaggregated travel-time elements requires very sophisticated estimation procedures, and may not always be feasible. However, insufficient research has been completed, so far, to determine the worth of this process.

*Estimation of Automobile Costs*

In all mode-choice models, the automobile usually features as one of the alternative modes. Given the omnipresence of the automobile in Western civilization, it is bound to pervade all travel-demand models. It is well known, however, that most drivers have very limited awareness of the real costs of operating their automobiles. The question must be raised, therefore, as to what are the appropriate automobiles costs to be used in behavioral travel-demand models. Unfortunately, this is another question to which a definitive answer has not yet been found.

Several researchers have investigated, empirically, the appropriate costs of the automobile from the viewpoint of average reported costs.[58] It is clear, from responses to questions on automobile operating costs, that a great diversity of costs are perceived by drivers. These generally range from nothing to values that are substantially larger than total real operating costs (including depreciation, garaging, taxes, insurance, etc.). In general, it appears that, for commuting trips, the best average automobile cost is direct out-of-pocket costs, such as parking and tolls, plus gasoline costs only. There is some evidence to suggest, however, that in the United States this should be reduced to parking and tolls only. For other types of trips, there has been much less empirical observation and analysis, and the best assumption is probably to use the out-of-pocket and gasoline costs again. However, it is clear that the correct specification of average "perceived" costs of using an automobile is of crucial importance in assessing any policies that relate to the control of automobile use or the increase of rates of utilization of mass transit.

*Specifications of Socioeconomic Variables*

Two principal questions arise in relation to the inclusion and specification of socioeconomic variables. The first relates to the appropriate variables to characterize homogeneity of choice processes, while the second relates to the mathematical procedure for including socioeconomic variables in the models.

It is probably appropriate to observe that correct specification of socioeconomic variables is highly dependent upon correct specification of the decision process, in terms of the attributes of the alternatives among which a choice is to be made. It is clear, from the preceding subsections, that this correct specification does not yet exist. Nevertheless, a number of attempts have been made to investigate the specifications of socioeconomic variables.

Many of the early studies assumed that certain variables should be important and used these without further testing. Most commonly, income was assumed to be an important variable, to which age, sex, and automobile availability were often added. If certain of these variables failed to enter the models significantly, they were dropped. One of the first pieces of research to consider seriously this issue was that of Eduardo Aldana,[59] who investigated the usefulness of a number of different variables including the stage in the family life cycle.[60] This is a compound variable made up of age, marital status, and ages of children (if any) living at home. Aldana found that this variable appeared to correlate very strongly, in certain aggregations, with revealed preferences for travel modes. This work has been followed by some further exploratory research aimed at attempting to determine whether this high correlation is generally evident and if other variables, such as age, sex, income, etc. are also important in combination with the stage in the family life cycle.[61] The results of this research are inconclusive so far.

Most of the early behavioral travel-demand models inserted socioeconomic variables as linear additive terms in the model. In a model of the logit type, a linear function for the exponent generates, as discussed earlier, an implicit difference formulation for the alternatives variables. It also implies that socioeconomic variables cannot be linear additive, *unless they are assumed to have choice-dependent coefficients*. Such an assumption has unfortunate implications, however. It requires that different coefficients must be found for each alternative included in the choice function. In addition, values must be determined a priori for the addition of a new alternative. This implication was not widely recognized in the early work (partly because this work was predominantly binary), with the consequence that many of the models used linear, additive terms.[62]

As an alternative, two strategies are possible. First, socioeconomic variables can enter as interactive variables with the characteristics (variables) describing the alternatives. The primary variable for which this method has been considered is income.[63] However, three problems arise in this method. The socioeconomic variables so used may only enter one or two terms of a multivariate utility function, or else severe multicollinearity problems arise. The number of socioeconomic variables that may enter, is likewise, very restricted and the choice of which variables they should interact with becomes crucial to model performance. Further, many socioeconomic variables are measured using grouped information, for example, age groups, income groups, occupational categories, etc. These groups provide, at best, only interval measures and may often provide nonmetric information. The use of such variables as quantitative interaction terms is clearly ill-advised.

The second method of reflecting the effect of socioeconomic variables on the choice process is to use these variables as the basis for stratifying the population. Within each stratum, a separate model is constructed, in terms only of the characteristics of the alternatives. Each model is then free to assume different weights (coefficients) for each such characteristic. By this means the effects of socioeconomic variables are reflected in the models. This strategy was first used by Stopher,[64] but has subsequently been used in several instances.[65] Clearly, it is to be hoped that such stratification processes will yield a pattern of variations in coefficients that might prove susceptible to exogenous estimation for predictive and forecasting uses of the models. Research in this area has, so far, failed to produce such patterns.

Two problems arise from the use of this method. First, the method requires substantially larger data sets for calibration, because of the need to have significant subpopulations in each stratum. Second, selection of ideal groupings within each socioeconomic variable and combinations of several such variables into multidimensional classification procedures are crucial to the success of the approach. Indeed, the entire approach is based upon an hypothesis that socioeconomic variables can be used to identify homogeneous subgroups of the population with respect to preferences and choice behavior. This hypothesis is open to testing and is clearly disputed by many psychologists.[66]

*Measurement of Attitudes, Preferences, and*
*"Nonquantitative" Variables*

Many of the early studies of behavioral travel-demand identified comfort
and convenience as being important level-of-service variables, in addition
to times and costs. However, for some years, these variables were dis-
missed as "unquantifiable." A few researchers attempted to include
dummy variables to measure some of the modal biases of comfort or
convenience.[67] Some of these attempts appear to be fairly successful, in the
sense that significant coefficients were obtained for the dummy variables
and the goodness of fit of the model to the data was improved. The use of
such measures, however, is not useful for planning applications, since
mode-specific dummy variables cannot be predicted for changing
technology and perceptions of comfort and convenience.

In the late 1960s and early 1970s, several attempts were made to use
attitudinal questions to obtain quantitative data on variables of this type.[68]
Generally, these attempts were unsuccessful. Eventually, the lack of
success was traced to the use of the terms "comfort" and "convenience,"
with the hypothesis that these terms are perceived differently by different
people.[69] After recognizing this fact, new efforts were undertaken[70] to
measure comfort and convenience through attitude and preference prob-
ing, but using hypothesized constituent elements of these two compound
factors. These elements were chosen with the view that they should be
unambiguous descriptors of attributes of modes of travel, so that problems
of interpretation would not arise.

To date, work in this area has used methods of scaling from the field of
psychometrics.[71] Two alternative approaches have been used
experimentally—unidimensional scaling and multidimensional scaling. In
essence, the scaling methods referred to here provide a mechanism
whereby psychological "distances" between attributes or objects can be
derived on, at least, interval scales, thereby permitting the derivation of
quantitative information. The difference between the two approaches, the
dimensionality, is conceptually a matter only of constraint. In unidimensional scaling, a prior hypothesis is made that the appropriate
measurement scale exists in only one dimension. For example, time might
be considered to be measured on a single dimension. In the work of Bruce
D. Spear,[72] an assumption was made that convenience is measured on such
a unidimensional scale.

Alternatively, multidimensional scaling relaxes this assumption and
allows the analyst to search for the most parsimonious dimensionality in
which a particular phenomenon can be represented. Measures have been
developed to provide indicators of what is an acceptable dimensionality.
This was the approach used by Gregory C. Nicolaidis[73] to measure com-

fort. Both of these measurement approaches have been successful, in the sense that comfort and convenience have each been converted into scale information, and the scale values have been shown to correlate highly with observed behavior of travelers.

Much work remains to be accomplished in this research area. First, the psychometricians are unsure of the linkages between revealed behavior and preferences and attitudes.[74] The transportation analyst is, therefore, pushing at the frontiers of knowledge in attempting to include psychological scale values in models of behavior. Second, for subsequent relevance to planning applications, the psychological measures must be linked to physical attributes of the transportation choice alternatives. Third, much work yet remains to explore the general applicability of the notions of comfort and convenience and their quantification, as developed by Nicolaidis and Spear. Fourth, as was mentioned briefly in the previous section, the application of scaling approaches is not restricted to the area of travel-mode characteristics, but is currently being used to identify destination characteristics. Similar issues must be confronted in this work as have just been discussed for the modal-attribute work.

*Aggregation Issues*

As was noted earlier in this chapter, the models and research that have been discussed under the rubric of behavioral travel-demand are all disaggregate by nature. One of the reasons for this is that behavioral hypotheses can be advanced and tested most easily by considering the decision-making unit in the behavioral context. Given the size of the planning unit for urban transportation planning, however, it appears that eventual aggregation of some degree is necessary. Earlier discussion in this book has been concerned with the problems and errors caused by aggregation. The philosophy of disaggregate modeling is partially based on the idea that the longer aggregation can be put off in the planning process, the fewer and smaller will be the errors introduced by aggregation. Thus, instead of carrying out aggregation before any system modeling is undertaken, as has been customary, it should be delayed until after the models have been constructed. This, however, leads to a dual set of problems.

First, aggregation of nonlinear relationships requires more information than would be needed for linear relationships. In a simple linear relationship, the calculation of mean attributes for specific population groupings would be sufficient as can be seen in Figure 16-4. In the case of aggregation from any two or more values of $G(X)$ in a linear relationship (within the range of the linear model), the mean value of $G(X)$ will produce the mean value of the probability. However, for a nonlinear relationship, such as a logit curve, this does not hold as is shown in Figure 16-5. Here, it can be seen that the probability, $\hat{\bar{p}}$, estimated from the mean of the attributes is different from $\bar{p}$, the mean of the probabilities of values $G^1(X)$ *and* $G^2(X)$. In general, the values $\hat{\bar{p}}$ and $\bar{p}$ will only coincide when $G^1(X)$ and $G^2(X)$ are equidistant from the zero value of $G(X)$. When multiple values of $G(X)$ are aggregated, the values of $\hat{\bar{p}}$, and $\bar{p}$ will generally be different. The value $\hat{\bar{p}}$ is the one obtained by naive aggregation. A number of alternative strategies are possible for aggregating nonlinear, behavioral travel-demand models. Talvitie[75] has proposed a method that uses a Taylor expansion in first and higher order moments of the attributes to aggregate model outputs. Richard B. Westin[76] has put forward an alternative method that necessitates the assumption of distributions for the attributes. Other methods have also been put forward with comparisons made both of their sensitivities over the range of probabilities[77] and of their comparative accuracies with those of aggregate models.[78]

Second, aggregation from disaggregate models also necessitates the aggregation of transportation system attributes on a spatial basis. Since the models are particularly sensitive to items such as walking, waiting, etc., the

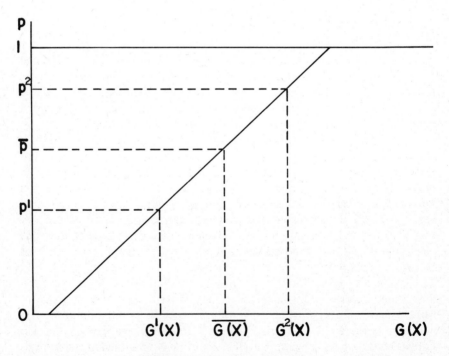

**Figure 16-4.** Comparison of Aggregate and Disaggregate Estimates from a Linear Model.

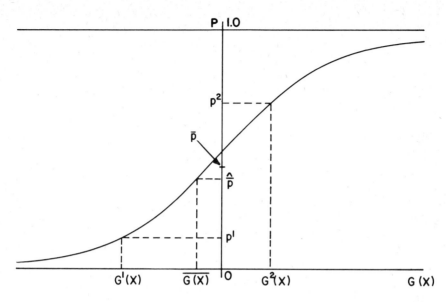

**Figure 16-5.** Comparison of Aggregate and Disaggregate Estimates from a Logit Model.

aggregation of transportation system attributes poses a serious potential for error. Methods for producing acceptable estimates of system attributes have been proposed by Yehuda Gur[79] and Antti P. Talvitie.[80]

Again, much yet remains to be accomplished in this area. It is, however, possible that aggregation is not necessary even at this level. Rather, it is plausible to suggest that disaggregate models could be used to predict changes in travel patterns that would result from various policies and investments. These changes could then be used either to factor a basic trip matrix or to estimate percentage changes in various appropriate travel movements. These strategies serve to delay aggregation yet further, to a point where it is debatable as to whether aggregation is actually carried out. Furthermore, it obviates the need for aggregation strategies of the type discussed by Frank S. Koppelman[81] and removes the requirement for system aggregation.

## Applications

The emphasis of this chapter has so far been on the theory and research issues of behavioral travel-demand models. This is appropriate, since most of the work in behavioral travel demand has been concerned with these areas. However, it would be remiss not to mention the applications that have been made of this approach. Understandably, the developers of the approach have been wary of applying prototype models too early. Recently, more applications have been attempted and these have worked sufficiently well to encourage further work in this area to proceed simultaneously with the research.

One of the earliest applications has already been mentioned. This was the use of multiple-choice models for the Washington airport access study and the San Diego study.[82] At about the same time as the San Diego study, models were also developed for the Department of Transportation of the state of Illinois for use in connection with studies of the feasibility of introducing feeder-bus service in suburban communities.[83] These models have been applied successfully in a number of situations.

More recently, the New York State Department of Transportation developed a mode-choice model for the Niagara Frontier Study.[84] In this application, tests were also made between the disaggregate model and the more conventional model that it was designed to replace. The best model obtained in the disaggregate calibration is given in equation 16.79 for long trips with auto available.

$$G(X) = 0.887 + 1.000TR \qquad (16.79)$$

where $G(X)$ = the logit exponent for the probability of using auto

and $TR$ = the travel-time ratio

A total of four models were constructed and their prediction results compared with the Niagara Frontier Study model. From these tests, it was found that the disaggregate model performed as well as the original model, but with substantially less data. However, it should be borne in mind that the original aggregate model[85] was a highly sophisticated trip-interchange model, constructed with household data, rather than zonal averages. Hence, it may be inferred that the disaggregate model would compare more favorably with most of the conventional modal-split models developed in past transporation studies.

With the success of these limited applications, there is an increasing concern with using the disaggregate models, particularly in the context of mode choice. A number of applications of the models are currently in progress, but have not yet been described in published material. It appears, however, that the disaggregate mode-choice model is now becoming an accepted planning tool and the need to produce behavioral, and possibly disaggregate, models for other choices is becoming increasingly apparent.

### The Way Ahead

This chapter has outlined an approach to travel forecasting that appears to hold the greatest potential for the improvement of policy-responsiveness and accuracy in the urban transportation-planning process. However, much research and development work is necessary before the full potentials of the approach can be realized. Clearly, while this work is in progress, continuing refinements and developments in the conventional models, outlined in the earlier chapters of this book, will occur. Nevertheless, the authors of this book feel that the way ahead for travel-forecasting methods lies principally in the behavioral travel-demand models described in this chapter, regardless of whether such models are developed as aggregate or disaggregate models. At numerous points in this chapter, reference has been made to further research needs and to developments now underway or about to be undertaken. It is clearly redundant to repeat each of these statements here. Rather, it is appropriate to take a broader view of the likely developments in behavioral travel-demand over the next few years.

The first direction that can be deduced is that of continued refinements in mode-choice models, which will be reflected as general refinements through all the choice steps by the preservation of strict utilities. These refinements appear most likely to affect the range of variables included, with particular emphasis on the inclusion of attitude-based information, and in the use of demographic and socioeconomic information to define homogeneous behavior groups in the population.

Allied to the work in mode choice, further developments seem likely in methods of aggregation or in changing the strategies of regional planning. Similarly, research into the separability of choices and the basic question of recursive, sequential models or simultaneously estimated models appear likely to be addressed. Together with these questions, research is currently underway into further extensions into choices of destinations, trip-making frequency, and time of day. The development of a total demand model, therefore seems to be likely within the next few years at least in prototype.

Third, it is apparent that an increasing number of applications of disaggregate models will be developed in the context of both local and regional planning. Most of these applications are likely to take place using present levels of knowledge about the behavioral travel-demand models. It is to be hoped that new knowledge will be applied in these operational models at an early stage, so that the maximum improvements in the accuracy and responsiveness of the planning process can be obtained.

# Notes

# Notes

## Chapter 1
### Introduction and Background

1. Radnor J. Paquette, Norman Ashford, and Paul H. Wright, *Transportation Engineering: Planning and Design*, New York, Ronald Press, 1972, pages 48-53; and "Highways, Safety, and Transit: An Analysis of the Federal-Aid Highway Act of 1973," Highway Users Federation, 1973, pages 3-4.

2. *Highway Maintenance: A Survey of State Laws*, Highway Research Board Special Report 84, 1965; Paquette, Ashford, and Wright, *Transportation Engineering*, pages 48-53.

3. U.S. Department of Transportation, "Urban Mass Transportation Act of 1964 as Amended through October 15, 1970," Washington, D.C. (unpublished).

4. "Highways, Safety, and Transit," pages 5-6.

5. "Brinegar Delineates Mass Transit Position," *American Highway and Transportation Monthly*, September 1974, Vol. 53, No. 7, page 10.

6. Jack E. Snell, "A Framework for the Analysis of Urban Transportation Research," Ph.D. dissertation, Department of Civil Engineering, Northwestern University, Evanston, Illinois, June 1966.

7. Automobile Manufacturers Association, Inc., *1972 Automobile Facts and Figures*, Washington, D.C., 1973, page 18.

8. Ibid., page 55.

## Chapter 2
### Systems Analysis and Principles of Modeling in Transportation

1. Charles J. Hitch and Roland N. McKean, *The Economics of Defense in the Nuclear Age*, Cambridge, Mass., Harvard University Press, 1960. Reprinted with permission. (Citation used from Atheneum edition, New York: Atheneum, 1965, page 41.)

2. C.J. Zwick, "Systems Analysis and Urban Planning," RAND Corporation, Santa Monica, 1963, page 5.

3. E.S. Quade (Editor), *Analysis for Military Decisions*, Netherlands, North Holland Publishing Co., 1964, page 4.

4. Arthur D. Hall, *A Methodology for Systems Engineering*, Princeton,

New Jersey, Van Nostrand, 1962, page 12. Reprinted by permission of Van Nostrand Reinhold Company. © 1962 by Litton Educational Publishing Co.

5. Richard De Neufville and Joseph H. Stafford, *Systems Analysis for Engineers and Planners*, New York, McGraw-Hill Book Co., 1971, page XI.

6. William Alonso, "The Quality of Data and the Choice and Design of Predictive Models," *Highway Research Board Special Report 97*, 1968, pages 178-192; P. Rao, "Some Notes on Misspecification in Multiple Regressions," *American Statistician*, 1971, Vol. 25, No. 5, pages 37-39; W.G. Cochran, "Some Effects of Errors of Measurement on Multiple Correlation," *Journal of American Statistical Accociation*, 1970, Vol. 65, No. 329, pages 22-34; J.B. Ramsey and P. Zarembka, "Specification Error Tests and Alternative Functional Forms of the Aggregate Production Function," *Journal of American Statistical Association* 1971, Vol. 66, No. 335, pages 471-477; J.J. Chai, "Correlated Measurement Errors and the Least Squares Estimation of the Regression Coefficient," *Journal of American Statistical Association*, 1971, Vol. 66, No. 335, pages 478-483.

## Chapter 3
### Economic Theory and Travel Demand

1. Walter Y. Oi and Paul W. Shuldiner, *An Analysis of Urban Travel Demands*, Evanston, Illinois, Northwestern University Press, 1962, Chapter II.

2. Paul A. Samuelson, *Economics: An Introductory Analysis,* New York, McGraw-Hill Book Co., 1967, page 59.

3. Ibid., pages 363-367.

4. Ibid., page 61.

5. Martin Wohl and B.V. Martin, *Traffic Systems Analysis for Engineers and Planners*, New York, McGraw-Hill Book Co., 1967, page 118.

6. John W. Dickey et al., *Metropolitan Transportation Planning*, Washington, D.C., Scripta Book Company, 1975, pages 128-129; and Frank A. Haight, *Mathematical Theories of Traffic Flow*, New York, Academic Press, 1963, page 72.

7. See primarily chapters 7, 8, and 9.

## Chapter 4
### The Urban Transportation-planning Process

1. Brian V. Martin, Frederick W. Memmott, III, and Alexander J.

Bone, *Principles and Techniques of Predicting Future Demand for Urban Area Transportation*, Cambridge, Mass., MIT Press, MIT Report No. 3, 1961, page 5; and Bruce G. Hutchinson, *Principles of Urban Transport Systems Planning*, Washington, D.C., Scripta Book Company, 1974, pages 21-23; Oi and Shuldiner, *Urban Travel Demands*, pages 24-27.

2. Roger L. Creighton, *Urban Transportation Planning*, Urbana, University of Illinois Press, 1970; John R. Meyer, John F. Kain, and Martin Wohl, *The Urban Transportation Problem*, Cambridge, Mass., Harvard University Press, 1965, Chapter 1; O.E.C.D., *The Urban Transportation Planning Process*, Paris, Organization for Economic Cooperation and Development (OECD), 1971, pages 15-21; S.C. Plowden, "Transportation Studies Examined," *Journal of Transport Economics and Policy*, January 1967, Vol. 1, No. 1, pages 5-27; R. Zettel and R.C. Carll, "Summary Review of Major Metropolitan Area Transportation Studies in the U.S.A.," Special Report, ITTE, University of California, Berkeley, 1962; Martin, Memmott, and Bone, *Principles and Techniques*, Part III; Oi and Shuldiner, *Urban Travel Demands*.

## Chapter 5
## Inventory

1. Martin, Memmott, and Bone, *Principles and Techniques*, pages 9-35; Oi and Shuldiner, *Urban Travel Demands*, pages 23-46.

2. U.S. Department of Commerce, *Traffic Assignment Manual*, Washington, D.C., U.S. Government Printing Office, 1964, Chapter III; Kenneth Shiatte, "Inventorying an Arterial Network for Computer Assignment—Methods and Implications" *Highway Research Record No. 41*, 1963, pages 13-28.

3. U.S. Bureau of Public Roads, *Manual of Procedures for Home-Interview Traffic Study*, Washington, D.C., U.S. Government Printing Office, 1954; Frederick W. Memmott, "Home-Interview Survey and Data-Collection Procedures," *Highway Research Record No. 41,* 1963, pages 7-12.

4. The reader will find a much more detailed treatment of questions of survey method, sampling theory, and sampling frames in: Frank Yates, *Sampling Methods for Censuses and Surveys*, London, Chas. Griffin & Co., 1965; Leslie Kish, *Survey Sampling*, New York, J. Wiley & Sons, 1967; W.G. Cochran, *Sampling Techniques*, New York, J. Wiley & Sons, 1966.

5. RAND Corporation, *A Million Random Digits with 100,000 Normal Deviates*, New York, Free Press, 1955.

6. Ibid.

7. Yates, *Sampling Methods*; Kish, *Survey Sampling*.

8. William R. McGrath and Charles Guinn, "Simulated Home Interview by Television," *Highway Research Record No. 41,* 1963, pages 1-6; C. Ben, Richard J. Bouchard and C.E. Sweet, Jr., "An Evaluation of Simplified Procedures for Determining Travel Patterns in Small Urban Areas," *Highway Research Record No. 88*, 1965, pages 137-170; Austin E. Brant, Jr. and Dana E. Low, "Cost-Saving Techniques for Collection and Analysis of Origin-Destination Data." *Highway Research Record No. 205*, 1967, pages 50-67.

## Chapter 6
## Land-use Forecasting

1. Britton Harris, "Quantitative Models of Urban Development: Their Role in Metropolitan Policy-Making" in Harvey Perloff and Lowdon Wingo, Jr. (Editors) *Issues in Urban Economics*, Baltimore, Johns Hopkins Press, 1968; Alan G. Wilson (Editor), *Urban and Regional Planning*, London, Pion Ltd., 1971.

2. Harvey S. Perloff with Vera W. Dodds, *How a Region Grows: Area Development in the U.S. Economy*, Committee for Economic Development, Supplementary Paper No. 17, March 1963; Irving Hoch, *Progress in Urban Economics: The Work of the Committee on Urban Economics 1959-1968 and the Development of the Field,* Washington, D.C., Resources for the Future, 1969, Appendix 1; Harvey S. Perloff et al., *Regions, Resources, and Economic Growth*, Baltimore, Johns Hopkins Press, 1960, particularly Chapters 4 and 5; Wilbur R. Thompson, "Urban Economics" in H. Wentworth Eldredge (Editor) *Taming Megalopolis: What is and What Could Be*, New York, Frederick A. Praeger, 1967, Vol. 1, Chapter 5.

3. Harvey S. Perloff and Lowdon Wingo, (Editors) *Issues in Urban Economics*, Baltimore, Johns Hopkins Press, 1968; Gerald Kraft, John R. Meyer, and Jean-Paul Valette, *The Role of Transportation in Regional Economic Development*, Lexington, Mass., Lexington Books, D.C. Heath and Co., 1971 (the Bibliography of this book is particularly useful); Eldredge, *Taming Megalopolis*, Vol. II, Chapter 14.

4. John R. Hamburg and Robert H. Sharkey, "Land Use Forecast," Chicago, *Chicago Area Transportation Study*, 1961, Document # 32,610; John R. Hamburg, "Land Use Projection for Transportation Planning," *Highway Research Board Bulletin No. 224,* 1959, pages 72-84; Carl N. Swerdloff and Joseph R. Stowers, "A Test of Some First Generation

Residential Land Use Models," *Highway Research Record No. 126*, 1966, pages 38-59.

    5. Swerdloff and Stowers, "Residential Land Use Models."

    6. Donald M. Hill, Daniel Brand, and Willard B. Hansen, "Prototype Development of Statistical Land-Use Prediction Model for Greater Boston Region," *Highway Research Record No. 114*, 1966, pages 51-69.

    7. Ibid., page 55.

    8. Hill, Brand, and Hansen, "Prototype Development"; Dickey et al., *Metropolitan Transportation Planning*, pages 155-173.

    9. John D. Herbert and Benjamin H. Stevens, "A Model for the Distribution of Residential Activity in Urban Areas," Philadelphia, Penn Jersey Transportation Study, PJ Papers No. 2, 1960.

    10. Ibid.

    11. David R. Seidman, "Report on the Activities Allocation Model," Philadelphia, Penn Jersey Transportation Study, PJ Papers No. 22, 1964.

    12. Ira S. Lowry, "Seven Models of Urban Development: A Structural Comparison," *Highway Research Board Special Report No. 97*, 1967, pages 139-141.

## Chapter 7
## Trip Generation

    1. See, for example, N.R. Draper and H. Smith, *Applied Regression Analysis,* New York, John Wiley & Sons, 1968, pages 1-35, Chapter 4.

    2. Draper and Smith, *Applied Regression Analysis*, pages 6-7; Peter R. Stopher, *Survey Sampling and Multivariate Analysis in Transportation,* Lexington, Mass., Lexington Books, D.C. Heath and Co., (forthcoming).

    3. H. Kassoff and H.D. Deutschman, "Trip Generation: A Critical Appraisal," *Highway Research Record No. 297*, 1969, pages 15-30; G.M. McCarthy, "Multiple-Regression Analysis of Household Trip Generation—A Critique," *Highway Research Record 297*, National Academy of Sciences, Washington, D.C., 1969, pages 31-43.

    4. McCarthy, "Multiple-Regression Analysis."

    5. Ibid., page 32. Used with permission.

    6. Chicago Area Transportation Study, *Volume 1: Survey Findings,* Chicago, December 1959, page 37 (83.8% of trips are home-based); Pittsburgh Area Transportation Study, *Volume 1: Study Findings*, Pittsburgh, November 1961, Table 30, page 92 (87.0% of trips are home-based); Traffic Research Corporation, Ltd., *Capital Region of British*

*Columbia Transportation Study,* March 1965, Figure 7, page 16 (80.0% of trips are home-based); Traffic Research Corporation, Ltd., *An Analysis Report on the 1964 Home Interview Survey,* Toronto, Metropolitan Toronto and Region Transportation Study, March 1965, Table 14, page 6 (88.8% of trips are home-based); London Traffic Survey, *Volume 1: Existing Traffic and Travel Characteristics in Greater London*, London, London County Council, July 1964, page 107, Table 6-16A (88.2% of trips are home-based); etc.

7. R. Hickman, "Generation of Business Trips in Central London," *Traffic Engineering and Control*, 1967, Vol. 8, No. 8, pages 384-387; M. Kolifrath and Paul Shuldiner, "Co-Variance Analysis of Manufacturing Trip Generation," *Highway Research Record No. 165*, 1967, pages 117-128; J. Th. Gantvoort, "Traffic Generation of a Large Department Store," *Traffic Engineering and Control*, 1967, Vol. 8, No. 6, pages 285-287 and 293; David N.M. Starkie, "Intensity of Commerical Traffic Generation by Industry," *Traffic Engineering and Control*, 1967, Vol. 7, No. 9, pages 558-560; Standing Conference on London and Southeast Regional Planning, "Trip Generation," Report of the Traffic Generation Subgroup, December 1966 (unpublished); Paul Prestwood-Smith and Geoffrey M. Lamb, "Traffic Generation Rates for Small- Scale Development Schemes Within the Central Area of London Based on the L.T.S." A Report of the Department of Highways and Transportation, Greater London Council, #TPS-15, March, 1967 (unpublished).

8. A. Ungar, "Traffic Attraction of Rural Outdoor Recreational Areas," *National Cooperative Highway Research Program Report No. 44*, 1967.

9. Starkie, "Commercial Traffic Generation," Arnim H. Meyburg and Peter R. Stopher, "Towards Trip Attraction Models for Freight Vehicle Trips to Shopping Plazas," *Transportation Research Forum Proceedings*, 1973, pages 233-242.


**Chapter 8**
**Trip Distribution**

1. Martin, Memmott, and Bone, *Principles and Techniques,* pages 126-138; T.J. Fratar, "Forecasting Distribution of Interzonal Vehicular Trips by Successive Approximations," *Highway Research Board Proceedings*, 1954, pages 376-385.

2. Isaac Newton, *Philosophiae Naturalis Principia Mathematica*, London, 2nd Edition, 1713, Book III, Prop. VII and Corr. II, page 414.

3. William J. Reilly, *The Law of Retail Gravitation,* New York, W.J. Reilly, 1931, page 9.

4. Ibid.

5. For Pallin see Torsten R. Astrom, "Laws of Traffic and Their Applications to Traffic Forecasts with Special Reference to the Sound Bridge Project," Stockholm, Royal Institute of Technology, 1973.

6. For example, Edwin L. Crow, Frances A. Davis, and Margaret W. Maxfield, *Statistics Manual,* New York, Dover Publications, pages 85-87.

7. For example, Sidney Seigel, *Nonparametric Statistics for the Behavioral Sciences,* New York, McGraw-Hill Book Co., 1956, pages 47-52.

8. Norman Ashford and D.O. Covault, "The Mathematical Form of Travel Time Factors," *Highway Research Record No. 283,* 1969, pages 30-47.

9. See chapter 10.

10. See chapter 9.

11. S.A. Stouffer, "Intervening Opportunities: A Theory Relating Mobility and Distance," *American Sociological Review*, 1940, Volume 5, No. 6, pages 845-867.

12. See Chicago Area Transportation Study, Final Report, Volume II, Chicago, 1960, pages 81-92 and 111.

13. Earl R. Ruiter, "Improvements in Understanding, Calibrating, and Applying the Opportunity Model," *Highway Research Record No. 165*, 1967, pages 9-10.

14. Ibid., page 11.

15. Ibid., pages 6-20.

16. F.B. Hildebrand, *Introduction to Numerical Analysis*, New York, McGraw-Hill Book Co., 1956, page 443.

17. Ruiter, "Improvements in the Opportunity Model," pages 10-13.

## Chapter 9
## Modal Split

1. Warren T. Adams, "Factors Influencing Mass Transit and Automobile Travel in Urban Areas," *Public Roads*, 1959, Vol. 30, pages 256-260; or Warren T. Adams, "Factors Influencing Transit and Automobile Use in Urban Areas," *Highway Research Board Bulletin No. 230*, 1959, pages 101-110.

2. Adams, "Transit and Automobile Use," page 104.

328

3. John J. Howe, "Modal Split of CBD Trips," *Chicago Area Transportation Study Research News*, Vol 2, No. 12, 1958, pages 3-10; Aristide E. Biciunnas, "Modal Split of First Work Trips—1956 and 1960," *Chicago Area Transportation Study Research News*, Vol. 6, No. 1, 1964, pages 12-13.

4. Martin J. Fertal et al., *Modal Split: Documentation of Nine Methods for Estimating Transit Usage*, U.S. Department of Commerce, 1966, pages 16-33; Louis E. Keefer, "Predicting the Modal Split in Pittsburgh," Journal of the Highway Division, *Proceedings of the American Society of Civil Engineers*, 1963, Vol. 89, No. HW1, pages 13-25; Louis E. Keefer, "The Illusory Demand for Mass Transit," *Traffic Engineering*, January 1966; Louis E. Keefer, "Characteristics of Captive and Choice Transit Trips in the Pittsburgh Metropolitan Area," *Highway Research Board Bulletin No. 347*, 1962, pages 24-33.

5. Fertal et al., *Modal Split*, pages 27-33; Alan M. Voorhees & Assoc., Inc., *Modal Split Model*, Erie Area Transportation Study, Staff Report No. 3, September 1963.

6. H. Basmaciyan and J.W. Schmidt, "Development and Application of a Modal Split Model for the Puget Sound Region," PSRTS Staff Report No. 12, May 1964.

7. Fertal et al., *Modal Split*, page 47.

8. Edward Weiner, *A Modal Split Model for Southeastern Wisconsin*, Technical Record, Vol. II, No. 6, Southeastern Wisconsin Regional Planning Commission, 1966.

9. H.D. Quinby, "Traffic Distribution Forecasts—Highway and Transit," *Traffic Engineering*, 1961, Vol. 31, No. 5, pages 22-29, 54 and 56.·

10. A discussion of this curve appears in chapter 16.

11. Donald M. Hill and Hans G. Von Cube, "Development of a Model for Forecasting Travel Mode Choice in Urban Areas," *Highway Research Record No. 38,* 1963, pages 78-96.

12. Ibid., page 30.

13. Ibid., pages 30-31.

14. Thomas B. Deen, William L. Mertz, and Neil A. Irwin, "Application of a Modal Split Model to Travel Estimates for the Washington Area," *Highway Research Record No. 38*, 1963, pages 97-123.

15. Metropolitan Toronto Planning Board, *Report 1*, Transportation Research Program, 1962, page 39.

16. Roger J. Forbord, "Twin Cities Modal Split Model," Minnesota Highway Department, January 1966.

17. Ibid., page 8.

18. Hill and Von Cube, "Development of a Model."

19. A.S. Goldberger, *Econometric Theory*, New York, John Wiley & Sons, 1964, Chapter 7.

20. See chapter 7.


**Chapter 10**
**Network Assignment**

1. E.F. Moore, "The Shortest Path Through a Maze," Proceedings, International Symposium on the Theory of Switching, Harvard University, Cambridge, Mass., 1957, pages 285-292.

2. Bureau of Public Roads, *Traffic Assignment Manual*, U.S. Department of Commerce, June 1964, Chapter 5.

3. A.S. Rathnau, "Capacity Restraint Method-Assignment Program," Chicago Area Transportation Study, January 1964.

4. Joyce Almond, "Traffic Assignment to a Road Network," *Traffic Engineering and Control*, 1965, Vol. 6, No. 10, pages 616, 617, 622; Joyce Almond, "Traffic Assignment with Flow-Dependent Journey Times," *Proceedings, Third International Symposium on Theory of Road Traffic Flow*, 1967.

5. Hill and Von Cube, "Forecasting Travel Mode Choice."

6. Hans G. Von Cube, R.J. Des Jardins, and Norman Dodd, "Assignment of Passengers to Transit Systems," *Traffic Engineering*, 1958, August, pages 12-14, 50.

7. J.E. Burrell, "Multiple Route Assignment and Its Application to Capacity Restraint," paper presented to Fourth International Symposium on the Theory of Traffic Flow, Karlsruhe, June 1968.

8. Freeman, Fox, Wilbur Smith and Associates, *London Transportation Study*, Phase III, Vol. 1, 1968 (unpublished); Robert Lane, Timothy J. Powell, and Paul Prestwood-Smith, *Analytical Transport Planning*, New York, John Wiley & Sons, 1973, pages 112-116.


**Chapter 11**
**Transportation-plan Evaluation**

1. Peter R. Stopher and Arnim H. Meyburg, *Transportation Systems Evaluation*, Lexington, Mass., Lexington Books, D.C. Heath and Co. (forthcoming).

2. C.H. Oglesby and L.I. Hewes, *Highway Engineering*, New York, John Wiley & Sons, 1963.

3. Daniel G. Haney, "The Value of Time for Passenger Cars: A Theoretical Analysis and Descriptions of Preliminary Experiments," Stanford Research Institute Contract CBR-11-0959, *Final Report, Vol. 1,* May 1957; Thomas C. Thomas and Gordon I. Thompson, "The Value of Time for Commuting Motorists as a Function of their Income Level and Amount of Time Saved," *Highway Research Record No. 369*, 1971, pages 104-117; Shalom Reichman, "Conceptual Problems in the Evaluation of Travel Time," *Transportation Research Board Special Report* (in press, 1975); Peter R. Stopher, "Value of Time from Mode Choice Analysis: Some Problems," *Transportation Research Board Special Report* (in press, 1975); Leon N. Moses and I.F. Williamson, Jr., *Value of Time, Choice of Mode, and the Subsidy Issue in Urban Transportation*, Research Report, The Transportation Center, Northwestern Univ.

4. J. Morley English (Editor), *Cost-Effectiveness—The Economic Evaluation of Engineered Systems*, New York, John Wiley & Sons, 1968; Edwin N. Thomas and Joseph L. Schofer, *Strategies for the Evaluation of Alternative Transportation Plans*, Final Report, National Cooperative Highway Research Program Project 8-4, Northwestern University, Evanston, Illinois, 1967.

**Chapter 12**
**Critique of the Conventional Urban**
**Transportation-planning Process**

1. Yehuda Gur, "An Accessibility-Sensitive Trip-Generation Model," Ph.D. dissertation, Department of Civil Engineering, Northwestern University, 1971; Mark H. Kellogg and Walter J. Diewald, "An Investigation of the Use of Accessibility in Direct Generation Models," Virginia Polytechnic Institute and State University, 1974.

2. Alan G. Wilson, "A Statistical Theory of Spatial Distribution Models," *Transportation Research*, 1967, Vol. 1.

3. Joseph L. Schofer, Workshop Report on "Demand Forecasting for Short-Range and Low-Capital Options," *Highway Research Board Special Report 143*, 1973, pages 27-33.

4. U.S. Department of Transportation, Urban Mass Transportation Administration, *Transportation Planning System (UTPS) Course Notes*, October 1972; U.S. Department of Transportation, Urban Mass Transportation Administration, *UMTA Transportation Planning System (UTPS) Reference Manual*, October 1972.

## Chapter 13
## Direct Traffic-estimation Method

1. Morton Schneider, "A Direct Approach to Traffic Assignment," *Highway Research Record No. 6,* Highway Research Board, Washington, D.C., 1963; Morton Schneider, "Direct Estimation of Traffic Volume at a Point," *Highway Research Record No. 165*, Highway Research Board, Washington, D.C., 1967.

2. Geoffrey Brown, and Albert M. Woehrle, "Program, Inputs and Calibration of the Direct Traffic Estimation Method," *Highway Research Record No. 250*, pages 18-24; William B. Mertz, "Direct Traffic Estimation Method—General Description and Calibration Results," *Interim Technical Report* 4112-7113, Tri-State Transportation Commission, New York, 1969; Albert H. Woehrle, "Direct Traffic Estimation—Test Case Results," *Interim Technical Report* 4032-1320, *Tri-State Transportation Commission,* New York, 1966; Albert H. Woehrle, "Direct Traffic Estimation Method—Systematic Inputs and Method of Computation," *Interim Technical Report* 4075-7111, *Tri-State Transportation Commission,* New York, 1967.

3. Schneider, "A Direct Approach."

4. Morton Schneider, "Access and Land Development," *Highway Research Board Special Report 97*, 1967, pages 164-177.

5. Ibid.

## Chapter 14
## Spatial-distribution Model Theory

1. *Van Nostrand's Scientific Encyclopedia*, Princeton, New Jersey, Van Nostrand Company, 1968, page 627.

2. Wilson, "Spatial Distribution Models."

3. *Van Nostrand's Scientific Encyclopedia*, page 1749.

4. Wilson, "Spatial Distribution Models."

5. Ibid.

6. Ibid.

7. Alan G. Wilson, "The Use of Entropy Maximizing Models in the Theory of Trip Distribution, Mode Split and Route Split," *Journal of Transport Economics and Policy*, 1969, Vol. 3, No. 1, page 112 et seq.; Alan G. Wilson, "Advances and Problems in Distribution Modelling," *Transportation Research*, 1970, Vol. 4, No. 1, page 10.

8. Wilson, "Spatial Distribution Models;" Wilson, "Entropy Maximizing Models," page 115 et seq.

9. Alan G. Wilson, " "Travel Demand Forecasting: Achievements and Problems," *Highway Research Board Special Report No. 143, 1973,* page 290.

10. See Chapter 16.

11. South-East Lancashire and North-East Cheshire Transportation Study. See for example, ibid., page 289.

12. Martin J. Beckmann and Thomas F. Golob, "On the Metaphysical Foundations of Traffic Theory: Entropy Revisited," GM Research Publication GMR-1091, 1971; or "A Critique for Entropy and Gravity in Travel Forecasting." Fifth International Symposium on the Theory of Traffic Flow and Transportation; Berkeley, California, 1971.

13. Alan G. Wilson, "Further Developments of Entropy Maximizing Transport Models," *Transportation Planning and Technology*, 1973, Vol. 1, No. 3, pages 184-185; Beckmann and Golob, "Metaphysical Foundations of Traffic Theory," Frank J. Cesario, "A Note on the Entropy Model of Trip Distribution," *Transportation Research*, 1973, Vol. 7, No. 3, pages 331-333.

## Chapter 15
## The Theory of Econometric Models

1. Kelvin J. Lancaster, "A New Approach to Consumer Theory," *Journal of Political Economy*, 1966, Vol. LXXIV, pages 132-157; and in Richard E. Quandt, *The Demand for Travel: Theory and Measurement*, Lexington, Mass., Lexington Books, D.C. Heath and Co., 1970, Chapter 2.

2. Quandt, *The Demand for Travel*, page 19. Used with permission of the University of Chicago Press.

3. Richard E. Quandt and William J. Baumol, "The Demand for Abstract Transport Modes: Theory and Measurement," *Journal of Regional Science*, 1966, Vol. 6, No. 2, pages 13-26; and in Quandt, *The Demand for Travel*, Chapter 4.

4. Marvin L. Manheim, "Practical Implications of Some Fundamental Properties of Travel Demand Models," *Highway Research Record No. 422*, 1973, pages 21-38.

5. Quandt and Baumol, "Demand for Abstract Transport Modes."

6. Richard E. Quandt and Kan H. Young, "Cross-Sectional Travel Demand Models: Estimates and Tests," *Journal of Regional Science*, Vol.

9, No. 2, 1969, pages 201-214; or in Quandt, *The Demand for Travel*, Chapter 6.

7. Richard E. Quandt, "Estimation of Modal Splits," in Quandt, *The Demand for Travel*, Chapter 7; Richard E. Quandt, "Abstract Transport Modes and Travel Demand Projections," *Rivista Internazionale di Scienze Economiche e Commerciali*, 1970, Anno XVII, No. 3, pages 201-215.

8. James M. McLynn and R.H. Watkins, "Multimode Assignment Model," Paper prepared for National Bureau of Standards, Washington, D.C., August 1965; James M. McLynn, Alan J. Goldman, P.R. Meyers, and R.H. Watkins, "Analysis of a Market-Split Model," Northeast Corridor Transportation Project, Technical Paper No. 8, April 1967.

9. McLynn and Watkins, "Multimode Assignment Model," page 14.

10. Gerald Kraft, "Demand for Intercity Passenger Travel in the Washington-Boston Corridor," Part V, Systems Analysis and Research Corporation, Boston, Mass., 1966.

11. Ibid.

12. Gerald Kraft and Martin Wohl, "New Directions for Passenger Demand Analysis and Forecasting," *Transportation Research*, 1967, Vol. 1, pages 205-230.

13. Antti P. Talvitie, *An Econometric Model for Downtown Work Trips*, Chicago Area Transportation Study, *Document No. 341,031*, 1971; and Antti P. Talvitie, "A Direct Demand Model for Downtown Work Trips," *Transportation*, 1973 (a), Volume 2, pages 121-152.

## Chapter 16
## Behavioral Travel-demand Models

1. Stanley L. Warner, *Stochastic Choice of Mode in Urban Travel: A Study in Binary Choice*, Evanston, Illinois, Northwestern University Press, 1962.

2. For example: David A. Quarmby, "Choice of Travel Mode for the Journey to Work: Some Findings," *Journal of Transport Economics and Policy*, 1967, Vol. 1, No. 3, pages 273-314; Thomas E. Lisco, "The Value of Commuters' Travel Time: A Study in Urban Transportation," Ph.D. dissertation, Department of Economics, University of Chicago, 1967; Charles A. Lave, "Modal Choice in Urban Transportation: A Behavioral Approach," Ph.D. dissertation, Department of Economics, Stanford University 1968; Peter R. Stopher, "A Probability Model of Travel Mode Choice for the Work Journey," *Highway Research Record No. 283*, 1969, pages 57-65.

3. R.D. Luce and H. Raiffa: *Games and Decisions*, New York, John Wiley & Sons, 1957.

4. J. Berkson, "Application of the Logistic Function to Bio-Assay," *Journal of the American Statistical Association*, 1944, Vol. 39, pages 357-365.

5. Peter R. Stopher, *Survey Sampling and Multivariate Analysis in Transportation*, Lexington, Mass., Lexington Books, D.C. Heath and Co., (forthcoming); Paul R. Rassam, Raymond Ellis, and John C. Bennett, "The N-Dimensional Logit Model: Development and Application," *Highway Research Record No. 369*, 1971, pages 135-147.

6. Daniel McFadden, "Conditional Logit Analysis of Qualitative Choice Behavior," in P. Zarembka (editor), *Frontiers of Econometrics*, New York, Academic Press, 1973.

7. Ibid.

8. W. Leontief, "Introduction to a Theory of the Internal Structure of Function Relationships," *Econometrica,* 1947, Vol. 15, No. 4; Daniel Brand, "Separable versus Simultaneous Travel-Choice Behavior," *Transportation Research Board Special Report No. 149*, 1974, pages 187-206; Moshe E. Ben-Akiva and Frank S. Koppelman, "Multidimensional Choice Models: Alternative Structures of Travel Demand Models," *Transportation Research Board Special Report No. 149,* 1974, pages 129-142.

9. For an example of this, see Daniel Brand, "Travel Demand Forecasting: Some Foundations and a Review," *Highway Research Board Special Report No. 143.* pages 251-252.

10. Ben-Akiva and Koppelman, "Multidimensional Choice Models," page 133.

11. R.D. Luce, *Individual Choice Behavior*, New York, John Wiley & Sons, 1959.

12. Draper and Smith, *Applied Regression Analysis.*

13. Peter L. Watson, "Choice of Estimation Procedure for Models of Binary Choice: Some Statistical and Empirical Evidence," *Regional and Urban Economics*, 1974, Volume 4, No. 2, pages 187-200.

14. Warner, *Stochastic Choice of Mode*; Quarmby, "Choice of Travel Mode;" Robert G. McGillivray, "Demand and Choice Models of Mode Split," *Journal of Transport Economics and Policy*, 1970, Vol. 4, No. 2, pages 192-207.

15. M.G. Kendall: *A Course in Multivariate Analysis*, London, Charles Griffin & Co., 1965, pages 144-170; Gerhard Tintner, *Econometrics*, New York, John Wiley & Sons, 1952, pages 96-102; R.A. Fisher, "The Use of

Multiple Measurements in Taxonomic Problems," *Annals of Eugenics*, 1936, Vol. 7, No. II, pages 179-188.

16. Quarmby, "Choice of Travel Mode," pages 301-314; Fisher, "The Use of Multiple Measurements," pages 179-188; Kendall, *Multivariate Analysis*; Stopher, *Multivariate Analysis*.

17. Watson, "Choice of Estimation Procedure;" Peter R. Stopher and John O. Lavender, "Disaggregate, Behavioral Demand Models: Empirical Tests of Three Hypotheses," *Transportation Research Forum Proceedings*, 1972, Vol. XIII, No. 1, pages 321-336.

18. D.J. Finney, *Probit Analysis*, Cambridge, England, Cambridge University Press, 1964, pages 8-22, 29-33, 48-50, 246-251.

19. Watson, "Choice of Estimation Procedure;" Stopher and Lavender, "Tests of Three Hypotheses."

20. Warner, *Stochastic Choice of Mode*, pages 44-47.

21. See Quinby, "Traffic Distribution Forecasts," and chapter 9 of this book.

22. See Wilson, "Spatial Distribution Model"; Wilson, "Entropy Maximizing Models"; and chapter 14 of this book.

23. See page 281 chapter 16.

24. Quandt and Baumol, "The Demand for Abstract Transport Modes."

25. McLynn and Watkins, "Multimode Assignment Model."

26. Warner, *Stochastic Choice of Mode*.

27. Quarmby, "Choice of Travel Mode;" Lisco, *The Value of Commuters' Travel Time*; Peter R. Stopher, "Factors Affecting Choice of Mode of Transport," Ph.D. dissertation, University of London, July 1967.

28. Hill and Von Cube, "Forecasting Travel Mode Choice."

29. Quarmby, "Choice of Travel Mode."

30. Lisco, *The Value of Commuters' Travel Time*.

31. Stopher, *Choice of Mode of Transport*.

32. Charles A. Lave, "A Behavioral Approach to Modal Split Forecasting," *Transportation Research*, 1969, Vol. 3, No. 4, pages 463-480.

33. McGillivray, "Demand and Choice Models."

34. Michael E. Beesley and Peter R. Stopher, "Time Values and Modal-Split Estimation," (forthcoming).

35. Francois X. de Donnea, *The Determinants of Transport Mode Choice in Dutch Cities*, Rotterdam, Rotterdam University Press, 1971.

36. David A. Hensher, "The Consumer's Choice Function: A Study of

Traveller Behavior and Values," Ph.D. dissertation, School of Economics, University of New South Wales, Australia, October 1972.

37. de Donnea, *Determinants of Transport Mode Choice.*

38. Haney, "The Value of Time for Passenger Cars;" Thomas and Thompson, "The Value of Time for Commuting Motorists."

39. Kenneth G. Rogers, Gillian M. Townsend, and Alex Metcalf, *Planning for the Work Journey*, Reading, England, Local Government Operational Research Unit, Report No. C67, April 1970; Kenneth G. Rogers et al., *Modal Choice and the Value of Time*, Reading, England, Local Government Operational Research Unit, Report No. C143, March 1973.

40. Rassam, Ellis, and Bennett, "The N-Dimensional Logit Model"; Peat, Marwick, Mitchell & Co., *Implementation of the N-Dimensional Logit Model.*

41. Peter L. Watson, *The Value of Time, Behavioral Models of Modal Choice*, Lexington, Mass., Lexington Books, D.C. Heath and Co., 1974.

42. Shalom Reichman, "Passengers on Arkia Services in November 1967," Jerusalem, August 1968; Shalom Reichman, "Subjective Time Savings in Interurban Travel: An Empirical Study," *Highway Research Record No. 446*, 1973, pages 21-27.

43. Reuben Gronau, *The Effect of Traveling Time on the Demand for Passenger Airline Transportation,* unpublished Ph.D. dissertation, Department of Economics, Columbia University, 1967.

44. Charles River Associates, Inc., *A Disaggregated Behavioral Model of Urban Travel Demand*, Final Report to U.S. Federal Highway Administration, USDOT, March 1972.

45. Moshe E. Ben-Akiva, "Structure of Passenger Travel Demand Models," *Transportation Research Record* 526, National Academy of Sciences, 1975, pp. 26-42.

46. Peter S. Liou and Antti P. Talvitie, "Disaggregate Access Mode and Station Selection Models for Rail Trips," *Transportation Research Record* (in press), 1975.

47. See discussions by Gerald Kraft, David T. Hartgen, and Peter R. Stopher on the papers cited in notes 45 and 46. (Source: *Transportation Research Record* (in press), 1975).

48. Staffan Algers, Stein Hansen, and Goran Tegner, "On the Evaluation of Comfort and Convenience in Urban Transportation—A Choice Analytic Approach," *Transportation Research Forum Proceedings*, 1974, Vol. XV, No. 1, pages 470-481.

49. K. Patricia Burnett, "A Bernoulli Model of Destination Choice," *Transportation Research Record* (in press), 1975; Susan Hanson, "On Assessing Individuals' Attitudes Towards Potential Travel Destinations: A

Research Strategy," *Transportation Research Forum Proceedings*, 1974, Vol. XV, No. 1, pages 363-370; Peter R. Stopher and Peter L. Watson, "Destination Choice Modeling: An Application of Psychometric Techniques," paper presented to APA Annual Meeting, Chicago, 1975; C. Gorman Gilbert, George L. Peterson, and D.W. Lime, "Toward a Model of Travel Behavior in the Boundary Waters Canoe Area," *Environment and Behavior*, 1972, Vol. 4, No. 2, pages 131-157.

50. Peter L. Watson, "Problems Associated with Time and Cost Data Used in Travel Choice Modeling and Valuation of Time," *Highway Research Record No. 369*, 1971, pages 148-158.

51. Joel Guttman, "Avoiding Specification Errors in Estimating the Value of Time," *Transportation Research Record* (forthcoming, 1975).

52. Quarmby, "Choice of Travel Mode."

53. John O. Lavender, "Stochastic Disaggregate Mode Choice Models: A Test of Three Hypotheses," M.S. thesis, Northwestern University, 1971; Stopher and Lavender, "Empirical Tests of Three Hypotheses."

54. Salvatore L. Bibona, "An Analysis of Total Travel Time and Cost Disutility Functions in Behavioral Mode Choice Modeling," M.S. thesis, Department of Civil Engineering, Northwestern University, Evanston, Illinois, August 1970.

55. Watson, *The Value of Time*.

56. Quarmby, "Choice of Travel Mode."

57. For example, Watson, *The Value of Time*; Charles River Associates, Inc., *A Disaggregated Behavioral Model*: Ben-Akiva, "Passenger Travel Demand Models;" Peter L. Watson, "The Homogeneity of Models of Transport Mode Choice: The Dimensions of Trip Length and Journey Purpose," *Journal of Regional Science*, 1974, Volume 14, No. 2, pages 247-257.

58. Quarmby, "Choice of Travel Mode;" Stopher, *Choice of Mode of Transport*; John B. Lansing and Gary Hendricks, *Automobile Ownership and Residential Density*, Michigan, Survey Research Center, University of Michigan, 1967, Chapter IV.

59. Eduardo Aldana, Richard deNeufville, and Joseph H. Stafford, "Microanalysis of Urban Transportation Demand," *Highway Research Record No. 446*, 1974, pages 1-11.

60. D. Wells and G. Gubar, "Life Cycle Concept in Marketing Research," *Journal of Marketing Research*, 1966, Volume 3, pages 355-363.

61. Peter R. Stopher and Arnim H. Meyburg, "The Effect of Social and Economic Variables on Choice of Travel Mode for the Work Trip," *Proceedings of the Sixth International Symposium on Transportation and Traffic Theory*, Sydney, Australia, August 1974, pages 685-713.

62. For example: Quarmby, "Choice of Travel Mode;" Lisco, *The*

*Value of Commuters' Travel Time*; Lave, "A Behavioral Approach"; McGillivray, "Demand and Choice Models."

63. Lave, "A Behavioral Approach"; Peter L. Watson and Peter R. Stopher, "The Effect of Income on the Usage and Valuation of Transport Modes," *Transportation Research Forum Proceedings*, 1974, Volume XV, No. 1, pages 460-469; Thomas C. Thomas, *The Value of Time for Passenger Cars: An Experimental Study of Commuter's Values*, Final Report, Volume II, Menlo Park, California, Stanford Research Institute, May 1967.

64. Stopher, *Choice of Mode of Transport*; Stopher, "A Probability Model."

65. For example: Watson, *The Value of Time*; Watson and Stopher, "The Effect of Income;" Stopher and Meyburg, "The Effect of Social and Economic Variables;" Lavender, *Stochastic Disaggregate Mode Choice*; Hensher, *The Consumers' Choice Function*.

66. V. Parker Lessig and John O. Tollefoon, "Market Segment Identification through Consumer Buying Behavior and Personal Characteristics," in James Engel, Henry F. Fiorillo and Murray A. Cayley, *Market Segmentation: Concepts and Applications*, New York, Holt, Rinehart and Winston, 1972, Chapter 26.

67. For example: Lave, "A Behavioral Approach"; F.C. Bock, "Factors Influencing Modal Trip Assignment," *Highway Research Board NCHRP Report No. 57*, 1968; Watson. *The Value of Time*.

68. Alistair Sherret, "Structuring an Econometric Model of Modal Choice," Ph.D. dissertation, Cornell University, June 1971; Alexis N. Sommers, "Expanding Nondemographic Factors in Modal Split Models," paper presented to 36th National Meeting of ORSA, Miami, Florida, November 1969; David T. Hartgen and George H. Tanner, "Investigation of the Effect of Traveler Attitudes in a Model of Mode Choice Behavior," *Highway Research Record No. 369*, 1971, pages 1-14; see also Peter R. Stopher, Bruce D. Spear, and Peter O. Sucher, "Towards the Development of Measures of Convenience for Travel Modes," *Highway Research Record* (in press), 1975.

69. Stopher, Spear and Sucher, "Development of Measures of Convenience."

70. Bruce D. Spear, "The Development of a Generalized Convenience Variable for Models of Mode Choice," Ph.D. dissertation, Cornell University, June 1974; Gregory C. Nicolaidis, "Quantification of the Comfort Variable," *Transportation Research*, 1975, Vol. 9, No. 1, pages 55-66; Stopher, Spear, and Sucher, "Development of Measures of Convenience."

71. For example: H.A. David, *The Method of Paired Comparisons*,

London, Charles Griffin & Co., 1963; W.S. Torgerson, *Theory and Methods of Scaling*, New York, John Wiley and Sons, 1958.

72. Spear, *A Generalized Convenience Variable*.

73. Nicolaidis, "Quantification of the Comfort Variable."

74. For example, Martin Fishbein, *Readings in Attitude Theory and Measurements*, New York, John Wiley & Sons, 1967; Jagdish N. Sheth, "Canonical Analysis of Attitude-Behavior Relationships," presented to 18th International Meeting, Institute of Management Sciences, 1971.

75. Antti P. Talvitie, "Aggregate Travel Demand Analysis with Disaggregate or Aggregate Travel Demand Models," *Transportation Research Forum Proceedings*, 1973, Vol. XIV, No. 1, pages 583-603.

76. Richard B. Westin, "Predictions from Binary Choice Models," *Journal of Econometrics*, Vol. II, No. 1, 1974, pages 1-16; Peter L. Watson and Richard B. Westin, "Transferability of Disaggregate Mode Choice Models," *Regional Science and Urban Economics*, 1975, Vol. 5, No. 2.

77. Frank S. Koppelman, "Prediction with Disaggregate Models: The Aggregation Issue," *Transportation Research Record* (in press), 1975.

78. Arnim H. Meyburg and Peter R. Stopher, "Aggregate and Disaggregate Travel-Demand Models," *ASCE Journal of Transportation Engineering*, Vol. 101, No. T.E.2, (in press), May 1975.

79. Yehuda Gur, E. Low, Anant Vyas and E.V. Ryan, "Urban Modal Split Modeling Using Monte-Carlo Simulation" (1975 Transportation Research Board paper) (in preparation).

80. Antti P. Talvitie and Thomas Leung, "A Parametric Access Network Model," *Transportation Research Board* (forthcoming, 1975).

81. Koppelman, "Prediction."

82. Rassam, Ellis, and Bennett, "The N-Dimensional Logit Model'; Peat, Marwick, Mitchell & Co., *Implementation of the N-Dimensional Logit Model*.

83. Nadeem Tahir, "Mode-Split Models for Homewood, Illinois," M.S. thesis, The Transportation Center, Northwestern University, 1973; Nadeem Tahir and Mark Hovind, "A Feasibility Study of Potential Feeder Bus Service for Homewood, Illinois," *Transportation Research Forum Proceedings*, 1973, Vol. XIV, No. 1, pages 553-570.

84. Peter S. Liou, Gerald S. Cohen, and David T. Hartgen, "An Application of Disaggregate Mode Choice Models to Systems-Level Travel Demand Forecasting," *Transportation Research Record* (forthcoming) 1975.

85. John R. Hamburg and C.R. Guinne, "A Modal-Choice Model—Description of Basic Concepts," New York State DOT, Publication TP080807, 1966.

# Index

abstract modes: concept, 269; hypothesis, 253-254; model, 257-269

accessibility, 65; function, 229, 232; in direct traffic estimation, 229; in modal split, 182-184, 187

accuracy in trip generation models, 115-117

aggregate model assumptions, 117-118; definition, 30-31; in trip generation, 117-118

aggregate-rates models, 115-117, 120

aggregate totals models, 114-117

aggregation: errors of, 313; naive, 314; of intervening-opportunity model, 160-163; of non-linear relationships, 313-315; to zones, 75

Aldana, E., 310

Algers, S., 306

alternative, 18, 20-21; choice, 278, 282; do-nothing, 10-11; examples, 23; independence axiom, 275-278, 282, 284, 304; strategies, 60

analogue model, 31

analytical model, 29

applications of behavioral models, 315-316

assigning rule in discriminant analysis, 291-292

assumptions in UTP models, 219

attitudes: measurement, 312-313; surveys, 94

automobile: estimation of costs, 309-310; in modal-split estimation, 179, 184-185

backward seeking model, 31

Baumol, W.J., 253, 256, 257, 261, 267, 270, 297

Bay Area Transportation Study: innovations, 224; modal-split model, 188-189, 191, 195, 295

behavioral model, 273, 297

Ben-Akiva, M.E., 305

benefits in economic evaluation, 216; maximum, 215; measurement of, 217; nonuser, 217; of transportation plans, 214; streams of, 214-215

blocks, 61

branch. *See* link

Bureau of Public Roads model package, 68

Burrell, J.E., 208

calibration: of abstract-mode model, 257; process for gravity model, 143-146; process for intervening-opportunity model, 164-168; use of data for, 92

capacity: changes of, 55-58; restraint, 202-205, 206, 207-208

Capital Grants Program, 6

captivity to transit, 185

category analysis. *See* cross-classification

Charles River Associates, 304

checking of survey data, 93-94

Chicago Area Transportation Study: capacity restraint, 204; intervening-opportunity model, 158; land-use model, 102-103; modal-split model, 178-180

Chi-square test for trip distribution, 144

classification of U.S. highways, 4-5

closure criterion: for gravity model, 144, 155; for growth-factor models, 129, 130, 131, 133; for intervening-opportunity model, 172

coding, 70; of the network, 202; system for the network, 75-76

column-factoring: example in gravity model, 148-149; example in intervening-opportunity model, 169-171

comfort from attitude measurement, 312-313; in behavioral models, 302

communications system, 12, 16

competition product-form demand model, 254; derivation, 256; examples of, 266-269; summary, 269-271

conceptual model, 26; role, 27

conductivity, 254; demand model, 254-256, 257-265, 269-271

consequences of plans, 94, 211; social and environmental, 220; system, 19

conservation rules: application to gravity model, 141-143; application to growth-factor models, 128, 133-138; application to intervening-opportunity model, 162-163; of trip distribution, 125-126

constraint, 19; equations for gravity model, 239, 245; equations for intervening-opportunity model, 243; equations for modal split, 247

consumer behavior theory in transportation, 46-47, 269, 273

continuing planning processes, 225, 226

convenience, 312-313

cordon, 76; external, 81, 86; internal, 76

cost-effectiveness, 217

costs: in economic evaluation, 216; least, 215; measurement of, 217; nonuser,

217; of planned strategies, 214;
streams of, 214-215
county roads funding, 5
criteria, 18-19; examples, 19, 23
cross-classification: in modal split, 180, 185,
187, 198; in nonresidential trip generation, 120-121; in residential trip generation, 111-114
cross-sectional model, 30; characteristic of
UTP models, 223

de Donnea, F.X., 302
demand, 47-48; curve, 48; elasticity of, 47;
for urban travel, 16; joint, 46; models,
223; relationship, 58
Demonstration Program of UMTA, 6
derived demand, 109
description, 26
descriptive model, 28-29
destinations, 64; choice models of, 305, 306,
317; survey of, 86
deterministic model, 29
direct demand model, 229, 253-271
direct traffic-estimation, 229; derivation,
230-234
disaggregate: elements of travel time, 308-
309; model definition, 30-31, 273;
model structure, 277; model theory,
274-282; travel demand model, 273-
317; trip generation, 118
discount rate, 216
discriminant analysis, applications, 299, 301,
302, 303; use in disaggregate models,
290-292
districts, 61
diversion curve, 182, 183, 188-189, 191, 198

ecological fallacy, 118, 123
economic growth, 115
economic theory, applications in transportation, 45-58, 278-282
elasticity, 255; assumptions in model, 267-
269; constant assumption, 255-256;
cross, 253, 283; direct, 253, 283; of
travel demand, 249; use to develop
abstract-mode models, 257-260, 262-
264, 266
EMPIRIC model, 103-104
entropy-maximizing: approach to demand
models, 227; approach to travel behavior, 237-251, 295; summary, 250-
251; theory, 238-242
environment, 18
equilibrium, of supply and demand, 54-55,
58, 224
Erie Transportation Study, 181-182
error: calibration, 41, 43; calibration in gravity model, 156-157; measurement, 33,

34-38, 41, 261, 295-297; measurement
in gravity model, 156-158; measurement in TRC modal-split model, 192-
193; prediction in abstract-mode
model, 260-262; prediction in logit
model, 295-297; propagation in UTP
process, 220; properties of models,
33; reporting, 33; sampling, 33-34;
specification, 34, 38-41, 42-43; variance in UTP models, 219
establishment accounting, 102
evaluation, 15, 20, 60; economic techniques,
216; of alternative plans, 94; process,
23, 211-217, 220; summary, 67

Federal Highway Administration survey
recommendations, 81; package, 68
forecasts: model use, 26; of land use, 60, 62,
of travel demand, 60, 94
forward-seeking model, 31; UTP process,
220
freight trip generation, 122
friction-factor. See travel-time factor

generalized cost, 232, 248, 250
goals, 18; examples, 19, 22; formulation
methods, 23-24; planning, 14; specification of, 20, 23; urban, 14, 20
Gompertz exponential curve, 189, 198
goodness-of-fit measures in discriminant
analysis, 292; in logit analysis, 295; in
probit analysis, 294; in regression, 289
gravity model, 125, 140, 158; as basis of direct traffic estimation, 229, 234; derivation, 140-143; econometric models,
253, 255; entropy derivation, 237,
238-242, 244-246; example, 146-151
Gronau, R., 304
growth-factor models, 125, 126-139;
average-factor, 128-129, 131-133, 139;
Detroit, 130-131, 133, 139; example of
use, 137-138; Fratar, 129-130, 133,
139; uniform-factor, 128, 131, 139
Gur, Y., 315

Hansen, S., 306
Hensher, D.A., 302
Herbert, 104
Herbert-Stevens Residential Model, 104-107
highway classification, 4-5; maintenance, 5
Highway Trust Fund creation, 3; use for
transit, 6
Hildebrand, F.B., 167
Hill, D.M., 195
home-based, 63; attractions, 119; proportion
in urban area, 119; trips in demand
analysis, 109
home interviews, 81

homomorphic model, 31
HUD Transit Planning Package, 68

impact, 15; environmental, 67
implementation, 220
interaction of UTP models, 220-221
interchange penalty, 209
interface, 18
Interstate Highway funding, 5
intervening-opportunity model of trip distri-
    bution, 125, 297; derivation, 159-163;
    derivation from entropy theory, 242-
    244, 251; example of, 168-171; forced
    model, 163; free model, 163; use with
    modal-split model, 179
inventory, 61-62, 69-97; of existing facilities,
    60; of land use, 60, 61, 80-81; of
    socio-economic characteristics, 60; of
    supply, 69, 76, 80; of travel, 60; of use
    of transportation system, 60
isomorphic model, 31

k-factors, 145-146, 156
Kolmogorov-Smirnov test, 144
Koppelman, F., 315
Kraft, G., 265-267, 270

Lagrange, 240, 243
Lancaster, K.J., 253
land development differential, 233; in direct
    traffic-estimation, 229, 232
land use: accounting, 101, 103, 104, 106; and
    trip generation, 115; categories, 80;
    classification, 80, 121; models of,
    101-107; succession, 101, 103, 104,
    106; surveys, 60-61, 80-81
Lave, C., 302
least harm, 215-216
legislation: freight transport, 6-7; Highway
    Trust Fund, 3, 6; UTP studies, 7
level of service, 65; elasticity, 255; in modal
    competition product-form model, 256
linear regression: assumptions, 115, 123, 289;
    calibration of econometric models,
    270; effects of measurement error,
    34-38; inapplicability to disaggregate
    models, 289-290; in intervening-
    opportunity model, 164; in nonresi-
    dential trip generation, 119, 121; in re-
    sidential trip generation, 111, 114-115;
    use in modal split, 176, 177, 181, 193-
    194, 197
link, 200; access, 202; loading, 75; network,
    75
Lion, P., 305
Lisco, T.E., 300, 301, 302
local feeder route funding, 5
Local Government Operations Research

Unit, 303
logit model applications, 300, 303, 304-306,
    315-316; for BATS modal-split model,
    189; from discriminant analysis, 292;
    from entropy, 248; in disaggregate ap-
    proach, 294-295
Lowry, I.S., 107
Luce, R.D., 275, 276

McCarthy, G.M., 118
McGillvray, R., 302
McLynn, J.M., 262, 265, 266, 267, 269, 270
major interurban arterials funding, 5
market-demand model, 106
mathematical model, 26; role, 27-28
maximum likelihood, iterative calibration,
    294, 295
measured times and costs, 307-308
measurement error. See error, measurement
minimum-cost path, 231, 232
minimum-impedance path, 66
minimum-time path, 66; algorithms, 199; in
    assignment, 199-200, 208, 210; tree,
    200
modal split, 65-66, 175-198; critique, 223; it-
    eration of, 221; model derivation from
    entropy theory, 247-248, 250; simul-
    taneous modeling, 226; trip-end mod-
    els, 175, 176-187, 196-198; trip-
    interchange models, 175, 187-196,
    196-198, 208
mode: addition of new, 260; categorization
    by, 63
mode choice, development of behavioral
    models, 298-304
model: aggregate, 30-31; analogue, 31; ana-
    lytical, 29-30; backward-seeking, 31;
    conceptual, 26, 27; cross-sectional,
    30; definition, 19; descriptive, 28-29;
    deterministic, 29; dimensions of,
    27-32; disaggregate, 30-31; examples,
    23; forward-seeking, 31; functions,
    26; homomorphic, 31; isomorphic, 31;
    mathematical, 26, 27-28; multidirec-
    tional, 31; physical, 26, 27-28; plan-
    ning, 28-29; predictive, 28; probabilis-
    tic, 29, 227, 273; simulation, 29-30;
    statistical, 29-30; system, 25-33; tem-
    poral, 30; unidirectional, 31. See also
    land use; modal split; mode choice;
    trip distribution; trip generation
Moore, E.F., 200
multidirectional model, 31
multiple logit model, applications in mode
    choice, 303; derivation, 275-282; elas-
    ticity properties, 282-284; structure of
    disaggregate models, 284
multiple regression. See linear regression

National mass transportation assistance act,
1974, 6
network, coding, 62, 75-76, 77f, 78f, 79f
network assignment, 66-67, 199-210, 221;
all-or-nothing, 66, 202, 203-205, 208,
210; capacity-restrained, 66; critique,
223; diversion, 66, 202, 206-207, 210;
highway, 202-208; incremental, 202;
in direct-traffic estimation, 234; in
UTP, 199-210; multi-path transit, 208;
multiple route, 207-208; partial, 205-
206, 210; proportional, 202, 207-208,
210; random, 205, 210; transit, 208-210
Newton, I., 140
Newton's Law of Gravitation, 140
Nicolaidis, G.C., 312-313
node, 75; definition, 200; for transit network,
208; load, 75
nonhome-based, 63, 65f; attractions, 199;
productions, 119; trips in travel-
demand analysis, 119

objectives, 18; examples, 19, 22; specification of, 20, 23; urban area, 14
offpeak, 121
origin-destination studies, 126-127
origins, 64, 65f; survey of, 86
output, 19

Pallin, 140
path, 200
path-finding algorithm, 176. See also
minimum-time path; minimum impedance path; minimum-cost path
peak, 121
peaking, 10, 11f
Pearson curves, 152
perceived times and costs, 307-308
person trips, 63, 120
physical model, 26; role, 27-28
Pittsburgh Area Transportation Study,
modal-split model, 180-182
planning, horizon, 212; model, 28-29
population forecasting, 99-100
prediction, 26
predictive model, 28
preferences, survey of, 94
price of travel, 49
price volume, curve, 49-54; relationship, 54
probabilistic model, 29, 227, 273
probability model. See probabilistic model
probit analysis, 292-294; application, 300,
301-302; and logit analysis, 295
problem, 19; transportation, 7-10; urban, 9
psychology of choice behavior, 273; theory
of travel behavior, 275-278
Puget Sound Transportation Study modal-
split model, 182-183

Quandt, R.E., 253, 256, 257, 261, 267, 270,
297
Quarmby, D.A., 300, 301, 302, 303

random selection, 90
random utility model, 279-281; structural
considerations, 284; summary, 288
Rassam, P.R., 303
Rathnau, A.S., 203
Reichman, S., 304
Reilley, W.J., 140
reported times and costs, 307-308
research on UTP models, 221, 226-227
resources, 19; specification, 20
Road Research Laboratory, capacity restraint, 204
roadside interviews, 80, 86
route-choice model from entropy, 249-250,
251
row-factoring, gravity model, 145, 147-148;
intervening-opportunity model, 163,
169-171

sample, 87
sampling, 87-93; bias, 91; error, 91-92
scaling, 312-313
Schneider, M., 158, 229, 231, 232
screen line, 80; survey, 86
sectors, 61
separability of choices, 284; in entropy approach, 250; implications, 284-285
sequential demand models, 269
shortcomings of UTP process, 219
short-cut techniques, 227
simulation model, 29-30
simultaneous demand model, 269, 287-288
site rent, 105-106
socio-economic variables: in behavioral
models, 299; methods of inclusion,
310-311
Southeastern Wisconsin Regional Planning
Study: innovations, 224; modal-split
model, 183-185
space mean speed, 50-51
Spear, B.D., 312, 313
specification error, 33, 34; effects, 38-39, 40f,
42f, 43f, 43
State Highway funding, 5
Stanford Research Institute, 303
statistical model, 29-30
Stevens, 104, 107
Stirling, 240
Stopher, P.R., 300, 301-302, 311
Stouffer, S.A., 158
stratification, 244, 311
strict utility model, 276-278, 279-280, 288
structure of models: comparison of, 284-288;
independent, 285-286; issues, 306-

# About the Authors

**Peter R. Stopher** is associate professor of civil engineering at Northwestern University. He was educated at the University of London, University College, where he received the B.Sc. in civil engineering in 1964 and the Ph.D. in 1967. From 1967 to 1968 he was a research officer with the Greater London Council. Subsequently he has held appointments at Cornell University, McMaster University (Ontario), and Northwestern University, specializing in urban transportation.

Dr. Stopher has been a consultant to a number of private firms and to governmental agencies on various aspects of urban transportation planning and travel demand. He has also written a number of technical papers, principally in travel-demand modeling and travel-time valuation, and also in urban goods movement, and in statistical and psychological methods. He is a member of several professional societies and committees.

**Arnim H. Meyburg** is an associate professor in the School of Civil and Environmental Engineering at Cornell University. He was educated at the University of Hamburg, Germany, the Free University of Berlin, Germany, and at Northwestern University, Evanston, Illinois. He received the Ph.D. from Northwestern University in 1971. From 1968 to 1969 he was a research associate at the Transportation Center at Northwestern University. Dr. Meyburg has been a faculty member at Cornell University since 1969.

Dr. Meyburg has also been a consultant to private industry and several governmental agencies. He has written a number of technical papers in the subject areas of travel-demand modeling, urban goods movements, and transportation systems analysis. In addition, he is a member of several professional societies and committees.